ATLAS
OF THE
WORLD

HarperCollins*Publishers*

First published by HarperCollins*Publishers* 1990

© Bartholomew 1990

Bartholomew is a Division of HarperCollins*Publishers*

ISBN 0 00 458368 X (outside the USA and Canada)

ISBN 0-06-276501-9 (USA and Canada)

Printed and bound in Great Britain by

HarperCollins*Manufacturing*, Glasgow
Reprint 10 9 8 7 6 5 4 3 2 1

CONTENTS

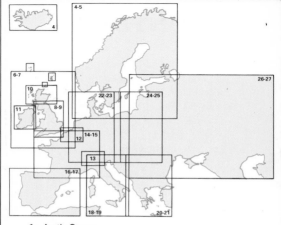

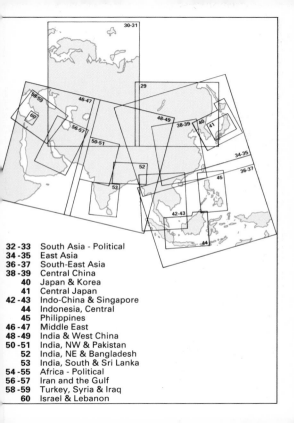

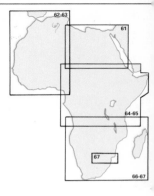

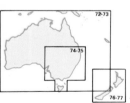

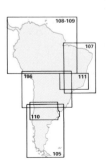

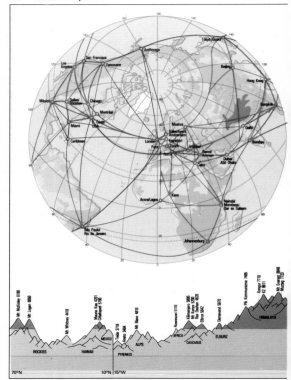

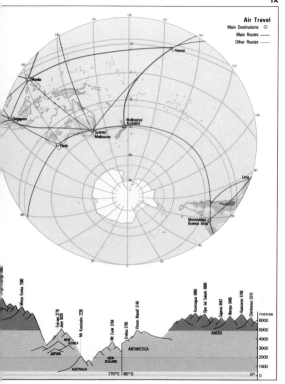

Air Travel

Main Destinations ○
Main Routes ——
Other Routes ——

Hawaii

Manila

Singapore

Perth

Sydney/
Melbourne

Wellington/
Auckland

Lima

Montevideo/
Buenos Aires

Metres Koxha 7590

Fuji-san 3776
Jaya 5029

Mt. Kosciusko 2230

Mt. Cook 3764

Erebus 3795

Vinson Massif 5140

Aconcagua 6960
Ojos del Salado 6908
Sajama 6542
Mercuy 6485
Huascaran 6768
Chimborazo 6310

NEW GUINEA

JAPAN

AUSTRALIA

NEW ZEALAND

ANTARCTICA

ANDES

metres
6000
5000
4000
3000
2000
1000
0

170°E   80°S   0°   0

• Denotes capital cities

Major Cities by Continent	
Oceania	**Pop.**
	'000
Sydney *Australia*	2874
Melbourne *Australia*	2578
Brisbane *Australia*	943
Adelaide *Australia*	883
Perth *Australia*	809
Auckland *New Zealand*	766
Asia	**'000**
Tōkyō *Japan*	11 696
Shanghai *China*	10 820
Calcutta *India*	9166
Beijing *China*	8626
Bombay *India*	8203

Sŏul *South Korea*	6879
Manila *Philippines*	5901
Jakarta *Indonesia*	5849
Delhi *India*	5277
Bangkok *Thailand*	5154
Tehran *Iran*	4496
Madras *India*	4280
Karachi *Pakistan*	4000
Shenyang *China*	3600
Dhākā *Bangladesh*	3459
Saigon *Vietnam*	3420
Baghdād *Iraq*	3206
T'ai-pei *Taiwan*	3050
Bangalore *India*	2914
Istanbul *Turkey*	2773

Europe	
	'000
London *UK*	12 075
Paris *France*	8613
Moskva *USSR*	8099
Leningrad *USSR*	4638
Madrid *Spain*	3188
Berlin *E.Ger.-W.Ger.*	3056
Roma *Italy*	2830
Birmingham *UK*	2748
Manchester *UK*	2687
Kiyev *USSR*	2144
Athínai *Greece*	2101
Budapest *Hungary*	2064
Bucureşti *Romania*	1934
Tashkent *USSR*	1779
Barcelona *Spain*	1755

North and Central America	'000
New York USA	16 120
México Mexico	14 750
Los Angeles USA	11 496
Chicago USA	7868
Philadelphia USA	5549
San Francisco USA	5182
Detroit USA	4618
Boston USA	3448
Houston USA	3102
Washington USA	3060
Toronto Canada	2999
Dallas USA	2975
Cleveland USA	2834
Montréal Canada	2828
Miami USA	2640

South America	'000
Buenos Aires Argentina	9910
São Paulo Brazil	8584
Rio de Janeiro Brazil	5184
Santiago Chile	4039
Lima Peru	3969
Bogotá Colombia	3831
Caracas Venezuela	2576
Belo Horizonte Brazil	1815
Salvador Brazil	1526
Medellín Colombia	1442
Fortaleza Brazil	1339
Montevideo Uruguay	1314
Recife Brazil	1241
Brasília Brazil	1203
Pôrto Alegre Brazil	1159

Africa	'000
Cairo Egypt	6588
Alexandria Egypt	2320
Kinshasa Zaire	2008
Casablanca Morocco	1753
Johannesburg South Africa	1536
Alger Algeria	1503
Lagos Nigeria	1477
El Giza Egypt	1247
Addis Ababa Ethiopia	1133
Cape Town South Africa	1108
Dar es Salaam Tanzania	870
Durban South Africa	851
Abidjan Ivory Coast	850
Ibadan Nigeria	847
Nairobi Kenya	835

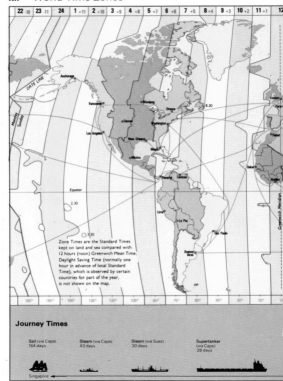

| 22 -10 | 23 -11 | 24 | 1 +11 | 2 +10 | 3 +9 | 4 +8 | 5 +7 | 6 +6 | 7 +5 | 8 +4 | 9 +3 | 10 +2 | 11 +1 | 12 |

Zone Times are the Standard Times
kept on land and sea compared with
12 hours (noon) Greenwich Mean Time.
Daylight Saving Time (normally one
hour in advance of local Standard
Time), which is observed by certain
countries for part of the year,
is not shown on the map.

180° 165° 150° 135° 120° 105° 90° 75° 60° 45° 30° 15°

DATE LINE

Monday
Sunday

Equator

Anchorage

Vancouver

Winnipeg
Ottawa
Denver
Washington
Los Angeles
New Orleans
Mexico
Miami
Panama
Caracas
Lima
La Paz
São Paulo
Buenos
Aires

8.30

London
Paris

Dakar
Abidjan

Greenwich Meridian

2.30

3.30

Journey Times

Sail (via Cape)
164 days

Steam (via Cape)
43 days

Steam (via Suez)
30 days

Supertanker
(via Cape)
28 days

Singapore ←

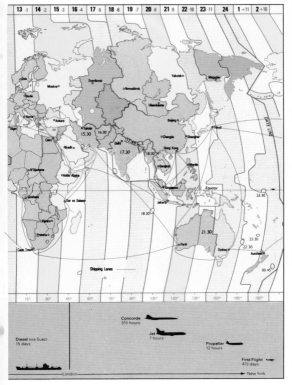

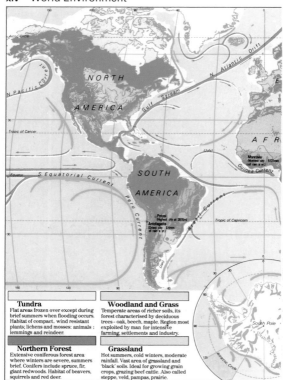

Tundra

Flat areas frozen over except during brief summers when flooding occurs. Habitat of compact, wind resistant plants; lichens and mosses: animals: lemmings and reindeer.

Northern Forest

Extensive coniferous forest area where winters are severe, summers brief. Conifers include spruce, fir, giant redwoods. Habitat of beavers, squirrels and red deer.

Woodland and Grass

Temperate areas of richer soils, its forest characterised by deciduous trees - oak, beech, maple. Region most exploited by man for intensive farming, settlements and industry.

Grassland

Hot summers, cold winters, moderate rainfall. Vast area of grassland and 'black' soils. Ideal for growing grain crops, grazing beef cattle. Also called steppe, veld, pampas, prairie.

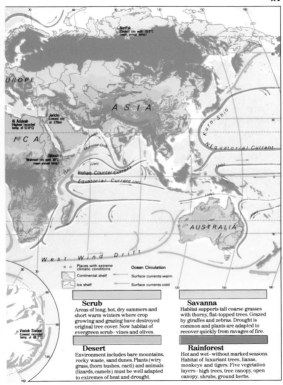

Scrub
Areas of long, hot, dry summers and short warm winters where crop growing and grazing have destroyed original tree cover. Now habitat of evergreen scrub–vines and olives.

Savanna
Habitat supports tall coarse grasses with thorny, flat-topped trees. Grazed by giraffes and zebras. Drought is common and plants are adapted to recover quickly from ravages of fire.

Desert
Environment includes bare mountains, rocky waste, sand dunes. Plants (wiry grass, thorn bushes, cacti) and animals (lizards, camels) must be well adapted to extremes of heat and drought.

Rainforest
Hot and wet–without marked seasons. Habitat of luxuriant trees, lianas, monkeys and tigers. Five vegetation layers– high trees, tree canopy, open canopy, shrubs, ground herbs.

BOUNDARIES

	International
	International under Dispute
	Cease Fire Line
	Autonomous or State
	Administrative
	Maritime (National)

LETTERING STYLES

CANADA	Independent Nation
FLORIDA	State, Province or Autonomous Region
Gibraltar (U.K.)	Sovereignty of Dependent Territory
Lothian	Administrative Area
LANGUEDOC	Historic Region
Loire *Vosges*	Physical Feature or Physical Region

TOWNS AND CITIES

Square symbols denote capital cities

Population

■ ●	**New York**	over 5 000 000
■ ●	**Montréal**	over 1 000 000
□ ○	Ottawa	over 500 000
■ ●	**Québec**	over 100 000
□ ○	St John's	over 50 000
○ ○	Yorkton	over 10 000
○ ○	Jasper	under 10 000
		Built-up-area

LAKE FEATURES

	Permanent
	Seasonal

OTHER FEATURES

	River
	Seasonal River
=	Pass, Gorge
	Dam, Barrage
	Waterfall, Rapid
	Aqueduct
	Reef
.4031	Summit, Peak
.717	Spot Height, Depth
	Well
▲	Oil Field
▲	Gas Field
	Oil/Natural Gas Pipeline
Gemsbok Nat. Pk	National Park
UR	Historic Site
	Main Railway
	Other Railway
	Under Construction
	Rail Tunnel
	Rail Ferry
	Canal
⊕	International Airport
✦	Other Airport

For pages 68-69, 70-71 only:

Sea Level
0
200m
2000m
4000m
6000m
Depth

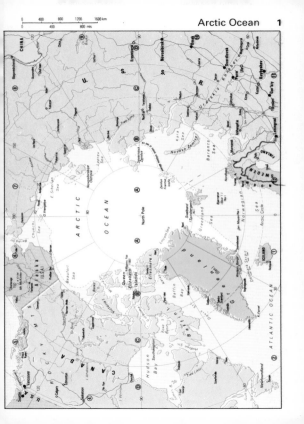

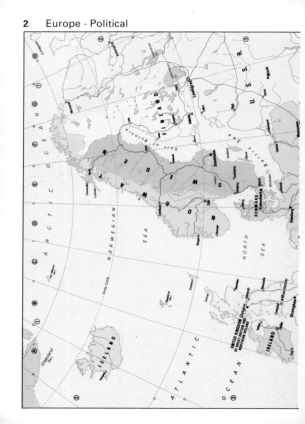

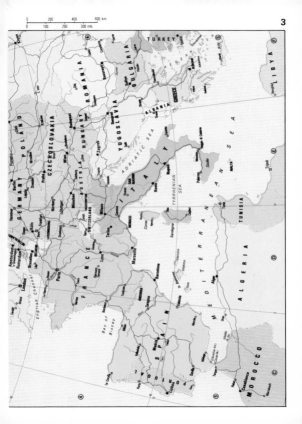

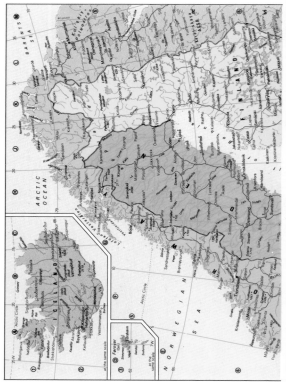

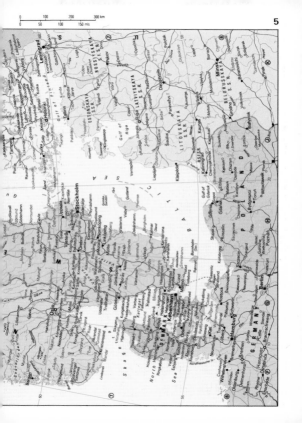

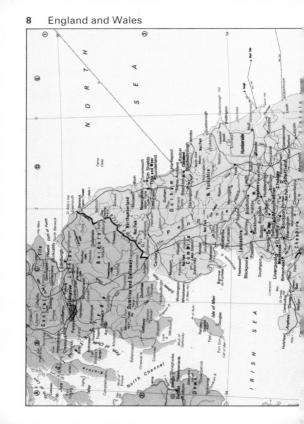

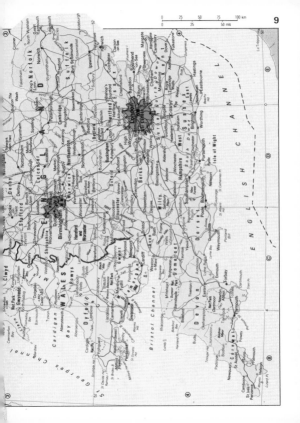

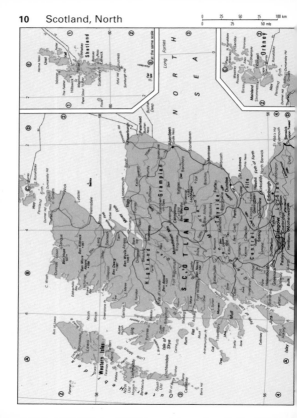

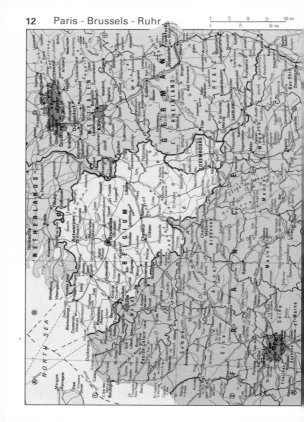

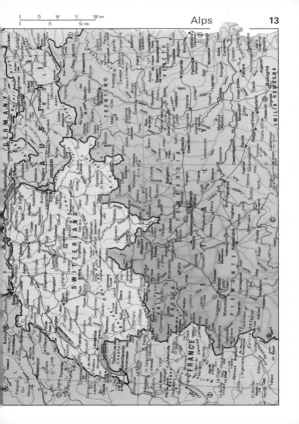

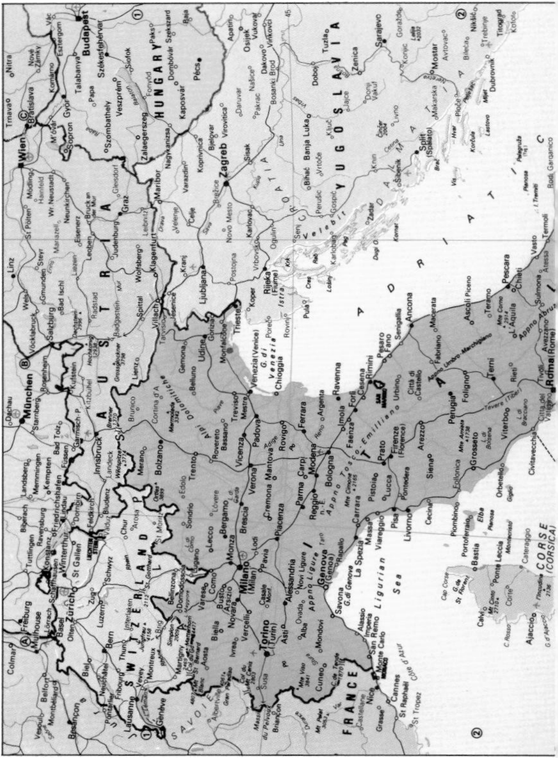
AUSTRIA
HUNGARY
YUGOSLAVIA
SWITZERLAND
FRANCE
CORSE (CORSICA)
Ligurian Sea
ADRIATIC
Wien
Budapest
Bratislava
Zagreb
Ljubljana
Graz
Linz
Salzburg
München
Innsbruck
Klagenfurt
Villach
Zürich
Bern
Basel
Genève
Lausanne
Lugano
Trieste
Udine
Venezia (Venice)
Padova
Verona
Vicenza
Treviso
Trento
Bolzano
Milano (Milan)
Bergamo
Brescia
Como
Torino (Turin)
Genova (Genoa)
Alessandria
Piacenza
Parma
Modena
Bologna
Ferrara
Ravenna
Rimini
Firenze (Florence)
Pisa
Livorno
Lucca
Siena
Perugia
Ancona
Pescara
L'Aquila
Roma (Rome)
Nice
Cannes
Monaco
San Remo
Savona
La Spezia
Rijeka (Fiume)
Split (Spalato)
Zadar
Sarajevo
Mostar
Dubrovnik
Banja Luka
Elba
Bastia
Ajaccio

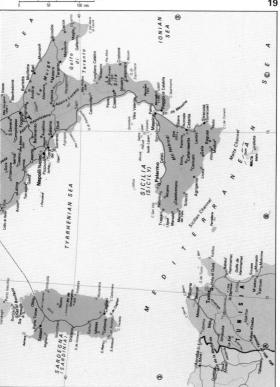

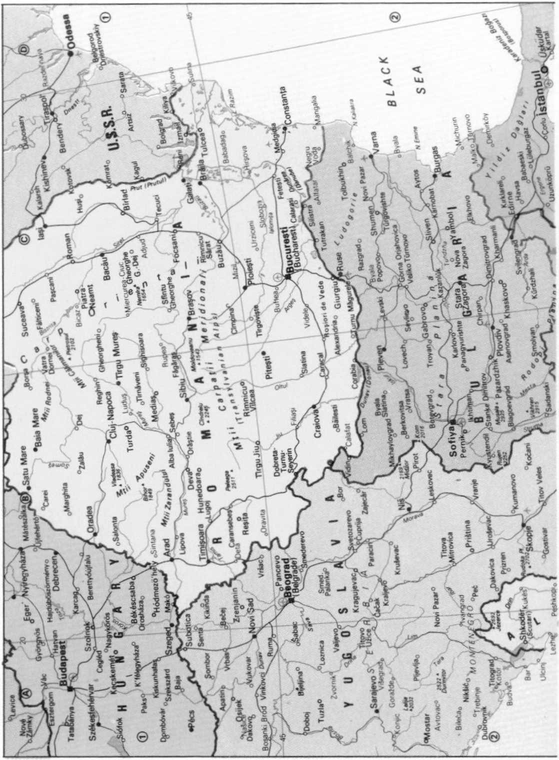
BLACK SEA
U.S.S.R.
Odessa
Tiraspol
Bendery
Kishinev
Iaşi
Galaţi
Brăila
Tulcea
Constanţa
Bucureşti (Bucharest)
Ploieşti
Braşov
Sibiu
Cluj-Napoca
Oradea
Arad
Timişoara
Craiova
Piteşti
Ruse
Varna
Burgas
Sofiya
Plovdiv
Istanbul
Üsküdar
Edirne
Beograd (Belgrade)
Novi Sad
Niš
Skopje
Sarajevo
Kragujevac
Budapest
Szeged
Debrecen
Pécs
Mostar
Dubrovnik
Titograd
Shkodër (Scutari)

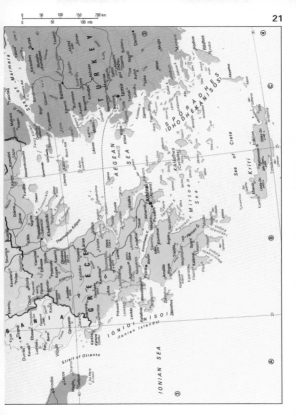

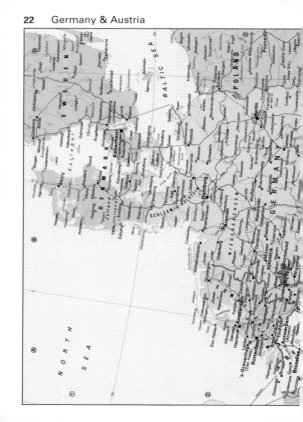

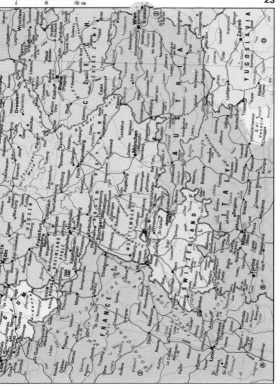

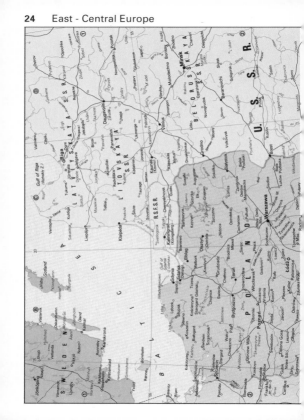

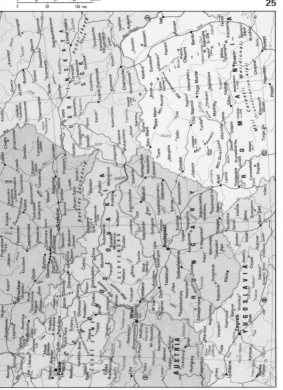

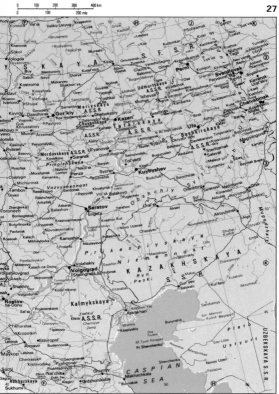

Scale bar:
0 100 200 300 400 km
0 100 200 mls

Y S K A Y A

R S F S R

Vologda · Konoshe · Vel'sk · Velikiy Ustyug · Krasavino · Grlva · Gayny · Solikamsk · Ust-Ula · Turinsk
Kharovsk · Tot'ma · Brusenets · Rosivatino · Nikol'sk · Murashi · Kirov · Omutninsk · Glazov · Vetluga · Perm · Kungur · Sverdlovsk
Sokol · Buy · Manturovo · Kotel'nich · Nolinsk · Vyatka · Balezino · Osa · Perm · Shamary · Pervoural'sk
Buy · Sharya · Sovetsk · Urzhum · Malmyzh · Sarapul · Chusovoy · Kasi
Kostroma · Kineshma · Shakhun'ya · Yoshkar-Ola · Izhevsk · Mozhga · Votkinsk · Chernushka · Nyazepetrovsk · Kasli
Ivanovo · Vichuga · Yur'evets · Cheboksary · Kazan' · Chistopol' · Al'met'evsk · Bashkirskaya · Zlatoust · Chelyabinsk
Kovrov · Shuya · Gor'kiy · Chuvashskaya · Kazan' · Tatarskaya · Ufa · A.S.S.R. · Miass
Dzerzhinsk · A.S.S.R. · Zelenodol'sk · Buguruslan · Sterlitamak · Salavat
Murom · Arzamas · Sergach · Leninogorsk · Belebey · Abdulino · Meleuz
Mordovskaya A.S.S.R. · Ul'yanovsk · Dimitrovgrad · Buzuluk · Orenburg
Ryazan' · Saransk · Privolzhskaya · Syzran' · Tol'yatti · Kuybyshev · Buzuluk · Orsk
Penza · Syzran' · Obshchiy Syrt · Orenburg
Michurinsk · Vozvyshennost' · Saratov · Engel's · Ural'sk
Tambov · Balashov · Krasnyy Kut · K A Z A K H S K A Y A
Saratov · Engel's · Novouzensk · S S R
Kamyshin · Prikaspiyskaya · Nizmennost'
Volzhskiy · Volgograd · Stalingrad · Astrakhan'
Rostov-na-Donu · Kalmykskaya · A.S.S.R. · Elista
Stavropol' · C A S P I A N
Makhachkala · S E A
Sochi · Ordzhonikidze
Sukhumi

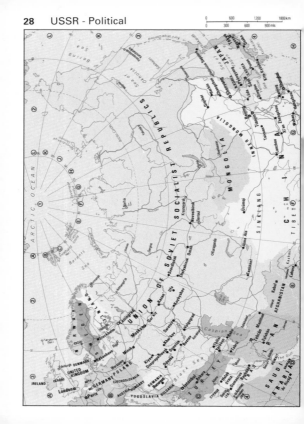

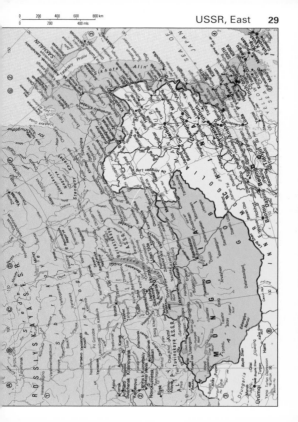

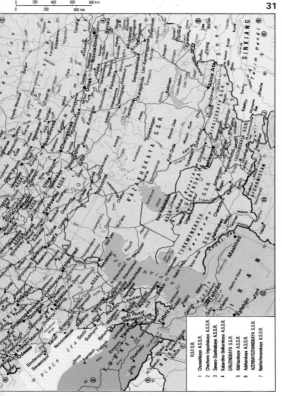

31

1 Chuvashskaya A.S.S.R.
2 Checheno-Ingushskaya A.S.S.R.
3 Severo-Osetinskaya A.S.S.R.
4 Kabardino-Balkarskaya A.S.S.R.
5 GRUZINSKAYA S.S.R.
6 Abkhazskaya A.S.S.R.
7 Nakhichevanskaya A.S.S.R.

AZERBAIDZHANSKAYA S.S.R.

R.S.F.S.R.

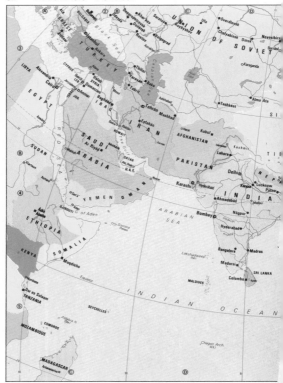

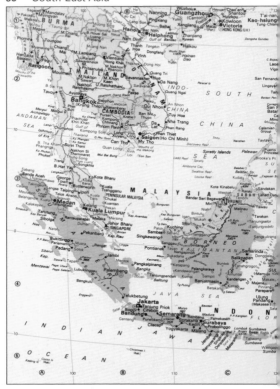

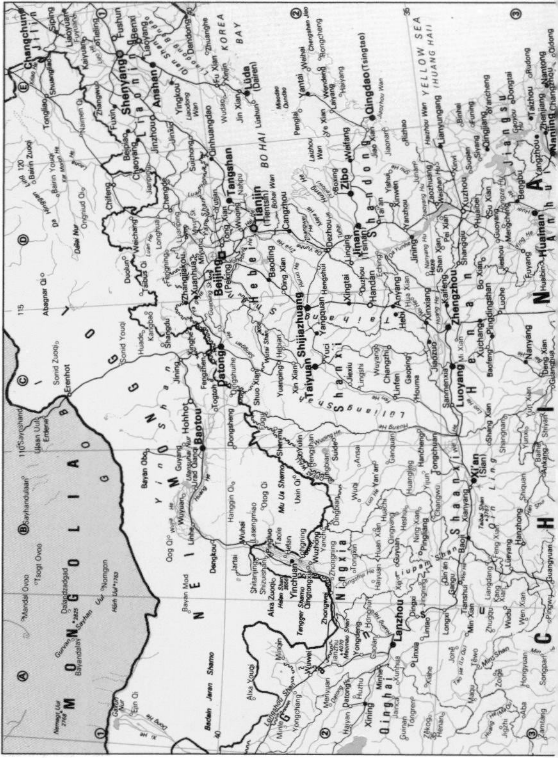
MONGOLIA
NEI MONGGOL
YIN SHAN
Hohhot
Baotou
Datong
Beijing (Peking)
Tianjin (Tientsin)
Tangshan
Shijiazhuang
Taiyuan
Shanxi
Hebei
Shandong
Jinan (Tsinan)
Qingdao (Tsingtao)
Zibo
Henan
Zhengzhou
Luoyang
Kaifeng
Anyang
Xi'an (Sian)
Shaanxi
Ningxia
Yinchuan
Lanzhou
Qinghai
Xining
Jiangsu
Anhui
Huainan
Liaoning
Shenyang
Anshan
Lüda (Dalian)
Changchun
Jilin
BO HAI
KOREA BAY
YELLOW SEA (HUANG HAI)
Mu Us Shamo
Tengger Shamo
Badain Jaran Shamo

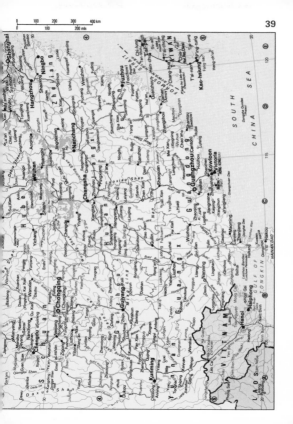

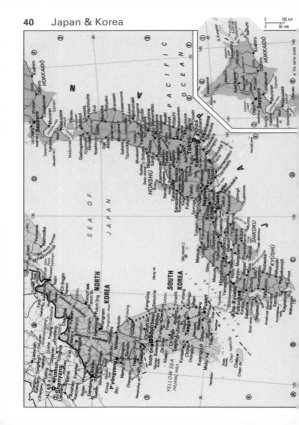

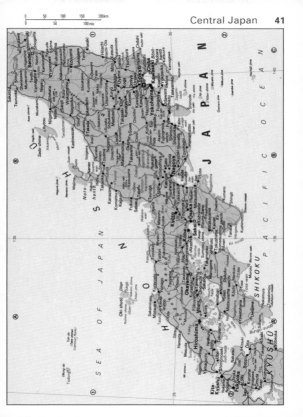

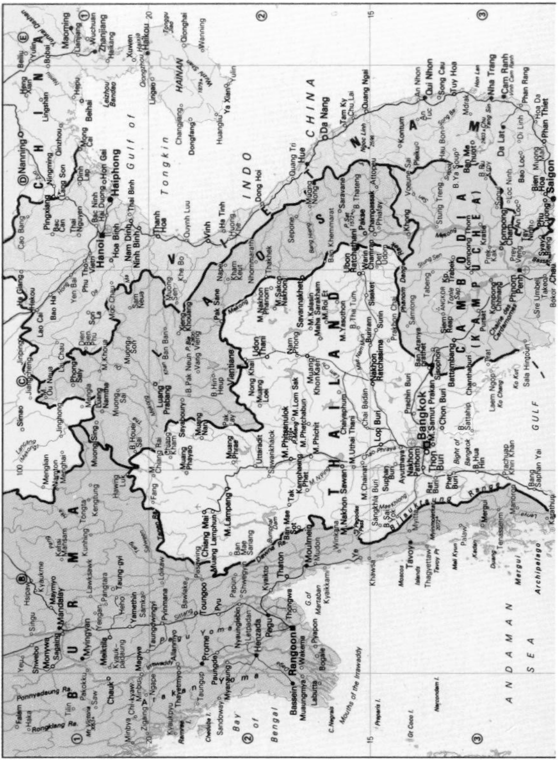
BURMA
THAILAND
LAOS
VIETNAM
CAMBODIA
(KAMPUCHEA)
CHINA
INDO CHINA
HAINAN
Gulf of Tongkin
Bay of Bengal
ANDAMAN SEA
Mergui Archipelago
Mouths of the Irrawaddy
Hanoi
Haiphong
Nanning
Vientiane
Luang Prabang
Bangkok
Rangoon
Mandalay
Moulmein
Saigon
Phnom Penh
Da Nang
Hue
Qui Nhon
Nha Trang
Da Lat
Chiang Mai
Udon Thani
Nakhon Ratchasima
Ubon Ratchathani
Savannakhet
Pakse
Battambang
Bassein
Prome
Toungoo
Tavoy
Mergui
Haikou
Zhanjiang

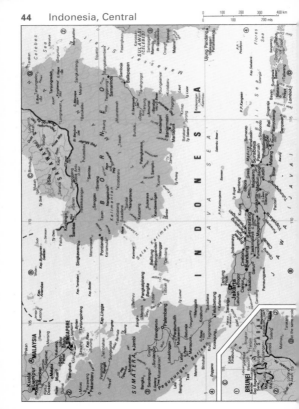

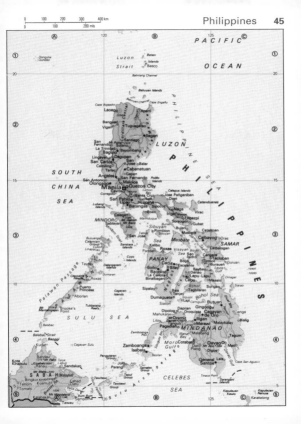

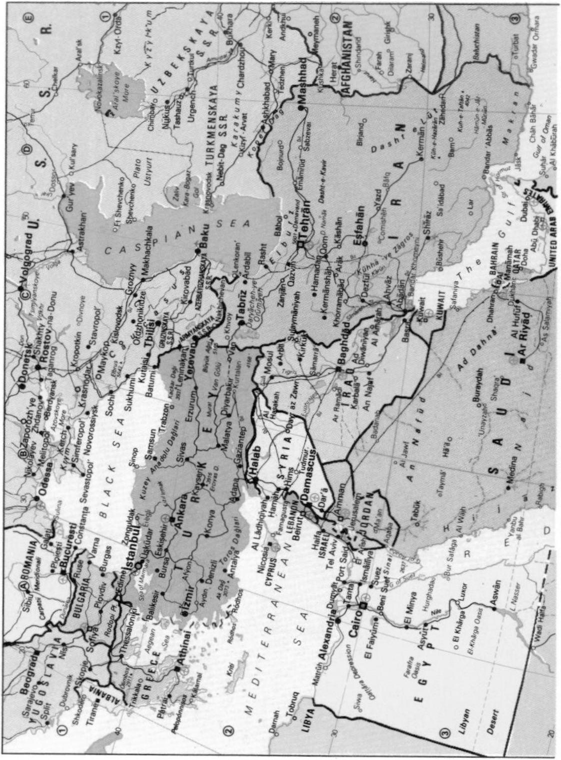
U. S. S. R.
UZBEKSKAYA S.S.R.
TURKMENSKAYA S.S.R.
AFGHANISTAN
IRAN
IRAQ
SYRIA
TURKEY
SAUDI ARABIA
JORDAN
LEBANON
ISRAEL
CYPRUS
KUWAIT
BAHRAIN
QATAR
UNITED ARAB EMIRATES
EGYPT
LIBYA
GREECE
ALBANIA
YUGOSLAVIA
BULGARIA
ROMANIA
CASPIAN SEA
BLACK SEA
MEDITERRANEAN SEA
The Gulf
Gulf of Oman
Aral'skoye More
Tehrān
Baghdād
Damascus
Ankara
Istanbul
Cairo
Alexandria
Beirut
Amman
Jerusalem
Ar Riyād
Mashhad
Esfahān
Tabrīz
Baku
Tbilisi
Yerevan
Halab
Mosul
Basra
Kuwait
Odessa
Volgograd
Rostov-na-Donu
Donetsk
Bucuresti
Beograd
Sofiya
Athinai
Izmir
Adana
Aswân
Medina
Dubai
Abū Dhabi
Doha
Manāmah

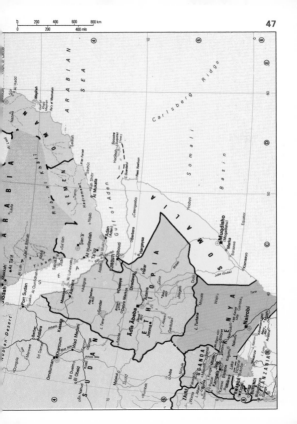

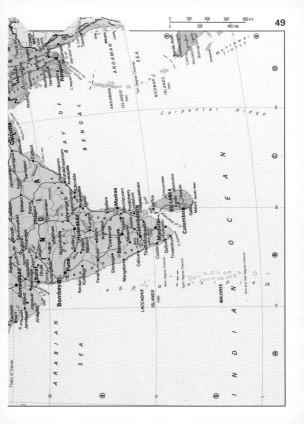

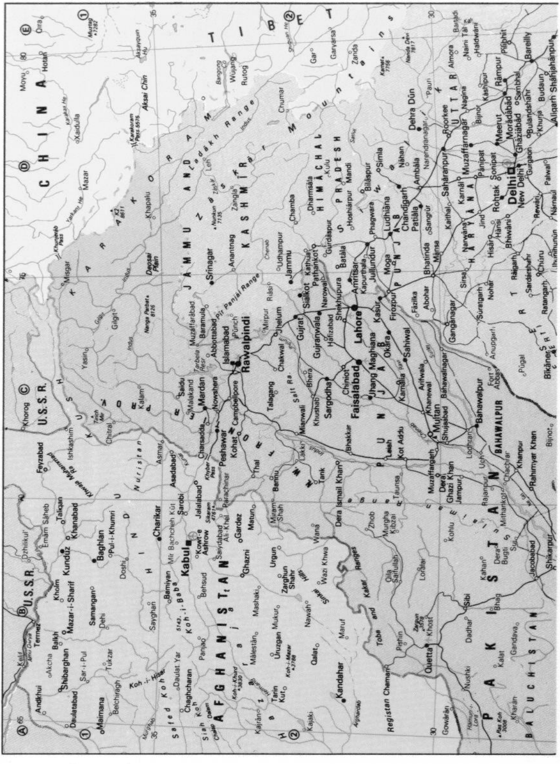
CHINA
U.S.S.R.
AFGHANISTAN
PAKISTAN
JAMMU AND KASHMIR
HIMACHAL PRADESH
PUNJAB
HARYANA
UTTAR
TIBET
BALUCHISTAN
BAHAWALPUR
Karakoram
Ladakh Range
Pir Panjal Range
Salt Ra.
Hindu Kush
Aksai Chin
Kabul
Rawalpindi
Islamabad
Lahore
Faisalabad
Delhi
New Delhi
Srinagar
Peshawar
Multan
Quetta
Kandahar
Ghazni
Jalalabad
Mardan
Gujranwala
Sialkot
Amritsar
Jullundur
Ludhiana
Chandigarh
Ambala
Simla
Dehra Dūn
Meerut
Moradabad
Bareilly
Rampur
Saharanpur
Muzaffarnagar
Rohtak
Panipat
Sonipat
Ghaziabad
Gurgaon
Patiala
Bhatinda
Firozpur
Jammu
Pathankot
Sargodha
Jhang Maghiana
Sahiwal
Okara
Kasur
Bahawalpur
Dera Ismail Khan
Dera Ghazi Khan
Muzaffargarh
Bannu
Kohat
Nowshera
Campbellpore
Jhelum
Gujrat
Chiniot
Mianwali
Shikarpur
Jacobabad
Sibi
Kalat
Chaman
Zhob
Mazar-i-Sharif
Kunduz
Baghlan
Termez
Balkh
Shiberghan
Maimana
Faryab
Feyzabad
Taloqan
Khanabad
Charikar
Gardez
Hotan
Chitral
Gilgit
Leh
Bikaner
Ganganagar
Hisar
Bhiwani
Karnal
Jind
Sirsa
Ratangarh
Churu
Aligarh
Shahjahanpur
Budaun
Khurja
Bulandshahr
Roorkee
Almora
Nainital
Haldwani
Pilibhit
Kashipur
Nagina
Bijnor

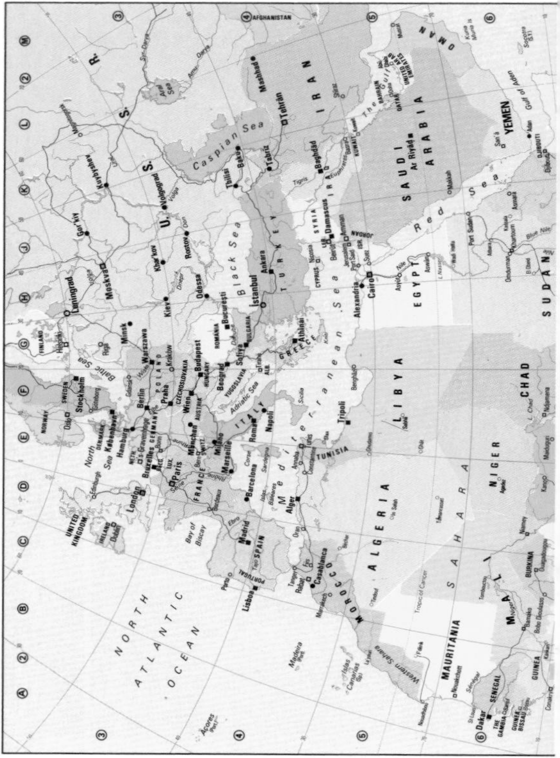
NORTH
ATLANTIC
OCEAN
Açores
Madeira
Islas Canarias
Western Sahara
MAURITANIA
SENEGAL
Dakar
THE GAMBIA
GUINEA-BISSAU
GUINEA
MALI
BURKINA
NIGER
ALGERIA
MOROCCO
Casablanca
Rabat
Tanger
Marrakech
Alger
Oran
TUNISIA
Tunis
LIBYA
Tripoli
Benghazi
CHAD
EGYPT
Cairo
Alexandria
Aswân
SUDAN
Khartoum
Omdurman
Port Sudan
Red Sea
SAUDI ARABIA
Ar Riyâd
YEMEN
Aden
Gulf of Aden
DJIBOUTI
OMAN
QATAR
BAHRAIN
UNITED ARAB EMIRATES
KUWAIT
IRAQ
Baghdad
IRAN
Tehrān
Mashhad
Tabriz
AFGHANISTAN
SYRIA
Damascus
JORDAN
Amman
LEB.
Beirut
ISR.
Jerusalem
CYPRUS
Nicosia
TURKEY
Ankara
Istanbul
Black Sea
Caspian Sea
Baku
Tbilisi
Aral Sea
U. S. S. R.
Moskva
Leningrad
Kuybyshev
Gor'kiy
Volgograd
Rostov
Khar'kov
Kiev
Odessa
Minsk
Riga
Helsinki
FINLAND
Baltic Sea
SWEDEN
Stockholm
NORWAY
Oslo
DENMARK
København
North Sea
UNITED KINGDOM
London
Edinburgh
IRELAND
Dublin
NETH.
Bruxelles
Paris
FRANCE
Bay of Biscay
SPAIN
Madrid
Barcelona
PORTUGAL
Lisboa
Porto
Hamburg
Berlin
POLAND
Warszawa
Kraków
Praha
CZECHOSLOVAKIA
Wien
AUSTRIA
München
SWITZ.
Milano
Marseille
ITALY
Roma
Napoli
Adriatic Sea
YUGOSLAVIA
Beograd
HUNGARY
Budapest
ROMANIA
Bucureşti
BULGARIA
Sofiya
ALB.
GREECE
Athinai
Mediterranean Sea
Sahara
Tropic of Cancer
Socotra

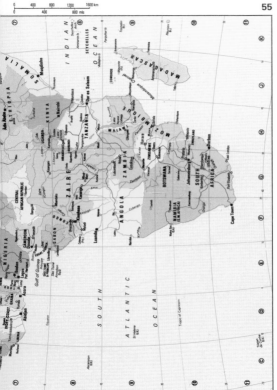

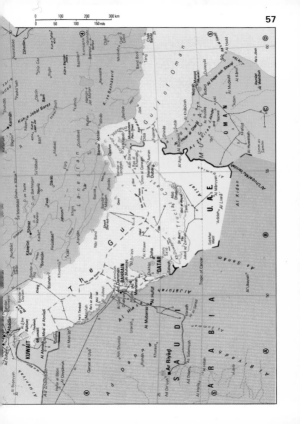

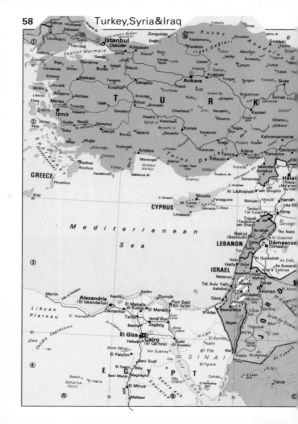

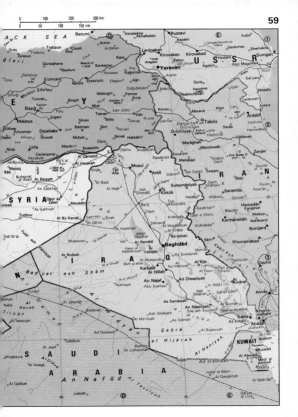

0   25   50   75   100 km
0   25   50   50 mls

CYPRUS

Paleokhoro Larnaca Larnaca Bay
Lefkara
Limassol Akrotiri Bay
C. Gata

MEDITERRANEAN

SEA

LEBANON
Beirut (Beyrouth)
Tripoli (Tarābulus esh Sham)
El Mina
El Hermel
Saida (Sidon)
Sür (Tyre, Sour)
Enn Nâqoûra

SYRIA
Damascus (Dimashq)

Naharlyya
Akko (Acre)
Haifa (Hefa)
'Atlit
Zikhron Ya'aqov
Pardes Hanna
Hadera
Netanya
Herzliyya
Ramat Gan
Tel Aviv
Yafo (Jaffa)
Holon
Rishon le Zion
Rehovot
Ashdod
Ashqelon
Gaza
Khan Yunis
Rafah

ISRAEL

Nazareth
Tiberias
Afula
Beyt She'an

Kefar Sava
Petah Tiqwa

Jerusalem (Yerushalayim)
Bethlehem (Beyt Lahm)
Hebron

Beersheba (Be'er Sheva)
Dimona

Gaza Strip

EGYPT

El 'Arîsh

NEGEV

JORDAN
Amman

Irbid
Mafraq
Zarqa

Madaba

Karak

Tafila

PETRA

Has Burûn
El Lahfan

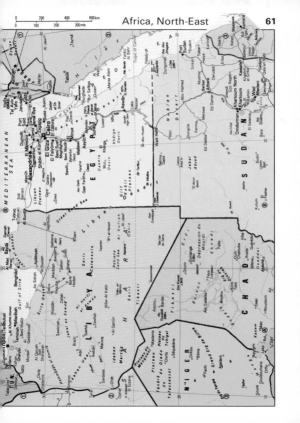

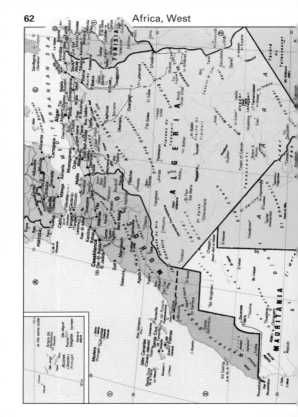

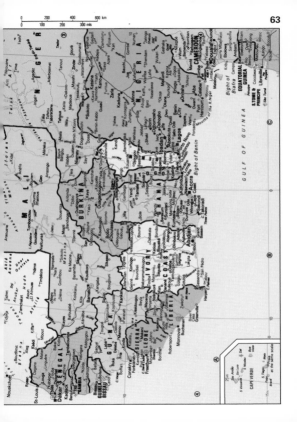

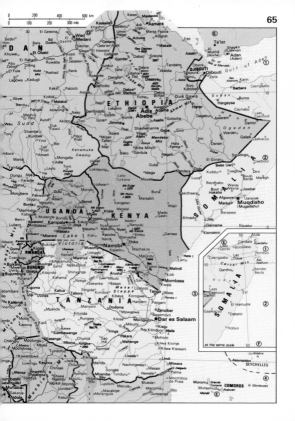

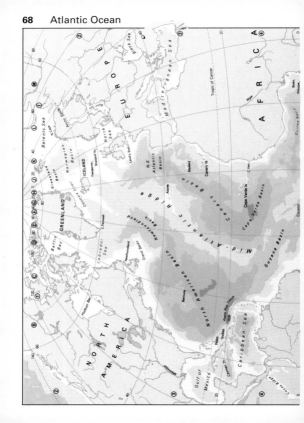

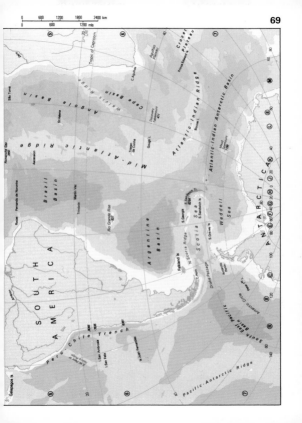

0   600   1200   1800   2400 km
0   600   1200 mls

Tropic of Capricorn

Agulhas Plateau
C. Agulhas
Crozet Plateau
Prince Edward I.
Atlantic-Indian Ridge

Säo Tomé

Walvis Ridge
Cape Basin
Angola Basin
Discovery Seamount 411
Bouvet I.
Meteor Seamount 1088

Atlantic-Indian Antarctic Basin

Stiegiaea

Tristan da Cunha
Gough I.

A N T A R C T I C A

Ascension
Rio Grande Gap 2000
Mid-Atlantic Ridge

Brazil Basin

Fernando de Noronha
Rocas

S. George
Scotia Sea
S. Sandwich Is.
S.Orkney Is.
Weddell Sea

Martin Vaz
Trindade

Rio Grande Rise 697

Argentine Basin

S O U T H
A M E R I C A

Scotia Ridge
Falkland Is.
Scotia Sea
Drake Passage
Antarctic Penin.
Peter I.

Galapagos Is.

Peru-Chile Trench
1 San Ambrosio
1 San Felix
a Juan Fernández

South East Pacific Basin
Amery Ice Shelf

Pacific-Antarctic Ridge

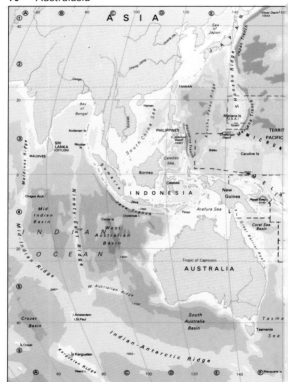

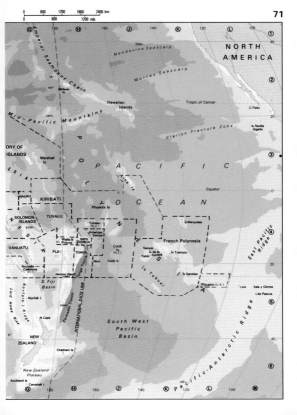

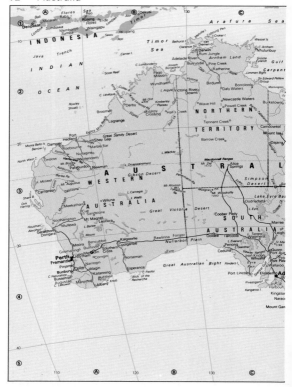

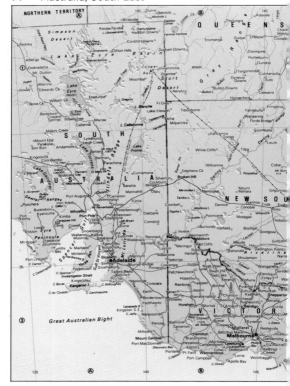

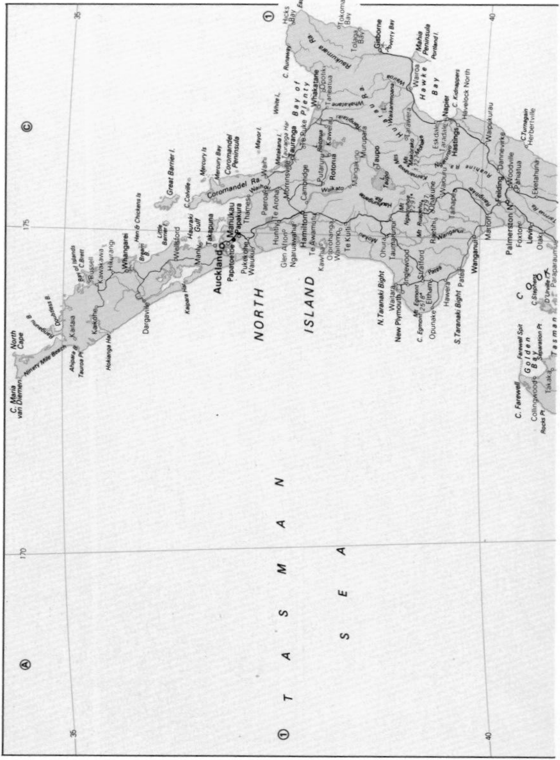

NORTH ISLAND
TASMAN SEA
C. Maria van Diemen
North Cape
Ninety Mile Beach
Kaitaia
Kaikohe
Hokianga Har.
Russell
Kawakawa
Hikurangi
Whangarei
Dargaville
Kaipara Har.
Wellsford
Hauraki Gulf
Great Barrier I.
Little Barrier I.
Hen & Chickens Is
Takapuna
Manukau
Auckland
Papatoetoe
Papakura
Pukekohe
Waiuku
Thames
Coromandel Ra.
Coromandel Peninsula
Mercury Is
Mercury Bay
C. Colville
Waihi
Mayor I.
Tauranga
Te Puke
White I.
Bay of Plenty
Whakatane
Opotiki
C. Runaway
East C.
Hicks Bay
Tokomaru Bay
Tolaga Bay
Gisborne
Poverty Bay
Mahia Peninsula
Portland I.
Raukumara Ra.
Wairoa
Hawke Bay
Napier
C. Kidnappers
Hastings
Havelock North
Waipukurau
Dannevirke
Woodville
Pahiatua
Eketahuna
C. Turnagain
Herbertville
Cambridge
Morrinsville
Te Aroha
Paeroa
Huntly
Hamilton
Te Awamutu
Otorohanga
Waitomo
Te Kuiti
Kawhia
Glen Afton
Ngaruawahia
Putaruru
Rotorua
Kawerau
Murupara
Mangakino
Taupo
L. Taupo
Waikato
Taumarunui
Ohura
Raetihi
Ohakune
Waiouru
Taihape
Wanganui
Marton
Feilding
Palmerston North
Foxton
Levin
Otaki
Paraparaumu
New Plymouth
Waitara
Inglewood
Stratford
Eltham
Hawera
Patea
Opunake
C. Egmont
Mt. Egmont
N. Taranaki Bight
S. Taranaki Bight
C. Farewell
Farewell Spit
Golden Bay
Collingwood
Takaka
Rocks Pt.
Separation Pt.
C. Stephens
D'Urville I.
35
40
170
175

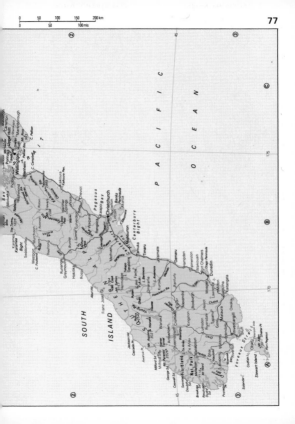

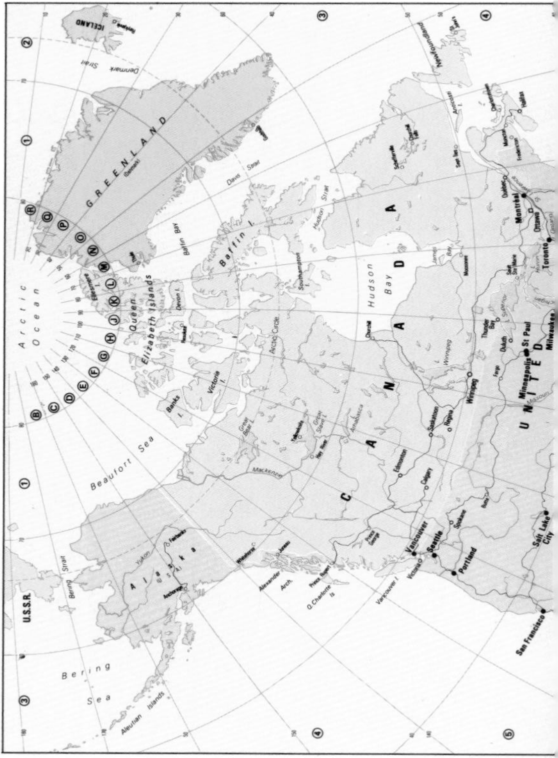
ICELAND
Reykjavík
Denmark Strait
GREENLAND
(Denmark)
Arctic Ocean
Davis Strait
Baffin Bay
Baffin I.
Hudson Strait
Hudson Bay
James Bay
Southampton I.
Ellesmere I.
Devon I.
Queen Elizabeth Islands
Victoria I.
Banks I.
Arctic Circle
Beaufort Sea
Great Bear L.
Great Slave L.
Athabasca
Mackenzie
Yellowknife
Hay River
CANADA
Churchill
L. Winnipeg
Winnipeg
Regina
Saskatoon
Edmonton
Calgary
Prince George
Prince Rupert
Q. Charlotte Is
Alexander Arch.
Juneau
Whitehorse
Yukon
Alaska
Fairbanks
Anchorage
Bering Strait
Bering Sea
Aleutian Islands
U.S.S.R.
Vancouver I.
Vancouver
Victoria
Seattle
Portland
Spokane
Butte
Salt Lake City
San Francisco
UNITED
Fargo
Minneapolis
St Paul
Duluth
Thunder Bay
Superior
Milwaukee
Sault Ste Marie
Huron
Toronto
Ottawa
Montreal
Quebec
Moosonee
Schefferville
Churchill Falls
Sept Îles
Anticosti I.
Newfoundland
St John's
Fredericton
Moncton
Charlottetown
Halifax

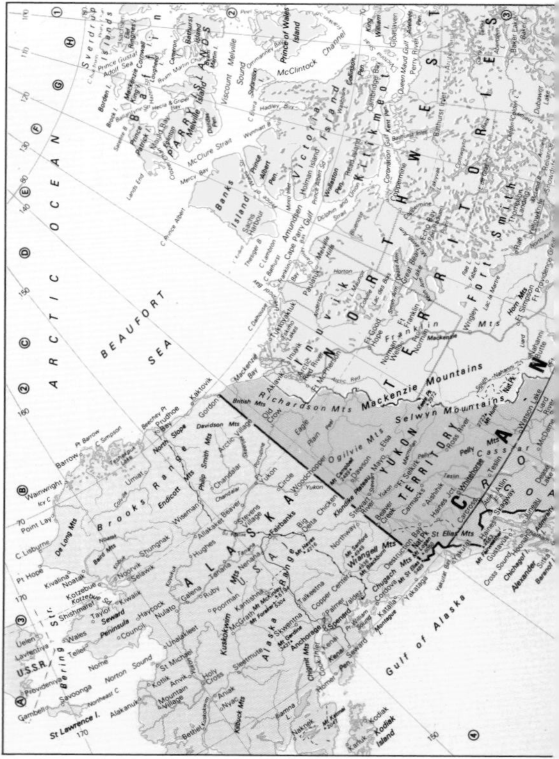
ARCTIC OCEAN
BEAUFORT SEA
Banks Island
Sachs Harbour
Prince Patrick I.
Melville Island
PARRY ISLANDS
Borden I.
Mackenzie King I.
Prince Gustaf Adolf Sea
Sverdrup Islands
Viscount Melville Sound
M'Clure Strait
Mercy Bay
Prince of Wales Island
McClintock Channel
Victoria Island
Prince Albert Pen.
Holman Island
Wollaston Pen.
Amundsen Gulf
Cape Parry
Dolphin and Union Strait
Coronation Gulf
Coppermine
Cambridge Bay
Queen Maud Gulf
King William I.
Gjoa Haven
Bathurst Inlet
Kent Pen.
Melville Hills
Paulatuk
Horton
Great Bear Lake
Port Radium
Echo Bay
Tuktoyaktuk
Inuvik
Aklavik
Ft McPherson
Arctic Red River
Mackenzie Bay
Colville Lake
Ft Good Hope
Norman Wells
Ft Norman
Ft Franklin
Franklin Mts
Mackenzie
Wrigley
Ft Simpson
Ft Providence
Horn Mts
Fort Smith
Fort Rae
Yellowknife
Snowdrift
Reliance
Thompson Landing
Baker Lake
Dubawnt Lake
NORTHWEST TERRITORIES
Kitikmeot
Inuvik
Mackenzie Mountains
Richardson Mts
British Mts
Old Crow
Eagle Plain
Ogilvie Mts
Selwyn Mountains
Keele Pk 2972
Mt Hunt
Nahanni Butte
Nat Pk
YUKON TERRITORY
Dawson
Mayo
Elsa
Ross River
Pelly
Ft Selkirk
Carmacks
Whitehorse
Teslin
Haines Jct
Aishihik
Beaver Creek
Klondike Plateau
Stewart River
Cassiar Mts
Watson Lake
Atlin
Carcross
Skagway
Haines
Juneau
St Elias Mts
Mt Logan
Mt St Elias
Yakutat
Yakataga
Glacier Bay
Destruction Bay
Kaktovik
Prudhoe Bay
Beechey Pt
Pt Barrow
C Simpson
Barrow
Wainwright
Icy C
Point Lay
C Lisburne
Pt Hope
Kivalina
Noatak
Kotzebue
Kotzebue Sd
Shishmaref
Seward Peninsula
Wales
Teller
Nome
Council
Haycock
Nulato
Galena
Ruby
Tanana
Unalakleet
St Michael
Norton Sound
Kotlik
Anvik
Holy Cross
Mountain Village
Aniak
Nyac
Bethel
Kilbuck Mts
Kuskokwim Mts
Alakanuk
Savoonga
Gambell
St Lawrence I.
Northeast C
Bering Str.
U.S.S.R.
Uelen
Lavrentiya
Provideniya
De Long Mts
Baird Mts
Noorvik
Selawik
Shungnak
Kiwalik
Brooks Range
Endicott Mts
Philip Smith Mts
Davidson Mts
North Slope
Umiat
Colville
Teshekpuk Lake
Wiseman
Allakaket
Beaver
Stevens Village
Chandalar
Arctic Village
Fort Yukon
Circle
Woodchopper
Eagle
Yukon
ALASKA
U.S.A.
Fairbanks
Nenana
Big Delta
Delta
Chicken
Northway
Hughes
Kantishna
Poorman
McGrath
Mt McKinley
Mt Foraker
Alaska Range
Talkeetna
Skwentna
Sleetmute
Anchorage
Palmer
Valdez
Copper Center
Chugach Mts
Wrangell Mts
Mt Sanford
Mt Blackburn
Cordova
Katalla
Seward
Kenai
Kenai Pen.
Cook Inlet
Homer
Chigmit Mts
Iliamna L.
Naknek
Mt Katmai
Kodiak
Kodiak Island
Karluk
Gulf of Alaska
Montague I.
Prince William Sound
Cross Sound
Chichagof I.
Baranof I.
Admiralty I.
Alexander Arch.
Sitka
Gustavus
Hoonah
Mt Fairweather

C A N A D A
MANITOBA
SASKATCHEWAN
ALBERTA
BRITISH COLUMBIA
ROCKY MOUNTAINS
NORTH DAKOTA
SOUTH DAKOTA
MINNESOTA
NEBRASKA
IOWA
Kansas
MONTANA
WYOMING
COLORADO
IDAHO
UTAH
NEVADA
OREGON
WASHINGTON
CALIFORNIA
UNITED STATES
Winnipeg
Regina
Saskatoon
Edmonton
Calgary
Vancouver
Victoria
Seattle
Tacoma
Olympia
Spokane
Portland
Salem
Eugene
Boise
Helena
Great Falls
Billings
Missoula
Butte
Bismarck
Fargo
Pierre
Rapid City
Sioux Falls
Omaha
Lincoln
Cheyenne
Casper
Denver
Boulder
Salt Lake City
Ogden
Provo
Reno
Carson City
Sacramento
San Francisco
Oakland
San Jose
Fresno
Stockton
Vancouver Island
Lake Winnipeg
Great Salt Lake
Lewis Range
Bitterroot Range
Big Horn Mts
Laramie Ra
Wind River Ra
Absaroka Ra
Monashee Mts
Selkirk Mountains
Blue Mts
Salmon River Mts

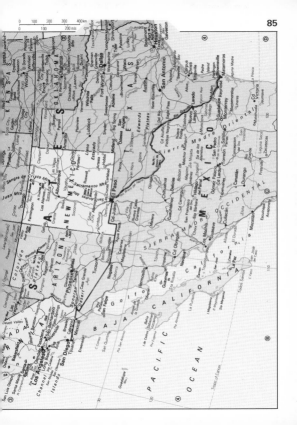

MANITOBA

ONTARIO

QUEBEC

NEW BRUNSWICK

MAINE

VERMONT

NEW HAMPSHIRE

NEW YORK

PENNSYLVANIA

WEST VIRGINIA

MICHIGAN

WISCONSIN

MINNESOTA

IOWA

ILLINOIS

INDIANA

OHIO

St. Lawrence

James Bay

LAKE SUPERIOR

L. HURON

L. MICHIGAN

Montreal

Toronto

Buffalo

Rochester

Syracuse

Albany

Boston

Providence

Hartford

New York

Philadelphia

Baltimore

Washington

Pittsburgh

Cleveland

Columbus

Cincinnati

Detroit

Chicago

Milwaukee

Madison

St. Paul

Minneapolis

Duluth

Thunder Bay

Sudbury

Sault Ste. Marie

Green Bay

Rockford

Peoria

Indianapolis

Davenport

Rochester

Des Moines

Council Bluffs

Kansas City

Lincoln

Omaha

Winnipeg

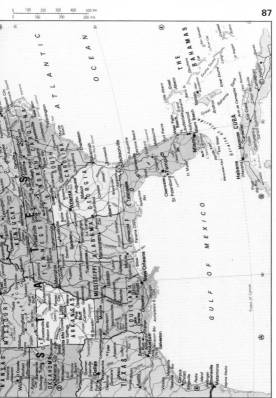

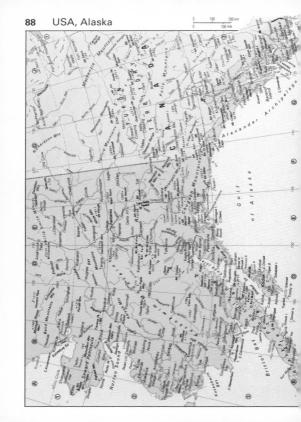

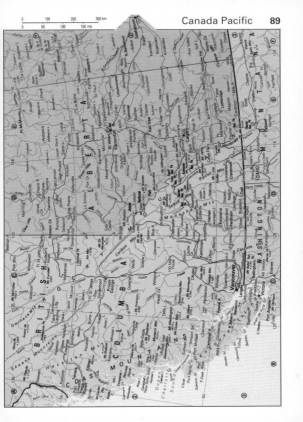

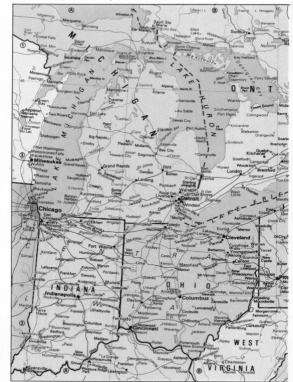

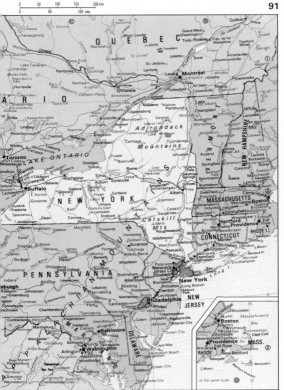

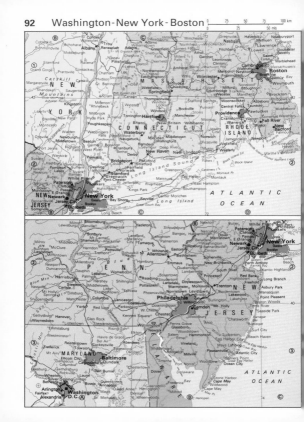

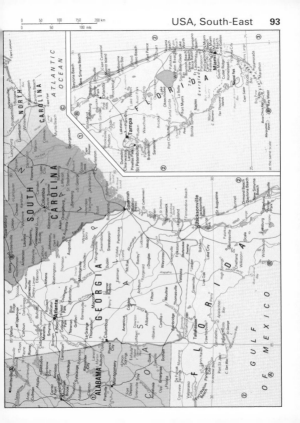

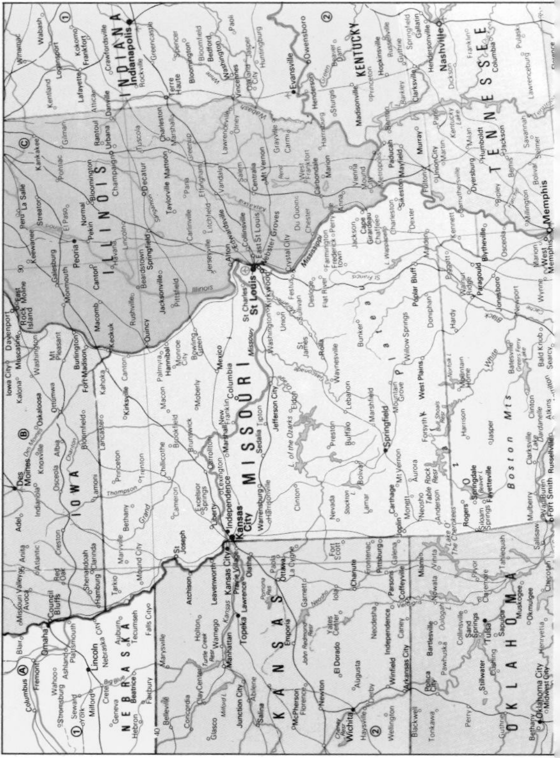

INDIANA

Indianapolis

KENTUCKY

Nashville

TENNESSEE

ILLINOIS

Springfield

Peoria

St. Louis

East St. Louis

Memphis

IOWA

Des Moines

MISSOURI

Columbia

Jefferson City

Springfield

Kansas City

Independence

St. Joseph

Boston Mts.

KANSAS

Topeka

Lawrence

Wichita

El Dorado

NEBRASKA

Lincoln

Omaha

Council Bluffs

OKLAHOMA

Tulsa

Oklahoma City

Stillwater

Muskogee

Bartlesville

Fort Smith

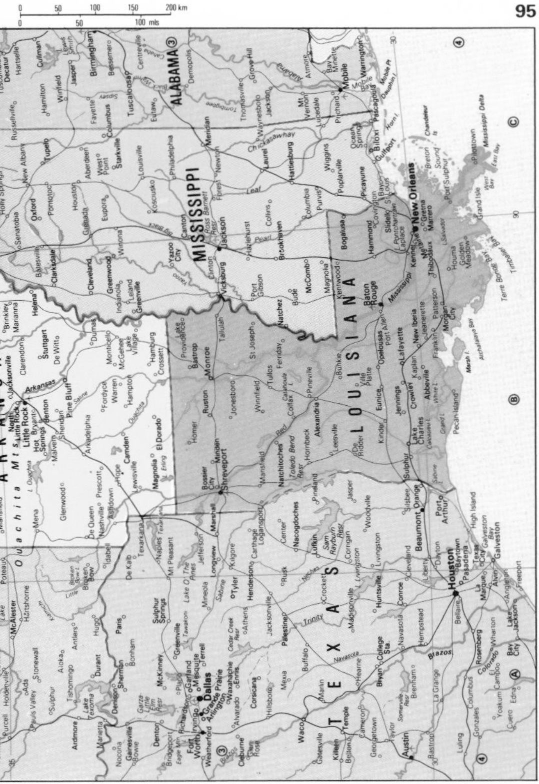

0 50 100 150 200 km
0 50 100 mi

ARKANSAS

MISSISSIPPI

ALABAMA

LOUISIANA

TEXAS

Ouachita Mts.

Little Rock

Pine Bluff

Shreveport

New Orleans

Baton Rouge

Jackson

Vicksburg

Houston

Dallas

Fort Worth

Austin

Beaumont

Galveston

Birmingham

Tuscaloosa

Mobile

Natchez

Alexandria

Lake Charles

Lafayette

Monroe

El Dorado

Texarkana

Longview

Tyler

Waco

Temple

Pasadena

Port Arthur

Orange

Mississippi Delta

| 0 | 50 | 100 | 150 | 200 km |
| 0 | 50 | 100 mls | | |

CANADA

Parksville · Qualicum Beach · Gibsons · Horseshoe Bay · Nanaimo · Vancouver · Princeton · Keremeos · Okanagan · Castlegar · Salmo · Creston

Ladysmith · Blaine · Abbotsford · Oroville · Grand Forks · Trail · Metaline Falls

Bamfield · Duncan · Sidney · Sumas · Chilliwack · Republic · Colville · Northport · Bonners Ferry

Port Renfrew · Victoria · Anacortes · Bellingham · Mt Baker 3285 · Okanogan · Omak · F.D. Roosevelt Lake · Sandpoint · Priest River

C. Flattery · Str. of Juan de Fuca · Port Angeles · Burlington · Concrete · Mt Logan 2751 · Brewster · Coulee Dam · Wilbur · Spirit Lake

Forks · Mt Olympus · Olympic Nat. Park · Marysville · Everett · Snohomish · Chelan · Davenport · Spokane · Coeur d'Alene

Edmonds · Mt Spokane · Medical Lake · Cheney

WASHINGTON

Seattle · Bremerton · Port Orchard · Renton · Snoqualmie · Wenatchee · Ephrata · Moses Lake · Ritzville · Odessa · Plummer

Tacoma · Kent · Auburn · Mt Rainier 4392 · Ellensburg · Othello · Cotax · Pullman · Moscow · Kendrick

Shelton · Olympia · Puyallup · Mt Rainier Nat. Park · Selah · Yakima · Sunnyside · Richland · Dayton · Clarkston · Lewiston

Hoquiam · Aberdeen · Centralia · Naches · Toppenish · Kennewick · Walla Walla

Raymond · Chehalis · Pe Ell · Mt St Helens 2549 · Mt Adams 3751 · Goldendale · Columbia · Umatilla · Wallowa

C. Disappointment · Winlock · Kelso · White Salmon · Arlington · Echo · Pendleton · Blue Mountains · Enterprise

Seaview · Astoria · St Helens · Vancouver · Camas · Hood River · The Dalles · Condon · La Grande · Wallowa Mtns

Seaside · Rainier · Portland · Hillsboro · Gresham · Mt Hood 3427 · Wallowa Mtns 2997

Tillamook · Lake Oswego · Newberg · Oregon City · Baker

McMinnville · Woodburn · Mt Wilson 1707

Lincoln City · Salem · Stayton · Mt Jefferson 3199 · Madras · Spray · Long Creek · Midvale

Newport · Corvallis · Albany · Lebanon · Idanha · Redmond · Dayville · Canyon City · John Day · Unity · Weiser

Yachats · Sweet Home · Three Sisters 3158 · Bend · Brothers · Payette · Ontario

Florence · Eugene · Springfield · Lowell · Burns · Brewsey · Vale · Emmett

OREGON

Reedsport · Cottage Grove · Oakridge · Crescent · High Desert · Harney Basin · Crane · Nampa · Caldwell

Coos Bay · N. Bend · Oakland · Roseburg · Chiloquin · Silver Lake · Harney L. · Malheur L. · Jordan Valley

C. Blanco · Myrtle Point · Myrtle Creek · Mt Thielsen 2799 · Mt Scott 2721

Port Orford · Canyonville · Prospect · Mt Bailey · Valley Falls

Gold Beach · Wolf Creek · Grants Pass · Central Point · Medford · Mt Scott · Copper · Klamath · Klamath Falls · Lakeview

Brookings · O'Brien · Ashland · Lakeview

Crescent City · Hornbrook · Yreka · Dorris · Clear L. · Willow Ranch · Denio · McDermitt

Klamath · Klamath Mts · Weed · Mt Shasta 4317 · Canby · Alturas · Black Rock Desert · Rosa Mtn

CALIFORNIA · Mount Shasta · Adin · NEVADA

Humboldt Bay · Arcata · Eureka · Durnsmuir · Winnemucca · Golconda

Fortuna · Weaverville · Project City · Redding · Lassen Pk 3187 · Eagle L. · Imlay · Battle Mtn

C. Mendocino · Susanville · Rye Patch Res · Mt Tobin 3276

USA, Hawaii

0   25   50   75   100 km

0   25   50 mls

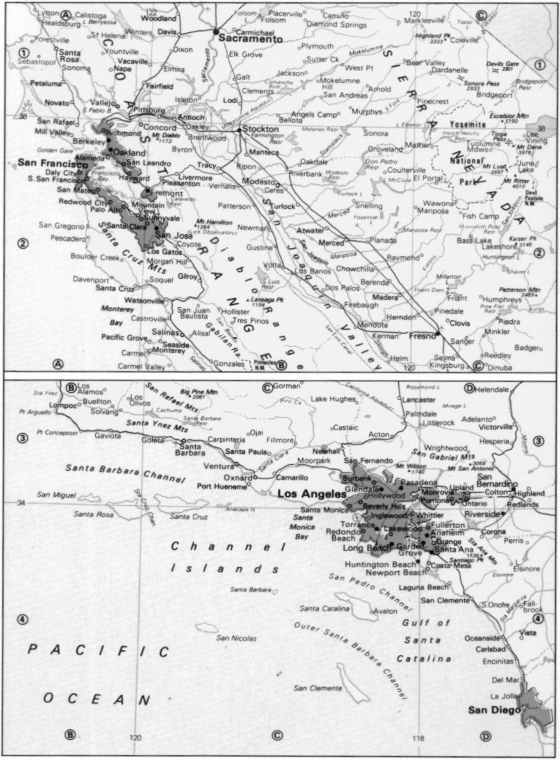

Lytton • Calistoga
Healdsburg • Middletown
St Helena
Santa • Sebastopol
Rosa • Sonoma • Yountville
Petaluma • Napa
Novato • Vallejo
San Rafael • Richmond
Mill Valley • Berkeley
Golden Gate • Oakland
San Francisco • Alameda • San Leandro
Daly City • Hayward
S. San Francisco • Fremont
San Mateo
Redwood City • Palo Alto
Mountain View
Santa Clara • Sunnyvale
San Jose
Pescadero
Boulder Creek • Morgan Hill
Coyote • Gilroy
Santa Cruz • Soquel
Davenport • Watsonville
Monterey • Castroville • Salinas
Pacific Grove • Monterey
Carmel
Carmel Valley

Woodland
Winters • Davis
Sacramento
Dixon
Elk Grove
Fairfield • Galt
Suisun City
Rio Vista • Lodi
Antioch
Pittsburg • Stockton
Concord
Byron • Manteca
Livermore • Ripon
Pleasanton • Modesto
Tracy • Turlock
Patterson
Newman
Gustine • Merced
Los Banos • Planada
Chowchilla
Dos Palos
Firebaugh • Madera
Mendota • Clovis
Kerman • **Fresno**
Selma
Reedley

Lincoln
Rocklin • Roseville
Folsom • Placerville
Camino
Diamond Springs
Plymouth
Sutter Ck
Jackson
Mokelumne Hill • San Andreas • Arnold
Angels Camp • Murphys
Sonora
Groveland • Coulterville
Mariposa
Raymond
Oakhurst
Fish Camp
Yosemite
National
Park
Lee Vining

Markleeville
Coleville
Bridgeport

PACIFIC

OCEAN

Channel
Islands

San Miguel
Santa Rosa
Santa Cruz
Anacapa I.
San Nicolas
Santa Catalina
Avalon
San Clemente

Santa Barbara Channel

Sta Ysabel • Los Olivos
Lompoc • Buellton • Solvang
Gaviota • Goleta
Santa Barbara
Carpinteria • Ojai
Santa Paula • Fillmore
Ventura • Moorpark
Oxnard • Camarillo
Port Hueneme
San Fernando
Thousand Oaks
Los Angeles
Santa Monica • Burbank • Pasadena
Beverly Hills • Hollywood
Torrance • Monrovia
Redondo Beach
Long Beach • Garden Grove
Huntington Beach
Newport Beach • Santa Ana
Costa Mesa • Orange • Anaheim • Fullerton
Laguna Beach • San Clemente
San Pedro Bay
San Bernardino
Colton • Highland
Riverside • Redlands
Perris
Elsinore
Oceanside
Carlsbad
Encinitas
Del Mar
La Jolla
San Diego

Gorman
Lake Hughes • Lancaster
Rosamond L. • Palmdale
Mirage L. • Littlerock • Adelanto
Wrightwood
Mt San Antonio
Hesperia • Victorville
Helendale

Gulf of
Santa
Catalina

San Pedro Channel
Outer Santa Barbara Channel

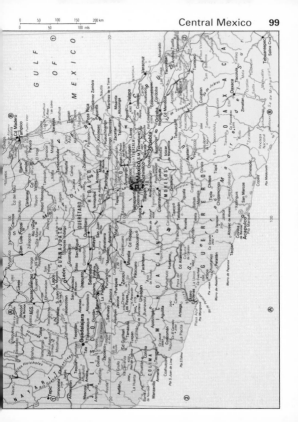

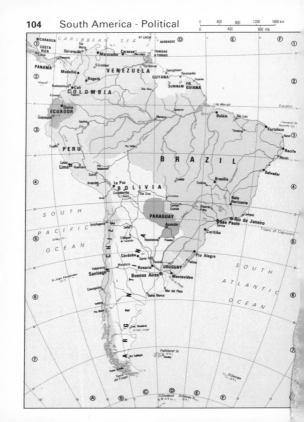

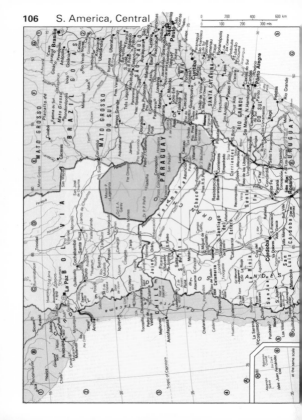

NICARAGUA
Bluefields
S. Carlos
San
José
Heredia Limón
Cartago
David
Santiago
Chitré
Armuelles
COSTA
RICA
Colón
Panama
PANAMA
G. de
Panamá

Barranquilla
Cartagena
Sta Marta
Ciénaga
Riohacha
Maicao
G. de Venezuela
Coro
Maracaibo
Cabimas
Valledupar
Machiques
Cd Ojeda
Barquisimeto
Maracay
Carac
VEN

Montería
Sincelejo
El Banco
Ocaña
Cúcuta
San Cristóbal
Mérida
Valera
Trujillo
Barinas
Guanare
San Fernando

Turbo
Bello
Medellín
Bucaramanga
Málaga
Tunja

Quibdó
Itagüí
Manizales
Pereira
Armenia
Bogotá
Chocontá
Orocuá
Pto Carreño

Buenaventura
Cali
Buga
Tuluá
Girardot
Villavicencio
Granada
COLOMBIA

Popayán
Santander
Neiva
Pto Inírida

Tumaco
Pasto
El Divisó
Florencia
Calamar

Esmeraldas
Ibarra
Ipiales
Pto Asís

Quito
ECUADOR
Coca
Lago Agrio
Tena

Manta
Guayaquil
Ambato
Riobamba
Macas
Iquitos

La Libertad
Cuenca
Machala
Zamora
Loja

Talara
Sullana
Piura
Chulucanas
Huancabamba
Yurimaguas

Chiclayo
Lambayeque
Ferreñafe
Chachapoyas
Tarapoto
Moyobamba

Chepén
Trujillo
Cajabamba
Pucallpa

Chimbote
Huaraz
Tingo María
Huánuco

Casma
Cerro de Pasco
La Merced

PACIFIC
OCEAN

Callao
Lima
Huancayo
PERU
Cuzco

Chincha Alta
Ica
Nazca
Ayacucho
Abancay
Sicuani

BOL

ISLAS
GALÁPAGOS
(ARCHIPEL.)
DO COLÓN)
Fernandina
Isabela
San Salvador
Santa Cruz
San Cristóbal
Santa María
Española
at the same scale

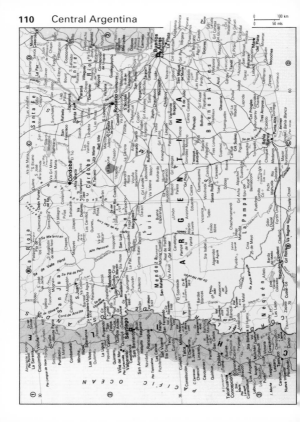

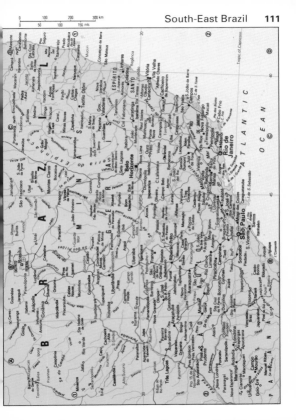

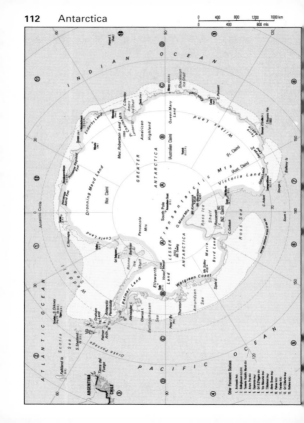

Index

In the index, the first number refers to the page, and the following letter and number refer to the section of the map in which the index entry can be found. For example, Paris 14C2 means that Paris can be found on page 14 where column C and row 2 meet.

Abbreviations used in the index

Name	Region	Code
Achao	*Chile*	105B4
Achensee, L	*Austria*	13D1
Achern	*W Germ*	12E2
Achill, I	*Irish Rep*	7A3
Achinsk	*USSR*	29B2
Acireale	*Italy*	19C3
Acklins, I	*Caribbean*	102C2
Acobamba	*Peru*	108C6
Aconcagua, Mt	*Chile*	109B3
Acopiara	*Brazil*	107D3
Acores, Is	*Atlantic O*	54B4
Acqui	*Italy*	13C2
Acraman, L	*Aust*	74A2
Acre, State	*Brazil*	108C5
Acton	*USA*	98C3
Actopan	*Mexico*	99B1
Ada	*USA*	95A3
Adam	*Oman*	57C5
Adama	*Eth*	65D2
Adamantina	*Brazil*	111A2
Adamaoua, Region	*Nig/Cam*	64B2
Adamello, Mt	*Italy*	13D1
Adams	*USA*	92C1
Adam's Bridge	*India/Sri Lanka*	53B3
Adams L	*Can*	89D2
Adams, Mt	*USA*	84A2
Adam's Peak, Mt	*Sri Lanka*	53C3
'Adan	*S Yemen*	47C4
Adana	*Turk*	58C2
Adapazari	*Turk*	26D5
Adavale	*Aust*	74B1
Ad Dahna', Region	*S Arabia*	57A4
Ad Damman	*S Arabia*	57B4
Ad Dibdibah, Region	*S Arabia*	57A4
Ad Dilam	*S Arabia*	57A5
Ad Dir'iyah	*S Arabia*	57A5
Addis Ababa	*Eth*	65D2
Ad Diwaniyah	*Iraq*	59D3
Ad Dil'	*S Yemen*	50D3
Ad Duwayd	*S Arabia*	59D3
Adelaide	*Aust*	72C4
Adelanto	*USA*	98D3
Aden, G of	*Yemen/Somalia*	47C4
Aderbissinat	*Niger*	63C3
Adhra	*Syria*	60C2
Adi, I	*Indon*	37E4
Adigrat	*Eth*	65D1
Adilabad	*India*	51D5
Adin	*USA*	96B2
Adirondack Mts	*USA*	91C3
Adi Ugai	*Eth*	61C3
Adiyaman	*Turk*	59C2
Adjud	*Rom*	20C1
Admiralty I	*USA*	80E4
Adoni	*India*	53A1
Adra	*Spain*	16A3
Adrano	*Italy*	19B3
Adrar, Region	*Maur*	62A2
Adrar, Mts	*Alg*	62C2
Adrar Soutouf, Region	*Mor*	62A2
Adré	*Chad*	64C2
Adri	*Libya*	61A2
Adria	*Italy*	13E2
Adrian, Michigan	*USA*	90B2
Adriatic S	*Italy/Yugos*	18B2
Aduwa	*Eth*	65D1
Adzopé	*Ivory Coast*	63B4
Aegean, S	*Greece*	21B3
Afghanistan, Republic	*Asia*	48B2
Afgooye	*Somalia*	65E2
Afikpo	*Nig*	63C4
Afjord	*Nor*	4G6
Aflou	*Alg*	62C1
Afmadu	*Somalia*	65D3
Afollé, Region	*Maur*	63A3
Afula	*Israel*	60B2
Afyon	*Turk*	58B2
Agadem	*Niger*	61A3
Agadez	*Niger*	63C3
Agadir	*Mor*	62B1
Agar	*India*	51D4
Agartala	*India*	52C2
Agassiz	*Can*	51D3
Agboville	*Ivory Coast*	63B4
Agdam	*USSR*	59E1
Agematsu	*Japan*	41B1
Agen	*France*	14C3
Agha Jari	*Iran*	56A3
Agordo	*Italy*	13E1
Agra	*India*	51D3
Agri	*Turk*	59D2
Agrigento	*Italy*	19B3
Agrinion	*Greece*	21B3
Agropoli	*Italy*	19B2
Agryz	*USSR*	27H2
Agto	*Greenland*	79C3
Aguadilla	*Puerto Rico*	103D3
Agua Prieta	*Mexico*	100B1
Aguascalientes	*Mexico*	100B2
Aguascalientes, State	*Mexico*	100B2
Aguas Formosas	*Brazil*	111C1
Agueda	*Port*	16A1
Aguelhok	*Mali*	62C3
Agüenit, Well	*Mor*	62A2
Aguilas	*Spain*	16B2
Aguililla	*Mexico*	100B2
Ahar	*Iran*	56B2
Ahmadabad	*India*	51C4
Ahmadnagar	*India*	53A1
Ahmar, Mts	*Eth*	65E2
Ahrgebirge, Region	*W Germ*	12D1
Ahuacatlán	*Mexico*	99A1
Ahualulco	*Mexico*	99A1
Ahus	*Sweden*	5G7
Ahuvan	*Iran*	56A3
Ahvaz	*Iran*	56A3
Aiajuela	*Costa Rica*	102A4
Aigle	*Switz*	13B1
Aiken	*USA*	91B1
Ailao Shan, Upland	*China*	39A5
Ain Beni Mathar	*Mor*	62B1
Ain el Hadjel	*Alg*	17C2
Ain Galakka	*Chad*	64C3
Ain Sefra	*Alg*	62B1
'Ain Sukhna	*Egypt*	58B4
Aioi	*Japan*	41A2
Aioun Abd el Malek, Well	*Maur*	62B2
Aïoun El Atrouss	*Maur*	63B3
Aiquile	*Bol*	106C2
Airdrie	*Can*	89E2
Aire	*France*	13B3
Airforce I	*Can*	82C3
Aishihik	*Can*	13C1
Aishihik L	*Can*	80E3
Aishihik L	*Can*	88G2
Aisne, Department	*France*	12B2
Aitape	*PNG*	37F4
Aixa Zungi	*China*	38B2
Aix-en-Provence	*France*	15D3
Aix-les-Bains	*France*	13A2
Aiyar Res	*India*	52B2
Aiyion	*Greece*	21B3
Aizpute	*USSR*	21B3
Aizuwakamatsu	*Japan*	40E3
Ajaccio	*Corse*	18A2
Ajalpan	*Mexico*	99B2
Ajdabiyah	*Libya*	61B1
Ajmer	*India*	60B2
Ajmer	*India*	51D3
Ajuchitan	*Mexico*	99B2
Akaishi-sanchi, Mts	*Japan*	41B1
Akalkot	*India*	53B1
Akaroa	*NZ*	77B2
Akashi	*Japan*	41A2
Akbulak	*USSR*	27J3
Akcakale	*Turk*	59C2
Ak Dag, Mt	*Turk*	21C3
Aketi	*Zaïre*	64C2
Akhalkalaki	*USSR*	59D1
Akhalsikhe	*USSR*	59D1
Akharnaí	*Greece*	21B3
Akhiok	*USA*	88D3
Akhisar	*Turk*	58A2
Akhmîm	*Egypt*	24H11
Akhnur	*India*	61C2
Akhtubinsk	*USSR*	27G4
Akhtyrka	*USSR*	26D4
Aki	*Japan*	41A2
Akimiski I	*Can*	83K4
Akita	*Japan*	40E3
Akjoujt	*Maur*	62A3
'Akko	*Israel*	60B2
Aklavik	*Can*	80E3
Akobo	*Sudan*	65D3
Akota	*Afghan*	50B1
Akola	*India*	51D4
Akot	*India*	51D4
Akpatok I	*Can*	82D3
Akranes	*Iceland*	4A2
Akron	*USA*	86B2
Aksai Chin, Mts	*China*	50D1
Aksaray	*Turk*	58B2
Aksay	*USSR*	27H3
Aksayquin Hu, L	*China*	50D1
Akshehir	*Turk*	58B2
Aksu	*USSR*	58B2
Aksenovo Zilovskoye	*USSR*	29D2
Aksha	*USSR*	34D1
Aksu	*China*	48C1

Aktogay *USSR* 31J5
Aktumsyk *USSR* 27J4
Aktyubinsk *USSR* 31G4
Akureyri *Iceland* 4B1
Akzhal *USSR* 31K5
Alabama, State *USA* 87B3
Alabaster *USA* 93A1
Ala Shan, Mts *China* 34C3
Alagir *USSR* 27F5
Alagna *Italy* 13B2
Alagoas, State *Brazil* 107D3
Alagoinhas *Brazil* 107D4
Alagón *Spain* 17B1
Al Ahmadi *Kuwait* 59E4
Alajuela *Costa Rica* 101D3
Alakanuk *USA* 88B2
Alakurtti *USSR* 4L5
Al Amarah *Iraq* 59E3
Alameda *USA* 97A2
Alamo *Mexico* 99B1
Alamogordo *USA* 85C3
Alamosa *USA* 85C3
Aland, I *Fin* 5H6
Alanya *Turk* 58B2
Alapayevsk *USSR* 31H4
Alasehir *Turk* 58A2
Alaska, State *USA* 80C3
Alaska, G of *USA* 80D4
Alassio *Italy* 18A2
Alatyr *USSR* 27G3
Alawoona *Aust* 74B2
Al'Ayn *UAE* 57C5
Alayskiy Khrebet, Mts *USSR* 48B2
Alba *Italy* 15D3
Al Bab *Syria* 58C2
Albacete *Spain* 17B2
Alba de Tormes *Spain* 16A1
Alba Iulia *Rom* 20B1
Albania, Republic *Europe* 20A2
Albany *Aust* 72A4
Albany, Georgia *USA* 93B1
Albany, New York *USA* 91D2
Albany, Oregon *USA* 84A2
Albardón *Arg* 110B2
Al Batinah, Region *Oman* 57C5
Al Bayda *Libya* 61B1
Albertville *France* 14D2
Al Bi'r *S Arabia* 58C4
Al Biyadh, Region *S Arabia* 57A5
Alborán, I *Spain* 16B2
Ålborg *Den* 5G7
Al Brayqah *Libya* 61A1
Al Bu Kamal *Syria* 59D3
Albuquerque *USA* 85C3

Al Buraymi *Oman* 57C5
Al Burdi *Libya* 61B1
Al Busayyah *Iraq* 59E3
Alcalá de Henares *Spain* 16B1
Alcaniz *Spain* 17B1
Alcântara *Brazil* 107C2
Alcaraz *Spain* 16B2
Alcazar de San Juan *Spain* 16B2
Alcira *Spain* 17B2
Alcoa *Brazil* 111D1
Alcolea de Pinar *Spain* 16B1
Alcoy *Spain* 17B2
Alcudia *Spain* 17C2
Aldabra, Is *Indian O* 55J8
Aldan *USSR* 29E2
Aldeburgh *Eng* 9E3
Alderney, I *UK* 14B2
Aldershot *Eng* 9D4
Aledo *Brazil* 63A3
Alegrete *Brazil* 106E4
Alejandro Roca *Arg* 110B2
Alejandro Selkirk, I *Chile* 106H6
Aleksandrovsk
   Sakhalinskiy *USSR* 29G2
Aleksevevka *USSR* 31J4
Aleksin *USSR* 26E3
Além Paraíba *Brazil* 111C2
Alençon *France* 15C2
Alenuihaha Chan *Hawaiian Is* 97C4
Alert *Can* 82D1
Ales *France* 14C3
Alessandria *Italy* 18A2
Ålesund *Nor* 30B6
Aleutian Range, Mts *USA* 88C3
Alexander Arch *USA* 80E4
Alexander Bay *S Africa* 66A3
Alexander City *USA* 93A1
Alexander I *Ant* 112C3
Alexandra *NZ* 77A3
Alexandra Fjord *Can* 82C2
Alexandria *Egypt* 61B1
Alexandria, Louisiana *USA* 87A3
Alexandria, Minnesota *USA* 86A2
Alexandria, Virginia *USA* 86C3
Alexandroúpolis *Greece* 21C2
Alexis Creek *Can* 89C2
Aley *Leb* 60B2
Aleysk *USSR* 31K4
Alfaro *Spain* 17B1
Alfatar *Bulg* 20C2
Al Faw *Iraq* 59E3
Alfenas *Brazil* 111B2
Alfonsine *Italy* 13D2
Alfonzo Cláudio *Brazil* 111C2
Alfredo Chaves *Brazil* 111C2
Alga *USSR* 27J4
Algarrobo del Aguila *Arg* 110B3
Algeciras *Spain* 16A2
Alger *Alg* 62C1
Algeria, Republic *Africa* 62C2
Alghero *Italy* 18A2
Algonquin Park *Can* 91C1

Al Hadd *Oman* 57C5
Al Hadithah *Iraq* 59D3
Al Hadithah *S Arabia* 58D2
Al Hadr *Iraq* 59D2
Al Hajar al Gharbi, Mts *Oman* 57C5
Al Hajar ash Sharqi, Mts *Oman* 57C5
Al Hariq *S Arabia* 57A5
Al Haruj al Aswad, Upland *Libya* 61A2
Al Hasa, Region *S Arabia* 57A4
Al Hasakah *Syria* 59D2
Al Hawja' *S Arabia* 59C4
Al Hayy *Iraq* 59E3
Al Hijanah *Syria* 60C2
Al Hillah *Iraq* 59D3
Al Hillah *S Arabia* 57A5
Al Hoceima *Mor* 62B1
Al Hufuf *S Arabia* 57A4
Al Humrah, Region *UAE* 57C5
Al Huwatsah *Oman* 57C5
Aliabad *Iran* 56A2
Aliabad *Iran* 57C4
Ali al Gharbi *Iraq* 59E3
Alibag *India* 53A1
Alicante *Spain* 17B2
Alice *USA* 85D4
Alice Springs *Aust* 72C3
Alicudi, I *Italy* 19B3
Aligarh *India* 50D3
Aligudarz *Iran* 56A3
Ali-Khel *Afghan* 50B2
Alimnia, I *Greece* 21C3
Alipur Duar *India* 52B1
Aliquippa *USA* 90B2
Alisal *USA* 97B2
Al'Iseiwiyah *S Arabia* 59C3
Aliwal North *S Africa* 66B4
Al Jaghbub *Libya* 61B2
Al Jalamid *S Arabia* 59D3
Al Jawb *S Arabia* 61B2
Al Jawf *S Arabia* 59C4
Aljezur *Port* 16A2
Al Jubayl *S Arabia* 57A4
Al Kamil *Oman* 57C5
Al Khaburah *Oman* 57C5
Al Khalis *Iraq* 59D3
Al Khasab *Oman* 57C4
Al Khawr *Qatar* 57B4
Al Khums *Libya* 61A1
Al Kidan, Region *S Arabia* 57B5
Al Kiswah *Syria* 60C2
Alkmaar *Neth* 22A2
Al Kut *Iraq* 59E3
Al Ladhiqiyah *Syria* 58C2
Allahabad *India* 52A1
Al Lajah, Mt *Syria* 60C2
Allakaket *USA* 88D1
Allanmyo *Burma* 42B2
Allatoona L *USA* 93B1
Allegheny Mts *USA* 86C3
Allendale *USA* 93B1
Allen, Mt *USA* 77A3
Allentown *USA* 91C2
Alleppey *India* 53B3
Allgäu, Mts *W Germ* 13D1

Alliance USA	84C2
Al Lith S Arabia	47C3
Al Liwa, Region UAE	57B5
Allora Aust	75D1
Alma, Michigan USA	90B2
Alma Ata USSR	48B1
Almada Port	16A2
Almagan, I Pacific O	37F2
Al Manamah Bahrain	57B4
Al Ma'niyah Iraq	59D3
Almanor, L USA	97A1
Almansa Spain	17B2
Alma Peak, Mt Can	89B1
Al Mariyyah UAE	57B5
Al Marj Libya	61B1
Almazán Spain	16B1
Almenara Brazil	111C1
Almeria Spain	16B2
Al'met'yevsk USSR	27H3
Almhult Sweden	22C1
Al Miqdadiyah Iraq	59E3
Almirante Latorre Chile	110A1
Almirós Greece	21B3
Al Mish'ab A Arabia	57A4
Almodóvar Port	16A2
Almora India	50D3
Al Mubarraz S Arabia	57A4
Al Mudawwara Jordan	58B3
Al Muhaylb Oman	57C5
Al Muharraq Bahrain	57B4
Al Mukalla S Yemen	47C4
Al Mukha Yemen	47C4
Al Musayyib Iraq	50B3
Alness Scot	10B3
Al Nu'maniyah Iraq	59E3
Alnwick Eng	8D2
Alor, I Indon	37D4
Alor Setar Malay	43C4
Alotau PNG	76E2
Aloysius, Mt Aust	72B3
Alpachiri Arg	110C3
Alpena USA	90B1
Alpes du Valais, Mts Switz	13B2
Alpi Dolomitiche, Mts Italy	13B1
Alpi Graie, Mts Italy	13B2
Alpine, Texas USA	85C3
Alpi Orobie, Mts Italy	13C1
Alpi Pennine, Mts Italy	13B2
Alpi Retiche, Mts Switz	13C1
Alpi Venoste, Mts Italy	13D1
Alps, Mts Europe	18A1
Al Qaddahiyah Libya	61A1
Al Qadmus Syria	60C1
Al Qa'im Iraq	59D3
Al Qalibah S Arabia	59C4
Al Qamishli Syria	59D2
Al Qaryah Ash Sharqiyah Libya	61A1
Al Qaryatayn Syria	58C3
Al Qatif S Arabia	57A4
Al Qatrun Libya	61A2
Al Qaysamah S Arabia	57A4
Al Quatayfah Syria	60C2
Al Qunaytirah Syria	58C3
Al Qunfidhah S Arabia	47C4
Al Qurnah Iraq	59E3
Al Qusayr Syria	60C1
Al Qutayfah Syria	58C3
Als, I Den	22B1
Alsace, Region France	15D2
Alsfeld W Germ	23B2
Alston Eng	8C2
Alta Nor	4J5
Alta Gracia Arg	105D2
Altagracia de Orituco Ven	103D5
Altai, Mts Mongolia	34A2
Altamira Brazil	109G4
Altamira Mexico	99B1
Altamura Italy	19C2
Altanbulag Mongolia	34C1
Altape PNG	37F4
Altata Mexico	100B2
Altay China	29B3
Altay Mongolia	29A3
Altay, Mts USSR	29A2
Altdorf Switz	13C1
Altenkirchen W Germ	12D1
Altkirch France	13D2
Alto Molócuo Mozam	67C2
Alton USA	86A3
Altoona USA	91C2
Alto Pencoso, Mts Arg	110C2
Alto Sucuriú Brazil	111A1
Altotonga Mexico	99B2
Altoyac de Alvarez Mexico	99B2
Altun Shan, Mts China	48C2
Alturas USA	96B2
Altus USA	85D3
Al'Ubaylah S Arabia	57B5
Alula Somalia	65F1
Al'Uruq al Mu'taridah, Region S Arabia	57B5
Alva USA	85D2
Alvarado Mexico	99B2
Alvarado USA	94A3
Alvdalen Sweden	5G6
Alvin USA	95A4
Alvsbyn Sweden	4J5
Al Wajh S Arabia	46B3
Alwar India	51D3
Alxa Yougi China	38A2
Alyat USSR	58E2
Alytus USSR	5J8
Alzey W Germ	12E2
Amadi Sudan	65D2
Amadiyah Iraq	59D2
Amadjuak L Can	82C3
Amakusa-shoto, I Japan	40B4
Åmål Sweden	5G7
Amaliás Greece	21B3
Amalner India	51D4
Amami, I Japan	35E4
Amami gunto, Arch Japan	35E4
Amanzimtoti S Africa	66C4
Amapá Brazil	109G3
Amapá, State Brazil	109G3
Amarillo USA	85C3
Amatitan Mexico	99A1
Amazonas Brazil	109E4
Amazonas, State Brazil	108D4
Amazonas, R Brazil	104C3
Ambala India	50D2
Ambalangoda Sri Lanka	53C3
Ambalavao Madag	67D3
Ambam Cam	64B2
Ambanja Madag	67D2
Ambarchik USSR	1C7
Ambato Ecuador	106B4
Ambato-Boeny Madag	67D2
Ambatolampy Madag	67D2
Ambatondrazaka Madag	67D2
Amberg W Germ	23C3
Ambergris Cay, I Belize	101D3
Ambikapur India	52A2
Ambilobe Madag	67D2
Amboasary Madag	67D3
Ambodifototra Madag	67D3
Ambohimahasoa Madag	67D3
Ambon Indon	37D4
Ambositra Madag	67D3
Ambovombe Madag	67D3
Ambriz Angola	64B3
Am Dam Chad	64C1
Amderma USSR	30H3
Amecameca Mexico	100B2
Amecacameca Mexico	99B2
Ameghino Arg	110C2
Ameland, I Neth	22B2
Amenia USA	92C2
American Samoa, Is Pacific O	71H4
Americus USA	93B1
Amersfoort S Africa	67F2
Amery Ice Shelf Ant	112C0
Amfilohkia Greece	21B3
Amfissa Greece	21B3
Amga USSR	29F1
Amga USSR	35F2
Amhara, Region Eth	65D1
Amherst Can	83D5
Amherst, Massachusetts USA	92C1
Amhur India	53B2
Amiens France	14C2
Amino Japan	41B1
Amioune Leb	60B1
Amirante Is Indian O	59K8
Amlekhgan Nepal	52B1
Amman Jordan	58C3
Ammänsaario Fin	4K6
Ammersfoort Neth	22B2
Amol Iran	56B2
Amos Can	83C5
Ampanihy Madag	67D3
Amparo Brazil	111B2
Amposta Spain	17C1
Amravati India	51C4
Amreli India	51C4
Amritsar India	50C2
Amsterdam Neth	22A2
Amsterdam S Africa	67H1
Amsterdam USA	91D2
Amu Darya, R USSR	54L3
Amund Ringes I Can	82A2
Amundsen G Can	86E6
Amundsen-Scott, Base Ant	46E
Amuntai Indon	44E3
Amur, R USSR	29E2
Anaco Ven	109E2

Anaconda USA	84B2	Angemuk, Mt Indon	37E4	Antalya Turk	58B2
Anacortes USA	96B1	Angers France	14B2	Antananarivo Madag	67D2
Anáfi, I Greece	21C3	Anglesey, I Wales	7C3	Antarctic Circle Ant	112C1
'Anah Iraq	59D3	Angleton USA	14C2	Antequera Spain	16B2
Anaheim USA	97B3	Angmagssalik Greenland	82G3	Anti-Atlas, Mts Mor	62B2
Anaimalai Hills India	53B2	Angoche Mozam	67D2	Anticosti I Can	83D5
Anakapalle India	49C4	Angol Chile	105B3	Antigua, I Caribbean	103E3
Anaktuvuk P USA	88E1	Angola, Republic Africa	66A2	Antioch USA	98A2
Analalaya Madag	67D2	Angoon USA	88H3	Antlers USA	95A3
Anamur Turk	58B2	Angoulème France	14C2	Antofagasta Chile	106B3
Anan Japan	41A2	Angra do Heroismo Acores	62A1	Antrim, County N Ire	11C1
Anantapur India	53B2	Angra dos Reis Brazil	111C2	Antrim N Ire	11C1
Anantnag India	53B2	Anguil Arg	110C3	Antseranana Madag	67D2
Anápolis Brazil	107B5	Anguilla, I Caribbean	103E3	Antsirabe Madag	67D2
Anar Iran	56C3	Anguilla Cays, Is Caribbean	102B2	Antsohihy Madag	67D2
Anarak Iran	56B3	Angumu Zaire	65C3	An Tuc Viet	42D3
Anatahan, I Pacific O	37F2	Anholt, I Den	22C1	Antwerpen Belg	12C1
Añatuya Arg	106D4	Anhua China	39C4	An Uaimh Irish Rep	11C2
Anbyon N Korea	40B3	Anhui, Province China	31D3	Anupgarh India	50C3
Ancapa Is USA	98C4	Aniak USA	88B3	Anuradhapura Sri Lanka	53C3
Anchorage USA	80D3	Anicuns Brazil	111B1	Anvik USA	80B3
Anchuma, Mt Bol	106C2	Anízy-le-Château France	12B2	Anxi China	26B2
Ancón Peru	108B6	Anjar USA	80C3	Anyang China	38C2
Ancona Italy	18B2	Anjou, Republic France	14B2	Anzac Can	89E1
Ancram USA	92C1	Anjouan, I Comoros	67D2	Anzhero-Sudzhensk USSR	31K4
Ancud Chile	105B4	Anjozorobe Madag	67D2	Anzio Italy	19B2
Anda China	35E2	Anju N Korea	40B3	Aomori Japan	40E2
Andacollo Arg	110A3	Ankang China	31B3	Aosta Italy	18A1
Andado Aust	74A1	Ankara Turk	58B2	Aoukâr, Desert Region Maur	62C2
Andahuaylas Peru	108C6	Ankaratra, Mt Madag	67D2	Aozou Chad	61A2
Andalsnes Nor	4F6	Ankazoabo Madag	67D3	Apalachicola USA	93B2
Andalucia, Region Spain	16A2	Ankazobe Madag	67D2	Apan Mexico	99B2
Andalusia USA	93A1	Anklam E Germ	22C2	Aparecida do Taboado Brazil	111A2
Andaman Is Burma	49D4	An Loc Viet	43D3	Aparri Phil	45B2
Andamooka Aust	74A2	Anlong China	39B4	Apatin Yugos	20A1
Andenes Nor	4H5	Anlu China	39C3	Apatzingan Mexico	100B3
Andermatt Switz	13C1	Anna USA	90B4	Apeldoorn Neth	22B2
Andernach W Germ	23B2	'Annaba Alg	62C1	Apiaí Brazil	111B2
Anderson, Indiana USA	9N2	An Nabk S Arabia	58C3	Apo, Mt Phil	45C4
Anderson, Missouri USA	94B2	An Nabk Syria	58C3	Apollo Bay Aust	74B3
Anderson, S Carolina USA	93B1	An Nafud, Desert Region S Arabia	58C3	Apo, Mt, Mt Phil	45C4
Andhra Pradesh, State India	53B1	An Najaf Iraq	59D3	Apopka, L USA	93B2
Andikithira, I Greece	21B3	Annan Scot	8C2	Apostle Is USA	86A2
Andizhan USSR	31J5	Annapolis USA	91C3	Apostle L USA	86A2
Andkhui Afghan	31H6	Annapurna, Mt Nepal	50B2	Apozol Mexico	99A1
Andong S Korea	40B3	Ann Arbor USA	92B2	Appalachian Mts USA	87B3
Andorra, Principality SW Europe	17C1	An Nasiriyah Iraq	60C1	Appenino Abruzzese, Mts Italy	18A2
Andover Eng	9D4	An Nasiriyah Iraq	59E3	Appennino Ligure, Mts Italy	18A2
Andradina Brazil	111A2	Annecy France	13B2	Appennino Lucano, Mts Italy	19C2
Andreafsky USA	88B2	Annemasse France	13B1	Appennino Napoletano, Mts Italy	18B2
Andria Italy	19C2	An Nhon Viet	42D3	Appennino Tosco-Emiliano, Mts Italy	18B2
Andros, I Bahamas	87C4	Anning China	39A5	Appennino Umbro-Marchigiano, Mts Italy	18B2
Andros, I Greece	21B3	Anniston USA	93A1	Appenzell Switz	13C1
Androth, I India	53A2	Annonay France	15C2	Appleby Eng	6C2
Andújar Spain	16B2	Annotto Bay Jamaica	103J1	Appleton, Wisconsin USA	90A2
Andulo Angola	66A2	Anqing China	39D3	Apucarana Brazil	106F3
Anécho Togo	63C4	Ansai China	38B2	Apulco Mexico	99B1
Anéfis Mali	63C3	Ansbach W Germ	18C3	'Aqaba Jordan	58C4
Añelo Arg	110B3	Anse d'Hainault Haiti	103C3	'Aqaba, G of Egypt/S Arabia	58B4
Angarsk USSR	29C2	Anshan China	38E1	'Aqda Iran	56B3
Ange Sweden	4H6	Anshun China	39B4		
Angel de la Guarda, I Mexico	100A2	Ansongo Mali	63C3		
Angeles Phil	45B2	Ansted USA	92B3		
Angelholm Sweden	5G7	Antakya Turk	58C2		
Angels Camp USA	98B1	Antalaha Madag	67E2		

Asansol India 52B2
Asbest USSR 27K2
Asbury Park USA 91D2
Ascension, I Atlantic O 69H5
Aschaffenburg W Germ 23B3
Aschersleben E Germ 22C2
Ascoli Piceno Italy 18B2
Ascona Switz 13C1
Asedjirad, Upland Alg 62C2
Asele Sweden 4H6
Aselle Eth 65D2
Asenovgrad Bulg 20B2
Asfeld France 12C2
Asha USSR 27J2
Ashburn USA 93B1
Ashburton NZ 77B2
Ashdod Israel 58B3
Ashdown USA 95B3
Asheville USA 87B3
Ashford Eng 9E4
Ashikaga Japan 40D3
Ashizuri-misaki, Pt Japan 41A2
Ashkhabad USSR 31G6
Ashland, Kentucky USA 91C3
Ashland, Nebraska USA 94A1
Ashland, Ohio USA 90B2
Ashland, Oregon USA 84A2
Ashley Aust 75C1
Ashokan Res USA 92B2
Ashqelon Israel 60B3
Ash Shabakh Iraq 59D3
Ash Sha'm UAE 57C4
Ash Sharqat Iraq 59D2
Ash Shatrah Iraq 59E3
Ash Shihr S Yemen 57A4
Ash Shumlul S Arabia 57A4
Ashtabula USA 90B2
Ashuanipi L Can 83D4
Asiago Italy 13D2
Asinara, I Medit S 19B3
Asino USSR 31K4
Askale Turk 59D2
Askersund Sweden 5G7
Asmar Afghan 50C1
Asmara Eth 61C3
Aso Japan 41A2
Asosa Eth 65D1
Aspiring, Mt NZ 77A2
Assab Eth 65E1
As Sabkhah Syria 59C2
As Salamiyah S Arabia 57A5
As Salamiyah Syria 58C2
As Salman Iraq 59D3
Assam, State India 52C1
As Samawah Iraq 59D2
As Sanam, Region S Arabia 57B5
As Sanamayn Syria 60C2
Assen Neth 22B2
Assens Den 22B1
As Sidrah Libya 61A1
Assiniboia Can 81H5
Assiniboine, Mt Can 81G4
Assis Brazil 106F3
As Sukhnah Syria 59C3
As Summan, Region S Arabia 57A5

Assumption, I Seychelles 65E3
As Suwayda' Syria 58C3
As Suwayrah Iraq 59D3
Astara USSR 59E2
Asti Italy 18A2
Astipálaia, I Greece 21C3
Astorga Spain 16A1
Astoria USA 84A2
Astrakhan' USSR 27G4
Asturias, Region Spain 16A1
Asunción Par 106E4
Aswân Egypt 46B3
Asyût Egypt 61C2
As Zilyif Egypt 58B3
Atakpamé Togo 63C4
Atar Maur 62A2
Atâsu USSR 31J5
Atchison USA 86A3
Atebubu Ghana 63C4
Atessa Italy 18B2
Ath Belg 12B1
Athabasca Can 89E2
Athabasca L Can 81H4
Athenry Irish Rep 11B2
Athens, Georgia USA 87B3
Athens, Ohio USA 90B3
Athens, Texas USA 95A3
Athínai Greece 21B3
Athlone Irish Rep 7B3
Athol USA 92C1
Athos, Mt Greece 21B2
Athy Irish Rep 11C2
Ati Chad 64B1
Atikokan Can 83A5
Atkarsk USSR 27F3
Atkins USA 99B2
Atlacomulco Mexico 99B2
Atlanta, Georgia USA 87B3
Atlanta, Michigan USA 90B2
Atlantic USA 94A1
Atlantic City USA 86C3
Atlantic Highlands USA 92B2
Atlas Saharien, Mts Alg 62C1
Atlin Can 80E4
Atlin L Can 80E4
'Atlit Israel 60B2
Atlixco Mexico 99B2
Atmore USA 87B3
Atofinandrahana Madag 67D3
Atognak I USA 98D3
Atoka USA 95D3
Atotonilco Mexico 99A1
Ataf, Region UAE 57B5
At Ta'if S Arabia 47C3
At Tall Syria 60C2
Attalla USA 93A1
Attapiskat Can 83A4
Attica, Indiana USA 90A2
Attigny France 12C2
Attleboro, Massachusetts USA 92D2
Attopeu Laos 42D3

Atvidaberg Sweden 5H7
Atwater USA 98B2
Aubagne France 15D3
Aube, Department France 12C2
Aubenas France 15C3
Auburn, Alabama USA 93A1
Auburn, California USA 97A2
Auburn, Indiana USA 90A2
Auburn, Nebraska USA 94A1
Auburn, New York USA 91C2
Auburn, Washington USA 96B1
Auch France 14C3
Auckland NZ 76B1
Auckland Is NZ 71G6
Auden Can 83B4
Audincourt France 13B1
Augathella Aust 75C1
Augsburg W Germ 23C3
Augusta Aust 72A3
Augusta, Georgia USA 87B3
Augusta, Kansas USA 94A2
Augusta, Maine USA 86D2
Augustów Pol 88D3
Augustus, Mt Aust 72A3
Aumale France 12A2
Auraiya India 51D3
Aurangabad India 51D5
Aurès, Mts Alg 62C1
Aurillac France 14C3
Aurora, Colorado USA 84C3
Aurora, Illinois USA 86B2
Aurora, Indiana USA 90B3
Aurora, Mississippi USA 94B2
Aus Namibia 73B1
Au Sable USA 90B2
Austin, Minnesota USA 86A2
Austin, Nevada USA 99B3
Austin, Texas USA 85D3
Australian Alps, Mts Aust 73D4
Austria, Fed Republic Europe 3E4
Autlán Mexico 100B3
Autun France 15C2
Auvergne, Region France 15C2
Auxerre France 15C2
Auxi-le-Chateaux France 12B1
Avallon France 15C2
Avalon USA 98C4
Avaré Brazil 111B2
Avaz Iran 56D3
Aveiro Brazil 109F4
Aveiro Port 16A1
Avellaneda Arg 105E2
Avellino Italy 19B2
Avesnes-sur-Helpe France 12B1
Avesta Sweden 5H6
Avezzano Italy 18B2
Aviemore Scot 10C3
Aviemore, L NZ 77B2
Avigliana Italy 13B2
Avignon France 15C3
Avila Spain 16B1
Aviles Spain 16A1
Avon, County Eng 9C4
Avonmouth Wales 9C4
Avon Park USA 93B2

Avtovac Yugos	20A2
Awarem Eth	65E2
Awarua Pt NZ	77A2
Awash Eth	65E2
Awa-shima, I Japan	41B1
Awbari Libya	61A2
Aweil Sudan	64C2
Awjilan Libya	61B2
Axel Heiburg I Can	82A2
Axminster Eng	9C4
Ayabe Japan	41B1
Ayacucho Arg	105E3
Ayacucho Peru	108C6
Ayaguz USSR	31K5
Ayakkum Hu, L China	48C2
Ayamonte Spain	16A2
Ayan USSR	29F2
Ayauiri Peru	108C6
Aydin Turk	58A2
Ayios Evstrátios, I Greece	21C3
Aylesbury Eng	9D4
Aylmer, Mt USA	89D2
'Ayn al Fijah Syria	60C2
Ayn Zalah Iraq	59D2
Ayod Sudan	65D2
Ayr Aust	73D2
Ayr Scot	8B2
Ayre, Pt of Eng	8B2
Aytthaya Thai	42C3
Ayutla Mexico	99A1
Ayvacik Turk	21C3
Ayvalik Turk	21C3
Azamgarh India	52A1
Azare Nig	63D3
A'Zaz Syria	58C2
Azerbaydzhanskaya SSR, Republic USSR	31F5
Azogues Ecuador	108B4
Azovskoya More, S USSR	26E4
Azrou Mor	62B1
Azucena Arg	110D3
Azúl Arg	105E3
Az-Zabdani Syria	60C2
Az Zahirah, Mts Oman	57C5
Az Zubayr Iraq	59E3

B

Ba'abda Leb	60B2
Ba'albek Leb	58C3
Ba'al Hazor, Mt Israel	60B3
Baardheere Somalia	65E2
Babadag Rom	20C2
Babaeski Turk	58A1
Babahoyo Ecuador	108B4
Babar, I Indon	37D4
Babati Tanz	65D3
Babayevo USSR	26E2
Baberton USA	90B2
Babîle I Can	8B1
Babol Iran	56B2
Babuyan Chan Phil	45B2
Babuyan Is Phil	45B2
Bacabal Brazil	107C2
Bacan, I Indon	37D4
Bacau Rom	26C4
Bac Can Viet	42D1
Bacchus Marsh Aust	74B3
Bachu China	48B2
Backbone Ranges, Mts Can	88J2
Bac Ninh Viet	42D1
Bacolod Phil	45B3
Baco, Mt Phil	45B3
Badagara India	53B2
Badain Jaran Shamo, Desert China	38A1
Badajoz Spain	16A2
Badalona Spain	17C1
Badanah S Arabia	59D3
Bad Bergzabern W Germ	12D2
Bad Ems W Germ	12D1
Baden Switz	13C1
Baden-Baden W Germ	23B3
Baden-Württemberg, State W Germ	23B3
Badgastein Austria	23C3
Badger USA	98C2
Bad-Godesberg W Germ	23B2
Bad Hersfeld W Germ	23B2
Bad Honnef W Germ	12D1
Badin Pak	51B4
Bad Ischl Austria	18B1
Bad-Kreuznach W Germ	23B3
Bad Nevemahr-hrweller W Germ	12D1
Bad Ragaz Switz	13C1
Bad Tolz W Germ	23C3
Badulla Sri Lanka	53C3
Baena Spain	16B2
Bafatá Guinea-Bissau	63A3
Baffin I Can	82C2
Bafia Cam	64B2
Bafoulabé Mali	63A3
Bafoussam Cam	64B2
Bafq Iran	56C3
Bafra Burun, Pt Turk	26E5
Baft Iran	57C4
Bafwasende Zaire	64C2
Bagaha India	52A1
Bagalkot India	53B1
Bagamoyo Tanz	65D3
Bagé Brazil	105F2
Bagherhat Bang	52B2
Baghin Iran	57C3
Baghlan Afghan	50B1
Bagnoa Ivory Coast	63B4
Bagnols-sur-Cèze France	15C3
Baguio Phil	45B2
Bahadurabad India	52B1
Bahamas, The, Is Caribbean	87C4
Baharampur India	52B1
Bahar Der Eth	65D1
Bahawahpur, Province Pak	51C3
Bahawalpur Pak	50C3
Bahawathagar Pak	51C3
Bahia, State Brazil	107C4
Bahia Blanca Arg	105D3
Bahia Kino Mexico	85B4
Bahraich India	52A1
Bahrain, Sheikdom Arabian Pen	46D3
Bahr al Milh, L Iraq	59D3
Baia dos Tigres Angola	66A2
Baia Mare Rom	26B4
Baïbokoum Chad	64B2
Baicheng China	35E2
Baie-Comeau Can	83D5
Baie-du-Poste Can	83C4
Baihe China	38B3
Ba'iji Iraq	59D3
Baikunthpur India	52A2
Bailesti Rom	20B2
Bailleul France	12B1
Baima China	38A3
Bainbridge USA	93B1
Baird Inlet USA	88B2
Baird Mts USA	80B3
Bairin Youqi China	38D1
Bairin Zuoqi China	38D1
Bairnsdale Aust	73D4
Bais Phil	45B4
Baja Hung	20A1
Baja California, State Mexico	85B3
Bakal USSR	27J2
Bakala CAR	64C2
Bakel Sen	63A3
Baker, Montana USA	84C2
Baker, Oregon USA	84B2
Baker Foreland, Pt Can	82A3
Baker L Can	80J3
Baker L Can	80J3
Baker, Mt USA	84A2
Bakersfield USA	85B3
Bakhardan USSR	56C2
Bakhardok USSR	56C2
Bakhmach USSR	26D3
Bako Eth	65D2
Bakouma CAR	64C2
Baku USSR	31F5
Balabac, I Phil	45A4
Balaikarangan Indon	74A2
Balakovo USSR	27G3
Balangir India	52A3
Balashov USSR	27F3
Balasore India	52B3
Balát Egypt	58B2
Balaton, L Hung	18C1
Balbniggan Irish Rep	11C2
Balcarce Arg	105E3
Balchik Bulg	20C2
Balclutha NZ	77B3
Bald Knob USA	94B2
Baldwin USA	93B1
Baldy Peak, Mt USA	85C3
Bale Pak	45B2
Balezino USSR	27H2
Bali Indon	72A1
Balikesir Turk	58A2
Balikpapan Indon	44A3
Balintang Chan Phil	44C4
Bali S Indon	44C4
Baliza Brazil	111A1
Balkh Afghan	50B1
Balkhash USSR	31J5
Ballachulish Scot	8B3
Ballaghaderreen Irish Rep	11B2
Ballantrae Scot	8B2

Ballantyne Str *Can*	80G2	
Ballapur *India*	53B2	
Ballarat *Aust*	73D4	
Ballater *Scot*	10C3	
Ballery is *Ant*	112C7	
Ballina *Irish Rep*	52A1	
Ballina *Aust*	75D1	
Ballinasloe *Irish Rep*	7B3	
Ballinrobe *Irish Rep*	11B2	
Ballycastle *N Ire*	11B2	
Ballycastle *N Ire*	11C1	
Ballyclare *N Ire*	11C1	
Ballymena *N Ire*	11C1	
Ballymoney *N Ire*	11C1	
Ballyshannon *Irish Rep*	11B2	
Ballyvaghan *Irish Rep*	74B3	
Balmoral *Aust*	74B3	
Balnearia *Arg*	110C2	
Balombo *Angola*	66A2	
Balotra *India*	51C3	
Balrampur *India*	52A1	
Balranald *Aust*	73D4	
Balsas *Brazil*	107B3	
Balsas *Mexico*	99B2	
Balta *USSR*	26C4	
Baltic S *N Europe*	5H7	
Baltim *Egypt*	58B3	
Baltimore *Irish Rep*	11B3	
Baltimore *USA*	86C3	
Baluchistan, Region *Pak*	50B3	
Balurghat *India*	52B1	
Bam *Iran*	57C4	
Bama *Nig*	64B1	
Bamako *Mali*	63B3	
Bambari *CAR*	64C2	
Bamberg *W Germ*	23C2	
Bambili *Zaire*	64C2	
Bambui *Brazil*	111B2	
Bamenda *Cam*	64B2	
Bamfield *Can*	89C3	
Bamiyan *Afghan*	50B2	
Bampur *Iran*	57D4	
Banalia *Zaire*	64C2	
Banamba *Mali*	63B3	
Ban Aranyaprathet *Thai*	42C3	
Ban Ban *Laos*	42C2	
Ban Betong *Thai*	43C4	
Banbridge *N Ire*	11C1	
Banbury *Eng*	9D3	
Banchory *Scot*	10C3	
Banco Chinchorro, S *Mexico*	101D3	
Bancroft *Can*	91C1	
Banda *India*	52A1	
Banda Aceh *Indon*	36A3	
Bandar Abbas *Iran*	57C4	
Bandar Anzali *Iran*	56A2	
Bandar-e Daylam *Iran*	57B4	
Bandar-e Lengheh *Iran*	57B4	
Bandar-e Maqam *Iran*	57B4	
Bandar-e Rig *Iran*	57B4	
Bandar-e Torkoman *Iran*	56B2	
Bandar Khomeyni *Iran*	57A3	
Bandar Seri Begawan *Brunei*	44C2	
Banda S *Indon*	37D4	
Band Bont *Iran*	57C4	
Bandeira, Mt *Brazil*	111C2	
Bandiagara *Mali*	63B3	
Bandirma *Turk*	26C5	
Bandon *Irish Rep*	11B3	
Bandundu *Zaire*	64B3	
Bandung *Indon*	44B4	
Banes *Cuba*	101E2	
Banff *Can*	89D2	
Banff *Scot*	10C3	
Bangalore *India*	53B2	
Bangassou *CAR*	64C2	
Banggi, I *Malay*	36D5	
Bangka, I *Indon*	44B3	
Bangko *Indon*	44A3	
Bangkok *Thai*	42C3	
Bangladesh, Republic *Asia*	48C3	
Bangong Co, L *China*	50D2	
Bangor, Maine *USA*	86D2	
Bangor *N Ire*	11D1	
Bangor, Pennsylvania *USA*	92B2	
Bangor *Wales*	8B3	
Bangsalsembera *Indon*	44D3	
Ban Saphan Yai *Thai*	42B3	
Bangued *Phil*	45B2	
Bangui *CAR*	64B2	
Bangweulu, L *Zambia*	66C2	
Ban Hat Yai *Thai*	43C4	
Ban Hin Heup *Laos*	42C2	
Ban Houei Sai *Laos*	42C1	
Ban Hua Hin *Thai*	42B3	
Bani Bangou *Niger*	63C3	
Bani Walid *Libya*	61A1	
Baniyas *Syria*	58C2	
Banja Luka *Yugos*	18C2	
Banjarmasin *Indon*	44D3	
Banjul *The Gambia*	63A3	
Ban Kantang *Thai*	43B4	
Ban Khemmarat *Laos*	42D2	
Banks I *Aust*	37F5	
Banks I, British Columbia *Can*	81E4	
Banks I, Northwest Territories *Can*	80F2	
Banks L *USA*	96C1	
Bankura *India*	52B2	
Ban Mae Sariang *Thai*	42B2	
Ban Mae Sot *Thai*	42B2	
Ban Me Thuot *Viet*	42D3	
Ban Na San *Thai*	43B4	
Baños Maule *Chile*	110A3	
Ban Pak Neun *Laos*	42C2	
Ban Pak Phanang *Thai*	43C4	
Ban Ru Kroy *Camb*	42D3	
Ban Sai Yok *Thai*	42B3	
Ban Sattahip *Thai*	42C3	
Banská Bystrica *Czech*	19D3	
Banswara *India*	51C4	
Ban Tha Kham *Thai*	43B4	
Ban Thateng *Laos*	42D2	
Ban Tha Tum *Thai*	42C2	
Bantry *Irish Rep*	7B3	
Ban Ya Soup *Viet*	42D3	
Banyuwangi *Indon*	44C4	
Baofeng *China*	38C3	
Bao Ha *Viet*	42C1	
Baoji *China*	38B3	
Bao Loc *Viet*	42D3	
Baoshan *China*	34B4	
Baotou *China*	38C1	
Bapatla *India*	53C1	
Bapaume *France*	12B1	
Ba'Qubah *Iraq*	59D3	
Baqueriro Morena *Ecuador*	108J7	
Bar *USSR*	20A2	
Bara *Sudan*	65D1	
Baraawe *Somalia*	65E2	
Barabai *Indon*	44D3	
Bara Banki *India*	52A1	
Barabinsk *USSR*	31J4	
Barabinskaya Step, Steppe *USSR*	31J4	
Baracaldo *Spain*	16B1	
Baracoa *Cuba*	102C2	
Baradine *Aust*	75C2	
Baramati *India*	53A1	
Baramula *Pak*	50C2	
Baran *India*	51D3	
Barangas *Phil*	45B3	
Baranof I *USA*	80E4	
Baranovichi *USSR*	26C3	
Baratta *Aust*	74A2	
Barauni *India*	52B1	
Barbacena *Brazil*	107C6	
Barbados, I *Caribbean*	103F4	
Barbastro *Spain*	17C1	
Barberton *S Africa*	67H1	
Barbezieux *France*	14B2	
Barbôsa *Colombia*	108C2	
Barbuda, I *Caribbean*	103E3	
Barcaldine *Aust*	73D3	
Barcelona *Spain*	19C3	
Barcelona *Spain*	17C1	
Barcelona *Ven*	109E1	
Barda del Medio *Arg*	110B3	
Bardai *Chad*	64C1	
Bardas Blancas *Arg*	105C3	
Barddhaman *India*	52B2	
Bardejov *Czech*	25C3	
Bardi *Italy*	13C2	
Bardonecchia *Italy*	13B2	
Bardsey, I *Wales*	9B3	
Bareilly *India*	50D3	
Barentsoya, I *Barents S*	30D2	
Barentu *Eth*	61C3	
Bargarh *India*	52A2	
Barge *Italy*	13B2	
Barguzin *USSR*	29D2	
Barhi *India*	52B2	
Bari *Italy*	19C2	
Barika *Alg*	17D2	
Barinas *Ven*	108C2	
Baripada *India*	52B2	
Bari Sadri *India*	51C4	
Barisal *Bang*	52C2	
Barkam *China*	39A3	
Barkley, L *USA*	94C2	
Barkly East *S Africa*	66B4	
Barkly Tableland, Mts *Aust*	72C2	
Bar-le-Duc *France*	12C2	
Barlee, L *Aust*	72A3	

Barlee Range, Mts *Aust*	72A3
Barletta *Italy*	23B3
Barmer *India*	51C3
Barmera *Aust*	74B2
Barmouth *Wales*	9B3
Barnard Castle *Eng*	8D2
Barnaul *USSR*	31K4
Barnegat *USA*	92B3
Barnesville, Georgia *USA*	93B1
Barnesville, Ohio *USA*	90B3
Barnsley *Eng*	8D3
Barnstaple *Eng*	9B4
Baro *Nig*	63C4
Barpeta *India*	52C1
Barquisimeto *Ven*	108D1
Barra *Brazil*	107C4
Barra, I *Scot*	10A3
Barraba *Aust*	75D2
Barra de Navidad *Mexico*	99A2
Barra de Piraí *Brazil*	111C2
Barra do Garcas *Brazil*	111A1
Barragem do Maranhao *Port*	16A2
Barra Mansa *Brazil*	107C6
Barranca *Peru*	108B6
Barrancabermeja *Colombia*	108C2
Barrancas *Ven*	109E2
Barranqueras *Arg*	106E4
Barranquilla *Colombia*	108C1
Barre *USA*	92C1
Barreal *Arg*	106C2
Barreiras *Brazil*	110B2
Barreiro *Port*	16A2
Barreiros *Brazil*	107D3
Barren Is *USA*	88D3
Barretos *Brazil*	107B6
Barrhead *Can*	89E2
Barrie *Can*	90C2
Barrière *Can*	89C2
Barrier Range, Mts *Aust*	74B2
Barrington, Mt *Aust*	73E4
Barrouaillie *St Vincent*	103N2
Barrow *USA*	80C2
Barrow Creek *Aust*	72C3
Barrow I *Aust*	72A3
Barrow-in-Furness *Eng*	8C2
Barrow, Pt *USA*	80C2
Barry's Bay *Can*	91C1
Barsi *India*	53B1
Barstow *USA*	85B3
Bar-sur-Aube *France*	15C2
Bartica *Guyana*	109F2
Bartin *Turk*	58B1
Bartle Frere, Mt *Aust*	73D2
Bartlesville *USA*	85D3
Bartolomeu Dias *Mozam*	67C3
Bartoszyce *Pol*	24C2
Barung, I *Indon*	44C4
Barwah *India*	51D4
Barwani *India*	51C4
Barysh *USSR*	27G3
Basankusu *Zaire*	64B2
Basavilbasa *Arg*	106E3
Basco *Phil*	45B1
Basel *Switz*	18A1
Bashaw *Can*	89E2
Bashi Chan *Phil*	45B1
Bashkirskaya ASSR, Republic *USSR*	27H3
Basilan, I *Phil*	45B4
Basildon *Eng*	9D4
Basin Region *USA*	84B2
Basra *Iraq*	59E3
Bas-Rhin, Department *France*	12D2
Bassano *Can*	89E2
Bassano *Italy*	18B1
Bassano del Grappa *Italy*	13D2
Bassari *Togo*	63C4
Bassas da India, I, *Mozam Chan*	67C3
Bassein *Burma*	42A2
Basse Terre *Guadeloupe*	103E3
Bassila *Benin*	63C4
Bass Lake *USA*	98C2
Bass Str *Aust*	73D4
Båstad *Sweden*	5G7
Bastak *Iran*	57B4
Basti *India*	52A1
Bastia *Corse*	18A2
Bastogne *Belg*	23B3
Bastrop, Louisiana *USA*	95B3
Bastrop, Texas *USA*	95A3
Bata *Eq Guinea*	64A2
Batakan *Indon*	44C3
Batala *India*	50D2
Batang *China*	34B3
Batangafo *CAR*	64B2
Batan Is *Phil*	45B1
Batatais *Brazil*	111B2
Batavia *USA*	91C2
Batemans Bay *Aust*	75D3
Batesburg *USA*	93B1
Batesville, Arkansas *USA*	94B2
Batesville, Mississippi *USA*	95C3
Bath *Eng*	9C4
Bath, New York *USA*	91C2
Bathgate *Scot*	73D4
Bathurst *Can*	83D5
Bathurst I *Aust*	72C2
Bathurst I *Can*	80H2
Batlow *Aust*	75C3
Batman *Turk*	59D2
Batna *Alg*	62C1
Baton Rouge *USA*	87A3
Batroun *Leb*	60B1
Battambang *Camb*	42C3
Batticaloa *Sri Lanka*	53C3
Battle Creek *USA*	96B2
Battle Harbour *Can*	83E4
Battle Mountain *USA*	96C2
Batukelau *Indon*	44D2
Batumi *USSR*	31F5
Batu Pahat *Malay*	43C5
Baturaja *Indon*	44A3
Bat Yam *Israel*	60B2
Baubau *Indon*	37D4
Bauchi *Nig*	63C3
Bauges, Mts *France*	13B1
Baumes-les-Dames *France*	13B1
Baunt *USSR*	29D2
Bauru *Brazil*	107B6
Baus *Brazil*	111A1
Bautzen *E Germ*	23C2
Baween, I *Indon*	44C4
Bawiti *Egypt*	61B2
Bawku *Ghana*	63B3
Bawlake *Burma*	42B2
Bawlen *Aust*	74A2
Baxley *USA*	93B1
Bayamo *Cuba*	101E2
Bayan *Indon*	44D4
Bayandalay *Mongolia*	38A1
Bayandzürh *Mongolia*	34C2
Bayan Har Shan, Mts *China*	34B3
Bayan Mod *China*	38A1
Bayan Obo *China*	38B1
Bayard, P *France*	13A2
Bayard, Mt *Can*	88J3
Baybay *Phil*	45B3
Bayburt *Turk*	59D1
Bay City, Michigan *USA*	90C2
Bay City, Texas *USA*	95A4
Bay Daglari *Turk*	58B2
Baydhabo *Somalia*	65E2
Bayeaux *France*	14B2
Bayerische Alpen, Mts *W Germ*	13D1
Bayern, State *W Germ*	23C3
Bayir *Jordan*	58C3
Baykalskiy Khrebet, Mts *USSR*	34C1
Baykit *USSR*	29B1
Baylik Shan, Mts *China/ Mongolia*	29B3
Baymak *USSR*	27J3
Bayombong *Phil*	45B2
Bayonne *France*	14B3
Bayreuth *W Germ*	23C3
Bay St Louis *USA*	95C3
Bay Shore *USA*	91D2
Baytik Shan, Mts *China*	34A2
Baytown *USA*	95B4
Baza *Spain*	16B2
Bazaliya *USSR*	25D3
Bazas *France*	14B3
Bazhong *China*	39B3
Bazman *Iran*	57D4
Bazovec *USA*	92C2
Bcharre *Leb*	60C1
Beach Haven *USA*	92B3
Beachy Head *Eng*	9E4
Beacon *USA*	92C2
Bealanana *Madag*	67D2
Beardstown *USA*	94B1
Bear Valley *USA*	98B1
Bearskin Lake *Can*	84D2
Beatrice *USA*	81F4
Beatton River *Can*	81F4
Beauchene Is *Falkland Is*	105E6
Beaudesert *Aust*	75D1
Beaufort S *Can*	1B5
Beaufort West *S Africa*	66B4
Beauharnois *Can*	91D1
Beauly *Scot*	10B3
Beaumont, California *USA*	97B3
Beaumont, Texas *USA*	87A3
Beaune *France*	15C2
Beauvais *France*	14C2
Beauval *Can*	89F1
Beaver, Alaska *USA*	88E1

Bergen Nor	5F6	
Bergen op Zoom Neth	12C1	
Bergerac France	14C3	
Bergisch-Gladbach W Germ	12D1	
Bering GI USA	88F2	
Bering Str USSR/USA	1C6	
Berizak Iran	57C4	
Berja Spain	16B2	
Berkeley USA	84A3	
Berkner I Ant	112B2	
Berkovitsa Bulg	20B2	
Berkshire, County Eng	9D4	
Berkshire Hills USA	92C1	
Berlin E Germ	22C2	
Berlin, New Hampshire USA	91D2	
Bermejo Bol	106D3	
Bermuda, I Atlantic O	79M5	
Bern Switz	18A1	
Bernardsville USA	9282	
Bernasconi Arg	110C3	
Bernburg E Germ	22C2	
Berner Oberland, Mts Switz	13B1	
Berri Aust	74B2	
Berriane Alg	62C1	
Berry, Region France	14C2	
Berryessa, L USA	98A1	
Berry Is Bahamas	87C4	
Bertoua Cam	64B2	
Berwick USA	91C2	
Berwick-upon-Tweed Eng	8C2	
Berwyn, Mts Wales	9C3	
Besalampy Madag	67D2	
Besancon France	15D2	
Beskidy Zachodnie, Mts Pol	25C3	
Besni Turk	59C2	
Bessemer USA	87B2	
Betafo Madag	67D2	
Betanzos Spain	16A1	
Bet Guvrin Israel	60B3	
Bethal S Africa	67G1	
Bethanie Namibia	66A3	
Bethany, Missouri USA	94B1	
Bethany, Oklahoma USA	94A2	
Bethel, Alaska USA	80B3	
Bethel, Connecticut USA	92C2	
Bethel Park USA	90B2	
Bethesda USA	91C3	
Bethlehem Israel	60B3	
Bethlehem S Africa	67G1	
Bethlehem USA	91C2	
Bethune France	14C1	
Betioky Madag	67D3	
Betoota Aust	74B1	
Betou Congo	64B2	
Betpak Dala, Steppe USSR	48A1	
Betroka Madag	67D3	
Betsiamites Can	83D5	
Bettiah India	52A1	
Bettles USA	88D1	
Béttola Italy	13C2	
Betul India	51D4	
Betzdorf W Germ	12D1	
Beverley, L USA	88C3	
Beverly USA	92D1	
Beverly Hills USA	97B3	
Beyla Guinea	63B4	
Beypore India	53B2	
Beysehir Turk	58B2	
Beysehir Gölü, L Turk	58B2	
Beyt Shean Israel	60B2	
Bezau Austria	13C1	
Bezhetsk USSR	26E2	
Béziers France	15C3	
Bezmein USSR	56C2	
Beznosova USSR	28B2	
Bhadgaon Nepal	52B1	
Bhadrachalam India	53C1	
Bhadrakh India	52B2	
Bhadra Res India	53B2	
Bhadravati India	53B2	
Bhagalpur India	52B1	
Bhakkar Pak	50C2	
Bhamo Burma	48D3	
Bhandara India	51D4	
Bharatpur India	51D3	
Bharuch India	51C4	
Bhatiapara Ghat Bang	52B2	
Bhatinda India	50C2	
Bhatkal India	53A2	
Bhatpara India	52B2	
Bhavnagar India	51C4	
Bhera Pak	50C2	
Bhilai India	52A2	
Bhilwara India	51C3	
Bhimavaram India	53C1	
Bhind India	51D3	
Bhiwani India	50D3	
Bhongir India	53B1	
Bhopal India	51D4	
Bhubaneshwar India	52B2	
Bhuj India	51B4	
Bhusawal India	51D4	
Bhutan, Kingdom Asia	48C3	
Biak, I Indon	37E4	
Biala Podlaska Pol	24C2	
Bialogrod Pol	24B2	
Bialystok Pol	24C2	
Biarjmand Iran	57C2	
Biarritz France	14B3	
Biasca Switz	13C1	
Biba Egypt	58B4	
Bibai Japan	40E2	
Bibala Angola	66A2	
Biberach W Germ	23B3	
Bibiani Ghana	63B4	
Bicaz Rom	20C1	
Bida Nig	63C4	
Bidar India	53B1	
Bidbid Oman	57C5	
Bideford Eng	9B4	
Bidon 5 Alg	62C2	
Bié Angola	66A2	
Biebrza Pol	24C2	
Biel Switz	13B1	
Bielawa Pol	25B2	
Bielefeld W Germ	22B2	
Bieler See, L Switz	13B1	
Biella Italy	18A1	
Bielsk Podlaski Pol	24C2	
Bien Hoa Viet	30D3	
Biga Turk	58A1	
Bigadic Turk	21C3	
Big Cypress Swamp USA	93B3	
Big Delta USA	80D3	
Bigent W Germ	15D2	
Biggar Can	89F2	
Biggar Kindersley Can	81H4	
Biggenden Aust	75D1	
Bigger, Mt Can	88G2	
Big I Can	82C1	
Bignasco Switz	13C1	
Bignona Sen	63A3	
Big Pine USA	97B3	
Big Pine Key USA	93B3	
Big Pine Mt USA	98B3	
Big Rapids USA	90A2	
Big River Can	81H4	
Big Spring USA	85C2	
Big Trout L Can	83A4	
Big Trout Lake Can	83B4	
Bihac Yugos	18C2	
Bihar India	52B1	
Bihar, State India	52B2	
Biharamulo Tanz	65D3	
Bihor, Mt Rom	26B4	
Bijapur India	53B1	
Bijapur India	53C1	
Bijar Iran	56A2	
Bijauri Nepal	52A1	
Bijeljina Yugos	20A2	
Bijie China	39B4	
Bijnor India	50D3	
Bijnot Pak	50D3	
Bikaner India	50C3	
Bikfaya Leb	60B2	
Bikin USSR	35F2	
Bikoro Zaïre	64B3	
Bilara India	51C3	
Bilaspur India	50D2	
Bilaspur India	52A2	
Bilauktaung Range, Mts Thai	42B3	
Bilbao Spain	16B1	
Bileca Yugos	20A2	
Bilecik Turk	58B1	
Biliran, I Phil	45B3	
Billings USA	84C2	
Bilma Niger	61A3	
Biloxi USA	87B3	
Bimbo Chad	64C3	
Bina-Etawa India	51D4	
Binalbagan Phil	45B3	
Bindura Zim	67C2	
Binga Zim	66B2	
Binga, Mt Zim	67C2	
Bingara Aust	75D1	
Bingen W Germ	23B3	
Bingham USA	86C2	
Bingkor Malay	44D?	
Bingöl Turk	59D2	
Binhai China	38D3	
Bintan, I Indon	44A3	
Bintuhan Indon	44A3	
Bintulu Malay	44A3	
Bioko, I Atlantic O	68J4	
Bir India	53B1	
Bira CAR	64C3	
Biratnagar Nepal	52B1	
Birch Creek USA	88E1	

Birchip *Aust*	74B3
Birch Mts *Can*	81G4
Bird *Can*	83A4
Birdsville *Aust*	72C3
Birdum *Aust*	72C2
Birganj *Nepal*	52A1
Birgui *Brazil*	111A2
Biriran *Iran*	56C3
Birkat Qarun, L *Egypt*	58B4
Birkenfeld *W Germ*	12D2
Birkenhead *Eng*	8C3
Birlad *Rom*	26C4
Birmingham *Eng*	9C3
Birmingham *USA*	87B3
Bir Moghrein *Maur*	62A2
Birnin N'Konni *Niger*	63C3
Birnin Kebbi *Nig*	63C3
Birobidzhan *USSR*	35F2
Birr *Irish Rep*	11C2
Bir Rabalou *Alg*	17C2
Birsay *Scot*	10C2
Birsk *USSR*	27J2
Biryusa *USSR*	29B2
Birzai *USSR*	5J7
Bischwiller *France*	12D2
Bishan *China*	39B4
Bishop *USA*	84B3
Bishop Auckland *Eng*	8C3
Bishop's Stortford *Eng*	9E4
Bishrampur *India*	52A2
Biskra *Alg*	62C1
Bislig *Phil*	45C4
Bismarck *USA*	84C2
Bissau *Guinea-Bissau*	63A3
Bissett *Can*	86A1
Bistcho L *Can*	81G4
Bitburg *W Germ*	23B3
Bitche *France*	12D2
Bitlis *Turk*	59D2
Bitola *Yugos*	21B2
Bitterfeld *E Germ*	22C2
Bitterfontein *S Africa*	66A4
Bitter Lakes *Egypt*	58B3
Bitteroot Range, Mts *USA*	84B2
Biwa-ko, L *Japan*	40D3
Biyo Kaboba *Eth*	65E1
Biysk *USSR*	31K4
Bizerte *Tunisia*	15B3
Bjelovar *Yugos*	18C1
Bj bou Arreridj *Alg*	17C2
Bjornoya, I *Barents S*	30C2
Blackall *Aust*	73D3
Blackburn *Eng*	8C3
Blackburn *USA*	80D3
Black Diamond *Can*	89E2
Black Hills *USA*	81H5
Blackman's *Barbados*	103R3
Black Mts *Wales*	9C4
Blackpool *Eng*	9C3
Black River *Jamaica*	103H1
Black Rock Desert *USA*	84B2
Black S *USSR/Europe*	31E5
Black Sugarloaf, Mt *Aust*	75C3
Blackwall *USA*	94A2
Blagoevgrad *Bulg*	20B2
Blagoveshchensk *USSR*	29E2
Blaine *USA*	96B1
Blair Atholl *Scot*	10C3
Blairgowrie *Scot*	10C3
Blakely *USA*	87B2
Blanche, L *Aust*	74A1
Blanc Sablon *Can*	83E4
Blandford Forum *Eng*	9C4
Blangy-sur-Bresle *France*	12A2
Blankenberge *Belg*	12B1
Blantyre *Malawi*	67C2
Blaye *France*	14B2
Blayney *USA*	75C2
Blenheim *NZ*	77B2
Blida *Alg*	62C1
Blind River *Can*	80B1
Blitar *Indon*	44C4
Block I *USA*	91D2
Bloemfontein *S Africa*	67G1
Bloemhof *S Africa*	67G1
Blommesteinmeer, L *Surinam*	109F3
Blonduós *Iceland*	4A1
Bloomfield, Indiana *USA*	90A3
Bloomfield, Iowa *USA*	84B3
Bloomington, Illinois *USA*	90B3
Bloomington, Indiana *USA*	90B3
Bloomsburg *USA*	92A2
Blora *Indon*	44C4
Blossville Kyst, Mts *Greenland*	82H3
Bludenz *Austria*	23B3
Bluefield *USA*	87B3
Bluefields *Nic*	108A1
Blue Mountain Peak, Mt *Jamaica*	103B3
Bluenose L *Can*	80G3
Blue Ridge Mts *USA*	87B3
Blue River *Can*	89B2
Blue Stack, Mt *Irish Rep*	11B1
Bluff *NZ*	77A3
Bluff Knoll, Mt *Aust*	72A4
Blumenau *Brazil*	106G4
Blundez *Austria*	23B3
Bly *USA*	96B2
Blyde River, R *S Africa*	67E2
Blyth *Eng*	8D2
Blythe *USA*	85B3
Blytheville *USA*	87B3
Boa Vista *Brazil*	110B2
Boac *Phil*	45B3
Boading *China*	38D2
Boardman *USA*	90B2
Boatou *China*	29C3
Boa Vista, I *Cape Verde*	63A4
Bobai *China*	42E1
Bóbbio *Italy*	13C2
Bobo Dioulasso *Burkina*	63B3
Bobruysk *USSR*	26C3
Boca Chica Key, I *USA*	93B2
Boca do Acre *Brazil*	108D5
Bocaiúva *Brazil*	111C1
Bocaranga *CAR*	64B2
Boca Raton *USA*	93B2
Bochnia *Pol*	25C3
Bocholt *W Germ*	20B2
Bochum *W Germ*	12D1
Bocoio *Angola*	66A2
Boda *CAR*	64B2
Bodaybo *USSR*	29D2
Bodega Head, Pt *USA*	96A2
Bodélé, Region *Chad*	61A3
Boden *Sweden*	4J5
Bodensee, L *Switz/W Germ*	13C1
Bodhan *India*	53B1
Bodinayakkanur *India*	53B2
Bodmin *Eng*	9B4
Bodmin Moor, Upland *Eng*	9B4
Bodo *Nor*	4G5
Bodorodskoye *USSR*	29G2
Bodrum *Turk*	21C3
Boende *Zaire*	64C3
Boffa *Guinea*	63A3
Bogale *Burma*	42B2
Bogalusa *USA*	95C3
Bogandé *Burkina*	63B3
Bogarnes *Iceland*	82H3
Bogazliyan *Turk*	58C2
Bogdanovich *USSR*	27K2
Bogda Shan, Mt *China*	34A2
Bogenfels *Namibia*	66A3
Boggabilla *Aust*	75D1
Boggabri *Aust*	75C2
Boggeragh Mts *Irish Rep*	11B2
Bogo *Phil*	45B3
Bogong, Mt *Aust*	75C3
Bogor *Indon*	44B4
Bogorodskoye *USSR*	27H2
Bogotá *Colombia*	108C5
Bogotol *USSR*	29A2
Bogra *Bang*	52B2
Bohain-en-Vermandois *France*	12B2
Böhmer-Wald, Upland *W Germ*	23C3
Bohol, I *Phil*	45B4
Bohol S *Phil*	45B4
Bois Blanc I *USA*	90B1
Boise *USA*	84B2
Bojnurd *Iran*	56C2
Boké *Guinea*	63A3
Boknafjord, Inlet *Nor*	5F7
Boko *Congo*	64B3
Bokor *Camb*	42C3
Bokungu *Zaire*	64B3
Bol *Chad*	64B1
Bolaanos *Mexico*	99A1
Bolama *Guinea-Bissau*	63A3
Bolbec *France*	14C2
Bole *Ghana*	63B4
Boleslawiec *Pol*	25B2
Bolgatanga *Ghana*	63B3
Bolgrad *USSR*	26C4
Bolívar *Arg*	110C3
Bolivar, Missouri *USA*	94B2
Bolivar, Tennessee *USA*	94C2
Bolivia, Republic *S America*	106C2

Bukittinggi *Indon* 36B4
Bukoba *Tanz* 65D3
Buku Gandadiwata, Mt *Indon* 44D3
Bula *Indon* 37E4
Bulan *Phil* 45B3
Bulandshahr *India* 50D3
Bulawayo *Zim* 66B3
Buldan *Turk* 21C3
Buldana *India* 51D4
Bulgan *Mongolia* 34C2
Bulgaria, Republic *Europe* 20B2
Bulle *Switz* 13B1
Buller, Mt *Aust* 75C3
Bullfinch *Aust* 72A4
Bulloo Downs *Aust* 74B1
Bulloo L *Aust* 74B1
Bull Shoals Res *USA* 94B2
Bulnes *Chile* 110A3
Bulolo *PNG* 37F4
Bultfontein *S Africa* 67G1
Bumpa *Zaire* 64C2
Buna *Kenya* 65D2
Bunbury *Aust* 72A4
Buncrana *Irish Rep* 11C1
Bundaberg *Aust* 73E3
Bundarra *Aust* 75D2
Bundi *India* 51D3
Bundoran *Irish Rep* 11B1
Bungo *Angola* 64B3
Bunguran, I *Indon* 36B3
Bunia *Zaire* 65D2
Bunker *USA* 94B2
Bunkie *USA* 95B3
Bunnell *USA* 93B2
Buntok *Indon* 44C3
Buol *Indon* 37D3
Burag *Syria* 60C2
Buram *Sudan* 64C1
Brauen *Phil* 45B3
Braydah *S Arabia* 46C3
Burbank *USA* 97B3
Burcher *Aust* 75C2
Burco *Somalia* 65E2
Burdur *Turk* 58B2
Bureinskiy Khrebet, Mts *USSR* 29F3
Burg *E Germ* 22C2
Burgas *Bulg* 20C2
Burgaw *USA* 93C1
Burgdorf *Switz* 13B1
Burgersdorp *S Africa* 66B4
Burgin *USSR* 31K5
Burgos *Spain* 16B1
Burgsvik *Sweden* 24B1
Burhaniye *Turk* 21C3
Burhanpur *India* 51D4
Burias, I *Phil* 45B3
Buriram *Thai* 42C2
Buritis *Brazil* 111B1
Burke *Can* 89B2
Burketown *Aust* 72C2
Burkina, Republic *Africa* 63B3
Burks Falls *Can* 91C1
Burley *USA* 84B2
Burlington, Iowa *USA* 86A2

Burlington, New Jersey *USA* 92B2
Burlington, Vermont *USA* 86C2
Burlington, Washington *USA* 96B1
Burma, Republic *Asia* 49D3
Burney *USA* 96B2
Burnham *USA* 92A2
Burnie *Aust* 73D5
Burns *USA* 8C3
Burns Lake *Can* 81F4
Burqin *China* 48C1
Burra *Aust* 74A2
Burragorang, L *Aust* 75D2
Burray, I *Scot* 10C2
Burren Junction *Aust* 75C2
Burrinjuck Res *Aust* 75C2
Bursa *Turk* 26C5
Bur Safâga *Egypt* 46B3
Burton *USA* 90B2
Burton upon Trent *Eng* 9D3
Burtrask *Sweden* 4J6
Burtundy *Aust* 74B2
Buru *Indon* 37D4
Burundi, Republic *Africa* 65C3
Burung *Indon* 44A2
Buryatskaya ASSR, Republic *USSR* 29D2
Burye *Eth* 65D1
Burynshik *USSR* 27H4
Bury St Edmunds *Eng* 9E3
Bushehr *Iran* 57B4
Buskozdroj *Pol* 24C2
Busra ash Sham *Syria* 60C2
Busselton *Aust* 72A4
Busto *Italy* 15D2
Busto Arsizio *Italy* 18A1
Busuanga, I *Phil* 45A3
Buta *Zaire* 64C2
Buta Ranquil *Arg* 110B3
Butare *Rwanda* 65C3
Bute, I *Scot* 8B2
Butha Qi *China* 35C2
Butler *USA* 84B2
Butte *USA* 84B2
Butterworth *Malay* 43C4
Button Is *Can* 82D3
Butuan *Phil* 45C4
Butung, I *Indon* 37D3
Buturlinovka *USSR* 27F3
Butwal *Nepal* 52A1
Buulo Barde *Somalia* 65E2
Buur Hakaba *Somalia* 65E2
Buy *USSR* 27F2
Buyant Ovvo *Mongolia* 35B2
Buynaksk *USSR* 27G5
Buyr Nuur, L *Mongolia* 29D3
Büyük Agri, Mt *Turk* 59D2
Buzuluk *USSR* 20C1
Byala *Bulg* 20C2
Byala Slatina *Bulg* 20B2
Byam Martin I *Can* 80H2
Bydgoszcz *Pol* 24B2
Bygland *Nor* 5F7

Bylot I *Can* 82C2
Byrock *Aust* 75C2
Byron *Aust* 99B3
Bytom *Pol* 25B2

C

Caacupé *Par* 106E4
Caála *Angola* 66A2
Caazapá *Par* 106E4
Cabanatuan *Phil* 45B2
Cabedelo *Brazil* 107E3
Cabeza del Buey *Spain* 16A2
Cabildo *Arg* 110C3
Cabildo *Chile* 110A2
Cabimas *Ven* 108C1
Cabinda *Angola* 64B3
Cabinda, Province *Angola* 64B3
Cabo Beata *Dom Rep* 103C3
Cabo Frio *Brazil* 111C2
Cabo Gracias à Dios *Honduras* 102A4
Cabonga, Res. *Can* 86C1
Cabora Bassa Dam *Mozam* 67C2
Caborca *Mexico* 100A1
Cabos *Mexico* 99B1
Cabot Str *Can* 83D5
Cabrera *Brazil* 106C4
Cabreira, Mt *Port* 16A1
Cabrera, I *Spain* 17C2
Cabrero *Chile* 110A3
Cacahuamilpa *Mexico* 99B2
Cacak *Yugos* 20A2
C A Carillo *Mexico* 99B2
Cáceres *Brazil* 106E2
Caceres *Spain* 16A2
Cache Creek *Can* 89C2
Cachi *Arg* 106C4
Cachimbo *Brazil* 109G5
Cachoeira *Brazil* 107D4
Cachoeira Alta *Brazil* 111A1
Cachoeira de Paulo Alfonso, Waterfall *Brazil* 107D3
Cachoeira do Sul *Brazil* 105F2
Cachoeiro de Itapemirim *Brazil* 107C6
Cachuma, L *USA* 98C3
Cacolo *Angola* 66A2
Caconda *Angola* 66A2
Cacu *Brazil* 111A1
Cadca *Czech* 25B3
Cader Idris, Mts *Wales* 9C3
Cadillac *USA* 86B2
Cadiz *Phil* 45B3
Cadiz *Spain* 16A2
Caen *France* 14B2
Caernarfon *Wales* 9B3
Caernarvon *Wales* 8B3
Caetité *Brazil* 107C4
Cafayate *Arg* 106C4
Caga Tepe *Turk* 58B2
Cagayan de Oro *Phil* 45B4
Cagayan Is *Phil* 45A4
Cagayan Sulu, I *Phil* 45A4
Cagliari *Sardegna* 19A3
Caguas *Puerto Rico* 103D3
Caha Mts *Irish Rep* 11B3

Capdepera Spain	17C2	
Cape Barren I Aust	75C4	
Cape Breton I Can	83E5	
Cape Coast Ghana	63B4	
Cape Dorset Can	82C3	
Cape Girardeau USA	94C2	
Cape Henrietta Maria Can	82B3	
Capelinha Brazil	111C1	
Cape Lisburne USA	80B3	
Capelongo Angola	66A2	
Cape May USA	91D3	
Cape Mendocino USA	81F5	
Capenda Camulemba Angola	64B3	
Cape Perry Can	80F2	
Cape Province S Africa	66B4	
Cape Tatnam Can	83A4	
Cape Town S Africa	66A4	
Cape Verde, Is Atlantic O	68G4	
Cape Yakataga USA	88F3	
Cap-Haitien Haiti	102C3	
Capo San Vito Italy	19B3	
Cap Pt St Lucia	103P2	
Capri, I Italy	19B2	
Caprivi Strip, Region Namibia	66B2	
Caracal Rom	20B2	
Caracaraí Brazil	109E3	
Caracas Ven	108D1	
Caraguatatuba Brazil	111B2	
Carahue Chile	105B3	
Caraí Brazil	111C1	
Carandaí Brazil	111C2	
Carangola Brazil	107C6	
Caransebes Rom	20B1	
Carappee Hill, Mt Aust	75A2	
Caratasca Honduras	102A3	
Caratinga Brazil	111C1	
Caravaca Spain	17B2	
Caravelas Brazil	111D1	
Carbondale, Illinois USA	94C2	
Carbonia Sardegna	19A3	
Carborear Can	83E5	
Carcaion Can	81G4	
Carcar Mts Somalia	65E1	
Carcassonne France	14C3	
Carcross Can	80E3	
Cardel Mexico	99B2	
Cardenas Cuba	101D2	
Cárdenas Mexico	99B1	
Cardiff Wales	9C4	
Cardigan Wales	9B3	
Cardston Can	89E2	
Carei Rom	20B1	
Careiro Brazil	109F4	
Carén Chile	110A2	
Carey USA	90B2	
Carhaix-Plouguer France	14B2	
Carhué Arg	105D3	
Cariacica Brazil	107C6	
Caribou Can	81J4	
Caribou Mts, Alberta Can	81G4	
Caribou Mts, British Columbia Can	81F4	
Carigara Phil	45B3	
Carignan France	12C2	
Caripito Ven	109E1	
Carleton Place Can	91C1	
Carletonville S Africa	67G1	
Carlisle USA	94C2	
Carlisle Eng	8C2	
Carlisle Eng	91C2	
Carlos Arg	110C3	
Carlow, County Irish Rep	11C2	
Carlow Irish Rep	11C2	
Carlsbad, California USA	97B3	
Carlsbad, New Mexico USA	85C3	
Carlyle Can	81H5	
Carmacks Can	88G2	
Carmagnola Italy	18B2	
Carmarthen Wales	9B4	
Carmel, California USA	98B2	
Carmel, New York USA	92C2	
Carmel, Mt Israel	60B2	
Carmelo Urug	110D2	
Carmel Valley USA	98B2	
Carmen, I Mexico	85B4	
Carmen de Patagones Arg	105D4	
Carmi USA	94C2	
Carmichael Brazil	97A2	
Carmo do Paranaiba Brazil	111B1	
Carmona Spain	17A2	
Carnarvon Aust	72A3	
Carnarvon S Africa	66B4	
Carncacá Brazil	111D1	
Carndonagh Irish Rep	11C1	
Carnegi, L Aust	72B3	
Carnot CAR	64B2	
Carol City USA	93B2	
Carolina Brazil	107B3	
Carolina S Africa	67H1	
Carolina Beach USA	93D2	
Caroline Is Pacific O	70F3	
Carpathians, Mts E Europe	26B4	
Carpatii Orientali, Mts Rom	25D3	
Carpentaria, G of Aust	72C2	
Carpenter Ridge Indian O	49C5	
Carpentras France	15B2	
Carpi Italy	18B2	
Carpinteria USA	98C3	
Carrabelle USA	93B2	
Carrara Italy	18B2	
Carrauntoohill, Mt Irish Rep	7B3	
Carrickmacross Irish Rep	11C2	
Carrick on Shannon Irish Rep	11B2	
Carrick-on-Suir Irish Rep	11C2	
Carrieton Aust	74A2	
Carrington USA	86A2	
Carroll USA	86A2	
Carrollton, Georgia USA	93A1	
Carrollton, Kentucky USA	90A3	
Carrollton, Missouri USA	94C2	
Carruthersville USA	94C2	
Carsamba Turk	26E5	
Carson City USA	84B3	
Carsonville USA	90B2	
Cartagena Colombia	102B4	
Cartagena Spain	17B2	
Cartago Costa Rica	101D4	
Carterton NZ	77C2	
Carthage, Missouri USA	94B2	
Carthage, New York USA	91C2	
Carthage, Texas USA	95B3	
Cartier I Timor S	72B2	
Cartwright Can	83E4	
Caruaru Brazil	107D3	
Carúpano Ven	109E1	
Carvin France	12B1	
Casablanca Chile	110A2	
Casablanca Mor	62B1	
Casa Branca Brazil	111B2	
Casa Grande USA	85B3	
Casale Monferrato Italy	18A1	
Casalmaggiore Italy	13D2	
Casares Arg	110C3	
Cascade Mts Can/USA	89C3	
Cascade Pt NZ	77A2	
Cascade Range, Mts USA	84A2	
Cascavel Brazil	106F3	
Caserta Italy	19B2	
Casey, Base Ant	112C10	
Cashel Irish Rep	11C2	
Casilda Arg	110C2	
Casino Aust	73E3	
Casma Peru	108B5	
Caspe Spain	17B1	
Casper USA	84C2	
Caspian S USSR	31G6	
Cass USA	90C3	
Cassamba Angola	66B2	
Cassel France	12B1	
Cassiar Can	88J3	
Cassiar Mts Can	80E3	
Cassilândia Brazil	111A1	
Cassino Italy	19B2	
Castaic USA	98C3	
Castelfranco Italy	13D2	
Castellane France	15B3	
Castelli Arg	110C3	
Castellon de la Plana Spain	17B2	
Castelo Brazil	107C3	
Castelo Branco Port	16A2	
Castelsarrasin France	14C3	
Castelvetrano Italy	19B3	
Casterton Aust	74B3	
Castilla La Nueva, Region Spain	16B2	
Castilla La Vieja, Region Spain	16B1	
Castlebar Irish Rep	7B3	
Castlebay Scot	10A3	
Castle Douglas Scot	8C2	
Castlegar Can	96C1	
Castleisland Irish Rep	7B3	
Castlemain Aust	74B3	
Castlerea Irish Rep	7B3	
Castlereagh Aust	75C2	
Castres France	14C3	
Castries St Lucia	103E4	
Castro Arg	106F4	
Castro Brazil	106F3	
Castro Alves Brazil	107D4	
Castrovillari Italy	19C3	
Castroville USA	98B2	
Cat, I Bahamas	101E2	
Catabalogan Phil	45B3	
Catacaos Peru	108A5	
Cataguases Brazil	111C2	

Catahoula L USA 95B3
Catalao Brazil 111B1
Cataluña, Region Spain 17C1
Catamarca Arg 106C4
Catamarca, State Arg 106C4
Catandica Mozam 67C2
Catanduanes, I Phil 45B3
Catanduva Brazil 107B6
Catania Italy 19C3
Catanzaro Italy 19C3
Catarman Phil 45B3
Catawissa USA 92A2
Cateman Mexico 99B2
Cater Corse 15D3
Cateraggio Corse 18A2
Catete Angola 64B3
Catio Guinea-Bissau 63A3
Cat Lake Can 83A4
Catlegar Can 78E3
Catoctin Mt USA 92A3
Cato, I Aust 73E3
Catonsville USA 91C3
Catrilo Arg 110C3
Catskill USA 91D2
Catskill Mts USA 91D2
Caucaia Brazil 107D2
Caucasia Colombia 108B2
Caudry France 12B1
Caungula Angola 64B3
Cauquenes Chile 105B3
Caurimun France 15D3
Cavalese Italy 13D1
Cavan, County Irish Rep 11C2
Cavan Irish Rep 11C2
Cavite Phil 45B3
Caxias Brazil 107C2
Caxias Brazil 108C4
Caxias do Sul Brazil 106F4
Caxito Angola 64B3
Cayce USA 93B1
Cayeli Turk 59D1
Cayenne French Guiana 109G3
Cayeux-sur-Mer France 12A1
Cayman Brac, I Caribbean 101E3
Cayman Is Caribbean 102A3
Cayman Trench Caribbean 102A3
Caynabo Somalia 65E2
Cayo Romana, I Cuba 101E2
Cayos Miskitos, Is Nic 101D3
Cay Sal, I Caribbean 102A2
Cazombo Angola 66B2
Ceara, State Brazil 107C3
Cebu Phil 45B3
Cebu, I Phil 45B3
Cecilton USA 92B3
Cecina Italy 18B2
Cedar City USA 84B3
Cedar Creek Res USA 95A3
Cedar L Can 81J4
Cedar Rapids USA 86A2
Cedartown USA 93A1
Cedros, I Mexico 100A2
Ceduna Aust 72C4
Ceelbuur Somalia 65E2
Ceerigaabo Somalia 65E1
Cefalù Italy 19B3
Cegléd Hung 25B3

Cela Angola 66A2
Celaya Mexico 100B2
Celebes S E Asia 36C3
Celina USA 90B2
Celje Yugos 18C1
Celle W Germ 22C2
Center USA 95B3
Center Moriches USA 92C2
Center Point USA 93A1
Central, Region Scot 10B3
Central African Republic Africa 64B2
Central Falls USA 92D2
Centralia, Illinois USA 94C2
Centralia, Washington USA 94B2
Central Range, Mts PNG 37D4
Centreville, Maryland USA 92A3
Cepu Indon 44C4
Ceram Sea Indonesia 37D4
Cereales Arg 110C3
Ceres Brazil 107B5
Ceres S Africa 66A4
Ceres USA 98B2
Cergy-Pontoise France 14C2
Cerignola Italy 19C2
Cernavoda Rom 26C5
Cerralvo, I Mexico 85C4
Cerritos Mexico 100B2
Cerro Aconcagua, Mt Arg 99B1
Cerro Azul Mexico 99C2
Cerro Campanario, Mt Chile 110A3
Cerro Champaqui, Mt Arg 110C2
Cerro Cuachala, Mt Mexico 99B1
Cerro de Astillero Mexico 99B1
Cerro de Olivares, Mt Arg/Chile 110B2
Cerro de Pasco Peru 108B6
Cerro de Punta, Mt Puerto Rico 103D3
Cerro El Cantado, Mt Mexico 99A2
Cerro El Nevado, Mt Chile 110B3
Cerro Grande, Mt Mexico 99A2
Cerro Juncal, Mt Arg/Chile 110A2
Cerro la Ardilla, Mts Mexico 99A1
Cerro las Tortolas, Mt Chile 110B1
Cerro Laurel, Mt Mexico 99A2
Cerro Mercedario, Mt Arg 110A2
Cerro Moro, Mt Chile 110A2
Cerron, Mt Ven 103C4
Cerro Payún, Mt Arg 110B3
Cerro Penón del Rosario, Mt Mexico 99B2
Cerro Sosneado, Mt Arg 110B2
Cerro Teotepec, Mt Mexico 99B2
Cerro Tupungato, Mt Arg/Chile 110B2
Cerro Yucuyacau, Mt Mexico 99B2
Cesena Italy 18B2
Cesis USSR 32D2
České Budějovice Czech 23C3
České Zemé, Region Czech 23C3
Českomoravská Vysočina, U Czech 25B3

Cesme Turk 21C3
Cessnock Aust 73E4
Ceuta N W Africa 62B1
Cevham Turk 58C2
Ceylanpinar Turk 59C2
Chaa-Khol USSR 29B2
Châteaudun France 14C2
Chablais, Region France 13B1
Chacabuco Arg 110C2
Chachapoyas Peru 108B5
Chacharramendi Arg 110B3
Chachran Pak 50C3
Chaco, State Arg 106D4
Chad, Republic Africa 64B1
Chadron USA 84C2
Chaffee USA 94C2
Chagai Pak 51A3
Chagda USSR 29F2
Chaghcharan Afghan 50C2
Chagos Arch Indian O 70B4
Chaguanas Trinidad 103L1
Chah Bahar Iran 57D4
Chai Badan Thai 42C2
Chaine des Cardamomes, Mts Camb 42C3
Chaine des Mitumba, Mts Zaïre 64C4
Chaiyaphum Thai 42C2
Chajari Arg 110D2
Chakwal Pak 50C2
Chala Peru 106B2
Chalabesa Zambia 66C2
Chalap Dalam, Mts Afghan 50A2
Chaling China 39C4
Chalisgaon India 51C4
Chalkyitsik USA 88F1
Challerange France 12C2
Châlons sur Marne France 12C2
Chalon sur Saône France 15C2
Cham W Germ 23C3
Chaman Pak 50B2
Chamba India 50D2
Chambersburg USA 91C3
Chambéry France 15D2
Chambly France 12B2
Chambor Kalat Pak 51A3
Chamgordan Iran 56B3
Chamonix France 13B2
Champa India 52A2
Champagne, Region France 15C2
Champagne Castle, Mt Lesotho 67G1
Champagnole France 13A1
Champaign USA 86B2
Champassak Laos 42D3
Champlain, L USA 86D2
Chamrajnagar India 53B2
Chanaral Chile 106B4
Chanco Chile 110A3
Chandalar USA 80D3
Chandausi India 50D2
Chandpur Bang 52C2
Chandrapur India 51D5
Chanf Iran 57D4
Changara Mozam 67C2
Changbai China 40B2

Changchun China 35E2
Changde China 39C4
Chang-hua Taiwan 34E4
Changjiang China 39D2
Chang Jiang, R China 39D3
Changjin N Korea 40B2
Changsha China 39C4
Changshu China 38E3
Changtu China 40A2
Changwu China 38B2
Changwon N Korea 40B3
Changzhi China 38C2
Changzhou China 39E3
Channel Is UK 14B2
Channel Is USA 85B3
Channel Port-aux-
Basques   Can 83E5
Chanthaburi Thai 42C3
Chantilly France 12B2
Chanute USA 94A2
Chaoan China 39D5
Chao'an China 39D5
Chao Hu, L China 39D3
Chaoyang China 38E1
Chapada Diamantina, Mts
Brazil 107C2
Chapadinha Brazil 107C2
Chapala Mexico 99B1
Chapala, Lac de, L Mexico 99A1
Chapayevo USSR 27H3
Chapecó Brazil 106F4
Chapeltown Jamaica 103H1
Chapleau Can 83B5
Chaplygin USSR 27E3
Charcot I Ant 112C3
Chardzhou USSR 46E2
Chari Baguirmi, Region
Chad 64B1
Charikar Afghan 50B1
Charity Guyana 109F2
Charkhari India 51D3
Charleroi Belg 12C2
Charleston, Illinois USA 94A2
Charleston, Missouri USA 94C2
Charleston, S Carolina USA 87B3
Charleston, W Virginia USA 86B3
Charlesville Zaïre 64C3
Charleville Aust 73D3
Charleville-Mézières France 15C2
Charlevoix USA 90A1
Charlotte, Michigan USA 90B2
Charlotte, N Carolina USA 87B1
Charlottesville USA 86C3
Charlottetown Can 83D5
Charlotteville Tobago 103H1
Charlton Aust 74B3
Charlton I Can 86C1
Charsadda Pak 50C2
Charters Towers Aust 73D3
Chartres France 14B2
Chascomús Arg 105E3
Chase Can 89D2
Châteaubriant France 14B2
Châteaudun France 14C2
Châteaulin France 14B2
Châteauroux France 14C2
Château-Salins France 12D2

Château-Thierry France 15C2
Châtelet Belg 12C1
Châtellerault France 14C2
Chatham Eng 9E4
Chatham, New Brunswick
Can 83D5
Chatham, New York USA 92C1
Chatham, Ontario Can 90B2
Châtillon France 15C2
Châtillon India 13B2
Chatsworth USA 92B3
Chattahoochee USA 93B1
Chattanooga USA 87B3
Chauk Burma 42A1
Chaumont France 15D2
Chauny France 12B2
Chau Phu Viet 43D3
Chaves Port 16A1
Chazaouet Alg 16B2
Chazón Arg 110C2
Chocontá Colombia 108C2
Cheb Czech 23C2
Cheboksary USSR 31F4
Cheboygan USA 86B2
Chech'on S Korea 40B3
Chechro Mali 51C3
Checotah USA 94A3
Cheduba I, Burma 42A2
Cheepie Aust 74B1
Chegga Maur 62B2
Chegutu Zim 66C2
Chehalis USA 96B1
Cheju S Korea 40B4
Cheju do, I S Korea 40B4
Chekunda USSR 29F2
Chelan, L USA 96B1
Cheleken USSR 56B2
Chelforo Arg 110B3
Chelkar USSR 46D1
Chelm Pol 25C2
Chelmno Pol 24B2
Chelmsford Eng 9E4
Cheltenham Eng 9C4
Chelyabinsk USSR 31H4
Chemba Mozam 67C2
Chenachen Alg 62B2
Cheney USA 96C1
Cheney Res USA 94A2
Chengde China 38D1
Chengdu China 39A3
Chengshan Jiao, Pt China 38E2
Chenxi China 39C4
Chen Xian China 39C4
Cheo Xian China 39D3
Chepén Peru 108B5
Chepes Arg 110B2
Cheran Mexico 99A2
Cheraw USA 93C1
Cherbourg France 14B2
Cherchell Alg 62C1
Cheremkhovo USSR 29C2
Cherepovets USSR 26E2
Cherkassy USSR 26D4
Cherkessk USSR 27F5
Chernigov USSR 26D3
Chernobyl USSR 26D3

Chernovtsy USSR 26C4
Chernushka USSR 27J4
Chernyakhovsk USSR 26B4
Chernyye Zemli, Region
USSR 27G6
Cherokees, L o'the USA 94A3
Cherquenco Chile 110A3
Cherrapunji India 52C2
Cherven' USSR 26C6
Chervonograd USSR 8C
Cheshire, County Eng 8C
Cheshire USA 92C
Chester, California USA 97A
Chester, Illinois USA 94C
Chester, Massachusets
USA 92C
Chester, Pennsylvania USA 91C
Chester, S Carolina USA 93B
Chesterfield Eng 8D
Chesterfield Inlet Can 82A
Chestertown USA 92A
Chetumal Mexico 101D
Chetwynd Can 89C
Chevak USA 88A
Cheviot NZ 77B
Cheviots, Hills Eng/Scot 8C
Chewelah USA 89D
Cheyenne USA 84C
Chhapra India 52A
Chhatak Bang 52C
Chhatarpur India 51D
Chhindwara India 51D
Chhuka Bhutan 52B
Chia'i Taiwan 39E
Chiange Angola 66A3
Chiang Kham Thai 42C
Chiang Mai Thai 42C
Chiavenna Italy 13C
Chiba Japan 40E
Chibasa India 52B
Chibia Angola 66A
Chibougamau Can 83C
Chiburi-jima, I Japan 41A
Chibuto Mozam 67C
Chicago USA 86B
Chicago Heights USA 90A
Chichagof I USA 88G
Chichaoua Mor 9D
Chichibu Japan 41B
Chichi-jima, I Japan 35G
Chickamauga L USA 87B
Chicksha USA 85D
Chicken USA 88F
Chiclayo Peru 108A
Chico USA 84A
Chico Mozam 67C
Chicopee USA 91D
Chicoutimi Can 83C
Chicualacuala Mozam 67C
Chidambaram India 53B
Chiefland USA 93B
Chiehn Lib 63B
Chiengi Zambia 65C
Chieri Italy 13B
Chiesa Italy 13C
Chieti Italy 18B

Chifeng *China* 38D1
Chiginigak, Mt *USA* 88C3
Chigmit Mts *USA* 80C3
Chignahuapán *Mexico* 99B2
Chignik *USA* 88C3
Chihuahua *Mexico* 100B2
Chik Ballapur *India* 53B2
Chikmagalur *India* 53B2
Chikuminuk L *USA* 88C2
Chikwawa *Malawi* 67C2
Chi-kyaw *Burma* 42A1
Chilakaluripet *India* 53C1
Chilapa *Mexico* 99B2
Chilaw *Sri Lanka* 53B3
Chile, Republic
Chilecito, Mendoza *Arg* 110B2
Chililabombwe *Zambia* 66B2
Chilka, L *India* 52B2
Chilko L *Can* 81F4
Chilko L *Chile* 110A3
Chillar *Arg* 110D3
Chillicothe, Missouri *USA* 94B2
Chillicothe, Ohio *USA* 90B3
Chilliwack *Can* 89C3
Chilmari *India* 52B2
Chilongozi *Zambia* 67C2
Chiloquin *USA* 96B2
Chilpancingo *Mexico* 100C3
Chiltern Hills, Upland *Eng* 9D4
Chilton *USA* 90A2
Chilumba *Malawi* 67C2
Chi-lung *Taiwan* 35E4
Chilwa, L *Malawi* 67C2
Chimay *Belg* 12C1
Chimbay *USSR* 31G5
Chimborazo, Mt *Ecuador* 108B4
Chimbote *Peru* 108B6
Chimkent *USSR* 31H5
Chimoio *Mozam* 67C2
China, Republic *Asia* 33E3
Chinandega *Nic* 101D3
Chincha Alta *Peru* 108B6
Chinchilla *Aust* 75D1
Chinde *Mozam* 67C2
Chingola *Zambia* 66B2
Chinguar *Angola* 66A2
Chinguetti *Maur* 62A2
Chinhae *S Korea* 40B3
Chinhoyi *Zim* 66C2
Chiniot *Pak* 50C2
Chinju *S Korea* 40B3
Chino *Japan* 41B1
Chinsali *Zambia* 67C2
Chioggia *Italy* 18B1
Chipata *Zambia* 67C2
Chipinge *Zim* 67C3
Chiplun *India* 53A1
Chippewa Falls *USA* 86A2
Chipuriro *Zim* 66C2
Chirala *India* 53C1
Chiredzi *Zim* 67C3
Chirfa *Niger* 61A2
Chiriqui, Mt *Panama* 108A2
Chirpan *Bulg* 20C2
Chirripo Grande, Mt
  Costa Rica 108A2

Chirundu *Zim* 66B2
Chisamba *Zambia* 66B2
Chita *USSR* 63B2
Chitado *Angola* 66A2
Chitembo *Angola* 66A2
Chitina *USA* 88F2
Chitradurga *India* 53B2
Chitral *Pak* 50C1
Chitré *Panama* 108A2
Chittagong *Bang* 52C2
Chittaurgarh *India* 51C4
Chittoor *India* 53B2
Chiume *Angola* 66A2
Chiusa *Italy* 13D1
Chivasso *Italy* 13B2
Chivilcoy *Arg* 105D2
Chizu *Japan* 41A1
Choele Choel *Arg* 105C3
Choix *Mexico* 100B2
Chojnice *Pol* 24B2
Choke, Mts *Eth* 65D1
Cholet *France* 14B2
Cholula *Mexico* 99B2
Choma *Zambia* 66B2
Chomo Yummo, Mt
  China/India 52B1
Chomutov *Czech* 23C2
Ch'onan *S Korea* 40B3
Chon Buri *Thai* 42C3
Chone *Ecuador* 108A4
Ch'ongjin *N Korea* 40B2
Chongju *N Korea* 40B3
Ch'ongju *S Korea* 40B3
Chongoroi *Angola* 66A2
Chongqing *China* 39B4
Chongup *S Korea* 40B3
Chonju *S Korea* 40B3
Chooyu, Mt *China/Nepal* 52D1
Chortkov *USSR* 25B3
Ch'orwon *N Korea* 40B3
Chorzow *Pol* 25B2
Chosh *Japan* 40E3
Chos-Malal *Arg* 110A3
Chosan *N Korea* 40B2
Chotanagpur, Region *India* 52B2
Chott Melrhir *Alg* 62C1
Chowchilla *USA* 98B2
Choybalsan *Mongolia* 29D3
Chraykovskiy *USSR* 27H2
Christchurch *NZ* 111B2
Christiana *S Africa* 67G1
Christian Sd *USA* 88H3
Christianshab *Greenland* 82E3
Christmas I *Indian O* 104B1
Christopol *USSR* 27G2
Chu *USSR* 31J5
Chubut, State *Arg* 110B3
Chudovo *USSR* 26C2
Chudskoye Ozer, L *USSR* 30D4
Chugach Mts *USA* 80D3
Chugiak *USA* 88E2
Chugoku-sanchi, Mts
  Japan 41A1
Chui *Brazil* 105F2
Chuillán *Chile* 105B3

Chukai *Malay* 43C5
Chu Lai *Viet* 42D2
Chula Vista *USA* 97B3
Chulitna *USA* 88E2
Chulman *USSR* 29E2
Chulucanas *Peru* 108A5
Chulumani *Bol* 106C2
Chulym *USSR* 31K4
Chumikan *USSR* 29F2
Chumphon *Thai* 43B3
Ch'unch'on *S Korea* 40B3
Chunchura *India* 52B2
Ch'ungju *S Korea* 40B3
Chunya *Tanz* 65D3
Chupara Pt *Trinidad* 103L1
Chuquibamba *Peru* 106C3
Chuquicamata *Chile* 106C3
Chur *Switz* 18A1
Churachandpur *India* 52C2
Churchill *Can* 83A4
Churchill L *Can* 81H4
Churchill R *Can* 81H4
Churu *India* 50C3
Churumuco *Mexico* 99A2
Chusovoy *USSR* 27J2
Chuvashskaya ASSR,
  Republic *USSR* 27G2
Chuxiong *China* 34B4
Chu Yang Sin, Mt *Viet* 42D3
Cianjur *Indon* 44B4
Ciano d'Enza *Italy* 13D2
Cianorte *Brazil* 111A2
Ciechanow *Pol* 24C2
Ciego de Avila *Cuba* 102C2
Ciénaga *Colombia* 108C1
Cienfuegos *Cuba* 101D2
Cieszyn *Pol* 25B3
Cieza *Spain* 17B2
Cihanbeyli *Turk* 58B2
Cihuatlán *Mexico* 99A2
Cijulang *Indon* 44B4
Cilacap *Indon* 44B4
Cimarron, R *USA* 96C2
Cincer, Mt *Yugos* 18C2
Cincinnati *USA* 86B3
Cindrelu, Mt *Rom* 20B1
Ciney *Belg* 12C1
Cipolletti *Arg* 110B3
Circle, Alaska *USA* 88D3
Circleville *USA* 90B3
Cirebon *Indon* 44B4
Cirencester *Eng* 9D4
Ciro *Italy* 13D2
Citadella *Italy* 13D2
Citlaltepetl, Mt *Mexico* 100C3
Citrusdal *S Africa* 66A4
Citta del Vaticano *Italy* 16C2
Citta di Castello *Italy* 16C2
Ciudad Acuña *Mexico* 100B2
Ciudad Altamirano *Mexico* 99A2
Ciudad Bolivar *Ven* 109E2
Ciudad Camargo *Mexico* 100B2
Ciudad del Carmen *Mexico* 101C3
Ciudad del Maiz *Mexico* 99B1
Ciudadela *Spain* 17C1
Ciudad Guayana *Ven* 109E2
Ciudad Guzman *Mexico* 100B3
Ciudad Hidalgo *Mexico* 99A2

Ciudad Juárez Mexico	100B1
Ciudad Lerdo Mexico	85C4
Ciudad Madero Mexico	100C2
Ciudad Mendoza Mexico	99B2
Ciudad Obregon Mexico	100B2
Ciudad Ojeda Ven	103C4
Ciudad Piar Ven	109E2
Ciudad Real Spain	16B2
Ciudad Rodrigo Spain	16A1
Ciudad Valles Mexico	100C2
Ciudad Victoria Mexico	100C2
Civitavecchia Italy	18B2
Cizre Turk	59D2
Clacton-on-Sea Eng	9E3
Claire, L Can	81G4
Clairton US	90C2
Clanton US	91C2
Clanwilliam S Africa	66A4
Clara Irish Rep	11C2
Claraz Arg	110D3
Clare, County Irish Rep	11B2
Clare US	90B2
Clare, I Irish Rep	11A2
Claremont US	91D2
Claremore US	94A2
Claremorris Irish Rep	11B2
Clarendon US	95B3
Clarenville Can	83E5
Claresholm Can	81G4
Clarinda US	94A1
Clarion, Pennsylvania USA	91C2
Clark Hill Res US	87B3
Clarksburg US	90B3
Clarksdale US	87A3
Clarks Point US	88C3
Clarkston US	96C1
Clarksville, Arkansas USA	94B2
Claromecó Arg	105D3
Clay Center US	94A2
Clayton, New Mexico USA	85C3
Clayton, New York USA	91C2
Clear Hills, Mts Can	89D1
Clear L US	97A2
Clear Lake Res US	96B2
Clearwater Can	89D2
Clearwater US	87B4
Clearwater L Can	89C2
Cleburne US	85D3
Clements US	91C2
Cleopatra Needle, Mt Phil	45A3
Clermont Aust	73D3
Clermont France	12B2
Clermont-en-Argonne France	12C2
Clermont-Ferrand France	15C2
Clervaux W Germ	12D1
Cles Italy	13D1
Cleve Aust	74A2
Cleveland, County Eng	8D2
Cleveland, Mississippi USA	95B3
Cleveland, Ohio USA	86B2
Cleveland, Tennessee USA	87B3
Cleveland, Texas USA	95A3
Clifden Irish Rep	11A2
Clifton Aust	75D1
Clifton, New Jersey USA	92B2
Clifton Hills Aust	74A1
Climax Can	89F3
Clinton, Arkansas USA	94B2
Clinton Can	81F4
Clinton, Connecticut USA	92C2
Clinton, Massachusetts USA	92D1
Clinton, Mississippi USA	95B3
Clinton, Missouri USA	94B2
Clinton, New Jersey USA	92B2
Clinton-Colden L Can	80H3
Clipperton I Pacific O	100B3
Clisa Bol	106C2
Clonakilty Irish Rep	11B3
Cloncurry Aust	73D3
Clones Irish Rep	11C1
Clonmel Irish Rep	11C3
Cloquet USA	86A2
Cloudy Mt USA	88C2
Clovis, California USA	98C2
Clovis, New Mexico USA	85C3
Cluj Rom	26B4
Cluj-Napoca Rom	20B1
Cluses France	13B1
Clusone Italy	13C2
Clwyd, County Wales	9C3
Clyde Can	82D2
Clyde NZ	77A3
Clyde US	92A2
Clydebank Scot	8B2
Coari Brazil	106B2
Coast Mts Can	81C4
Coast Ranges, Mts USA	84A2
Coatbridge Scot	8B2
Coatepec Mexico	99B2
Coatesville US	92B3
Coaticook Can	92B1
Coats I Can	82B3
Coatzacoalcos Mexico	101C3
Cobalt Can	83C5
Cobán Guatemala	101C3
Cobar Aust	73D4
Cobargo Aust	75C3
Cobh Irish Rep	11B3
Cobija Bol	108D6
Cobleskill US	92B1
Cobourg Can	83C5
Coburg W Germ	23C2
Coca Ecuador	108B4
Coca US	93B2
Cochabamba Bol	106C2
Cochem W Germ	12D1
Cochin India	53B3
Cochrane, Alberta Can	83E5
Cochrane, Ontario Can	89B5
Cockburn Aust	74B2
Cockeysville US	92A3
Cockpit Country, The Jamaica	103H1
Cocobeach Gabon	64A2
Cocos Is Indian O	70C4
Cocula Mexico	99A1
Codfish I NZ	77A3
Cod I Can	83D4
Codigoro Italy	13E2
Cod Brazil	107C2
Codogno Italy	13C2
Cody US	84C2
Coesfeld W Germ	22B2
Coffeyville US	85D3
Coff's Harbour Aust	75D2
Cofre de Perote, Mt Mexico	99B2
Cognac France	14B2
Cohoes US	91D2
Cohuna Aust	75B3
Coihaique Chile	105B5
Coimbatore India	53B2
Coimbra Port	16A1
Cojimies Ecuador	108A3
Colac Aust	73D4
Colatina Brazil	107C5
Colchester Eng	9E4
Colebrook US	92C2
Col de la Faucille France	13B1
Cold L Can	89E2
Col du Grand St Bernard, P Switz/Italy	18A1
Col du Lautaret, P France	13B2
Col du Mont Cenis, P Italy/France	18A1
Coldwater US	90B2
Coleman, Michigan USA	90B2
Colenso S Africa	67G1
Coleraine N Ire	11C1
Coleridge, L NZ	77B2
Colesberg S Africa	66B4
Coleville USA	98C1
Colfax, California USA	98B3
Colfax, Louisiana USA	95B3
Colfax, Washington USA	96C1
Colima Mexico	100B3
Colima, State Mexico	99A2
Colina Chile	110A2
Coll, I Scot	8B3
Collarenebri Aust	75C1
Colle de Tende, P Italy/France	18A2
College US	88E2
College Park, Georgia USA	95C3
College Park, Washington US	92A3
College Station USA	95A3
Collie Aust	72A4
Collines de L'Artois, Mts France	12A1
Collines De Thiérache France	12C2
Collingwood Can	90B2
Collingwood NZ	78B2
Collins, Mississippi USA	95C3
Collinsville USA	73D3
Collinsville, Illinois USA	94C2
Collinsville, Oklahoma USA	94A2
Collipulli Chile	110A3
Colomba Brazil	111B2
Colombia, Republic S America	108B3
Colombia USA	91C3

Coronel Brandsen *Arg*	110D3
Coronel Dorrego *Arg*	110C3
Coronel Fabriciano *Brazil*	111C1
Coronel Oviedo *Par*	106E4
Coronel Pringles *Arg*	105D3
Coronel Suárez *Arg*	110C3
Coronel Vidal *Arg*	110D3
Coropuna, Mt *Peru*	106B2
Corowa *Aust*	75C3
Corps *France*	15D3
Corpus Christi *USA*	85D4
Corpus Christi, L *USA*	85D4
Corregidor, I *Phil*	45B3
Corrientes *Arg*	106E4
Corrientes, State *Arg*	106E4
Corrigan *USA*	95B3
Corrigin *Aust*	72A4
Corringe Is *Aust*	75C2
Corryong *Aust*	75C3
Corse, I *Medit S*	18A2
Corsewall, Pt *Scot*	8B2
Corsicana *USA*	85D3
Corte *Corse*	18A2
Cortez *USA*	58C3
Cortina d'Ampezzo *Italy*	18B1
Cortland *USA*	91C2
Coruca de Catalan *Mexico*	99A2
Corum *Turk*	21F1
Corumbá *Brazil*	106E2
Corumbaiba *Brazil*	111B1
Corvallis *USA*	96B2
Corvo, I *Acores*	62A1
Corwen *Wales*	9C3
Coscomatopec *Mexico*	99C3
Cosenza *Italy*	19C3
Cosmoledo, Is *Seychelles*	67D1
Cosquín *Arg*	110C2
Costa Blanca, Region *Spain*	17B2
Costa Brava, Region *Spain*	17C1
Costa de la Luz, Region *Spain*	16B2
Costa del Sol, Region *Spain*	16B2
Costa Mesa *USA*	98D4
Cotabato *Phil*	45B4
Cotagaita *Bol*	106C3
Côte d'Azur, Region *France*	15D3
Côtes de Meuse, Mts *France*	12C2
Cotonou *Benin*	63C4
Cotopaxi, Mt *Ecuador*	108B4
Cotswold Hills, Upland *Eng*	9C4
Cottage Grove *USA*	96B2
Cottbus *E Germ*	22C2
Couer d'Alene L *USA*	96C1
Coulommiers *France*	12B2
Coulterville *USA*	98B2
Council *USA*	80B3
Council Bluffs *USA*	84D2
Courmayeur *Italy*	13B2
Courtenay *Can*	89B3
Coutances *France*	14B2
Coventry *Eng*	9D3
Covilha *Spain*	16A1
Covington, Georgia *USA*	53B1
Covington, Louisiana *USA*	95B3
Cowal, L *Aust*	75C2
Cowangie *Aust*	74B3
Cowansville *Can*	91D1
Coward Springs *Aust*	74A1
Cowell *Aust*	74A2
Cowes *Aust*	74C3
Cowichan L *Can*	96B1
Cowra *Aust*	75C2
Coxim *Brazil*	106F2
Coxsackie *USA*	92C1
Cox's Bazar *Bang*	52C2
Coyote *USA*	98B2
Coyuca de Benitez *Mexico*	99A2
Cradock *S Africa*	66B4
Craig *USA*	84C2
Crailsheim *W Germ*	23C3
Craiova *Rom*	20B2
Cranberry L *USA*	91D2
Cranbrook *Can*	81G5
Crane, Oregon *USA*	96C2
Cranston *USA*	92D2
Crater L *USA*	96B2
Crateus *Brazil*	107C3
Crato *Brazil*	107C3
Crawfordsville *USA*	90A2
Crawfordville *USA*	93B1
Crawley *Eng*	9D4
Cree L *Can*	81H4
Creil *France*	12B2
Crema *Italy*	13C2
Cremona *Italy*	18B1
Crépy-en-Valois *France*	12B2
Cres, I *Yugos*	18B2
Crescent City *USA*	96B2
Crespo *Arg*	110C2
Creston *USA*	89D3
Creston *USA*	94B1
Crestview *USA*	93A1
Creswick *Aust*	74B3
Crêt de la Neige, Mt *France*	13A1
Crete *USA*	94A1
Crete, S of *Greece*	21B3
Crewe *Eng*	9C3
Crianlarich *Scot*	10B3
Criciúma *Brazil*	106G4
Crieff *Scot*	10C3
Crillon, Mt *USA*	88G3
Cristalina *Brazil*	111B1
Croatia, Region *Yugos*	18C1
Crocker Range, Mts *Malay*	44D1
Crockett *USA*	95A3
Crook I *Aust*	72C2
Cromarty *Scot*	10C3
Cromer *Eng*	9E3
Cromwell *NZ*	77A3
Crooked, I *Bahamas*	87C4
Crookston *USA*	84D2
Croppa Creek *Aust*	75D1
Crossett *USA*	87A3
Crotone *Italy*	19C3
Crowley *USA*	95B3
Crown Pt *Tobago*	103Q2
Crows Nest *Aust*	75D1
Croydon *Aust*	73D2
Croydon *Eng*	9D4
Crozet Basin *Indian O*	70B5
Crozier Chan *Can*	80F2
Cruz Alta *Brazil*	106F4
Cruz del Eje *Arg*	105D2
Cruzeiro *Brazil*	111C2
Cruzeiro do Sul *Brazil*	108C5
Crysdale, Mt *USA*	89C1
Crystal Brook *Aust*	74A2
Crystal City, Missouri *USA*	94B2
Crystal Falls *USA*	90A1
Cuamba *Mozam*	67C2
Cuangar *Angola*	66A2
Cuauhtémoc *Mexico*	100B2
Cuautla *Mexico*	99B2
Cuba, Republic *Caribbean*	101D3
Cuchi *Angola*	66A2
Cuchillo Có *Arg*	110C3
Cucui *Brazil*	108D3
Cúcuta *Colombia*	108C2
Cuddalore *India*	53B2
Cuddapah *India*	53B2
Cue *Aust*	72A3
Cuenca *Ecuador*	108B4
Cuenca *Spain*	17B1
Cuernavaca *Mexico*	100C3
Cuero *USA*	95A4
Cuiabá *Brazil*	106E2
Cuicatlan *Mexico*	99B2
Cuillin Hills, Mts *Scot*	10A3
Cuito Cunavale *Angola*	66A2
Cuitzeo *Mexico*	99A2
Cu Lao Hon, I *Viet*	43D3
Culcairn *Aust*	75C3
Culiacán *Mexico*	100B2
Culion, I *Phil*	45A3
Cullman *USA*	93A1
Culoz *France*	13A2
Culpeper *USA*	91C3
Culpepper, I *Ecuador*	108J7
Culter Ridge *USA*	93B2
Culverden *NZ*	77B2
Cumana *Ven*	109E1
Cumberland, Maryland *USA*	86C3
Cumbria *Eng*	8C2
Cummings *USA*	97A2
Cummins *Aust*	74A2
Cumnock *Scot*	8C4
Cunco *Chile*	110A3
Cuneo *Italy*	18A2
Cunnamulla *Aust*	73D3
Cupar *Scot*	10C3
Cuprija *Yugos*	20B2
Curacao, I *Caribbean*	103D4
Curacautin *Chile*	110A3
Curanilahue *Chile*	110A3
Curepto *Chile*	110A3
Curicó *Chile*	105B2
Curitiba *Brazil*	106G4
Curnamona *Aust*	74A2
Curvelo *Brazil*	107C5
Cushing *USA*	84B3
Cuthbert *USA*	93B1
Cuttack *India*	52B2
Cuvelai *Angola*	66A2
Cuxhaven *W Germ*	22B2
Cuyahoga Falls *USA*	91B2
Cuyo Is *Phil*	45B3

Cuzco *Peru*	108C6	
Cyangugu *Zaïre*	65C3	
Cypress Hills, Mts *Can*	89F3	
Cyprus, Republic *Medit S*	58B3	
Czechoslovakia, Republic *Europe*	25B3	
Czestochowa *Pol*	25B2	

D

Da'an *China* 35E2
Dab'a *Jordan* 60C3
Dabajuro *Ven* 103C4
Dabaro *Somalia* 65E2
Daba Shan, Mts *China* 39B3
Dabat *Eth* 65D1
Dabhoi *India* 51C4
Dabie Shan, U *China* 39C3
Dabola *Guinea* 63A3
Dabou *Ivory Coast* 63B4
Dabrowa Gorn *Pol* 25B2
Dachau *W Germ* 23C3
Dachstein, Mt *Austria* 18B1
Dade City *USA* 93B2
Dadhar *Pak* 50B3
Dadu *Pak* 51B3
Daet *Phil* 45B3
Dafang *China* 39B4
Dagabur *Eth* 65E2
Dagana *Sen* 63A3
Dagestanskaya ASSR, Republic *USSR* 31F5
Dagupan *Phil* 45B2
Dahab *Egypt* 58B4
Da Hinggan Ling, Mts *China* 29E3
Dahlonega *USA* 93B1
Dahod *India* 51C4
Dahra, Region *Alg* 17C2
Dailekh *Nepal* 52A1
Daireaux *Arg* 110C3
Daito Is, *Pacific Oc* 35F4
Dajarra *Aust* 72C3
Dakar *Sen* 63A3
Dakhla *Mor* 62A2
Dakhla Oasis *Egypt* 61B2
Dakoro *Niger* 63C3
Dakovica *Yugos* 20B2
Dakovo *Yugos* 20A1
Dala *Angola* 66B2
Dalaba *Guinea* 63A3
Dalai Nur, L *China* 38D1
Dalandzadgad *Mongolia* 34C2
Dalanganem Is *Phil* 45B4
Dalanjargalan *Mongolia* 34C2
Da Lat *Viet* 42D3
Dalby *Aust* 73E3
Dalen *Nor* 5F7
Dales, The, Upland *Eng* 8C2
Daleville *USA* 93A1
Dalhart *USA* 85C3
Dallas *USA* 85D3
Dalles, The *USA* 96B1
Dall I *USA* 81E4
Dalli Rajhara *India* 52A2
Dalmatia, Region *Yugos* 18C2

Dal'nerechensk *USSR* 35F2
Daloa *Ivory Coast* 63B4
Dalou Shan, Mts *China* 39B4
Daltenganj *India* 52A2
Dalton, Georgia *USA* 93B1
Dalton, Massachusetts, *USA* 92C1
Daly City *USA* 97A2
Daly Waters *Aust* 72C2
Damaguete *Phil* 45B4
Daman *India* 51C4
Damanhûr *Egypt* 58B3
Damar, I *Indon* 37D4
Damara *CAR* 64B2
Damascus *Syria* 58C3
Damascus *USA* 92A3
Damaturu *Nig* 63D3
Damavand *Iran* 56B2
Damba *Angola* 64B3
Dambulla *Sri Lanka* 53C3
Damghan *Iran* 56B2
Damoh *India* 51D4
Damot *Eth* 65E2
Damour *Leb* 60B2
Dampier *Aust* 72A3
Dana, Mt *USA* 98C2
Danané *Lib* 63B4
Da Nang *Viet* 42D2
Danao *Phil* 45B3
Danau Tobu, L *Indon* 36A3
Danau Tuwuti, L *Indon* 37D4
Danbu *China* 39A3
Danbury *USA* 92D2
Dandeldhura *Nepal* 52A1
Dandeli *India* 53A1
Dandenong *Aust* 74C3
Dandong *China* 38C1
Danger Pt *S Africa* 66A4
Dangila *Eth* 65D1
Danguard Jenson Land, Region *Can* 82D1
Daniels Harbour *Can* 83E4
Dannebrogs Oy, I *Greenland* 82G3
Dannevirke *NZ* 76C2
Dansteware *India* 53C1
Danvang *Nig* 63C3
Danville, Illinois *USA* 86B2
Danville, Kentucky *USA* 87B3
Danville, Pennsylvania *USA* 92A3
Danville, Virginia *USA* 87C3
Dao Xian *China* 39C4
Daozhen *China* 39B4
Dapiak, Mt *Phil* 45B4
Dapitan *Phil* 45B4
Da Qaidam *China* 34B3
Daqing *China* 60C2
Dar'a *Syria* 58C3
Darab *Iran* 57B4
Daraj *Libya* 61A1
Daran *Iran* 56B3
Dar es Salkhad *Syria* 58C3
Dardanelles *USA* 52B1
Dardanelle *USA* 98C1
Dardanelle, L *USA* 94B2
Dar es Salaam *Tanz* 65D3
Dargaville *NZ* 76B1
Darien *USA* 93B1
Darjiling *India* 52B1

Darling, R *Aust* 73D4
Darling Downs *Aust* 75C1
Darlington *Aust* 74B2
Darlington *Eng* 8D2
Darlington *USA* 93C1
Darmstadt *W Germ* 23B3
Darnah *Libya* 61B1
Darnick *Aust* 74B2
Daroca *Spain* 17B1
Dar Rounga, Region *CAR* 64C2
Dartmoor, Moorland *Eng* 7C3
Dartmouth *Can* 83D5
Dartmouth *Eng* 9C4
Daru *PNG* 73D1
Daruvar *Yugos* 18C1
Darwin *Aust* 72C2
Daryacheh-ye Bakhtegan, L *Iran* 57B4
Daryacheh-ye Maharlu, L *Iran* 57B4
Daryacheh-ye Namak, Salt Flat *Iran* 56B3
Daryacheh-ye-Sistan, Salt Lake *Iran/Afghan* 56D3
Daryacheh-ye Tashk, L *Iran* 57B4
Daryacheh-ye Urumiyeh, L *Iran* 31F6
Darzin *Iran* 57C4
Das, I *UAE* 57B4
Dashennonglia, Mt *China* 39C3
Dasht *Iran* 56C2
Dasht, R *Iran* 51B3
Datong *China* 38A2
Datong *China* 38C1
Datu Piang *Phil* 45B4
Daugavpils *USSR* 26C2
Dauguard Jensen Land *Greenland* 82D1
Daulatabad *Afghan* 50A1
Daulpur *India* 51D3
Daun *W Germ* 12D1
Daund *India* 53A1
Dauphin *Can* 81H4
Dauphin *USA* 92B2
Dauphiné, Region *France* 15D2
Daura *Nig* 63C3
Dausa *India* 51D3
Davangere *India* 53B2
Davao *Phil* 45C4
Davao G *Phil* 45C4
Davenport, California *USA* 98A2
Davenport, Iowa *USA* 86A2
David *Panama* 108A2
Davidson Mts *USA* 80D3
Davis *USA* 97A2
Davis, Base *Ant* 112C0
Davis *Can* 83D4
Davis Str *Greenland/Can* 82E3
Davlekanovo *USSR* 27J3
Davos *Switz* 13C1
Dawa *China* 38A2
Dawan *China* 39B4
Dawat Yar *Afghan* 50B2
Dawna Range, Mts *Burma* 42B2
Dawson *Can* 80E3
Dawson, Georgia *USA* 93B1
Dawson Creek *Can* 81F4
Dawson, Mt *Can* 89D2

Diablo Range, Mts USA	97A2
Diamante Arg	110C2
Diamantina Brazil	107C5
Diamond Harbours India	52B2
Diamond Springs USA	98B1
Diba UAE	57C4
Dibaya Zaire	64C3
Dibrugarh India	52C1
Dickinson USA	84C2
Dickson USA	1B10
Dickson City USA	91C2
Didsbury Can	89E2
Didwana India	51C3
Diebougou Burkina	63B3
Diekirch Lux	12D2
Diéma Mali	63B3
Dien Bien Phu Viet	42C1
Diepholz W Germ	22B2
Dieppe France	14C2
Diest Belg	12C1
Dieuze France	12D2
Digby Can	83D5
Digne France	15D3
Digoin France	15C2
Digos Phil	45C4
Dijon France	15C2
Dik Chad	63D3
Dikhil Djibouti	65E1
Diksmuide Belg	12B1
Dilaram Afghan	48A2
Dili Indon	72B1
Di Linh Viet	42D3
Dillenburg W Germ	12E1
Dilling Sudan	65C1
Dillingham USA	88C3
Dillon USA	84B2
Dillsburg USA	92A2
Dilolo Zaire	66B2
Dimbelenge Zaire	64C3
Dimbokro Ivory Coast	63B4
Dimitrovgrad Bulg	20C2
Dimitrovgrad USSR	27G3
Dimona Israel	60B3
Dimapur India	52C1
Dinagat, I Phil	45C3
Dinajpur India	52B1
Dinan France	14B2
Dinant Belg	12C1
Dinar Turk	58B2
Dindigul India	58B3
Dingbian China	38B2
Dinggyê China	52B1
Dingle Irish Rep	7A3
Dinguiraye Guinea	63A3
Dingwall Scot	10B3
Dingxi China	38A2
Ding Xian China	38D2
Dinh Lap Viet	42D1
Dinuba USA	98C2
Dioulououlou Sen	63A3
Diphu India	52C1
Diredawa Eth	65E2
Dirk Hartog, I Aust	72A3
Dirkou Niger	61A3
Dirranbandi Aust	75C1
Dirri Somalia	65E2
Disappointment, L Aust	72B3
Disentis Muster Switz	13C1
Disko Greenland	82E3
Diskorjord Greenland	82E3
Distrito Federal, Federal District Brazil	111B1
Diu India	51C4
Diuat Mts Phil	45C4
Divinopolis Brazil	107C6
Divnoye USSR	27F4
Divrigi Turk	59C2
Dixon, California USA	98B1
Dixonville Can	89D1
Diyarbakir Turk	31F6
Djado, Plat du Niger	61A2
Djambala Congo	64B3
Djanet Alg	62C2
Djebel Bouhalla, Mt Mor	16A2
Djelfa Alg	62C1
Djéma CAR	64C2
Djenné Mali	63B3
Djibo Burkina	63B3
Djibouti Djibouti	65E1
Djibouti, Republic E Africa	65E1
Djolu Zaire	64C2
Djougou Benin	63C4
Djúpivogur Iceland	6C2
Djurdjura, Mts Alg	17C2
Djugu Zaire	65D2
Dmitrov USSR	26E2
Dnepr, R USSR	26D4
Dneprodzerzhinsk USSR	26D4
Dnepropetrovsk USSR	26E4
Dneprovskaya Nizmennost', Region USSR	26C4
Dno USSR	26D2
Doba Chad	64B2
Dobele USSR	24C1
Doblas Arg	110C3
Doda Indon	37E4
Doboj Yugos	20A2
Dobrush USSR	26D3
Doda Eth	65E2
Doda Betta, Mt India	51B3
Dodge City USA	86D3
Dodoma Tanz	65D3
Dodo, I Japan	41A1
Dogondoutchi Niger	57B4
Dogubayazit Turk	59D2
Doha Qatar	57B4
Dolbeau Can	83C5
Dole France	15D2
Dolgellau Wales	7C3
Dolo Eth	65E2
Dolomitche, Mts Italy	13D1
Dolores Arg	110D2
Dolores Urug	110D2
Dolores Hidalgo Mexico	99A1
Dolores, Mt Indon	37G6
Dombarovskiy USSR	31G4
Dombas Nor	4F6
Dombasle-sur-Meurthe France	12D2
Dombóvár Hung	20A1
Domfront France	14B2
Dominica, I Caribbean	103E3
Dominican Republic Caribbean	103C3
Domino Can	83E4
Domna USSR	34D1
Domodossola Italy	18A1
Dompu Indon	44D4
Domuyo, Mt Arg	105B3
Domville, Mt Aust	75D1
Dom-yarskoya USSR	31H4
Don, R USSR	27F4
Donaghadee N Ire	11C1
Donauwörth W Germ	23C3
Don Benito Spain	16A2
Doncaster Eng	8D3
Dondo Angola	64B3
Dondo Mozam	67C2
Donegal, County Irish Rep	11B1
Donegal Irish Rep	6B3
Donegal B Irish Rep	11B1
Donetsk USSR	26E4
Dong'an China	39C4
Dongara Aust	72A3
Dongchuan China	39A4
Dongfang China	42D2
Dongfeng China	40B2
Donggala Indon	36C4
Donggi Cona, L China	34B3
Dongguan China	40A3
Donghai Dao, I China	39C5
Dong Hoi Viet	42D2
Dongola Sudan	61C3
Dongshan China	39B5
Dongtai China	38E3
Dongting Hu, L China	39C4
Dongxing China	39B5
Dongzhi China	39D3
Doniphan USA	94B2
Donji Vakuf Yugos	18C2
Dønna, I Nor	4G5
Donner, P USA	97A2
Donnersberg, Mt W Germ	12D2
Donnybrook S Africa	67G1
Don Pedro Res USA	98B2
Doonerak, Mt USA	88D1
Dopolong Phil	45B4
Dorbirn Austria	15D2
Dorchester Eng	9C4
Dordrecht Neth	22A2
Dore, L Can	89F2
Dore Lake Can	89F2
Dori Burkina	63B3
Dormans France	12B2
Dornbirn Austria	23B3
Dornoch Scot	10B3
Dornoch Firth, Estuary Scot	10B3
Dorotea Sweden	4H6
Dorrigo Aust	75D2
Dorris USA	96B2
Dorset, County Eng	9C4
Dorsten W Germ	22B2
Dortmund W Germ	22B2
Doruma Zaire	64C2
Dosatuy USSR	29D2
Doshi Afghan	50B1
Dos Palos USA	98B2
Dosso Niger	63C3
Dossor USSR	31G5

Dothan *USA*	87B3
Douai *France*	15C1
Douala *Cam*	64A2
Double Island Pt *Aust*	75D1
Douentza *Mali*	63B3
Douglas, Arizona *USA*	85C3
Douglas *Eng*	8B2
Douglas, Georgia *USA*	93B1
Douglas Chan *Can*	89B2
Douglas, Mt *USA*	84C2
Doullens *France*	12B1
Doun, County *N Ire*	11C1
Dourados *Brazil*	106F3
Dover, Delaware *USA*	91C3
Dover *Eng*	9E4
Dover, New Hampshire	
USA	91D2
Dover, New Jersey *USA*	92B2
Dover, Ohio *USA*	90B2
Downington *USA*	92B3
Downpatrick *N Ire*	8B2
Downton, Mt *Can*	89C2
Doylestown *USA*	92B2
Dozen, I *Japan*	41A1
Dracena *Brazil*	111A2
Dracut *USA*	88D1
Draguignan *France*	15D3
Drakensberg, Mts *S Africa*	67C3
Drakensberg, Mt *S Africa*	67G1
Dráma *Greece*	21B2
Drammen *Nor*	5G7
Drangajökull *Iceland*	4A1
Drayton Valley *Can*	89D2
Dreaux *France*	15C2
Dreux *France*	14C2
Drewsey *USA*	96C2
Drogheda *Irish Rep*	11C2
Drogobych *USSR*	25C3
Dr P.P. Pená *Par*	106D3
Drumheller *Can*	81G4
Drummond I *USA*	90B1
Drummondville *Can*	91D1
Druskininkai *USSR*	24C2
Dryden *Can*	83A5
Dry Harbour Mts *Jamaica*	103H1
Duang, I *Burma*	42B3
Duarte, Pico *Dom Rep*	57C4
Dubawnt L *Can*	80H3
Dubbo *Aust*	73D4
Dublin, County *Irish Rep*	11C2
Dublin *Irish Rep*	11C2
Dublin *USA*	93B1
Dubna *USSR*	26E2
Dubno *USSR*	26C3
Du Bois *USA*	91C2
Dubose, Mt *Can*	89B2
Dubrovica *USSR*	24D2
Dubrovnik *Yugos*	16D2
Dubuque *USA*	86A2
Dudelange *Lux*	12D2
Dudinka *USSR*	1C10
Dudley *Eng*	9C3
Duekoué *Ivory Coast*	63B4
Dufftown *Scot*	10C3
Dugi Otok, I *Yugos*	18B2

Duisburg *W Germ*	22B2
Dukan *Iraq*	59E3
Duk Faiwil *Sudan*	65D2
Dukhan *Qatar*	57B4
Dukou *China*	39A4
Dulan *China*	34B3
Dulit Range, Mts *Malay*	44C2
Dullabchara *India*	52C2
Duluth *USA*	86A2
Dumai *Syria*	60C2
Dumai *Indon*	44A2
Dumaran, I *Phil*	45A3
Dumas *USA*	85C3
Dumayr *Syria*	60C2
Dumbarton *Scot*	8B2
Dumfries *Scot*	8C2
Dumfries and Galloway,	
Region *Scot*	8B2
Dumka *India*	52B2
Dumoine, L *Can*	91C1
Dumont d'Urville, Base *Ant*	112C8
Dumyat *Egypt*	61C1
Dunary Head, Pt *Irish Rep*	11C2
Dunayevtsy *USSR*	25D3
Duncan *USA*	89C3
Duncannon *USA*	92A2
Duncansby Head, Pt *Scot*	10C2
Dundalk *Irish Rep*	11C1
Dundalk *USA*	92A3
Dundas Greenland	82D2
Dundas *Scot*	67H1
Dundee *S Africa*	67H1
Dundee *Scot*	10C3
Dundoo *Aust*	74B1
Dunedin *NZ*	77B3
Dunedin *USA*	93B2
Dunedoo *Aust*	75C2
Dunfermline *Scot*	10C3
Dungarpur *India*	51C4
Dungarvan *Irish Rep*	11C2
Dungeness *Eng*	9E4
Dungog *Aust*	75D2
Dungu *Zaïre*	65C2
Dungunab *Sudan*	61C2
Dunhuang *China*	34B2
Dunkerque *France*	12B1
Dunkirk *USA*	86C2
Dunkur *Eth*	65D1
Dunkwa *Ghana*	63B4
Dun Laoghaire *Irish Rep*	11C2
Dunmanway *Irish Rep*	11B3
Dunmore Town *Bahamas*	102B1
Dunnet Head, Pt *Scot*	10C2
Duns *Scot*	8C2
Dunsmuir *USA*	96B2
Dunstan Mts *NZ*	77A2
Dun-sur-Meuse *France*	12C2
Duolun *China*	38D1
Duque de Braganca *Angola*	64B3
Du Quoin *USA*	90C3
Dura *Israel*	60C3
Durango *Mexico*	100B2
Durango *Spain*	16B1
Durango *USA*	85C3
Durano *Urug*	105E2
Durant *USA*	85D3
Durayksh *Syria*	60C1
Durban *S Africa*	67H1

Duren *W Germ*	12D1
Durg *India*	52A2
Durgapur *India*	52B2
Durham, County *Eng*	8D2
Durham *Eng*	8D2
Durham, N Carolina *USA*	87C3
Durham, New Hampshire	
USA	92D1
Durham Downs *Aust*	74B1
Durmitor, Mt *Yugos*	20A2
Durness *Scot*	10B2
Durrës *Alb*	21A2
Durrie *Aust*	74B1
Dursey, I *Irish Rep*	11A3
Dursunbey *Turk*	21C3
D'Urville I *NZ*	76B2
Dushak *USSR*	56D2
Dushan *China*	39B4
Dushanbe *USSR*	48A2
Düsseldorf *W Germ*	22B2
Duyun *China*	39B4
Düzce *Turk*	58B1
Dwarka *India*	51B4
Dyersburg *USA*	87B3
Dyfed, County *Wales*	9B3
Dykh Tau Daglari, Mt *USSR*	27F5
Dynevor Downs *Aust*	74B1
Dzag *Mongolia*	34B2
Dzamin Uüd *USSR*	29C3
Dzaoudzi *Mayotte*	67D2
Dzarnin Uüd *Mongolia*	34C2
Dzhezkazgan *USSR*	46E1
Dzerzhinsk *USSR*	27F2
Dzhalinda *USSR*	29E2
Dzhambul *USSR*	31J5
Dzhankoy *USSR*	26D4
Dzhezkazgan *USSR*	31H4
Dzhilikul' *USSR*	50B1
Dzhungarskiy Alatau, Mts	
USSR	31J5
Dzierzoniow *Pol*	25B2
Dzungaria, Basin *China*	48C1

E

Eabamic L *Can*	83B4
Eagle, Alaska *USA*	88F2
Eagle L *Can*	96B2
Eagle Mountain L *USA*	95A3
Eagle Pass *USA*	85C4
Eagle Plain *Can*	80E3
Eagle River *USA*	88E2
Earlimart *USA*	97B2
Easley *USA*	93B1
East Aurora *USA*	91C2
Eastbourne *Eng*	9F4
East Chicago *USA*	90A2
East China Sea *China/Japan*	35E3
Eastern Ghats, Mts *India*	49B3
East Falkland, I *Falkland Is*	105E6
Eastgate *USA*	97B2
East Germany, Republic	
Europe	22C2
Easthampton *USA*	92C1
East Hampton *USA*	92C2
East Lake *USA*	94B2
East Liverpool *USA*	90B2

Father Can 89D1	Figuig Mor 62B1	Florence, Oregon USA 96B2
Fatima du Sul Brazil 106F2	Fiji, Is Pacific O 71G4	Florence, S Carolina USA 87C1
Fauresmith S Africa 67G1	Filadelfia Par 106D3	Florencia Colombia 108E3
Favergas France 13B2	Filiasi Rom 20B2	Florennes Belg 12C2
Faya Chad 72C3	Filiatrá Greece 21B3	Flores Guatemala 101D3
Fayetteville, Arkansas USA 95B3	Filicudi, I Italy 19B3	Flores, I Azores 62A1
Fayetteville, N Carolina USA 87C3	Fillmore, California USA 97B3	Flores, I Indon 72B4
Faylakah, I Kuwait 45E4	Findlay USA 86B2	Flores, I Indon 36C3
Fazilka India 50C2	Findlay, Mt Can 89D2	Floriano Brazil 107C2
Fdérik Maur 62A2	Finger Lakes USA 91C2	Florianópolis Brazil 106C4
Fécamp France 14C2	Fingoè Mozam 66C1	Florida, State USA 87C3
Federación Arg 110D2	Finike Turk 58B2	Florida Urug 105C4
Federal Arg 110D2	Finke Flood Flats Aust 74A1	Florida City USA 93E4
Federated States of	Finland, Republic N Europe 30D3	Florida Keys, Is USA 87B4
Micronesia, Is Pacific O 37F3	Finland, G of N Europe 5J7	Florida, Strs of USA 87B4
Fehmarn, I W Germ 22C2	Finlay Forks Can 81F4	Flórina Greece 21B2
Feijó Brazil 108C5	Finley Aust 74C3	Floro Nor 4F6
Feilding N Z 76C2	Finnsnes Nor 4H5	Fluchthorn, Mt Austria 13D1
Feira Zambia 66C2	Finschhafen PNG 37F4	Focsani Rom 20C1
Feira de Santan Brazil 107D4	Finsterarahorn, Mt Switz 13C1	Foggia Italy 19C2
Feke Turk 58C2	Finsterwalde E Germ 22C2	Fogo, I Cape Verde 63A4
Feldkirch Austria 23B3	Fintona N Ire 11C1	Foix France 14C3
Felixstowe Eng 7D3	Fiordland Nat Pk NZ 77A3	Foley I Can 82C2
Feltre Italy 13D1	Fiq Syria 60B2	Foligno Italy 18B2
Femund, L Nor 4G6	Firebaugh USA 98B2	Folkestone Eng 9E3
Fengcheng China 40A2	Firenze Italy 18B2	Folkston USA 93B1
Fengdu China 39B4	Firmat Arg 110C2	Follonica Italy 18B2
Fenging China 38B1	Firozabad India 51D3	Folsom USA 98B2
Fengjie China 39B3	Firozpur India 50C2	Folsom L, L USA 98B2
Feng Xian China 38B3	Firspäng Sweden 5H7	Fond-du-Lac Can 81H4
Fengzhen China 38C1	Firth of Clyde, Estuary Scot 8B2	Fond du Lac USA 86B2
Fenoarivo Atsinanana	Firth of Forth, Estuary Scot 10C3	Fontainebleau France 14C2
Madag 67D2	Firth of Lorn, Estuary Scot 10A3	Fontenac USA 94B2
Feodosiya USSR 26E5	Firth of Tay, Estuary Scot 10C3	Fontenay-le-Comte France 14B2
Ferdow Iran 56C3	Firuzabad Iran 57B4	Fonyód Hung 18C1
Fère-Champenoise France 12B2	Fish Camp USA 98C2	Foraker, Mt USA 88D3
Fergana USSR 48J5	Fishers I USA 92C2	Forbach France 12D2
Fermanagh, County N Ire 11C1	Fishguard Wales 7B4	Forbes Aust 76C2
Fermoy Irish Rep 11B2	Fiskenaesset Greenland 82E3	Forcados I A... 63C4
Fern, Mt Austria 13D1	Fismes France 12B2	Forde Nor 4F6
Fernandina, I Ecuador 108J7	Fitchburg USA 91D2	Fords Bridge Aust 74C1
Fernandina Beach USA 93B1	Fitful Head, Pt Scot 10D2	Fordyce USA 95B3
Fernando de Noronha, I	Fitzgerald USA 93B1	Forécarian Guinea 62A3
Atlantic O 69G5	Fitzroy Crossing Aust 73B1	Forel, Mt Greenland 82C2
Fernandópolis Brazil 111A2	Fitzwilliam I Can 90B1	Forest Can 90B1
Ferndale USA 96B1	Fizi Zaire 65C3	Forest Park USA 93B1
Fernley USA 97B2	Flagstaff USA 85B3	Forestville USA 98A2
Ferrara Italy 18B2	Flaming Gorge Res USA 84C2	Forfar Scot 10C3
Ferreñafe Peru 108B5	Flannan Isles, Is Scot 10A2	Forges-les-Eaux France 12A1
Ferriday USA 95B3	Flathead L USA 84B2	Forks USA 96B1
Fès Mor 62B1	Flat River USA 94B2	Forlì Italy 18B2
Festus USA 94B2	Fleetwood Eng 8C3	Formentera, I Spain 17C2
Fetesti Rom 20C2	Flekkefjord Nor 5F7	Formia Italy 19B2
Fethiye Turk 58A2	Flemish Deep Pacific Oc 35G4	Formigas, I Azores 62A1
Fetisovo USSR 27H5	Flemington USA 92B2	Formosa Arg 106E3
Fetlar, I Scot 10D1	Flensburg W Germ 22B2	Formosa Brazil 107B2
Feyzabad Afghan 31J6	Fleurier Switz 13B1	Formosa, State Arg 106D3
Fianarantsoa Madag 67D3	Flinders, I Aust 72C4	Fornovo di Taro Italy 13D2
Fiche Eth 65D2	Flinders, I Aust 73D4	Forres Scot 10C3
Ficksburg S Africa 67G1	Flinders Range, Mts Aust 72C4	Forrest Aust 72B4
Fidenza Italy 13D2	Flin Flon Can 81H4	Forrest City USA 87A3
Fier Alb 21A2	Flint USA 86B2	Forsayth Aust 73D2
Fiera Di Primeiro Italy 13D1	Flint Wales 8C3	Forssa Fin 5J6
Fife, Region Scot 10C3	Flixecourt France 12B1	Forster Aust 75D2
Figeac France 14C3	Florala USA 93A1	Forsyth, Missouri USA 94B3
Figueira da Foz Port 16A1	Florence, Alabama USA 87B3	Fort Abbas Pak 50C3
Figueras Spain 17C1	Florence, Kansas USA 94A3	

Fort Albany *Can*	83B4
Fortaleza *Brazil*	107D2
Fort Augustus *Scot*	10B3
Fort Beaufort *S Africa*	66B4
Fort Bragg *USA*	97A2
Fort Collins *USA*	84C2
Fort Coulogne *Can*	91C1
Fort de France *Martinique*	103E4
Fort Deposit *USA*	93A1
Fort Dodge *USA*	86A2
Fort Frances *Can*	83A5
Fort Franklin *Can*	80F3
Fort George *Can*	83C4
Fort Good Hope *Can*	80F3
Fort Grey *Aust*	74B1
Fort Hope *Can*	83B4
Fortin Uno *Arg*	110B3
Fort Laird *Can*	80F3
Fort Lallemand *Alg*	62C1
Fort Lauderdale *USA*	88B2
Fort Mackay *Can*	81G4
Fort Macleod *Can*	81G5
Fort McMurray *Can*	81G4
Fort McPherson *Can*	80E3
Fort Madison *USA*	94B2
Fort Morgan *USA*	84C2
Fort Myers *USA*	87B4
Fort Nelson *Can*	81F4
Fort Norman *Can*	80F3
Fort Payne *USA*	93A1
Fort Peck Res *USA*	84C2
Fort Pierce *USA*	87B4
Fort Providence *Can*	80G3
Fort Resolution *Can*	81G3
Fort Rousset *Congo*	64B3
Fort Rupert *Can*	83C4
Fort St James *Can*	81F4
Fort St John *Can*	89C1
Fort Saskatchewan *Can*	89E2
Fort Scott *USA*	94B2
Fort Selkirk *Can*	80E3
Fort Severn *Can*	83A3
Fort Shevchenko *USSR*	27H5
Fort Simpson *Can*	81G3
Fort Smith *Can*	87A3
Fort Smith *USA*	87A3
Fort Stockton *USA*	85C3
Fortuna, California *USA*	96B2
Fort Vermillion *Can*	81G4
Fort Walton Beach *USA*	93A1
Fort Wayne *USA*	86B2
Fort William *Scot*	10B3
Fort Worth *USA*	85D3
Fort Yukon *USA*	88E1
Foshan *China*	39C5
Fossano *Italy*	13B2
Foster, Mt *USA*	88C3
Fougamou *Gabon*	64B3
Fougères *France*	14B2
Foulness I *Eng*	9E4
Foumban *Cam*	64B3
Fournies *France*	15C1
Fournoi, I *Greece*	21C3
Fouta Djallon, Mts *Guinea*	63A3
Fowey *Eng*	9B4
Fox Creek *Can*	89D2
Foxe Basin, G *Can*	82B3
Foxe Chan *Can*	82B3
Foxton *NZ*	76C2
Fox Valley *Can*	89F2
Foynes *Irish Rep*	11B2
Foz do Cuene *Angola*	66A2
Foz do Iguacu *Brazil*	106F4
Frackville *USA*	92A2
Fraga *Arg*	110B2
Framingham *USA*	92D1
Franca *Brazil*	107B6
France, Republic *Europe*	16C2
Frances *Can*	86A2
France Ville *Gabon*	64B3
Franche Comté, Region *France*	15D2
Francistown *Botswana*	66B3
François L *Can*	86B2
Frankfort, Indiana *USA*	90A2
Frankfort, Kentucky *USA*	87B3
Frankfort *S Africa*	67G1
Frankfurt am Main *W Germ*	12E1
Frankfurt-an-der-Oder *E Germ*	22C2
Fränkische Alb, Upland *W Germ*	23C3
Franklin, Indiana *USA*	90A3
Franklin, Louisiana *USA*	90A3
Franklin, Massachusetts *USA*	92D1
Franklin, New Jersey *USA*	92D1
Franklin, Pennsylvania *USA*	90C2
Franklin, Region *Can*	80G2
Franklin D Roosevelt L *USA*	96C1
Franklin Mts *Can*	80F3
Frankovsk *USSR*	22D3
Franz Josef Glacier *NZ*	77B2
Fraserburgh *Scot*	10D3
Fraser I *Aust*	75D1
Fraser L *Can*	89B2
Frasne *France*	13C1
Frauenfeld *Switz*	13C1
Fray Bentos *Urug*	110D2
Frazerburgh *Scot*	6C2
Fredericia *USA*	92B3
Fredericia *Den*	22B1
Frederick, Maryland *USA*	91C3
Fredericksburg, Virginia *USA*	91C3
Fredericktown *USA*	94B2
Fredericton *Can*	83D5
Frederikshab *Greenland*	82E3
Frederikshavn *Den*	5G7
Fredonia *USA*	91C2
Fredrikstad *Nor*	5G7
Freehold *USA*	92B2
Freeport *Bahamas*	102B1
Freeport, Texas *USA*	95A4
Freetown *Sierra Leone*	63A4
Freiburg *W Germ*	23C3
Freistadt *Austria*	23C3
Fremantle *Aust*	72A4
Fremont, California *USA*	96B2
Fremont, Nebraska *USA*	94A1
Fremont, Ohio *USA*	90B2
French Guiana, Dependency *S America*	109G3
Frenchmans Cap, Mt *Aust*	75C4
French Polynesia, Is *Pacific O*	71J4
Fresnillo *Mexico*	100B2
Fresno *USA*	84B3
Fretigney *France*	13A1
Frévent *France*	12B1
Fria *Guinea*	63A3
Friant *USA*	98C2
Friant Dam *USA*	98C2
Fribourg *Switz*	18A1
Friedrichshafen *W Germ*	23B3
Frobisher Bay *Can*	82D3
Frobisher L *Can*	81H4
Frolovo *USSR*	27F4
Frome *Eng*	9C4
Frome, L *Aust*	72C4
Frontera *Mexico*	101C3
Front Royal *USA*	91C3
Frosinone *Italy*	19B2
Frunze *USSR*	48B1
Fuchuan *China*	39C5
Fuding *China*	39E4
Fuerte Olimpo *Par*	106E3
Fuerteventura, I *Canary Is*	62A2
Fugong *China*	38C2
Fugu *China*	38C2
Fuhai *China*	34A2
Fuji *Japan*	41B1
Fujian, Province *China*	39D4
Fujin *China*	35F2
Fujinomiya *Japan*	41B1
Fuji-san, Mt *Japan*	40D3
Fujisawa *Japan*	41B1
Fuji-Yoshida *Japan*	41B1
Fukang *China*	29A3
Fukuchiyima *Japan*	40C3
Fukui *Japan*	40C3
Fukuoka *Japan*	40C4
Fukushima *Japan*	40E3
Fukuyama *Japan*	40C4
Fulda *W Germ*	23B2
Fuling *China*	39B4
Fullarton *Trinidad*	103L1
Fullerton *USA*	98D4
Fulton, Kentucky *USA*	94C2
Fulton, New York *USA*	91C2
Fumay *France*	12C1
Funabashi *Japan*	41C1
Funchal *Medeira*	62A1
Fundao *Brazil*	111C1
Funhalouro *Mozam*	67C3
Funing *China*	38D3
Funing *China*	39B5
Funtua *Nig*	63C3
Fuqing *China*	39D4
Furancungo *Mozam*	67C2
Furg *Iran*	57C4
Furka, P *Switz*	13C1
Furneaux Group, Is *Aust*	73D5
Fürstenwalde *E Germ*	22C2
Fürth *W Germ*	23C3
Furukawa *Japan*	40D3
Fury and Hecla Str *Can*	82B3
Fushun, Liaoning *China*	40A2

Fushun, Sichuan China	39A4	Gamba China	52B1	Garza-Little Elm, Res USA	95A3
Fusong China	40B2	Gambaga Ghana	63B3	Gasan Kuli USSR	56B2
Füssen W Germ	23C1	Gambell USA	80A3	Gascogne, Region France	14B3
Fu Xian China	38E2	Gambia, The, Republic		Gashaka Nig	64B2
Fuxin China	38E1	Africa	63A3	Gashua Nig	63D3
Fuyang China	38D3	Gamboma Congo	64B3	Gaspé Can	86D2
Fuyuan, Liaoning China	38E1	Gambos Angola	66A2	Gatchina USSR	26C2
Fuyuan, Yunnan China	39A4	Gampola Sri Lanka	53C3	Gateshead Eng	8D2
Fuyun China	34A2	Gananoque Can	91C2	Gatesville USA	95A3
Fuzhou China	39D4	Ganda Angola	66A2	Gatineau Can	91C1
Fyn, I Den	22C1	Gandajika Zaire	64C3	Gatineau Can	91C1
		Gandava Pak	50B3	Gatton Aust	75D1
		Gander Can	83E5	Gauháti India	52C1
G		Gandhinagar India	51C4	Gauri Phanta India	52A1
		Gandhi Sagar, L India	51D4	Gaviota USA	98B3
Gaalkacyo Somalia	65E2	Gandia Spain	17B2	Gävle Sweden	5H6
Gabbs USA	97B2	Ganga, R India	52B2	Gawler Ranges, Mts Aust	74A2
Gabela Angola	66A2	Ganganar India	51C3	Gaxun Nur, L China	38A1
Gabe's Tunisia	62D1	Gangaw Burma	52C2	Gaya India	52A2
Gabilan Range, Mts USA	64B3	Gangca China	38A2	Gaya Niger	63C3
Gabon, Republic Africa	64B3	Gangdise Shan, Mts China	48C2	Gaylord USA	90B1
Gaborone Botswana	66B3	Gangtok India	52B1	Gayndah Aust	75D1
Gabrovo Bulg	20C2	Gangu China	38B3	Gayny USSR	27H1
Gach Saran Iran	57B3	Gannett Peak, Mt USA	86A1	Gaysin USSR	26C4
Gadsden, Alabama USA	93A1	Ganquan China	38B2	Gaza Israel	58B3
Gads I, Can	86A1	Gantsevichi USSR	5K8	Gaziantep Turk	52B3
Gaeta Italy	19B2	Ganzhou China	39D4	Gbarnga Lib	63B4
Gaferut, I Pacific O	37F3	Gao Mali	63C3	Gdansk Pol	59B2
Gafsa Tunisia	62C1	Gaolan China	38A2	Gdansk Sweden	54F2
Gagarin USSR	26D2	Gaoping China	38C2	Gdansk, G of Pol	58B2
Gagnon Can	83F4	Gaoua Burkina	63B3	Gdov USSR	5K7
Gagra USSR	27F5	Gaoual Guinea	63A3	Gdynia Pol	59B2
Gaibanda India	52B1	Gaoyou Hu, L China	38D3	Gebel Halâl, Mt Egypt	24B2
Gaimán Arg	105C4	Gaozhou China	39C5	Gebel Hamata, Mt Egypt	60A3
Gainesville, Florida USA	93B2	Gap France	15D3	Gebel Katherina, Mt Egypt	61C2
Gainesville, Georgia USA	93B1	Gapan Phil	45B2	Gebel Libni, Mt Egypt	58B4
Gainesville, Texas USA	9B3	Gar China	50D2	Gebel Maghâra, Mt Egypt	60A3
Gainsborough Eng	8D3	Garah Aust	75C1	Gedaref Sudan	64B2
Gairdner, L Aust	74A2	Garanhuns Brazil	107D3	Gedser Den	65D1
Gairloch Scot	10B3	Garberville USA	97A1	Geel Belg	22C2
Gaithersburg USA	92A3	Garca Brazil	111B2	Geelong Aust	12C1
Gajendragarh India	65E2	Garcas Brazil	111A2	Geeveston Aust	74B3
Galadi Eth	65E2	Garda Italy	13D2	Geidam Nig	75C3
Galapagos Is Pacific O	69D5	Garden City USA	85C3	Geilenkirchen W Germ	63D3
Galashiels Scot	8C2	Gardez Afghan	50B2	Geita Tanz	12D1
Galati Rom	20C1	Gardey Arg	110D3	Gejiu China	65D3
Galena, Alaska USA	80C3	Gardiners I USA	92C2	Gela Italy	39B3
Galena, Kansas USA	18B2	Gardner I USA	92D1	Geldern W Germ	19B3
Galeota Pt Trinidad	103L1	Gardone Italy	13D2	Gelibolu Turk	12D1
Galera Pt Trinidad	103L1	Gardula Eth	65D2	Gelidonya Burun Turk	21C2
Galesburg USA	86A2	Gargano Italy	52A2	Gelsenkirchen W Germ	58B2
Galeton USA	91C2	Gargarsa China	48C2	Gelting W Germ	12D1
Galich USSR	27F2	Gargano I USA	90A2	Gemas Malay	5F8
Galicia, Region Spain	16A1	Garhakota India	51D4	Gembloux Belg	43C5
Galina Pt Jamaica	103J1	Gari USSR	27K2	Gemena Zaire	12C1
Gallabat Sudan	65D1	Garies S Africa	66A4	Gemerek Turk	58C2
Gallarate Italy	13C2	Garissa Kenya	65D3	Gemlik Turk	58A1
Galle Sri Lanka	53C3	Garland USA	95A3	Gemona Italy	18B1
Gallipoli Italy	21A2	Garmisch-Partenkirchen		Gemsbok Nat Pk,	
Gallivare Sweden	4J5	W Germ	23C3	Botswana	66B3
Galloway, District	8B2	Garmsar Iran	56B2	Geneina Sudan	64C1
Gallup USA	84C3	Garnett USA	94A2	General Acha Arg	110C3
Galt USA	98B1	Garnett Peak, Mt USA	86A1	General Alvear, Buenos	
Galveston USA	101C2	Garut Indon	44B4	Aires Arg	110C3
Galvez Arg	110C2	Garwa India	52A2	General Alvear, Mendoza	
Galvi Corse	15D3	Gary USA	90A2	Arg	110C3
Galway, County Irish Rep	11B2	Garyarsa China	48C2	General Arenales Arg	110C2
Galway Irish Rep	7B3	Gary L Can	80H3	General Belgrano Arg	110D3

eneral Belgrano, Base Ant	112B2
eneral Bernardo O'Higgins, Base Ant	112C2
ieneral Conesa, Buenos Aires Arg	110D3
ieneral Eugenio A Garay Par	106D3
ieneral Guido Arg	110C3
ieneral La Madrid Arg	110C3
ieneral Levalle Arg	110C3
ieneral Manuel Belgrano, Mt Arg	106C4
ieneral Paz, Buenos Aires Arg	110D3
ieneral Pico Arg	110C3
ieneral Pinto Arg	110C2
ieneral Pirán Arg	110D3
ieneral Roca Arg	105C3
ieneral Santos Phil	45C4
ieneral Viamonte Arg	110C3
ieneral Villegas Arg	110C3
ieneseo USA	91C2
ieneva, Nebraska USA	94A1
ieneva, New York USA	91C2
ieneve Switz	18A1
ienoa Aust	75C3
ienova Italy	18A2
ienova, I Ecuador	108J7
ient Belg	12B1
ienteng Indon	44B4
enthin E Germ	22C2
ieokchay USSR	59E1
ieorge S Africa	66B4
eorge, L Aust	75C2
eorge, L Florida USA	93B3
eorge, L New York USA	91D2
eorge Town Aust	75C4
ieorgetown, Delaware USA	91C3
ieorgetown Guyana	109F2
ieorgetown, Kentucky USA	90B3
eorgetown St Vincent	103N2
ieorgetown, S Carolina USA	93C1
ieorgetown, Texas USA	95A3
ieorgetown The Gambia	63A3
eorgia, State USA	93B1
ieorgiu-Dezh USSR	26E3
ieorgiyevsk USSR	27F5
iera E Germ	22C2
ieraardsbergen Belg	12B1
ieraldine NZ	77B2
ieraldton Aust	72A3
eraldton Can	86B2
ierdine, Mt USA	80C3
erdova Peak, Mt USA	88E2
ierik Malay	43C4
ierlachovsky, Mt Pol	26B4
iermanson Lodge Can	89C1
iermiston S Africa	67G1
iermiston USA	80B2
ierona Spain	17C1
ieseke W Germ	12E1
ietafe Spain	16B1
Gettysburg, Pennsylvania USA	92A3
Gevas Turk	59D2
Gevgelija Yugos	21B2
Gex France	13B1
Ghabaghib Syria	60C2
Ghadamis Libya	62C1
Ghaem Shahr Iran	56B2
Ghana, Republic Africa	63B4
Ghanzi Botswana	66B3
Ghardaïa Alg	62C1
Gharyan Libya	61A1
Ghat Libya	61A2
Ghazi Khan Pak	50D3
Ghazni Afghan	50B2
Gheorgheni Rom	20C1
Gheorghiu G Dei Rom	20C1
Ghudamis Alg	54E4
Ghurian Afghan	56D3
Gialo Libya	61B2
Giamame Somalia	65E2
Giarre Italy	19C3
Gibeon Namibia	66A3
Gibraltar, Colony SW Europe	16A2
Gibson Desert Aust	72B3
Gibsons Can	96B1
Giddalur India	53B1
Giessen W Germ	23B3
Gifford USA	93B2
Gifu Japan	40D3
Gigha, I Scot	8B2
Giglio, I Italy	18B2
Gijón Spain	16A1
Gilbert, Mt Can	90A2
Gilé Mozam	67C2
Gilead, Region Jordan	60B2
Gilf Kebir Plat Egypt	61B2
Gilgandra Aust	75C2
Gilgit Pak	50C1
Gilgunnia Aust	74C2
Gillam Can	83A4
Gilles, L Aust	74A2
Gill I Can	89B2
Gills Rock USA	90A1
Gilman USA	90A1
Gilroy USA	99B2
Gimli Can	84D1
Gingindlovu S Africa	67H1
Gingoog Phil	45C4
Ginir Eth	65E2
Gióna, Mt Greece	21B3
Gippsland, Mts Aust	75C3
Girard USA	90B2
Girardot Colombia	108C3
Giresun Turk	59C1
Gir Hills India	51C4
Giridih India	52B2
Girvan Scot	8B2
Gisborne NZ	77C2
Gisors France	12A2
Gitega Burundi	69C3
Giurgiu Rom	20C2
Givet Belg	12C1
Gizycko Pol	24C2
Gjirokastër Alb	21B2
Gjoatlaven Can	80J3
Gjovik Nor	5G6
Glace Bay Can	83D5
Glacier Nat Mon USA	88G3
Glacier Nat Pk, USA/Can USA	89E3
Glacier Peak, Mt USA	96B1
Gladstone, Queensland Aust	73E3
Gladstone, S Aust Aust	74A2
Gladstone, Tasmania Aust	75C4
Gladstone USA	90A1
Glama, Mt Iceland	4A1
Glarner, Mts Switz	13C1
Glarus Switz	13C1
Glasco USA	94A2
Glasgow, Montana USA	84C2
Glasgow Scot	8B2
Glassboro USA	92B3
Glastonbury Eng	9C4
Glazov USSR	27H2
Gleisdorf Austria	25B3
Glen Afton NZ	76C1
Glen Burnie USA	92A3
Glencoe S Africa	67H1
Glendale, Arizona USA	85B3
Glendale, California USA	98C3
Glenhallen USA	88E2
Glen Innes Aust	75D1
Glenmorgan Aust	75D1
Glenreagh Aust	75D2
Glen Rock USA	92A3
Glen Rose USA	95A3
Glenrothes UK	10C3
Glens Falls USA	91D2
Glenties Irish Rep	11B1
Glenwood, Arkansas USA	95B3
Glenwood Springs USA	84C3
Glittertind, Mt Nor	5F6
Gliwice Pol	25B2
Globe USA	85B3
Głogów Pol	24B2
Glomfjord Nor	4G5
Gloucester Aust	75D2
Gloucester Eng	9C4
Gloucester USA	92D1
Glubokoye USSR	24D1
Glukhov USSR	26D3
Gmünd Austria	25B3
Gmunden Austria	23C3
Gniezno Pol	24B2
Goabeg Namibia	66A3
Goa, Daman and Diu, Union Territory India	53A1
Goalpara India	52C1
Goba Eth	65D2
Gobabis Namibia	66A3
Gobernador Crespo Arg	110C2
Gobernador Duval Arg	110C3
Gobi, Desert China/Mongolia	38B1
Gobo Japan	41B2
Godag India	53B1
Goderich Can	90B2
Godhavn Greenland	82E3
Godhra India	51C4
Godoy Cruz Arg	110B2

Gross Venediger, Mt Austria 13E1
Grosvenor, L USA 88C3
Groveland USA 98B2
Grover City USA 97A2
Groveton USA 91D2
Groznyy USSR 27G5
Grudziadz Pol 24B2
Grünau Namibia 66A3
Grutness Scot 10D2
Gruzinskaya SSR, Republic USSR 31F5
Gryazi USSR 27F3
Gryazovets USSR 27E2
Grytviken South Georgia 105G8
Gt Blasket, I Irish Rep 11A2
Guacui Brazil 111C2
Guadalajara Mexico 99A1
Guadalajara Spain 16B1
Guadalcanal, I Solomon Is 73E1
Guadalupe Mexico 100B2
Guadalupe, I Mexico 79G6
Guadeloupe, I Caribbean 103E3
Guadix Spain 16B2
Guajará Mirim Brazil 108D6
Gualaceo Ecuador 108B4
Gualeguay Arg 110D2
Gualeguaychú Arg 110D2
Guam, I Pacific O 37F2
Guamini Arg 110C3
Gua Musang Malay 43C5
Guanajuato Mexico 99A1
Guanajuato, State Mexico 99A1
Guanare Ven 108D2
Guane Cuba 101D2
Guangdong, Province China 39C5
Guanghan China 39A3
Guanghua China 38C3
Guangmao Shan, Mt China 39B5
Guangnan China 39B5
Guangyuan China 38B3
Guangze China 39A4
Guanghzou China 33F3
Guanhães Brazil 111C1
Guantánamo Cuba 102B2
Guanting Shuiku, Res China 38D1
Guanxi, Province China 39B5
Guan Xian China 39A3
Guapa Colombia 108B2
Guaqui Bol 106C2
Guaranda Ecuador 108B4
Guarapuava Brazil 106F4
Guaratinguetá Brazil 111B3
Guarda Port 16A1
Guarda Mor Brazil 111B1
Guasave Mexico 85C4
Guastalla Italy 47D2
Guatemala Guatemala 101C3
Guatrachè Arg 110C3
Guaxupé Brazil 111B2
Guayaguayare Trinidad 103L1
Guayaquil Ecuador 108A4
Guaymas Mexico 99A2
Guba Eth 65D2
Guba Zaïre 66B2

Guban, Region Somalia 65E2
Gubat Phil 45B3
Gubin Pol 22C2
Gudur India 53B2
Guelpho Can 90B2
Guelta Zemmur Mor 62A2
Guanabacoa Cuba 102A2
Guéréda Chad 64C1
Guéret France 14C2
Guernsey, I UK 14B2
Guerrero, State Mexico 99A2
Gughe, Mt Eth 65D2
Gugigu China 29E2
Guguan, I Pacific O 37F2
Guidong China 39C4
Guiglo Ivory Coast 63B4
Guildford Eng 9D4
Guilin China 39C4
Guillestre France 13B2
Guinan China 38A2
Guinea, Republic Africa 63A3
Guinea, G of W Africa 63C4
Guinea-Bissau, Republic Africa 63A3
Guinès France 68H4
Güiria Ven 109E1
Guise France 12B2
Guiuan Phil 45C3
Gui Xian China 39B5
Guiyang China 39B4
Guizhou, Province China 39B4
Gujarat, State India 51C4
Gujrat Pak 50C2
Gulbarga India 53B1
Gulbene USSR 24D1
Guledagudda India 53B1
Gulf, The S W Asia 46D3
Gulgong Aust 75C2
Gulin China 39B4
Gulkana USA 4D3
Gull L Can 89F2
Gulu Uganda 65D2
Guluguba Aust 75C1
Gumel Nig 63C3
Gummersbach W Germ 12D1
Gumpla India 52A2
Gümüshane Turk 59C1
Guna India 51D4
Guna, Mt Eth 65D1
Gundagai Aust 75C3
Gungu Zaïre 64B3
Gunnedah Aust 75D2
Guntakal India 53B1
Guntersville USA 93A1
Guntersville L USA 93A1
Guntur India 53C1
Gunung Batu Putch, Mt Malay 43C5
Gunung Besar, Mt Indon 44D3
Gunung Bulu, Mt Indon 44D2
Gunung Gedang, Mt Malay 44C2
Gunung Lawit, Mt Malay 44C2
Gunung Lawu, Mt Indon 44C4

Gunung Menyapa, Mt Indon 44D2
Gunung Niapa, Mt Indon 44D2
Gunung Patah, Mt Indon 44A3
Gunung Raung, Mt Indon 44A3
Gunung Resag, Mt Indon 44A3
Gunung Sarempaka, Mt Indon 44D3
Gunung Sumbing, Mt Indon 44C4
Gunung Tahan, Mt Malay 43C5
Gunung Talakmau, Mt Indon 44A2
Gunza Angola 66A2
Guoyang China 38D3
Gurdaspur India 50D2
Gurkha Nepal 52A1
Gürün Turk 58C2
Gurvan Sayhan Uul, Upland Mongolia 38A1
Gur'yev USSR 27H4
Gusau Nig 63C3
Gus'khrustalnyy USSR 27F2
Gustavus USA 88G3
Gustine USA 98B2
Guston USA 87B3
Gütersloh W Germ 22B2
Guthrie, Kentucky USA 94C2
Guthrie, Oklahoma USA 94C3
Gutiérrez Zamora Mexico 99B1
Guyana, Republic S America 109F3
Guyana Basin Atlantic O 68F4
Guyang China 38C1
Guyenne, Region France 14B3
Guymon USA 85C3
Guyra Aust 75D2
Guyuan China 75C2
Gwabegar Aust 75C2
Gwalior India 51D3
Gwanda Zim 66B3
Gwane Zaïre 64C2
Gwardar Pak 48A3
Gwelo Zim 55G9
Gwent, County Wales 9C4
Gwynedd, County Wales 9C3
Gyangzê China 52C1
Gyaring Hu, L China 34B3
Gyirong China 52B1
Gympie Aust 75D1
Gyöngyös Hung 25B3
Györ Hung 25B3

H

Haapajärvi Fin 4K6
Haapsalu USSR 26B4
Haarlem Neth 22A2
Haarstrang, Region W Germ 12D1
Habana Cuba 101D2
Habiganj Bang 52C2

Harstad Nor	4H5	Hawker Aust	74A2	Helensburgh Scot	10B
Hårteigen, Mt Nor	5F6	Hawng Luk Burma	42B1	Hellin Spain	17B
Hartford, Connecticut USA	92C2	Hawr al Habbaniyah, L Iraq	59D3	Hellweg, Region W Germ	12D
Hartford, Michigan USA	90A2	Hawr al Hammár, L Iraq	59E3	Helm USA	98B
Hartkjolen, Mt Nor	4G6	Hawthorne USA	97B2	Helmeringhausen Namibia	66A
Hart, L Aust	74A2	Hay Aust	74C3	Helmond Neth	12C
Hartland Pt Eng	9B4	Hayange France	12D2	Helmsdale Scot	10C
Hartlepool Eng	8D2	Haycock USA	80B3	Helong China	40B
Hartshorne USA	95A3	Hayes Halvo, Region Greenland	82D2	Helsingborg Sweden	5G
Hartwell Res USA	93B1	Hayes, Mt USA	88E2	Helsinger Den	22C
Harwich Eng	9E4	Hay River Can	81G3	Helsinki Fin	4..
Haryana, State India	50D3	Haysville USA	94A2	Helston Eng	9B
Hasa Jordan	60B3	Hayward, California USA	98A2	Helwân Egypt	58B
Hasbaiya Leb	60B2	Hazaribag India	52B2	Hempstead USA	95A
Haselmere Eng	9D4	Hazebrouck France	12B1	Hemse Sweden	5H
Hashimoto Japan	41B2	Hazelhurst USA	92B3	Henan China	38A
Hashtpar Iran	56A2	Hazelton Can	81F4	Henan, Province China	38A
Hashtrud Iran	56A2	Hazelton Mts Can	89B1	Hen and Chicken Is NZ	76B
Hassan India	53B2	Hazen L Can	82C1	Henderson, Kentucky USA	90A
Hasselt Belg	22B2	Hazeva Israel	60B3	Henderson, Nevada USA	85B
Hassi Inifel Alg	62C2	Hazleton USA	92B2	Henderson, Texas USA	95A
Hassi Messaoud Alg	62C1	Healdsburg USA	98A1	Heng-ch'un Taiwan	39E
Hastings Aust	74C3	Healesville Aust	74C3	Hengduan Shan, Mts China	34B
Hastings Eng	9E4	Healy USA	88E2	Hengelo Neth	22B
Hastings, Nebraska USA	84D2	Heard I Indian O	70B6	Hengshan China	38B
Hastings NZ	76C1	Hearne USA	95A3	Hengshui China	38C
Hatfield Aust	74B2	Hearst Can	86B2	Heng Xian China	42D
Hatham Inlet USA	88B1	Hebei, Province China	38D2	Hengyang China	39C
Hathras India	51D3	Hebel Aust	75C1	Henhoaha Nicobar Is	43A
Ha Tinh Viet	42D2	Hebi China	38C2	Henley-on-Thames Eng	9D
Hattah Aust	74B2	Hebian China	38C2	Henryetta USA	94A
Hattiesburg USA	95C3	Hebron Can	83D4	Hentiyn Nuruu, Mts Mongolia	34C
Hatvan Hung	78E3	Hebron Israel	60B3	Heppner USA	96B
Hau Bon Viet	42D3	Hebron, Nebraska USA	94A1	Hepu China	39B
Haud, Region Eth	65E2	Hecate I USA	88H3	Herat Afghan	46E
Haugesund Nor	5F7	Hechi China	39B5	Herbert Can	81H
Hauhungaroa Range, Mts NZ	76C1	Hector, Mt NZ	77C2	Herbertville NZ	76C
Hauraki G NZ	76B1	Hede Sweden	4G6	Herborn W Germ	12D
Hauroko, L NZ	77A3	Hedemora Sweden	5H6	Heredia Costa Rica	102A
Hausstock, Mt Switz	13C1	He Devil Mt USA	96C1	Hereford Eng	9C
Haut Atlas, Mts Mor	62B1	Heerenveen Neth	22B2	Hereford & Worcester, County Eng	9C
Haute Kotto, Region CAR	64C2	Heerlen Neth	12C1	Herentals Belg	12C
Hautes Fagnes, Mts Belg	13D1	Hefei China	39D3	Héricourt France	13B
Hautmont Belg	13B2	Hefeng China	38B2	Herington USA	94A
Hauts Plateaux, Mts Alg	62B1	Hegang China	35F2	Heriot NZ	77A
Hauzdar Iran	56D3	Hegura-jima, I Japan	41B1	Herisau Switz	13C
Havana USA	94B1	Heide W Germ	22B2	Herkimer USA	91D
Havankulam Sri Lanka	53B3	Heidelberg, Transvaal S Africa	67G1	Hermidale Aust	75C
Havelock North NZ	76C1	Heidelberg W Germ	23B3	Hermitage NZ	77A
Haverfordwest Wales	9B4	Heilbron S Africa	67G1	Hermosillo Mexico	100A
Haverhill USA	92D1	Heilbronn W Germ	23B3	Herndon, Pennsylvania USA	92A
Haveri India	53B2	Heiligenstadt E Germ	22C2	Herndon, California USA	98C
Haverstraw USA	92C2	Heinola Fin	4K6	Herne W Germ	12D
Hlavlickuv Brod Czech	25B3	Hejiang China	39B4	Herning Den	12D
Havre USA	84C2	Hekla, Mt Iceland	32J3	Herowabad Iran	56A
Havre de Grace USA	92A3	Hekou Viet	39B4	Herrera del Duque Spain	16A
Havre-St-Pierre Can	83D4	Hekou Yaozou Zizhixian China	39A5	Hershey USA	92A
Havsa Turk	20C2	Helan China	38B2	Hertford, County Eng	9D
Hawaii, i Hawaiian Is	*	Helan Shan, Mt China	38B2	Herzliyya Israel	60B
Hawaii Volcanoes Nat Pk Hawaiian Is	97C4	Helena, Arkansas USA	95B3	Hesbaye, Region Belg	12C
Hawea, L NZ	77A2	Helena, Montana USA	84B2	Hesdin France	12B
Hawera NZ	76B1	Helendale USA	97C4	Heshui China	38B
Hawick Scot	8C2	Helen Reef, I Pacific O	37E3	Hesperia USA	98D
Hawkdun Range, Mts NZ	77A2			Hessen, State W Germ	12D

Hetch Hetchy Res USA	98C2
Hexham Eng	8C2
He Xian China	39C5
Heyuan China	39C5
Heywood Aust	74B3
Heze China	38D2
Hialeah USA	93B2
Hibbing USA	86A2
Hicks Bay NZ	76C1
Hicks, Pt Aust	75C3
Hidalgo, State Mexico	100B2
Hidalgo del Parral Mexico	100B2
Hidrolândia Brazil	111B1
Hierro, I Canary Is	62A2
Higashima Japan	41C1
High Desert USA	96B2
High Island USA	95B4
Highland, Region Scot	10B3
Highland USA	98D3
Highland Peak, Mt USA	96B3
Highlands Falls USA	92B2
High Point USA	87B3
High Prairie Can	89D1
High River Can	81G4
High Springs USA	91C3
Hightstown USA	92B2
High Wycombe Eng	9D4
Hiiumaa, I USSR	5J7
Hijaz, Region S Arabia	46B3
Hikigawa Japan	41B2
Hikone Japan	41B2
Hikurangi NZ	76B1
Hildago Mexico	85C4
Hidalgo del Parral Mexico	85C4
Hildesheim W Germ	22B2
Hillaby, Mt Barbados	103R3
Hillerod Den	22C1
Hillsboro, Ohio USA	90B3
Hillsboro, Oregon USA	96B1
Hillsboro, Texas USA	95A3
Hillston Aust	74C2
Hillswick Scot	10D1
Hilo Hawaiian Is	97C4
Hilvan Turk	59C2
Hilversum Neth	22B2
Himachal Pradesh, State India	50D2
Himalaya, Mts Asia	48B3
Himatnagar India	51C4
Himeji Japan	40C4
Hims Syria	58C3
Hinchinbrook Entrance USA	88E2
Hinchinbrook I USA	88E2
Hindaun India	51D3
Hindu Kush, Mts Afghan	50B1
Hindupur India	53B2
Hines Creek Can	89D1
Hinganghat India	51D4
Hinggan Ling, Upland China	35E2
Hingoli India	51D5
Hinnoya, I Nor	4H5
Hinsdale USA	94C1
Hinton Can	89D2
Hipolito Itrogoyen Arg	110B2
Hirakud Res India	52A2
Hirfanli Baraji, Res Turk	58B2
Hirihar India	53B2
Hirosaki Japan	40E2
Hiroshima Japan	40C4
Hirson France	12C2
Hirsova Rom	22B1
Hirtshals Den	22B1
Hisar India	50D3
Hispaniola, I Caribbean	102C3
Hisyah Syria	60C1
Hit Iraq	60C2
Hitachi Japan	40E3
Hitachi-Ota Japan	41C1
Hitchin Eng	9D4
Hitra, I Nor	4F6
Hiwasa Japan	41A2
Hjorring Den	22B1
Ho Ghana	63C4
Hoa Binh Viet	42D1
Hoa Da Viet	42D3
Hobart Aust	75C4
Hobbs USA	96C3
Hobro Den	22B1
Hobson's I Can	89C2
Hobyo Somalia	65E2
Hochkonig, Mt Austria	23C3
Hódmező'hely Hung	20B1
Hodonin Czech	23D3
Hoeryong N Korea	40B2
Hof W Germ	23C2
Hofsjökull, Mts Iceland	4B2
Hofu Japan	40C4
Hoggar, Upland Alg	62C2
Hoh Ach, Mt W Germ	12D1
Hohhot China	38C1
Höhn Iceland	82J3
Hoh Sai Hu, L China	34B3
Hoh Xil Shan, Mts China	48B2
Hoima Uganda	65D2
Hojai India	52C1
Hojo Japan	41A2
Hokitika NZ	77B2
Hokkaido Japan	40E2
Hokmabad Iran	58D3
Holbrook Aust	75C3
Holbrook USA	85B3
Holdenville USA	95A2
Hole Narsipur India	53B2
Holetown Barbados	103R3
Holguin Cuba	102B2
Holitika K2	77B2
Hollabrunn Austria	25B3
Holland USA	90A2
Hollister USA	98B2
Holly Springs USA	95C3
Hollywood, California USA	98C3
Hollywood, Florida USA	93B2
Holman Island Can	80G2
Holmsund Sweden	4J6
Holon Israel	60B2
Holstebro Den	22B1
Holsteinborg Greenland	82E3
Holt USA	90B2
Holton USA	94A2
Holy Cross USA	88C2
Holyhead Wales	9D2
Holy I Eng	8D2
Holy I Wales	9B3
Holyoke, Massachusetts USA	92C1
Homalin Burma	52C2
Homer, Alaska USA	88B3
Homer, Louisiana USA	95B3
Homer Tunnel NZ	77A2
Homerville USA	91B3
Homestead USA	93B2
Homewood USA	93A1
Homnabad India	53B1
Homoine Mozam	67C3
Honduras, G of Honduras	101D3
Honefoss Nor	5G6
Honesdale USA	91C2
Honey L USA	97A1
Hon Gai Viet	42D1
Hongguo China	39A4
Hong Hu, L China	39C4
Honghui China	38B2
Hongjiang China	39C4
Hong Kong, Colony S E Asia	39C5
Hongor Mongolia	34D2
Hongyuan China	38A3
Hongze Hu, L China	38D3
Honiara Solomon Is	73E1
Hon Khoai, I Camb	43C4
Hon Lan, I Viet	42D3
Honnigsvåg Nor	4K4
Honolulu Hawaiian Is	97C4
Hon Panjang, I Viet	43C4
Honshu, I Japan	40D3
Hood, Mt USA	96B1
Hood River USA	96B1
Hoonah USA	88G3
Hooper Bay USA	88A2
Hoopstad S Africa	67G1
Hoorn Neth	22A2
Hoover Dam USA	85B3
Hope, Alaska USA	88E2
Hope, Arkansas USA	95B3
Hope Can	89C4
Hopedale Can	83D4
Hopen, I Barents S	30D2
Hopetoun Aust	74B3
Hopetown S Africa	66B3
Hopkinsville USA	94C2
Hoquiam USA	96B1
Horasan Turk	59D1
Hordiyo Somalia	65F1
Horgen Switz	13C1
Horizon Depth Pacific O	71H5
Horn Austria	25B3
Hornavan, L Sweden	4H5
Hornbrook USA	96B2
Hornby NZ	77B2
Hornepayne Can	83B5
Horn Mts Can	80F3
Hornsea Eng	8D3
Horn Uul, Mt Mongolia	38B1
Horqueta Par	106E3
Horseheads USA	91C2
Horsens Den	22C1
Horseshoe Bay Can	96B1
Horsham Aust	74B3

Horsham *Eng*	9D4		Hubli *India*	53B1		Huntly *NZ*	76C1
Horten *Nor*	5G7		Hucal *Arg*	110C3		Huntly *Scot*	10C3
Hose Mts *Malay*	44C2		Huch'ang *N Korea*	40B2		Hunt, Mt *Can*	88J2
Hoshangabad *India*	51D4		Huddersfield *Eng*	8D3		Huntsville, Alabama *USA*	93A1
Hoshiarpur *India*	50D2		Hudiksvall *Sweden*	5H6		Huntsville *Can*	91C1
Hospet *India*	53B1		Hudson, Florida *USA*	93B2		Huntsville, Texas *USA*	95A3
Hoste, I *Chile*	105C7		Hudson, Michigan *USA*	90B2		Huong Khe *Viet*	42D2
Hotan *China*	48B2		Hudson, New York *USA*	92C1		Huonville *Anst*	75C4
Hot Springs, Arkansas *USA*	95B3		Hudson Bay *Can*	81H4		Hurghada *Egypt*	46B3
Hot Springs, S. Dakota *USA*	84C2		Hudson's Hope *Can*	89C1		Huron, S. Dakota *USA*	84D2
Hottah *Can*	80G3		Hue *Viet*	42D2		Huron, L *USA/Can*	90B1
Houdan *France*	12A2		Huejutla *Mexico*	99B1		Hurtado *Chile*	110A2
Houma *China*	38A2		Huelva *Spain*	16A2		Husavik *Iceland*	4B1
Houma *USA*	95B4		Hueramo *Mexico*	99B2		Husi *Rom*	20C1
Houston *Can*	89B2		Huercal Overa *Spain*	17B2		Huskvarna *Sweden*	5G7
Houston, Mississippi *USA*	95C3		Huesca *Spain*	17B1		Husn *Jordan*	60B2
Houston, Texas *USA*	95A4		Huexotla, Hist Site *Mexico*	99B2		Husum *W Germ*	22B2
Houtman, Is *Aust*	72A3		Huize *China*	39A4		Huzhu *China*	39B2
Hovd *Mongolia*	34B2		Huizhou *China*	39C5		Hvar, I *Yugos*	18C2
Hövsgöl Nuur, L *Mongolia*	34C1		Hujuápan de Léon *Mexico*	99B2		Hwange *Zim*	66B2
Howard City *USA*	90A2		Hulin *China*	35F2		Hwange Nat Pk *Zim*	66B2
Howard P *USA*	88C1		Hull *Can*	91C1		Hyannis *USA*	91D2
Howick *S Africa*	67H1		Hull *Eng*	8D3		Hyaryas Nuur, L *Mongolia*	34B2
Hoy, I *Scot*	7D2		Hultsfred *Sweden*	24B1		Hydaburg *Can*	81E4
Hoyanger *Nor*	5F6		Hulun Nur, L *China*	29D3		Hyde Park *USA*	92C2
Hradec-Králové *Czech*	25B2		Huma *China*	35E1		Hyderabad *India*	53B1
Hranice *Czech*	25B3		Humaita *Brazil*	109E5		Hyderabad *Pak*	51B3
Hsin-chu *Taiwan*	39E5		Humansdorp *S Africa*	66B4		Hyères *France*	15D3
Hsüeh Shan, Mt *Taiwan*	39E5		Humberside, County *Eng*	8D3		Hyndman Peak, Mt *USA*	84B2
Huachi *China*	38B2		Humboldt *Can*	81H4		Hyrynsalmi *Fin*	4K6
Huacho *Peru*	108B6		Humboldt Gletscher, Gl *Greenland*	82D2		Hythe *Can*	89D1
Huade *China*	38C1		Humboldt L *USA*	97B2		Hyuga *Japan*	40C4
Huaibei *China*	38D3		Humeburn *Aust*	74C1		Hyvikää *Fin*	5J6
Huaibin *China*	38D3		Hume, L *USA*	75C3			
Huaihua *China*	39C4		Humpata *Angola*	66A2		**I**	
Huaiji *China*	39C5		Humphreys *USA*	98C2			
Huainan *China*	38D3		Hunan, Province *China*	39C4		Iacu *Brazil*	107C4
Hua-lien *Taiwan*	35E4		Hunchun *China*	40C2		Iasi *Rom*	20C1
Huallanca *Peru*	108B5		Hundred Mile House *Can*	89C2		Ibadan *Nig*	63C4
Huamachuco *Peru*	108B5		Hunedoara *Rom*	54B1		Ibagué *Colombia*	108B3
Huambo *Angola*	100A2		Hungary, Republic *Europe*	25B3		Ibarra *Ecuador*	108B3
Huanay *Bol*	106C2		Hungerford *Aust*	74B1		Ibiá *Brazil*	111B1
Huancabamba *Peru*	108B5		Hungnam *N Korea*	40B3		Ibiza *Spain*	17C2
Huancavelica *Peru*	108B6		Hunjiang *China*	40B2		Ibiza, I *Spain*	17C2
Huancayo *Peru*	108B6		Hunsrück, Mts *W Germ*	12D2		Ibo *Mozam*	67D2
Huangchuan *China*	38D3		Hunstanton *Eng*	8E3		Ibotirama *Brazil*	107C4
Huangling *China*	38B2		Hunter, Is *Aust*	89D2		'Ibri *Oman*	57C5
Huangliu *China*	42D2		Hunter Is *Aust*	75C4		Ica *Peru*	108B6
Huangpi *China*	39C3		Hunter, Mt *USA*	88D2		Icana *Brazil*	108D3
Huangshi *China*	39C3		Huntingburg *USA*	90A3		Iceland, Republic *N Atlantic*	4A1
Huanguelén *Arg*	110D3		Huntingdon, Indiana *USA*	90A2		Ice Mt *Can*	89C2
Huangyan *China*	39E4		Huntingdon *USA*	86B2		Ichalkaranji *India*	53A1
Huanren *N Korea*	40B2		Huntington *USA*	98C4		Ichihara *Japan*	40E3
Huanuco *Peru*	108B5		Huntington Beach *USA*	98C4		Ichinomiya *Japan*	41B3
Huanuni *Bol*	106C2		Huntington L *USA*	98C2		Ichinoseki *Japan*	40E3
Huan Xian *China*	38B2					Idabell *USA*	95B3
Huaraz *Peru*	108B5					Idaho Falls *USA*	84B2
Huarmey *Peru*	108B6					Idanha *USA*	96B2
Huascarán, Mt *Peru*	108B5					Idar Oberstein *W Germ*	12D2
Huasco *Chile*	106B4					Idehan Marzug, Desert *Libya*	61A2
Huatusco *Mexico*	99B2					Idehan Ubari, Desert *Libya*	61A2
Huauchinango *Mexico*	99B1						
Huautla *Mexico*	99B2						
Hua Xian *China*	38C2						
Hubei, Province *China*	39C3						

Idelés Alg	62C2
Idfu Egypt	61C2
Idhi Óros, Mt Greece	21B3
Ídhra, I Greece	21C3
Idiofa Zaïre	64B3
Idlib Syria	58C2
Idritsa USSR	5K7
Idutywa S Africa	66B4
Ierápetra Greece	21C3
Ifakara Tanz	65D3
Ifalik, I Pacific	37F3
Ifanadiana Madag	67D3
Ife Nig	63C4
Iférouane Niger	63C3
Igan Malay	44C2
Iggesund Sweden	5H6
Iglesias Sardegna	19A3
Igloolik Can	82B3
Ignace Can	86A2
Igoumenitsa Greece	21B3
Igra USSR	27H2
Ihosy Madag	67D3
Iida Japan	40D3
Iide-san, Mt Japan	41B1
Iisalmi Fin	4K6
Iizuka Japan	41A2
Ijebu Ode Nig	63C4
Ijsselmeer, S Neth	22B2
Ikaria, I Greece	21C3
Ikeda Japan	40E2
Ikela Zaïre	64C3
Ikhtiman Bulg	20B2
Ilagan Phil	45B2
Ilam Iran	56A3
Ilanz Switz	13C1
Ile à la Crosse Can	89F1
Ile à la Crosse, L Can	89F1
Ilebo Zaïre	55G8
Ile de Jerba, I Tunisia	62D1
Ile de Noirmoutier, I France	14B2
Ile de Ré, I France	14B2
Iles des Pins, I Nouvelle Calédonie	73F3
Ile d'Ouessant, I France	14A2
Ile d'Yeu, I France	14B2
Iles Bélèp Nouvelle Calédonie	73F2
Iles Chesterfield Nouvelle Calédonie	73E2
Iles d'Hyleres, Is France	15D3
Ilfracombe Eng	9B4
Ilgaz Daglari, Mts Turk	58B1
Ilha Bazaruto, I Mozam	67C3
Ilha de Maracá, I Brazil	109G4
Ilha de Marajó, I Brazil	109G4
Ilha de Sao Sebastião, I Brazil	111B2
Ilha do Bananal, Region Brazil	109G6
Ilha Grande, I Brazil	111C2
Ilha Santo Amaro, I Brazil	111B2
Ilhas Selvegens, I Atlantic O	62A1
Ilhéus Brazil	107M6
Iligan Phil	45B4
Il'inskiy USSR	29G3
Iliodhrómia, I Greece	21B3
Illapel Chile	110A2
Illéla Niger	63C3
Illinois, State USA	80C4
Illinois, State USA	86A2
Illizi Alg	62C2
Ilo Peru	106B2
Iloilo Phil	45B3
Ilomantsi Fin	4L6
Ilorin Nig	63C4
Imabari Japan	41A2
Imalchi Japan	41B1
Imatra Fin	26C1
Imbituba Brazil	106G4
Imi Eth	65E2
Imlay USA	96C2
Immenstadt W Germ	13D1
Imola Italy	18B2
Imperatriz Brazil	107B3
Imperia Italy	18A2
Impfondo Congo	64B2
Imphal India	43G4
Imst Austria	13D1
Imuruk L USA	88B1
Ina Japan	41B1
Inamba-jima, I Japan	41B2
Inari Fin	4K5
Inarijärvi, L Fin	4K5
In Belbel Alg	62C2
Ince Burun, Pt Turk	58B1
Incekum Burun, Pt Turk	58B2
Inch'on S Korea	40B3
Independence, California USA	97B2
Independence, Kansas USA	94A2
Independence, Missouri USA	94A2
Inderborskly USSR	27H4
Indian Republic India	40B3
Indiana, State USA	90A3
Indiana, State USA	91C2
Indian-Antarctic Ridge	70C6
Indianapolis USA	90A3
Indian Harbour Can	83E4
Indian O	70B4
Indianola, Iowa USA	94B2
Indianola, Mississippi USA	95B3
Indio USA	111B1
Indo-China, Region S E Asia	42D2
Indonesia, Republic S E Asia	36C4
Indore India	51D4
Indramayu Indon	44B4
Indus, R Pak	51B3
Inebolu Turk	26D5
In Ecker Alg	62C2
Inegöl Turk	58A1
In Ezzane Alg	62D2
Ingal Niger	63C3
Ingersoll Can	90B2
Ingham Aust	76D2
Inglefield Land, Region Can	82D2
Inglewood NZ	76B1
Inglewood, Queensland Aust	75D1
Inglewood USA	98C4
Inglewood, Victoria Aust	74B3
Ingólfshöfdi, I Iceland	4B2
Ingolstadt W Germ	23C3
Ingraj Bazar India	52B2
Inhambane Mozam	67C3
Inharrime Mozam	67C3
Inhumas Brazil	111B1
Inishbofin, I Irish Rep	11A2
Inishkea, I Irish Rep	11A1
Inishmaan, I Irish Rep	11B2
Inishmore, I Irish Rep	11B2
Inishmurray, I Irish Rep	11B1
Inishowen, District Irish Rep	11C1
Inishshark, I Irish Rep	11A2
Inishturk, I Irish Rep	11A2
Injune Aust	75C1
Inklin Can	88H3
Inland L USA	88C1
Innamincka Aust	74B1
Inner Mongolia, Autonomous Region China	34C2
Innisfail Aust	76D2
Innsbruck Austria	23C3
Inongo Zaïre	64B3
Inowroclaw Pol	24B2
In Salah Alg	62C2
Interlaken Switz	13B1
Intexpec Mexico	100C3
Intra Italy	13C2
Intu Indon	44D3
Inukjuac Can	83C4
Inuvik Can	80E3
Inveraray Scot	10B3
Invercargill NZ	77A3
Inverell Aust	75D1
Invermere Can	89D2
Inverness Scot	10B3
Inverurie Scot	10C3
Inya USSR	34A1
Inyanga Zim	67C2
Inyokern USA	97B2
Ioánnina Greece	21B3
Iola USA	94A2
Iona I Scot	10A3
Iôna Nat Pk Angola	66A2
Ione USA	96C1
Ionian S Italy/Greece	21A3
Iónioi Nísoi, Is Greece	21B3
Ios, I Greece	21C3
Iowa USA	86A2
Iowa City USA	94B2
Ipameri Brazil	111B1
Ipanema Brazil	111C1
Ipatovo USSR	27F4
Ipiales Colombia	108B3
Ipoh Malay	43C5
Iporá Brazil	106F2

Ipsala Turk	21C2
Ipswich Aust	75D1
Ipswich Eng	9E3
Ipswich USA	92D1
Iquique Chile	106B3
Iquitos Peru	108C4
Iráklion Greece	21C3
Iran, Republic S W Asia	46D2
Iranshahr Iran	57D4
Irapuato Mexico	99A1
Iraq, Republic S W Asia	59D3
Irbid Jordan	60B2
Irbit USSR	27K2
Ireland, Republic NW Europe	2C3
Iri S Korea	40B3
Irian Jaya, Province Indon	37E4
Iriba Chad	61B3
Iriga Phil	45B3
Iringa Tanz	65D3
Iriomote, I Japan	35E4
Irish S Eng/Irish Rep	3B3
Irkutsk USSR	29C2
Irlysh USSR	31J4
Iron Knob Aust	74A2
Iron Mountain USA	90A1
Iron Range Aust	73D2
Iron River USA	90A1
Irontown USA	90B3
Ironwood USA	86A2
Iroquois Falls Can	86B2
Irrawaddy, Mouths of the Burma	42A2
Irtysh, R USSR	31H4
Irun Spain	17B1
Irvine Scot	8B2
Irving USA	95A3
Isabela Phil	45B4
Isabela, I, Ecuador	108J7
Isachsen Can	80H2
Ósafjörthur Iceland	82H3
Isahaya Japan	40C4
Isangi Zaïre	64C2
Isbister Scot	10D1
Ischgl Austria	50C1
Ischia, I Italy	19B2
Ise Japan	41B2
Iseo Italy	13D2
Iserlohn W Germ	12D1
Isernia Italy	19B2
Ishigaki, I Japan	35E4
Ishim USSR	31H4
Ishinomaki Japan	40E3
Ishioka Japan	41C1
Ishkashim Afghan	50C1
Ishpeming USA	90A1
Isil'kul USSR	31J4
Isiolo Kenya	65D2
Isiro Zaïre	64C2
Iskenderun Turk	58C2
Iskür R Bulg	58B1
Iskitim USSR	31K4
Isla Mexico	99B2
Isla Bermejo, I Arg	110C3
Isla Blanquilla Ven	103E4
Isla Coiba, I Panama	108A2
Isla de Cedros, I Mexico	85B4
Isla de Chiloé, I Chile	105B4
Isla de Cozumel, I Mexico	101D2
Isla de la Gonâve Cuba	102C3
Isla de la Juventud, I Cuba	102A2
Isla de las Lechiguanas, I Arg	110D2
Isla del Coco, I Costa Rica	79K8
Isla del Maiz, I Caribbean	101D3
Isla de Lobos, I Mexico	99B1
Isla de los Estados, I Arg	105D6
Isla de Marajó, I Brazil	104E2
Isla de Pascua, I Pacific O	71L5
Isla de Providencia, I Caribbean	102A2
Isla de San Andres, I Caribbean	102A4
Isla de Santa Catarina, I Brazil	106G4
Isla du Diable, I French Guiana	109G2
Isla Fernando de Noronha, I Brazil	107E2
Isla Grande de Tierra del Fuego, I Arg/Chile	105C6
Isla la Tortuga, I Ven	103D4
Isla Magdalena, I Mexico	100A2
Isla Margarita Ven	109E1
Isla Mocha Chile	110A3
Islamorada USA	93B2
Island L Can	86A1
Isla Puná, I Ecuador	108A4
Isla San Ambrosia, I Pacific O	69D6
Isla San Félix, I Pacific O	69D6
Isla Santa Margarita, I Mexico	100A3
Isla Santa Maria, I Chile	110A3
Islas Baleares, Is Spain	17C2
Islas Canarias, Is Atlantic O	62A2
Islas Columbretes, Is Spain	17C2
Islas de la Bahía, Is Honduras	101D3
Islas del Maiz, Is Caribbean	102A4
Islas de Margarita, Is Ven	109E1
Islas Diego Ramírez, Is Chile	105C7
Islas Galapagos, Is Pacific O	108J7
Islas Juan Fernández Chile	106H6
Islas los Roques, Is Ven	103D4
Islas Revilla Gigedo, Is Pacific O	71L3
Islas Wollaston, Is Chile	105C7
Isla Tidra, I Maur	60C1
Islas Wellington, Is Chile	105B5
Islas Amsterdam, I Indian O	70B5
Isle of Wight, I Eng	9D4
Isle Royale, I USA	86B2
Isle St Paul, I Indian O	70B5
Isles Crozet, I Indian O	70A6
Isles de la Société Pacific O	71J4
Isles Gambier, Is Pacific O	71K5
Isles Glorieuses, Is Madg	67D2
Isles Kerguelen, Is Indian O	70B6
Isles Marquises, Is Pacific O	71K4
Isles Tuamotu, Is Pacific O	71J4
Isles Tubai, Is Pacific O	71J5
Isleton USA	98B1
Ismâ'iliya Egypt	58B3
Isoanala Madag	67D3
Isoka Zambia	65D5
Isola Egadi, I Italy	19B3
Isola Ponziane, I Italy	18B2
Isole Lipari, Is Italy	19B3
Isoles Tremiti, Is Italy	18C2
Isosaki Japan	41B1
Isparta Turk	58B2
Israel, Republic S W Asia	60B2
Issoire France	14C2
Issoudun France	15C2
Istanbul Turk	58A1
Istiáia Greece	21B3
Istmo de Tehuantepec Isthmus, Mexico	101C3
Istokpoga, L USA	93B2
Istranca Daglari, Upland Turk	20C2
Itabaianha Brazil	111B1
Itabira Brazil	111C2
Itabirito Brazil	111C2
Itabuna Brazil	107D4
Itacoatiara Brazil	109F4
Itagui Colombia	108B2
Itaituba Brazil	109F4
Itajai Brazil	106G4
Itajuba Brazil	111C2
Italy, Republic Europe	18B2
Itamaraju Brazil	111D1
Itamarandiba Brazil	111C1
Itambacuri Brazil	111C1
Itambé, Mt Brazil	111C1
Itanagar India	52C1
Itanhaém Brazil	111C1
Itanhém Brazil	111C1
Itaobim Brazil	111C1
Itapecerica Brazil	111C2
Itaperuna Brazil	111C2
Itapetinga Brazil	111B2
Itapetininga Brazil	111B2
Itapeva Brazil	111B2
Itapipoca Brazil	111B1
Itapuranga Brazil	111B1
Itaqui Brazil	106E4
Itarantim Brazil	111C1
Itauba Brazil	111C2
Itauna Brazil	111C1
Ithaca USA	91C2
Itinga Brazil	111C1
Itivdleg Greenland	82E3
Ito Japan	41B2
Itoigawa Japan	40D3
Itumbiara Brazil	111B2
Itumbiara Brazil	111B1
Iturama Brazil	111A1
Iturbe Arg	106C3
Iturutaba Brazil	111B1
Itzehoe W Germ	12C2
Ivacevichi USSR	24D2
Ivalo Fin	4K5
Ivangrad Yugos	20A2
Ivanhoe Aust	74B2
Ivano USSR	30D5

Jelena Gora *Pol*	25B2
Jelgava *USSR*	26B2
Jember *Indon*	44C4
Jena *E Germ*	23C2
Jenaja, I *Indon*	44B2
Jenbach *Austria*	13D1
Jenin *Israel*	60B2
Jennings *USA*	95B3
Jenseniky, Upland *Czech*	25B2
Jensen Nunatakker, Mt *Greenland*	82F3
Jens Munk, I *Can*	82B3
Jeparit *Aust*	74B3
Jequié *Brazil*	107D4
Jequitinhonha *Brazil*	111C1
Jerez de la Frontera *Spain*	16A2
Jerez de los Caballeros *Spain*	16A2
Jericho *Israel*	60B3
Jerilderie *Aust*	74C3
Jersey, I *UK*	14B2
Jersey City *USA*	86C2
Jersey Shore *USA*	91C2
Jerseyville *USA*	94B2
Jerusalem *Israel*	58C3
Jesenice *Yugos*	18B1
Jessore *Bang*	52B2
Jesup *USA*	87B3
Jesus Maria *Arg*	110C2
Jewett City *USA*	92D2
Jezerce, Mt *Alb*	20A2
Jeziora Mamry, L *Pol*	24C2
Jezioro Sniardwy, L *Pol*	24C2
Jezzine *Leb*	60B2
Jhabua *India*	51C4
Jhalawar *India*	51D4
Jhang Maghiana *Pak*	50C2
Jhansi *India*	51D3
Jharsuguda *India*	52A2
Jhelum *Pak*	50C2
J H Kerr L, *USA*	87C3
Jhunjhunun *India*	50D3
Jiamusi *China*	35F2
Ji'an, Jiangxi *China*	39C4
Ji'an, Jilin *China*	38B2
Jiande *China*	39D4
Jiang'an *China*	39B4
Jiangbiancun *China*	39D4
Jiangcheng *China*	39A5
Jiangmen *China*	39C5
Jiangsu, Province *China*	38D3
Jiangxi, Province *China*	39C4
Jiangyou *China*	39A3
Jianping *China*	38D1
Jianshui *China*	39A5
Jianyang *China*	39D4
Jiaonan *China*	38E2
Jiao Xian *China*	38E2
Jiaozuo *China*	38C2
Jiaxiang *China*	39E3
Jiayuguan *China*	34B3
Jiddah *S Arabia*	47B3
Jieshou *China*	38D3
Jiexiu *China*	38C2
Jigzhi *China*	38A3
Jihlava *Czech*	25B3
Jilib *Somalia*	65E2
Jilin *China*	35E2
Jiménez, Coahuila *Mexico*	85C4
Jimma *Eth*	65D2
Jinan *China*	38D2
Jind *India*	50D3
Jingbian *China*	38B2
Jingdezhen *China*	39D4
Jinghong *China*	42C1
Jingmen *China*	39C3
Jinging *China*	38B2
Jing Xiang *China*	38B2
Jinhua *China*	39D4
Jining, Nei Monggol *China*	38C1
Jining, Shandong *China*	38D2
Jinja *Uganda*	65D2
Jinping *China*	42C1
Jinshi *China*	39C4
Jinxi *China*	38E1
Jin Xian *China*	38E2
Jinzhou *China*	38E1
Jipijapa *Ecuador*	108A4
Jiquilpan *Mexico*	99A2
Jīroft *Iran*	57C4
Jishou *China*	39B4
Jisr ash Shughur *Syria*	58C2
Jiujiang *China*	39D4
Jiulong *China*	39A4
Jixi *China*	35F2
Jiza *Jordan*	60B3
Jizan *S Arabia*	50C3
Jō *Sen*	63A3
Joal *Sen*	63A3
Joao Monlevade *Brazil*	111C1
Joao Pessoa *Brazil*	107E3
Joao Pinheiro *Brazil*	111B1
Jocoli *Arg*	110B2
Jodhpur *India*	51C3
Joensuu *Fin*	4K6
Joeuf *France*	12C2
Joffre, Mt *Can*	89D2
Jogbani *India*	52B1
Jog Falls *India*	53A2
Johannesburg *S Africa*	67G1
Johannesburg *USA*	100B2
John Day *USA*	96C2
John O'Groats *Scot*	10C2
John Redmond Res *USA*	94A2
Johnson City, Tennessee *USA*	
Johnston *USA*	93B1
Johnston Pt *St Vincent*	103N2
Johnstown, Pennsylvania *USA*	91C2
Johor Bharu *Malay*	43C5
Joigny *France*	15C2
Joinville *Brazil*	106G4
Jokkmokk *Sweden*	4H5
Jolfa *Iran*	59E2
Joliet *USA*	86B2
Joliette *Can*	83C5
Jolo *Phil*	45B4
Jolo, I *Phil*	45B4
Joma, Mt *USSR*	24C1
Jonava *USSR*	24C1
Jonesboro, Arkansas *USA*	94B3
Jonesboro, Louisiana *USA*	95B3
Joniskis *USSR*	24C1
Jönköping *Sweden*	5G7
Joplin *USA*	87A3
Jordan, Kingdom *S W Asia*	65D2
Jordan Valley *USA*	96C2
Jorhat *India*	52C1
Jörn *Sweden*	4J5
Jorong *Indon*	44C3
Jorpeland *Nor*	5F7
Jose Pañganiban *Phil*	45B3
Joseph Bonaparte G *Aust*	72B2
Jotunheimen, Mt *Nor*	30B3
Jouai'ya *Leb*	60B2
Jounié *Leb*	60B2
Jowal *India*	52C1
Jowhar *Somalia*	65E2
Joy, Mt *Can*	88H2
Juan de Nova, I *Mozam Chan*	67D2
Juárez *Arg*	110D3
Juazeiro *Brazil*	107C3
Juazeiro do Norte *Brazil*	107D3
Juba *Sudan*	65D2
Jubail *S Arabia*	60B1
Jubbah *S Arabia*	59D3
Juchatengo *Mexico*	99B2
Juchitlan *Mexico*	99A1
Juchitán *Mexico*	99A1
Jugandh *Austria*	23C3
Juigalpa *Peru*	106B2
Juiz de Fora *Brazil*	107C6
Jujuy, State *Arg*	106C3
Juli *Peru*	106C2
Julianatop, Mt *Surinam*	109F3
Julianehab *Greenland*	82F3
Jülich *W Germ*	12D1
Jullundur *India*	50D2
Jumla *Nepal*	52A1
Jum Suwwana, Mt *Jordan*	60B3
Junagadh *India*	51C4
Junan *China*	38D2
Junction City *USA*	85D3
Jundiaí *Brazil*	107B6
Juneau *USA*	80E4
Junee *Aust*	73D4
June Lake *USA*	98C2
Jungfrau, Mt *Switz*	18A1
Junín *Arg*	105D2
Junlian *China*	39A4
Juquiá *Brazil*	107B6
Jura, I *Scot*	12D1
Jura, Mts *France*	15D2
Jura, Sound of, Chan *Scot*	10B3
Jurf ed Darawish *Jordan*	60B3
Jurmala *USSR*	26B2
Jusiyah *Syria*	60C1
Justo Daract *Arg*	110B2
Juticalpa *Honduras*	101D3
Juymand *Iran*	56C3
Jyväskylä *Fin*	4K6

K

K2, Mt *China/India*	48B2
Kaakhka *USSR*	56C2
Kaapmuiden *S Africa*	67H1
Kabaena, I *Indon*	37D4
Kabala *Sierra Leone*	63A4

abale Rwanda	65D3	Kaiyuan, Liaoning China	39A5	Kalush USSR	25C3
abalo Zaïre	64C3	Kaiyuan, Yunnan China	40A2	Kalyandurg India	53B2
abambare Zaïre	64C3	Kaiyuh Mts USA	88C2	Kalyazin USSR	26E2
abarole Uganda	65D2	Kajaani Fin	4K6	Kamaishi Japan	40E3
abinda Zaïre	64C3	Kajaki Afghan	50B2	Kamalia Pak	50C2
abir Kuh, Mts Iran	56A3	Kajiado Kenya	65D3	Kamanawa Mts NZ	76C1
abompo Zambia	66B2	Kajran Afghan	50B2	Kamanjab Namibia	66A2
abongo Zaïre	64C3	Kaka Sudan	65D1	Kamat, Mt India	50D2
abul Afghan	50B2	Kakamega Kenya	65D2	Kamban India	53B3
achchh, G of India	51B4	Kake Japan	41A2	Kambarka USSR	27H2
achkanar USSR	27J2	Kake USA	88H3	Kambia Sierra Leone	63A4
achug USSR	29C2	Kakhonak USA	88D3	Kamenets Podolskiy USSR	25D3
adan Burma	42B3	Kakhovskoye		Kamenka USSR	27F3
adapongan, I Indon	44D3	Vodokhranilishche,		Kamen-na-Obi USSR	31K4
adi India	51C4	Res USSR	31E5	Kamensk USSR	27K2
adina Aust	74A2	Kaki Iran	57B4	Kamensk-Ural'skiy USSR	27K2
adinhani Turk	58B2	Kakinada India	53C1	Kamilukak L Can	81H3
adiri India	51B2	Kakogawa Japan	41A2	Kamina Zaïre	64C3
adiyevka USSR	26E4	Kaktovik USA	80D2	Kaminak L Can	83A3
adoma Zim	66B2	Kakuda Japan	41C1	Kaminoyama Japan	41C1
adugli Sudan	65C1	Kalabáka Greece	21B3	Kamloops Can	81F4
aduna Nig	63C3	Kalabakan Malay	44D1	Kamo Japan	59E1
adur India	53B2	Kalabo Zambia	66B2	Kamogawa Japan	41C1
aedi Maur	63A3	Kalach USSR	27F3	Kampala Uganda	65D2
aena Pt Hawaiian Is	97C4	Kalach-na-Donu USSR	27F4	Kampar Malay	43C5
aesong N Korea	40B3	Kalajoki Fin	4J6	Kampen Neth	22B2
afanchan Nig	63C4	Kalakan USSR	29D2	Kamphaeng Phet Thai	42B2
affrine Sen	63A3	Kalakepen Indon	36A1	Kampot Camb	43C3
afrun Bashur Syria	60C1	Kalam Pak	50C1	Kamsar Iran	57D4
afue Zambia	66B2	Kalámai Greece	21B3	Kamskoye	
afue Nat Pk Zambia	66B2	Kalamazoo USA	86B2	Vodokhranilishche,	
aga USSR	40D3	Kalat Pak	50B3	Res USSR	27J2
agan USSR	31H6	Kalecik Turk	58B1	Kamthi India	51D4
agizman Turk	59D1	Kalembau, I Indon	44D1	Kamyshin USSR	27G3
agnashima Japan	40B3	Kalémié Zaïre	65C3	Kamyshlov USSR	27K2
agok Iran	56C2	Kalevala USSR	4L5	Kananga Zaïre	64C3
ahama Tanz	65D3	Kalewa Burma	52C2	Kanash USSR	27G2
ahan Pak	50B3	Kalgin I USA	88D2	Kanayama Japan	41B1
ahemba Zaïre	64B3	Kalgoorlie Aust	72B4	Kanazawa Japan	40D3
ahler Asten, Mt W Germ	46B1	Kalianda Indon	44B8	Kanbisha USA	80C3
ahnuj Iran	57C4	Kalibo Phil	45B3	Kanchipuram India	53B2
ahoka USA	94B1	Kalima Zaïre	64C3	Kandahar Afghan	50B2
ahoolawe, I Hawaiian Is	97C4	Kalimantan, Province Indon	44C3	Kandalaksha USSR	30E3
ahramannaras Turk	58C2	Kálimnos, I Greece	21C3	Kandi Benin	63C3
ahuku Pt Hawaiian Is	97C4	Kalimpang India	52B1	Kandos Aust	75C2
aiapoil NZ	77B2	Kalinin USSR	26E2	Kandy Sri Lanka	53C3
aieteur Fall Guyana	109F2	Kaliningrad USSR	26B3	Kane USA	91C2
aifeng China	38C3	Kalinkovichi USSR	26C3	Kanem, Desert Region Chad	64B1
aikohe NZ	76B1	Kalispell USA	84B2	Kangaba Mali	63B3
aikoura NZ	77B2	Kalisz Pol	24B2	Kangal Turk	58C2
aikoura Range, Mts NZ	77B2	Kaliua Tanz	65D3	Kangâmiut Greenland	82E3
ailsa NZ	39B4	Kalkfeld Namibia	66A3	Kangan Iran	57B4
ailua Hawaiian Is	97C4	Kalkrand Namibia	66A3	Kangar Malay	43C4
aimana Indon	37E4	Kallávesi, L Fin	4K6	Kangaroo I Aust	72C4
ainan Japan	41B2	Kalmar Sweden	5H7	Kanga'tsiaq Greenland	82E3
ainji Res Nig	63C3	Kalmytskaya ASSR,		Kangavar Iran	56A3
aiping China	39C5	Republic USSR	27G4	Kangbao China	38C1
airouan Tunisia	62D1	Kalomo Zambia	66B2	Kangding China	39A4
aiser Peak, Mt USA	98C2	Kalone Peak, Mt USA	89B2	Kangetpet Kenya	65D2
aiserslautern W Germ	23B3	Kalpeni, I India	53C4	Kanggye N Korea	40B2
aishantun China	40B2	Kalpi India	51D3	Kangiqsualujjuaq Can	83D4
aisiadorys USSR	24D2	Kalskag USA	88B2	Kangiqsujuaq Can	82C3
aista NZ	76B1	Kaltag USA	88C1	Kangnung S Korea	40B3
aitangata NZ	77A3	Kaluga USSR	26E3	Kango Gabon	64B2
aithai India	50D3	Kalundborg Den	5G7	Kangto, Mt China	34B4
aiwi Chan Hawaiian Is	97C4			Kang Xian China	38B3
ai Xian China	39B3			Kanh Hung Viet	43D4

Kaniama Zaire	64C3	Kara Tau, Mts USSR	31H5	Kasese Uganda	65D2
Kani Giri India	53B1	Karathuri Burma	42B3	Kashan Iran	56B2
Kanin Nos, Pt USSR	30F3	Karatsu Japan	40B4	Kashegelok USA	88C2
Kankaanpää Fin	5J6	Karaz Iran	57B4	Kashi China	48B2
Kankakee USA	90A2	Karbala' Iraq	59D3	Kashipur India	50D3
Kankan Guinea	63B3	Karcag Hung	25C3	Kashiwazaki Japan	40D3
Kanker India	52A2	Kardhitsa Greece	21B3	Kashmar Iran	56C2
Kanniyakuman India	53B3	Karel'skaya ASSR,		Kashmir, State India	32D5
Kano Nig	63C3	Republic USSR	30E3	Kasimov USSR	27F3
Kanoya Japan	40C4	Karesvando Sweden	4J5	Kasko Fin	4J6
Kanpur India	52A1	Karet, Desert Region Maur	62B2	Kasli USSR	27K2
Kansas, State USA	85D3	Kargasok USSR	31K4	Kaslo Can	81G5
Kansas City USA	86A3	Kari Nig	63D3	Kasonga Zaïre	64C3
Kanshi China	39D6	Kariba Zim	66B2	Kasonga-Lunda Zaïre	64B3
Kansk USSR	29B2	Kariba, L Zim/Zambia	66B2	Kásos, I Greece	21C3
Kantchari Burkina	63C3	Kariba Dam Zim/Zambia	66B2	Kaspiyskiy USSR	27G4
Kanthi India	52B2	Karima Sudan	61C3	Kassala Sudan	61C3
Kantishna USA	88D2	Karimganj Bang	44B3	Kassel W Germ	22B2
Kanye Botswana	34D4	Karimnagar India	53B1	Kassérine Tunisia	62C1
Kao-hsiung Taiwan	34D4	Karin Somalia	65E1	Kassinga Angola	66A2
Kaoka Veld Plain, Namibia	66A2	Karis Fin	5J6	Kastamonou Turk	58B1
Kaolack Sen	63A3	Karishimbe, Mt Zaïre	65C3	Kastélli Greece	21B3
Kaoma Zambia	66B2	Káristos Greece	21B3	Kastellorizon, I Greece	58A2
Kapaau Hawaiian Is	97C4	Karkal India	53A2	Kastória Greece	21B2
Kapanga Zaire	64C3	Karkar, I PNG	37F4	Kástron Greece	21C3
Kapelliskär Sweden	5H7	Karlik Shan, Mt China	29B3	Kasugai Japan	40D3
Kapiri Zambia	66B2	Karlino Pol	24B2	Kasumi Japan	41A1
Kapit Malay	44C2	Karl Marx Stadt E Germ	23C2	Kasungu Malawi	67C2
Kaplan USA	95B3	Karlobag Yugos	18C1	Kasur Pak	50C2
Kaplice Czech	23C3	Karlovac Yugos	18C1	Kataba Zambia	66B2
Kapoe Thai	43B4	Karlovo Bulg	20B2	Katako-kombe Zaïre	64C3
Kapona Zaïre	65C3	Karlovy Vary Czech	23C2	Katalla USA	80D3
Kaposvár Hung	18C1	Karlshamn Sweden	5G7	Katangli USSR	29G2
Kapsukas USSR	26B3	Karlskoga Sweden	5G7	Katanning Aust	72A4
Kapunda Aust	74A2	Karlskrona Sweden	5H7	Katerini Greece	21B2
Kapurthala India	50D2	Karlsruhe W Germ	23B3	Kates Needle, Mt Can/USA	81E4
Kapuskasing Can	83B5	Karlstad Sweden	5G7	Katha Burma	48D3
Kaputar, Mt Aust	75D2	Karluk USA	88D3	Katherine Aust	72C2
Kapydzhik, Mt USSR	59E2	Karnafuli Res Bang	52C2	Kathmandu Nepal	52B1
Karabük Turk	58B1	Karnal India	50D2	Kathua India	50D2
Karacabey Turk	21C2	Karnataka, State India	53A1	Katihar India	52B1
Karachi Pak	51B4	Karnobat Bulg	20C2	Katima Mulilo Namibia	66B2
Karad India	53A1	Karoi Zim	66B2	Katmai, Mt USA	80C4
Kara Daglari, Mt Turk	26E5	Karonga Malawi	65D3	Katmai Nat Mon USA	88D3
Karafitt USSR	34D1	Karora Sudan	61C3	Katni India	52A2
Karaganda USSR	31J5	Karossa Indon	44A3	Katoomba Aust	75D2
Karagayly USSR	31J5	Kárpathos, I Greece	21C3	Katowice Pol	25B2
Karaikal India	53B2	Karrats Fjord Greenland	82E2	Katrineholm Sweden	5H7
Karaj Iran	56B2	Kars Turk	59D1	Katsina Nig	63C3
Karak Jordan	58C3	Karsakpay USSR	31H4	Katsina Ala Nig	63C4
Kara Kalpakskaya,		Karsava USSR	24D1	Katsuta Japan	41C1
Republic USSR	31G5	Karshi USSR	46E2	Katsuura Japan	41C1
Karakelong, I Indon	37D3	Karstula Fin	4J6	Katsuyama Japan	41B1
Karakoram, Mts India	50D1	Kartal Turk	20C2	Kattakurgan USSR	31H6
Karakoram, P India/China	50D1	Kartaly USSR	27K3	Kauai, I Hawaiian Is	97C4
Karakumy, Desert USSR	31G6	Karwar India	53A2	Kauai Chan Hawaiian Is	97C4
Karama Jordan	60B3	Kasaji Zaïre	66B2	Kaulakahi Chan Hawaiian Is	97C4
Karaman Turk	58B2	Kasama Zambia	67C2	Kaunakaki Hawaiian Is	97C4
Karamay China	31K5	Kasanga Tanz	65D3	Kaunas USSR	26B3
Karamea NZ	77B2	Kasaragod India	53A2	Kaura Namoda Nig	63C3
Karanja India	51D4	Kasba L Can	81H3	Kautokeino Nor	4J5
Karapinar Turk	58B2	Kasempa Zambia	66B2	Kavadarci Yugos	21B2
Kara S USSR	30H2	Kasenga Zaïre	66B2	Kavajë Alb	21A2
Karasburg Namibia	66A3			Kavali India	53B2
Karasjok Nor	4K5			Kavalla Greece	21B2
Karasuk USSR	31J4			Kavda India	51B4
Karatas Turk	58C2			Kawagoe Japan	41B1

Khanaqin Iraq 59E3
Khandwa India 51D4
Khanewal Pak. 50C2
Khan ez Zabib Jordan 60C3
Khanh Hung Viet 43D4
Khania Greece 21B3
Khanpur Pak 50C3
Khanty-Mansiysk USSR 31H3
Khan Yunis Egypt 60B3
Khapalu India 50D1
Khapcheranga USSR 34C2
Kharabali USSR 27G4
Kharagpur India 52B2
Kharan Iran 57C4
Kharan Pak 50B3
Kharanaq Iran 56B3
Kharg, Is Iran 56B3
Khârga Oasis Egypt 61C2
Khargon India 51D4
Khar'Kov USSR 26E4
Kharmanli Bulg 20C2
Kharovsk USSR 27F2
Khartoum Sudan 61C3
Khartoum North Sudan 61C3
Khasan USSR 40C2
Khashm el Girba Sudan 61C3
Khasi-Jaintia Hills India 52C1
Khaskovo Bulg 20C2
Khatanga USSR 1B9
Khawsa Burma 42B3
Khe Bo Viet 42C2
Khed Brahma India 51C4
Khemis Alg 17C2
Kherrata Alg 17D2
Kherson USSR 26D4
Khilok USSR 29D2
Khíos Greece 21C3
Khios, I Greece 21C3
Khmel'nitskiy USSR 26D4
Khodorov USSR 25C3
Kholm Afghan 50B1
Khong Laos 42D3
Khonj Iran 57B4
Khor USSR 35F2
Khoramshahr Iran 56C3
Khorog USSR 50C1
Khorramabad Iran 56A3
Khosf Iran 56C3
Khost Pak 50B2
Khotin USSR 26C4
Khotol, Mt USA 88C2
Khoyniku USSR 26C3
Khrebet Dzhugdzhur, Mts USSR
Khrebet Kopet Dag, Mts USSR 29F2
Khrebet Pay-khoy, Mts USSR 30H3
Khrebet Tarbagatay, Mts USSR 48C1
Khrebet Tukuringra, Mts USSR 29E2
Khulna Bang 52B2
Khunjerab, P China/India 50D1
Khunsar Iran 56B3
Khurays S Arabia 57A4
Khurda India 52B2

Khurja India 50D3
Khushab Pak 50C2
Khushniyah Syria 60B2
Khust USSR 25C3
Khuwei Sudan 65C1
Khuzdar Pak 51B3
Khvali Iran 56D3
Khvalynsk USSR 27G3
Khvor Iran 56C3
Khvormuj Iran 57B4
Khvoy Iran 59D2
Khwaja Muhammad, Mts Afghan 50C1
Khyber P Afghan/Pak 50C2
Kiambi Zaïre 65C5
Kiana USA 88B1
Kibangou Congo 64B3
Kibaya Tanz 65D3
Kibombo Zaïre 64C3
Kibondo Tanz 65D3
Kibungu Rwanda 65D3
Kicevo Yugos 21B2
Kicking Horse P Can 81G4
Kidal Mali 63C3
Kidderminster Eng 9C3
Kidira Sen 63A3
Kiel W Germ 22C2
Kielce Pol 25D2
Kifab USSR 48E2
Kiffa Maur 63A3
Kigali Rwanda 55H8
Kigluaik Mts USA 88C3
Kigoma Tanz 65C3
Kii-sanchi, Mts Japan 41B2
Kikinda Yugos 20B1
Kikládhes, Is Greece 21B3
Kikori PNG 37F4
Kikwit Zaïre 64B3
Kilauea Crater, Mt Hawaiian Is 97C4
Kilbuck Mts USA 80C3
Kilchu N Korea 40B2
Kilcoy Aust 75D1
Kildare, County Irish Rep 11C2
Kildare Irish Rep 11C2
Kilgore USA 95B3
Kilifi Kenya 65D3
Kilimanjaro, Mt Tanz 65D3
Kilindoni Tanz 65D3
Kilis Turk 58C2
Kilkee Irish Rep 11B2
Kilkenny, County Irish Rep 11C2
Kilkenny Irish Rep 11C2
Kilkis Greece 21B2
Killaloe Irish Rep 11B2
Killarney Aust 75D1
Killarney Irish Rep 7B3
Killeen USA 95A3
Killin Scot 10B3
Killini, Mt Greece 21B3
Killybegs Irish Rep 11B1
Kilmarnock Scot 8B4
Kil'mez USSR 27H2
Kilosa Tanz 65D3
Kilrush Irish Rep 7B3
Kilwa Zaïre 65C3
Kilwa Kisiwani Tanz 65D3
Kilwa Kivinje Tanz 65D3

Kimba Aust 74A2
Kimball, Mt USA 88F2
Kimball USA 89D3
Kimberley S Africa 67F1
Kimberley Plat Aust 72B2
Kimch'aek N Korea 40B2
Kimch'on S Korea 40B3
Kimi Greece 21B3
Kimry USSR 26E2
Kinabalu, Mt Malay 36C3
Kincardine Can 90B2
Kincolith Can 89B1
Kinder USA 95B3
Kindersley Can 89F2
Kindia Guinea 63A3
Kindu Zaïre 64C3
Kinel' USSR 27H3
Kineshma USSR 27F2
Kingaroy Aust 75D1
King City USA 97A2
Kingcome Inlet Can 81F4
King George Is Can 83C4
King I Aust 73D4
King I Can 89B2
Kingisepp USSR 26B2
King Leopold Range, Mts Aust 72B2
Kingman USA 85B3
Kingombe Zaïre 64C3
Kingonya Aust 74A2
Kingsburg USA 98C2
Kings Canyon Nat Pk USA 97B2
Kingscote Aust 74A3
Kingsford USA 90A1
Kingsland USA 93B1
King's Lynn Eng 9E3
Kings Park USA 92C2
Kings Peak, Mt USA 84B2
Kingsport USA 91C3
Kingston Can 83C5
Kingston Jamaica 101E3
Kingston, New York USA 91D2
Kingston NZ 77A3
Kingston St Vincent 103E4
Kingsville USA 85D4
Kingussie Scot 10B3
King William I Can 80J3
King William's Town S Africa 66B4
Kinkala Congo 64B3
Kinna Sweden 5G1
Kinnairds Head, Pt Scot 10D3
Kinomoto Japan 41B1
Kinross Scot 10C3
Kinsale Irish Rep 11B3
Kinshasa Zaïre 64B3
Kintap Indon 44D3
Kinuso Can 89D1
Kinyeti, Mt Sudan 65D2
Kiparissía Greece 21B3
Kiparissiakós Kólpos, G Greece 21B3
Kipawa, L Can 90C1
Kipili Tanz 65D3
Kipnuk USA 88B3
Kippure, Mt Irish Rep 11C2
Kipushi Zaïre 65C5

Kirensk *USSR*	29C2	
Kirgizskaya SSR, Republic *USSR*	31J5	
Kirgizskiy Khrebet, Mts *USSR*	31J5	
Kiri *Zaïre*	48B1	
Kiribati, Is *Pacific O*	71G4	
Kirikkale *Turk*	56A2	
Kirishi *USSR*	26D2	
Kirithar Range, Mts *Pak*	58B3	
Kirk Bulag Dagh, Mt *Iran*	56A2	
Kirkby *Eng*	8C2	
Kirkcaldy *Scot*	10C3	
Kirkcudbright *Scot*	8B2	
Kirkenes *Nor*	4K5	
Kirkland Lake *Can*	83B5	
Kirkpatrick, Mt *Ant*	46E	
Kirksville *USA*	86A2	
Kirkuk *Iraq*	59D2	
Kirkwall *Scot*	10C2	
Kirkwood *USA*	94B2	
Kirov *USSR*	26D3	
Kirov *USSR*	27G2	
Kirovabad *USSR*	31P5	
Kirovakan *USSR*	59D1	
Kirovograd *USSR*	27J2	
Kirovograd *USSR*	26D4	
Kirovsk *USSR*	30E3	
Kirovskiy *USSR*	27H2	
Kirs *USSR*	29F2	
Kirsehir *Turk*	22C2	
Kiruna *Sweden*	22C2	
Kiryu *Japan*	41B1	
Kisangani *Zaïre*	64C2	
Kisarazu *Japan*	41B1	
Kishangarh *India*	52B1	
Kishangarh *India*	51C3	
Kishinev *USSR*	26C4	
Kishiwada *Japan*	41B2	
Kisii *Kenya*	65D3	
Kisiju *Tanz*	65D3	
Kiskunhalas *Hung*	25B3	
Kislovodsk *USSR*	31F5	
Kismaayo *Somalia*	65E3	
Kiso-sammyaku, Mts *Japan*	41B1	
Kissidougou *Guinea*	63A4	
Kississimmee, L *USA*	93B2	
Kisumu *Kenya*	65D3	
Kisvárda *Hung*	25C3	
Kita *Mali*	63B3	
Kitab *USSR*	31H6	
Kitakata *Japan*	41C1	
Kita-Kyushu *Japan*	40C4	
Kitale *Kenya*	65D2	
Kitalo, I *Japan*	35G4	
Kitami *Japan*	40E2	
Kitchener *Can*	82C3	
Kitgum *Uganda*	65D2	
Kithira, I *Greece*	21B3	
Kithnos, I *Greece*	21B3	
Kitimat *Can*	81F4	
Kitsuki *Japan*	41A2	
Kittanning *USA*	91C2	
Kittilä *Fin*	4D3	
Kitunda *Tanz*	65D3	
Kitwanga *Ca*	89B1	
Kitwe *Zambia*	66B2	
Kitzbühel *Austria*	23C3	
Kitzbühler Alpen, Mts *Austria*	13E1	
Kitzingen *W Germ*	23C3	
Kiumbi *Zaïre*	64C3	
Kivalina *USA*	88B1	
Kivu, L, *Zaïre/Rwanda*	65C3	
Kiwalik *USA*	80B3	
Kiyev *USSR*	26D3	
Kizel *USSR*	27J2	
Kizyl-Arvat *USSR*	46D2	
Kizyl-Atrek *USSR*	56B2	
Kladno *Czech*	23C2	
Klagenfurt *Austria*	23C3	
Klaipeda *USSR*	26B2	
Klamath *USA*	84A2	
Klamath Falls *USA*	84A2	
Klamath Mts *USA*	96B2	
Klatovy *Czech*	23C3	
Klawak *USA*	88H3	
Kleiat *Leb*	60B1	
Klerksdorp *S Africa*	67G1	
Klin *USSR*	26E2	
Klintehamn *Sweden*	24B1	
Klintsy *USSR*	26D3	
Kljuc *Yugos*	18C2	
Klodzko *Pol*	25B2	
Klondike Plat *USA/Can*	80D3	
Klosterneuburg *Austria*	25B3	
Kluane *Can*	88G2	
Kluane Nat Pk *Can*	88G2	
Kluczbork *Pol*	25B2	
Klukwan *USA*	88G3	
Klutina L *USA*	88E2	
Knight I *USA*	88E2	
Knighton *Wales*	9C3	
Knin *Yugos*	18C2	
Knokke-Heist *Belg*	13B2	
Knox Coast *Ant*	112C9	
Knoxville, Tennessee *USA*	87B3	
Knud Ramussens Land, Region *Greenland*	82H3	
Koba *Indon*	44B3	
Kobbermirebugt *Greenland*	82F3	
København *Den*	22C1	
Koblenz *W Germ*	23B2	
Kobrin *USSR*	26B3	
Kocani *Yugos*	19E2	
Ko Chang, I *Thai*	42C3	
Koch Bihar *India*	52B1	
Kochel *W Germ*	13D1	
Koch I *Can*	82C3	
Kochi *Japan*	40C4	
Kochi *USA*	40C4	
Kodiak *USA*	88D3	
Kodiak I *USA*	88D3	
Kodikkarai *India*	53B2	
Kodok *Sudan*	65D2	
Koes *Namibia*	66A3	
Koffiefontein *S Africa*	67G1	
Koforidua *Ghana*	63B4	
Kofu *Japan*	40D3	
Koga *Japan*	41B1	
Koge *Den*	5G7	
Kohat *Pak*	50C2	
Koh-i-Baba, Mts *Afghan*	50B2	
Koh-i-Hisar, Mts *Afghan*	50B1	
Koh-i-Khurd, Mt *Afghan*	50B2	
Kohima *India*	52C1	
Koh-i-Mazar, Mt *Afghan*	50B1	
Kohlu *Pak*	58B2	
Kohtla Järve *USSR*	26C2	
Koide *Japan*	41B1	
Koidern *Can*	88F2	
Koihoa, Is *Nicobar Is*	43A4	
Koje-do, I *S Korea*	40B4	
Kokchetav *USSR*	31H4	
Kokemaki, L *Fin*	5J6	
Kokkola *Fin*	4J6	
Kokoda *PNG*	73D1	
Kokomo *USA*	90A2	
Kokonau *Indon*	37E4	
Kokpekty *USSR*	31K5	
Kokstad *S Africa*	66B4	
Ko Kut, I *Thai*	42C3	
Kola *USSR*	4L5	
Kolaka *Indon*	37D4	
Ko Lanta, I *Thai*	43A4	
Kolar *India*	53B2	
Kolar Gold Fields *India*	53B2	
Kolda *Sen*	63A3	
Kolding *Den*	5F7	
Kolhapur *India*	53A1	
Koligarek *USA*	88C4	
Kolín *Czech*	25B2	
Köln *W Germ*	23B2	
Kolo *Pol*	24B2	
Kolobrzeg *Pol*	24B2	
Kolokani *Mali*	63B3	
Kolomna *USSR*	26E2	
Kolomyya *USSR*	26C4	
Kolpashevo *USSR*	31K4	
Kolpekty *USSR*	34A2	
Kólpos Singitikós, G *Greece*	21B2	
Kólpos Strimonikós, G *Greece*	21B2	
Kólpos Toronaíos, G *Greece*	21B2	
Kolvereid *Nor*	4G6	
Kolwezi *Zaïre*	66B2	
Kolyma, R *USSR*	1C7	
Kom, Mt *Bulg/Yugos*	20B2	
Koma *Eth*	65D2	
Komárno *Czech*	25B3	
Komatsu *Japan*	41A2	
Komatsushima *Japan*	41A2	
Komi, Republic *USSR*	30G3	
Komodo, I *Indon*	36C4	
Komoran, I *Indon*	37E4	
Komoro *Japan*	41B1	
Komotini *Greece*	21C2	
Kompong Cham *Camb*	42D3	
Kompong Chhnang, Mts *Camb*	42C3	
Kompong Som *Camb*	42C3	
Kompong Thom *Camb*	42D3	
Kompong Trabek *Camb*	42D3	
Komsomol'sk na Amure *USSR*	29F2	
Kondoa *Tanz*	65D3	
Kondukur *India*	53B1	

Kong Christian IX Land, Region *Greenland*	82G3
Kong Frederik VI Kyst, Mts *Greenland*	82F3
Kong Karls Land, Is *Barents S*	30C2
Kongkemul, Mt *Indon*	44D2
Kongolo *Zaire*	64C3
Kongsberg *Den*	5F7
Kongsvinger *Nor*	5G6
Konin *Pol*	24B2
Konjic *Yugos*	20A2
Konosha *USSR*	18G3
Konotop *USSR*	26D3
Konsk *USSR*	29B2
Konskie *Pol*	25C2
Konstanz *W Germ*	13B3
Kontagora *Nig*	63C3
Kontum *Viet*	42D3
Konya *Turk*	58B2
Kopargaon *India*	51C5
Kópasker *Iceland*	82J3
Koper *Yugos*	18B1
Kopet Dag, Mts *Iran/USSR*	46D2
Kopeysk *USSR*	27K2
Ko Phangan, I *Thai*	43C4
Ko Phuket, I *Thai*	43B4
Köping *Sweden*	5H7
Koppal *India*	53B1
Koprivnica *Yugos*	18C1
Korangi *Pak*	51B4
Koraput *India*	53C1
Korbach *W Germ*	23B2
Korçë *Alb*	21B2
Korcula, I *Yugos*	18C2
Korec *USSR*	25D2
Körglu Tepesi, Mt *Turk*	58B1
Korhogo *Ivory Coast*	63B4
Korl Creek *India*	51B4
Korinthiakós Kólpos, G *Greece*	21B3
Kórinthos *Greece*	21B3
Koriyama *Japan*	40E3
Korkino *USSR*	27K3
Korkuteli *Turk*	58B2
Korla *China*	48C1
Kornat, I *Yugos*	18C2
Köroglu Tepesi, Mt *Turk*	26D5
Korogwe *Tanz*	65D3
Koroit *Aust*	74B3
Koror, Palau Is *Pacific O*	37E3
Korosten *USSR*	26C3
Koro Toro *Chad*	61A3
Korovin, I *USSR*	88B3
Korsakov *USSR*	35G2
Korsør *Den*	5H7
Kortrijk *Belg*	22A2
Kós, I *Greece*	21C3
Ko Samui, I *Thai*	43C4
Koscierzyna *Pol*	24B2
Kosciusko, Mt *Aust*	73D4
Kosciusko I *USA*	88H3
Koshikijima-retto, I *Japan*	40B4
Kosice *Czech*	25C3
Kosong *N Korea*	40B3
Kosovska Mitrovica *Yugos*	20B2
Kossou, L *Ivory Coast*	63B4
Koster *S Africa*	67G1
Kosti *Sudan*	65D1
Kostopol' *USSR*	25D2
Kostroma *USSR*	18G4
Kostrzyn *Pol*	22C2
Koszalin *Pol*	5H8
Kota *India*	51D3
Kotaagung *Indon*	44A4
Kotabaharu *Indon*	44C3
Kotabaru *Indon*	44A3
Kota Bharu *Malay*	43C4
Kotabum *Indon*	44A3
Kot Addu *Pak*	50C2
Kota Kinabulu *Malay*	44D1
Kotapad *India*	53C1
Kotel'nich *USSR*	27G2
Kotel'nikovo *USSR*	27F4
Kotka *Fin*	5K6
Kotlas *USSR*	30F3
Kotlik *USA*	88B2
Kotor *Yugos*	20A2
Kotovsk *USSR*	26C4
Kotri *Pak*	51B3
Kottagudem *India*	53C1
Kottayam *India*	53B3
Kotzebue *USA*	88B1
Kouande *Benin*	63C3
Kouango *CAR*	64C2
Koudougou *Burkina*	63B3
Koulamoutou *Gabon*	64B3
Koulikoro *Mali*	63B3
Koupéla *Burkina*	63B3
Kourou *French Guiana*	109G2
Kouroussa *Guinea*	63B3
Kousséri *Cam*	64B1
Kouvola *Fin*	5K6
Kovel *USSR*	26B3
Kovrov *USSR*	27F2
Kovylkino *USSR*	27F3
Ko Way, I *Thai*	43C4
Kowloon *Hong Kong*	39C5
Kowt-e-Ashrow *Afghan*	50B2
Köycegiz *Turk*	58A2
Koydor *USSR*	4L5
Koyna Res *India*	53A1
Koyuk *USA*	88B2
Koyukuk *USA*	88C2
Kozan *Turk*	58C2
Kozani *Greece*	21B2
Koz'modemyansk *USSR*	27G2
Koztroma *USSR*	27F2
Kozu-shima, I *Japan*	41B2
Krageno *Nor*	5F7
Kragujevac *Yugos*	20B2
Kra, Isthmus of *Burma/Malay*	43B3
Krak des Chevaliers, Hist Site *Syria*	60C1
Kraków *Pol*	25B2
Kraljevo *Yugos*	20B2
Kramatorsk *USSR*	26E4
Kramfors *Sweden*	4H6
Kranj *Yugos*	18B1
Krapotkin *USSR*	27F4
Krasavino *USSR*	27G1
Krashnokamsk *USSR*	27J2
Krasino *USSR*	30G2
Krasnik *Pol*	25C2
Krasnoarmeysk *USSR*	27G3
Krasnoarmeysk *USSR*	27G5
Krasnodar *USSR*	27E4
Krasnotur'insk *USSR*	27K2
Krasnoufimsk *USSR*	27J2
Krasnousol'-skiy *USSR*	27J3
Krasnovishersk *USSR*	31G3
Krasnovodsk *USSR*	31G5
Krasnoyarsk *USSR*	29B2
Krasnyy *USSR*	25C2
Krasnyy Kut *USSR*	27G3
Krasnyy Luch *USSR*	26E4
Krasnyy Yar *USSR*	27G4
Kratie *Camb*	42D3
Kraulshavn *Greenland*	82E2
Krefeld *W Germ*	22B2
Kremenchug *USSR*	26D4
Kremenchugskoye Vodokhranilische, Res *USSR*	26D4
Kremennes *USSR*	25D2
Krements *USSR*	64A2
Krichev *USSR*	26D3
Krimml *Austria*	13E1
Krinstinestad *Fin*	4J6
Krishnagiri *India*	53B2
Krishnanagar *India*	52B2
Kristiansand *Nor*	5F7
Kristianstad *Sweden*	30B3
Kristiansund *Nor*	5G7
Kristinehamn *Sweden*	5G7
Kriti, I *Greece*	21B3
Krivoy Rog *USSR*	26D4
Krk, I *Yugos*	18B1
Kronpris Frederik Bjerge, Mts *Greenland*	82G3
Kronshtadt *USSR*	5K7
Kroonstad *S Africa*	67G1
Kropotkin *USSR*	31F5
Krugersdorp *S Africa*	67G1
Krui *Indon*	44A4
Kruje *Alb*	21A2
Krupki *USSR*	24D2
Krusevac *Yugos*	20B2
Krustpils *USSR*	5K7
Kruzof I *USA*	88G3
Krymsk *USSR*	26E5
Krzyz *Pol*	24B2
Ksar El Boukhari *Alg*	62C1
Ksar el Kebir *Mor*	62B1
Kuala *Indon*	36A3
Kuala Dungun *Malay*	43C5
Kuala Kerai *Malay*	43C4
Kuala Kubu Baharu *Malay*	43C5
Kuala Lipis *Malay*	43C5
Kuala Lumpur *Malay*	43C5
Kuala Trengganu *Malay*	43C4
Kuamut *Malay*	44D1
Kuandian *China*	40A2
Kuantan *Malay*	43C5
Kubar *PNG*	59E1
Kuching *Malay*	44C2

Kudat *Malay* 36C3
Kudus *Indon* 44C4
Kudymkar *USSR* 27H2
Kufstein *Austria* 23C3
Kuh Duren, Upland *Iran* 56C3
Kuh e Bazman, Mt *Iran* 57C4
Kuh-e Dinar, Mt *Iran* 56B3
Kuh-e-Hazar Masjed, Mts *Iran* 56C2
Kuh-e Jebal Barez, Mts *Iran* 57C4
Kuh-e Karkas, Mts *Iran* 56B3
Kuh-e Laleh Zar, Mt *Iran* 57C4
Kuh-e Sahand, Mt *Iran* 56A2
Kuh-e Taftan, Mt *Iran* 57D4
Kuhhaye Sabalan, Mts *Iran* 56A2
Kuhja-ye Zagros, Mts *Iran* 56A3
Kuhmo *Fin* 4K6
Kuhpayeh *Iran* 56B3
Kuhpayeh, Mt *Iran* 56C3
Kuh ye Bashakerd, Mts *Iran* 57C4
Kuh ye Sabalan, Mt *Iran* 56A2
Kuibis *Namibia* 66A3
Kuigillingok *USA* 80B4
Kuiu I *USA* 88H3
Kuji *Japan* 40E2
Kuju-san, Mt *Japan* 41A2
Kukalek L *USA* 88C3
Kukës *Alb* 20B2
Kukup *Malay* 43C5
Kula *Turk* 21C3
Kulakshi *USSR* 27J4
Kulal, Mt *Kenya* 65D2
Kulata *Bulg* 21B2
Kuldiga *USSR* 26B2
Kul'sary *USSR* 27K5
Kulu *India* 50D2
Kulu *Turk* 58B2
Kulunda *USSR* 31J4
Kulwin *Aust* 74B2
Kumagaya *Japan* 41B1
Kumai *Indon* 44C3
Kumamoto *Japan* 40C4
Kumano *Japan* 41B2
Kumanovo *Yugos* 20B2
Kumara *China* 63B4
Kumba *Cam* 64A2
Kumbakonam *India* 53B2
Kumasi *Ghana* 64B4
Kumertau *USSR* 27J3
Kumhwa *S Korea* 40B3
Kumla *Sweden* 5H7
Kumta *India* 53A2
Kümüx *China* 48C1
Kunda *USSR* 5K7
Kundla *India* 51C4
Kunduz *Afghan* 50B1
Kungsbacka *Sweden* 5G7
Kungur *USSR* 27J2
Kunhing *Burma* 42B1
Kunlun Shan, Mts *China* 48B2
Kunming *China* 39A4
Kunsan *S Korea* 40B3
Kuopio *Fin* 4K6
Kupang *Indon* 72B2
Kupiano *PNG* 73D2
Kupreanof I *USA* 88H3
Kupyansk *USSR* 26E4

Kuqa *China* 48C1
Kurabe *Japan* 41B1
Kurashiki *Japan* 40C4
Kurayoshi *Japan* 41A1
Kurdistan, Region *Iran* 56A2
Kurdzhali *Bulg* 20C2
Kure *Japan* 40C4
Kurgan *USSR* 31H4
Kurikka *Fin* 4J6
Kurnool *India* 53B1
Kuroiso *Japan* 41C1
Kurow *NZ* 77B2
Kurri Kurri *Aust* 75D2
Kursk *USSR* 26E3
Kuruman *S Africa* 66B3
Kurume *Japan* 40C4
Kurunegala *Sri Lanka* 53C3
Kusa *USSR* 27J2
Kus Gölü, L *Turk* 21C2
Kushimoto *Japan* 40D4
Kushiro *Japan* 40E2
Kushtia *Bang* 52B2
Kushka *Afghan* 31G4
Kushva *USSR* 88C2
Kuskokwim Mts *USA* 88C2
Kusma *Nepal* 52A1
Kussharo-ko, L *Japan* 40E2
Kustanay *USSR* 31H4
Kitahya *Turk* 58A2
Kutná Hora *Czech* 25B3
Kutno *Pol* 24B2
Kutu *Zaïre* 64B3
Kutubdia I *Bang* 52C2
Kutum *Sudan* 64C1
Kuujjuaq *Can* 83D4
Kuusamo *Fin* 4K5
Kuvandyk *USSR* 27J3
Kuwait *Kuwait* 59E4
Kuwait, Sheikdom *S W Asia* 46C3
Kuwana *Japan* 41B1
Kuybyshev *USSR* 31G4
Kuybyshev *USSR* 31J4
Kuybyshevskoye Vodokhranilishche, Res *USSR* 27G3
Kuytun *USSR* 29C2
Kuzey Anadolu Daglari, Mts *Turk* 26E5
Kuznetsk *USSR* 27G3
Kvichak *USA* 88C3
Kvigtind, Mt *Nor* 4G5
Kvikkjokk *Sweden* 4H5
Kwale *Kenya* 65D3
Kwangju *S Korea* 40B3
Kwekwe *Zim* 66B2
Kwethluk *USA* 80B3
Kwidzyn *Pol* 24B2
Kwoka, Mt *Indon* 37E4
Kyabram *Aust* 74C3
Kyaikkami *Burma* 42B2
Kyaikto *Burma* 42B2
Kyakhta *USSR* 34C1
Kyancutta *Aust* 74A2
Kyaukme *Burma* 42B1
Kyauk-padaung *Burma* 42B1
Kyaukpyu *Burma* 42A2
Kyle of Lochalsh *Scot* 6B2

Kyneton *Aust* 74B3
Kyoga, L *Uganda* 65D2
Kyogle *Aust* 75D1
Kyongju *S Korea* 40B3
Kyoto *Japan* 40D3
Kyshtym *USSR* 31H4
Kyushu, I *Japan* 40C4
Kyushu-Palau Ridge Pacific O 70E3
Kyustendil *Bulg* 20B2
Kyzyl *USSR* 34B1
Kyzylkum, Desert *USSR* 31H5
Kzyl Orda *USSR* 31H5

L

Laas Caanood *Somalia* 65E2
Laasphe *W Germ* 12E1
Laas Qoray *Somalia* 65E2
La Asunción *Ven* 109E1
La Barca *Mexico* 99A1
Labé *Guinea* 63A3
Labelle *Can* 91D1
Labé *USA* 93B2
Labé, L *Can* 88G2
Labi *Brunei* 44D1
La Biche, L *Can* 89E2
Labinsk *USSR* 27F5
Laboué *Leb* 60C1
Laboulaye *Arg* 110C2
Labrador, Region *Can* 83D4
Labrador City *Can* 83D4
Labrador S *Greenland/Can* 83E4
Labrea *Brazil* 109E5
Labuan, I *Malay* 44D1
Labuhan *Indon* 44B4
Labutta *Burma* 42A2
Labytnangi *USSR* 31H3
La Capelle *France* 13B3
La Carlota *Arg* 110C2
La Carlota *Phil* 45B3
Lac Belot, L *Can* 80F3
Lac Bienville, L *Can* 83C4
Laccadive Is *India* 53A3
Lac d'Annecy, L *France* 13B2
Lac de Gras, L *Can* 80G3
Lac de Joux, L *Switz* 13B1
Lac de Neuchâtel, L *Switz* 13B1
Lac de Patzcuaro, L *Mexico* 99A2
Lac de Sayula, L *Mexico* 99A2
Lac du Bonnet, L *Can* 80F3
Lac du Bourget, L *France* 13B2
La Ceiba *Honduras* 101D3
La Châtre *France* 14C2
La-Chaux-de-Fonds *Switz* 13B1
Lachish, Hist Site *Israel* 60B3
La Chorrera *Panama* 108B2
Lachute *Can* 91D1
Lac Joseph, L *Can* 83D4
Lackawanna *USA* 91C2
La Ciotat *France* 81G4
La Martre, L *Can* 80G3
La Ronge, L *Can* 81H4
Lac l'eau Claire *Can* 83C4
Lac Léman, L *Switz/France* 13B1
Lac Manouane *Can* 82C3
Lac Manouane, L *Can* 86C1

Lac Megantic Can	91D1
Lac Mistassini, L Can	83C4
Lacombe Can	89E2
Laconia USA	91D2
La Coruña Spain	16A1
La Crosse USA	86A2
Las Cruces USA	85C3
Lac Seul, L Can	83A4
La Cygne USA	94B2
Ladakh Range India	50D2
Ladnun India	51C3
Ladozhskoye Ozero, L USSR	26D1
Lady Barron Aust	75C4
Ladybrand S Africa	67G1
Ladysmith Can	89C3
Ladysmith S Africa	67G1
Lae PNG	37F4
Laem Ngop Thai	42C3
Laeso, I Den	22C1
Lafayette, Indiana USA	86B2
Lafayette, Louisiana USA	87A3
La Fère France	12B2
La-Ferté-sous-Jouarre France	12B2
Lafia Nig	63C4
Lafiagi Nig	63C4
La Flèche France	14B2
La Galite, I Tunisia	62C1
Lagarto Brazil	107D4
Laghouat Alg	62C1
Lagoa de Araruama Brazil	111C2
Lagoa Feia Brazil	111C2
Lagoa Agrio Ecuador	108B4
Lagoa Juparana, L Brazil	111C1
Lagoa mar Chiquita, L Arg	105D2
Lagoa Mirim, L Urug/Brazil	105F2
Lago Argentino, L Arg	105B7
Lago Buenos Aires, L Arg	105B6
Lago Cochrane, L Chile/Arg	105B5
Lago Colhué Huapi, L Arg	105C5
Lago de Chapala, L Mexico	100B2
Lago de Chiriqui, L Panama	108A2
Lago de Cuitzeo, L Mexico	99A2
Lago de la Laja, L Chile	105B5
Lago del Coghinas, L Sardegna	19A2
Lago de Maracaibo, L Ven	108B2
Lago de Nicaragua, L Nic	101D3
Lago de Perlas, L Nic	101D3
Lago di Bolsena, L Italy	18B2
Lago di Bracciano, L Italy	18B2
Lago di Como, L Italy	18B1
Lago di Garda, L Italy	18B1
Lago di Lecco, L Italy	13C2
Lago di Lugano, L Italy	13C2
Lago d'Iseo, L Italy	13C2
Lago d'Orta, L Italy	13C2
Lago General Carrera, L Chile	105B6
Lago Maggiore, L Italy	18A1
Lago Musters, L Arg	105C5
Lagon France	14B3
Lago Nahuel Huapi, L Arg	105B4
Lago O'Higgins, L Chile	105B5
Lago Omodeo, L Sardegna	19A2
Lago Poopó, L Bol	106C2
Lago Ranco, L Chile	105B5
Lago Rogaguado, L Bol	108D6
Lagos Nig	63C4
Lagos Port	16A2
Lago San Martin, L Chile/Arg	105B6
Lagos de Moreno Mexico	100B2
Lago Titicaca Bol/Peru	106C2
Lago Viedma, L Arg	105B6
La Grande Canada	84B2
Lagrange Aust	72B2
La Grange, Georgia USA	87B3
La Grange, Kentucky USA	86B3
La Grange, Texas USA	95A4
La Gran Sabana, Mts Ven	106F2
La Grave France	13B2
Lagronho Spain	14B3
Laguna Aluminé, L Arg	105B5
Laguna Beach USA	97B3
Laguna Colorada Grande, L Arg	110C3
Laguna de Chiriquí, L Panama	101D4
Laguna de Managua, L Nicaragua	101D3
Laguna de Nicaragua, L Nicaragua	101D3
Laguna de Pueblo Viejo, L Mexico	99B1
Laguna de Yuriria, L Mexico	99A1
Laguna la Altamira Mexico	99B1
Laguna Mar Chiquita, L Arg	110C2
Laguna Nahuel Huapi, L Arg	105B4
Laguna Paiva Arg	105B4
Laguna Ranco Chile	105B5
Laguna Seca Mexico	85C4
Laguna Tortugas, L Mexico	95B3
Lahad Datu Malay	36C3
Lahat Indon	44A3
Lahia Fin	4J6
Lahijan Iran	56B2
Lahnstein W Germ	12D1
Lahore Pak	50C2
Lahti Fin	5K6
La Huerta Mexico	99A2
Lai Chad	64B3
Laibin China	39B5
Lai Chau Viet	42C1
Laingsburg S Africa	66B4
Lairg Scot	10B2
Lais Indon	44A3
Lais Phil	45C4
Laiyang China	38E2
Lajes Brazil	106F4
La Jolla USA	98D4
La Junta USA	85C3
Lake Cargelligo Aust	75C2
Lake City, Florida USA	93B1
Lake City, S Carolina USA	93C1
Lake District, Region Eng	8C2
Lake Elsinore USA	98D4
Lake Eyre Basin Aust	72C3
Lakefield Can	91C2
Lake Harbour Can	82D3
Lake Hughes USA	98C3
Lakehurst USA	92B2
Lake Jackson USA	95A4
La Biche Can	89E2
Lakeland USA	93B2
Lake of the Woods Can	83A5
Lake Oswego USA	96B1
Lakeport USA	97A2
Lake Providence USA	95B3
Lake Pukaki NZ	77B2
Lakes Entrance Aust	75C3
Lakeshore USA	98C2
Lake Stewart Aust	74B1
Lake Traverse Can	91C1
Lakeview USA	84A2
Lakeview USA	96B1
Lake Village USA	95B3
Lake Wales USA	93B2
Lakewood, California USA	98C4
Lakewood, New Jersey USA	92B2
Lakewood, Ohio USA	90B2
Lake Worth USA	93B2
Lakhimpur India	52A1
Lakhpat India	51B4
Lakki Pak	50C2
Lakonikós Kólpos, G Greece	21B3
Lakota Ivory Coast	63B4
Lakselv Nor	4K4
Laksefjord, Inlet Nor	4K4
La Laguna Arg	110C2
La Libertad Ecuador	108A4
La Ligua Chile	110A2
La Linea Spain	16A2
Lalitpur India	51D4
La Loche Can	81H4
La Loche, L Can	89F1
La Louvière Belg	12C1
La Luz Nic	102A4
La Malbaie Can	83C5
La Malinche, Mt Mexico	99B2
La Mancha, Region Spain	16B2
Lamar, Colorado USA	85C3
Lamar, Missouri USA	94B2
La Marque USA	95A4
Lambaréné Gabon	64B3
Lambayeque Peru	108A5
Lambert Gl Ant	112B0
Lambertville USA	92B2
Lamego Port	16A1
La Meije, Mt France	13B2
La Merced Peru	108B6
Lamesa USA	97B3
Lamia Greece	21B3
Lammermuir Hills Scot	8C2
Lammhult Sweden	5G7
Lamon USA	94B1
Lamotrek, I Pacific O	37F3
Lampeter Wales	9B3
Lamu Kenya	65E3
Lana Italy	13D1
Lanai, I Hawaiian Is	97C4
Lanai City Hawaiian Is	97C4

Lanark Scot	8C2		Lappland, Region Sweden/Fin	4H5
Lanbi, I Burma	42B3		Laprida Arg	110C3
Lancashire, County Eng	8C3		Laptev S USSR	1B8
Lancaster, California USA	97B3		Lapua Fin	4J6
Lancaster Eng	8C2		Lapu-Lapu Phil	45B3
Lancaster, Mississippi USA	94B1		La Purisima Mexico	85B4
Lancaster, New Hampshire USA	91D2		La Quiaca Arg	106C3
Lancaster, Ohio USA	90B3		L'Aquila Italy	18B2
Lancaster, Pennsylvania USA	86C3		Lar Iran	57B4
Lancaster, S Carolina USA	93B1		Larache Mor	52B1
Landau W Germ	12E2		Laramie USA	84C2
Landeck Austria	23C3		Laramie Range, Mts USA	84C2
Lander USA	84C2		Laredo USA	85D4
Landeta Arg	110C2		Larestan, Region Iran	57B4
Langenhagen W Germ	22B2		L'Argentiere France	13B2
Langenthal Switz	13B1		Largo USA	93B2
Langholm Scot	8C2		Lari Iran	56A2
Langjökull, Mts Iceland	4A2		La Rioja Arg	106C4
Langkawi, I Malay	43B4		La Rioja, State Arg	106C4
Langley Can	89C3		Lárisa Greece	21B3
Langnau Switz	13B1		Larkana Pak	51B3
Langres France	15D2		Larnaca Cyprus	58B3
Langsa Indon	36A3		Larne N Ire	11D1
Lang Shan, Mts China	34C2		La Robla Spain	16A1
Lang Son Viet	42D1		La Roche-en-Ardenne Belg	12C1
Languedoc, Region France	14C3		La Rochelle France	14B2
Lanin, Mt Arg	105B3		La Roche-sur-Foron France	13B1
Lanoa, L, L Phil	45B4		La Roche-sur-Yon France	14B2
Lansdale USA	92B2		La Roda Spain	17B2
Lansdowne House Can	83B4		La Romana Dom Rep	103D3
Lansford USA	92B2		La Ronge Can	81H4
Lansing USA	86B2		La Ronge, L Can	81H4
Lanslebourg France	13B2		Larvik Nor	5F7
Lanzarote, I Canary Is	62A2		La'ryak USSR	31J3
Lanzhou China	38A2		La Sagra, Mt Spain	16B2
Lanzo Torinese Italy	13B2		La Salle Can	91D1
Laoag Phil	45B2		La Salle USA	90B2
Lao Cai Viet	42C1		La Sarre Can	83C5
Laois, County Irish Rep	11C2		Las Avispas Arg	110A2
Laon France	12B2		Las Cabras Chile	110A2
La Oroya Peru	108B6		Lascombe Can	81G4
Lapalisse France	15C2		Las Cruces USA	85C3
La Palma Panama	108B2		Lasengmia China	38A1
La Palma, I Canary Is	62A2		La Serena Chile	106B4
La Pampa, State Arg	110B3		Las Flores Arg	105E3
La Paragua Ven	109E2		La Sila, Mts Italy	19C3
La Paz Arg	110C2		Lashio Burma	42B1
La Paz Arg	110B2		Lasjerd Iran	90A2
La Paz Bol	106C2		Las Lajas Chile	110A3
La Paz Mexico	100A2		Las Marismas, Marshland Spain	16A2
La Piedad Mexico	99A1		Las Palmas de Gran Canaria Canary Is	62A2
La Pine USA	97B2		La Spezia Italy	18A2
Laplace USA	95B3		Las Plumas Arg	105C4
La Placita Mexico	99A2		Las Rosas Arg	110C2
La Plata Arg	105E2		Lassen Peak, Mt USA	97B2
La Plonge, L Can	89F1		Lassen Volcanic Nat Pk USA	96B2
La Porte USA	90A2		Las Tinaji Mexico	99B2
Lappeenranta Fin	5K6		Lastoursville Gabon	64B3
			Lastovo, I Yugos	18C2
			Las Tres Marias, Is Mexico	100B2
			Las Varillas Arg	110C2

Las Vegas USA	85C3
Latina Italy	19B2
La Toma Arg	110B2
La Tortuga, I Ven	108D1
La Trinidad Phil	45B2
Latrobe Aust	75C2
Latrun Israel	60B3
La Tuque Can	83C5
Latur India	53B1
Latviyskaya SSR, Republic USSR	26B2
Lough Carlingford, L N Ire	11C1
Lough Oughter, L Irish Rep	11C1
Launceston Aust	73D5
Launceston Eng	9B4
La Unión Chile	105B4
La Unión El Salvador	101D3
La Unión Mexico	99A2
La Unión Peru	108B5
Laura Aust	73D2
Laurel, Delaware USA	91C3
Laurel, Maryland USA	92A3
Laurel, Mississippi USA	87B3
Laurens USA	93B1
Laurinburg USA	93C1
Lausanne Switz	18A1
Laut, I Indon	44D0
Lautaro, Mt Chile	105B5
Lauterbach W Germ	12D2
Laval Can	91D1
Laval France	14B2
Laveaga Peak, Mt USA	98B2
Laveno Italy	13C2
Lavras Brazil	107B6
Lavrentiya USSR	80A3
Lavumisa Swaziland	67H1
Lawas Malay	44D1
Lawksawk Burma	42B1
Lawrence, Kansas USA	94A2
Lawrence, Massachusetts USA	91D2
Lawrence NZ	77A3
Lawrenceville, Illinois USA	85D3
Lawton USA	85D3
Layla S Arabia	57A5
Laylo Sudan	65D2
La'youn Mor	62A2
Lázaro Cárdenas Mexico	99A2
Laz Daua Somalia	65E1
Lazi Phil	45B4
Lead USA	84C2
Leader Can	89F2
Leavenworth USA	94A2
Leba Pol	24B2
Lebanon, Missouri USA	94B2
Lebanon, Oregon USA	96B2
Lebanon, Pennsylvania USA	91C2
Lebanon, Republic S W Asia	58C3
Lebombo, Mts Mozam/S Africa/Swaziland	67C3
Lebork Pol	24B2
Le Bourg-d'Oisans France	13B1
Le Brassus Switz	13B1
Lebu Chile	105B3
Le Buet, Mt France	13B1
Le Cateau France	12B1
Lecce Italy	21A2

uckenwalde E Germ	22C2	
uckhoff S Africa	67F1	
ucknow India	52A1	
ucusse Angola	66B2	
uda China	38E2	
udenscheid W Germ	12D1	
uderitz Namibia	66A3	
udhiana India	50D2	
udington USA	90A2	
udlow Eng	9C3	
udogorie, Upland Bulg	33B1	
udowici USA	93B1	
udus Rom	20B1	
udvika Sweden	5H6	
udwigsburg W Germ	23B3	
udwigshafen W Germ	23B3	
udwigslust E Germ	22C2	
uebo Zaïre	64C3	
uena Angola	66A2	
ueyang China	38B3	
ufeng China	39D5	
ufkin USA	87A3	
uga USSR	26C2	
ugano Switz	18A1	
ugela Mozam	67C2	
ugo Spain	16A1	
ugoj Rom	20B1	
uhuo China	38A3	
uiana Angola	66B2	
uiano Italy	13C2	
ujan China	39D5	
uik USSR	30E4	
ukolela Zaïre	64B3	
uków Pol	24C2	
ukulu Zambia	66B2	
uleå Sweden	4J5	
uleburgaz Turk	20C2	
uliang Shan, Mts China	38C2	
uling USA	95A4	
umbala Angola	66B2	
umberton USA	87C3	
umbis Indon	44D1	
umding India	52C1	
umeje Angola	66B2	
umsden NZ	77A3	
und Sweden	5G7	
undazi Zambia	67C2	
undy, I Eng	9B4	
uneburg W Germ	12D2	
unéville France	12D2	
unglei Indon	52C2	
uninec USSR	24D2	
uobomo Congo	64B3	
uocheng China	39B5	
uoding China	39B5	
uohe China	38C3	
uoxiao Shan, Hills China	39C4	
uoyang China	38C3	
uozi Zaïre	64B3	
upane Zim	66B2	
upilichi Mozam	67C2	

Luque Par	106E4
Lurgan N Ire	11C1
Luristan, Region Iran	56A3
Lusaka Zambia	66B2
Lusambo Zaïre	64C3
Lushnje Alb	21A2
Lushoto Tanz	65D3
Lushui China	34B4
Lüshun China	38E2
Luton Eng	9D4
Lutsk USSR	26C3
Luuq Somalia	65E2
Luwingu Zambia	66C2
Luwuk Indon	37D4
Luxembourg, Grand Duchy N W Europe	12D2
Luxembourg Lux	15D2
Luxi China	39A5
Luxor Egypt	61C2
Luza USSR	27G1
Luzern Switz	18A1
Luzhai China	39B5
Luzhi China	39B4
Luzhou China	39B4
Luziânia Brazil	111B1
Luzon, I Phil	45B2
L'vov USSR	25C3
Lybster Scot	10C2
Lycksele Sweden	4H6
Lydenburg S Africa	66B3
Lyell, Mt Aust	84B3
Lykens USA	92A2
Lyme Regis Eng	9C4
Lynchburg USA	87C3
Lyndhurst Aust	74A2
Lynn USA	91D2
Lynn Haven USA	93A1
Lynn Lake Can	81H3
Lyon France	15C2
Lyons, Georgia USA	93B1
Lys-Va USSR	27J2

M

Ma'agan Jordan	60B2
Ma'alot Tarshiha Israel	60B2
Ma'an Jordan	58C3
Ma'anshan China	39D3
Ma'arrat an Nu'man Syria	58C3
Maasek Belg	12C1
Maasin Phil	45B3
Maastricht Belg	23B2
Mabalane Mozam	67C2
Mabaruma Guyana	109F2
Mablethorpe Eng	8E3
Mabote Mozam	67C3
Mabrita USSR	24C2
M'adel USSR	24D2
Macaé Brazil	111C2
McAlester USA	85D3
McAllen USA	85D4

Macaloge Mozam	67C2
Macapá Brazil	109G3
Macaraní Brazil	111C1
Macas Ecuador	108B4
Macaú Brazil	70D3
Macau, Dependency China	39C5
McBride Can	89C2
McCarthy USA	88F2
McCauley I Can	89A2
Macclesfield Eng	8C3
McClintock Chan Can	80H2
McClure USA	92A2
McClure, L USA	98B2
McComb USA	95B3
McCook USA	84C2
McCusker, Mt Can	89C1
McDame Can	89F2
McDermitt USA	96C2
Macdonnell Ranges, Mts Aust	72C3
Macedo de Cavaleiros Port	16A1
Maceió Brazil	111B2
Macenta Guinea	63B4
Macerata Italy	18B2
Macfarlane, L Aust	74A2
McGehee USA	95B3
MacGillycuddys Reeks, Mts Irish Rep	11B3
McGrath USA	80C3
Machado Brazil	111B2
Machaila Mozam	67C3
Machakos Kenya	65D3
Machala Ecuador	108B4
Machaze Mozam	67C3
Macherla India	53B1
Machgharab Leb	60B2
Machilipatnam India	53C1
Machiques Ven	108C1
Machu-Picchu, Hist Site Peru	108C6
Macia Mozam	67C3
Mackay Aust	73D3
Mackay, L Aust	72B3
McKeesport USA	92C2
Mackenzie Can	89C1
Mackenzie, R Can	80F3
Mackenzie, Region Can	80F3
Mackenzie King I Can	80G2
Mackenzie Mts Can	80E3
Mackinaw City USA	90B1
McKinley, Mt USA	88D2
McKinney USA	95A3
Macksville Aust	75D2
McLaughlin, Mt USA	96B2
Maclean Aust	75D1
Maclear S Africa	66B4
McLennan Can	81G4
McLeod, L Aust	72A3
McLeod Lake Can	89C1
Macmillan P Can	80E3
McMinnville, Oregon USA	96B1
McMurdo, Base Ant	112B7
McNaughton L Can	89D2
Macomb USA	94B1
Macomer Sardegna	19A2
Macomia Mozam	67C2
Mâcon France	15C2

Macon, Georgia *USA*	87B3
Macon, Missouri *USA*	95B3
Macondo *Angola*	66B2
McPherson *USA*	94A2
Macquarie, Is *Aust*	70F6
Macquarie, L *Aust*	75D2
McRae *USA*	93B1
MacRobertson Land, Region *Ant*	112B1
Macroom *Irish Rep*	11B3
M'Sila *Alg*	62C1
Macunaga *Italy*	13C2
M'yárdvár *Hung*	25B3
Madaba *Jordan*	60B3
Madagascar, I *Indian O*	55J0
Madama *Niger*	61A2
Madang *PNG*	37F4
Madaoua *Niger*	61A2
Madaripur *Bang*	52C2
Madau *USSR*	56B2
Madeira, I *Atlantic O*	62A1
Madeira, R *Brazil*	109E5
Madera *USA*	97A2
Madgaon *India*	52B1
Madhubani *India*	52B1
Madhya Pradesh, State *India*	52A2
Madikeri *India*	53B2
Madimba *Zaïre*	64B3
Madingo Kayes *Congo*	64B3
Madingou *Congo*	64B3
Madison, Indiana *USA*	86B3
Madison, Wisconsin *USA*	100A1
Madisonville, Kentucky *USA*	94C2
Madisonville, Texas *USA*	95A3
Madiun *Indon*	44C4
Mado Gashi *Kenya*	65D2
Madonna Di Campiglio *Italy*	13C2
Madras *India*	53C2
Madras *USA*	96B2
Madre de Dios, I *Chile*	105A6
Madrid *Spain*	16B1
Madridejos *Spain*	16B2
Madura, I *Indon*	44C4
Madurai *India*	100A1
Maebashi *Japan*	41B1
Maevatanana *Madag*	67D2
Mafeteng *Lesotho*	67G1
Maffra *Aust*	75C3
Mafia, I *Tanz*	65D3
Mafikeng *S Africa*	67E2
Mafra *Brazil*	106G4
Mafraq *Jordan*	58C3
Magangué *Colombia*	108C2
Magdalena *Arg*	110D3
Magdalena *Mexico*	85B3
Magdalena *Mexico*	100A1
Magdalena, B *Colombia*	102C4
Magdalena, Mt *Malay*	44D1
Magdalen Is *Can*	83D5
Magdeburg *E Germ*	22C2
Mage *Brazil*	107C6
Magelang *Indon*	44C4
Maghágha *Egypt*	58B4
Magherafelt *N Ire*	11C1
Maglie *Italy*	21A2
Magnitogorsk *USSR*	27J3
Magnolia *USA*	95B3
Magóe *Mozam*	67C2
Magog *Can*	91D1
Magosal *Mexico*	99B1
Magrath *Can*	89E2
Maguse River *Can*	83A3
Magwe *Burma*	42B1
Mahabad *Iran*	56A2
Mahabharat Range, Mts *Nepal*	52B1
Mahad *India*	53A1
Mahadeo Hills *India*	52B1
Mahajanga *Madag*	67D2
Mahalapye *Botswana*	66B3
Mahanoro *Madag*	67D2
Mahanoy City *USA*	92A2
Maharashtra, State *India*	52A2
Mahasamund *India*	52A2
Maha Sarakham *Thai*	42C2
Mahbubnagar *India*	53B1
Mahdia *Tunisia*	62D1
Mahe *India*	53B2
Mahekar *India*	51D4
Maheli, I *Comoros*	51D4
Mahendragarh *India*	52A2
Mahenge *Tanz*	65D3
Mahesana *India*	51C4
Mahoba *India*	51D3
Mahón *Spain*	17C2
Mahony L *Can*	88J1
Mahrès *Tunisia*	62D1
Mahuva *India*	51C4
Maicao *Colombia*	108C1
Malche *France*	13B1
Maidstone *Eng*	9E4
Maiduguri *Nig*	64B1
Maihar *India*	52A2
Maijdi *Bang*	52C2
Mail Kyun, I *Burma*	42B3
Maimana *Afghan*	50A1
Main Chan *Can*	90B1
Mai-Ndombe, L *Zaïre*	64B4
Maine, State *USA*	86D2
Maine, Region *France*	14B2
Mainland, 1 *Scot*	10C2
Mainpuri *India*	51D3
Maintenon *France*	12A2
Maintirano *Madag*	67D2
Mainz *W Germ*	23B2
Maio, I *Cape Verde*	63A4
Maipó, Mt *Arg/Chile*	110D3
Maipú *Arg*	110D3
Maiquetía *Ven*	108D1
Mairabari *India*	52C1
Maiskhal I *Bang*	52C2
Maitland, New South Wales *Aust*	73E4
Maitland, S Australia *Aust*	74A2
Maizuru *Japan*	40D3
Majene *Indon*	36C4
Maji *Eth*	65D2
Makale *Eth*	65D2
Makale *Indon*	36C4
Makalu, Mt *China/Nepal*	52B1
Makarska *Yugos*	18C2
Makaryev *USSR*	27F2
Makat *USSR*	27H…
Makeni *Sierra Leone*	63A4
Makeyevka *USSR*	26E4
Makgadikgadi, Salt Pan *Botswana*	66B3
Makhachkala *USSR*	27G1
Makindu *Kenya*	65D3
Makkovik *Can*	83B3
Makó *Hung*	25C3
Makokou *Gabon*	64B2
Makorako, Mt *NZ*	76C1
Makoua *Congo*	64B3
Makrana *India*	51C3
Makran Coast Range, Mts *Pak*	51A3
Maktar *Tunisia*	62C1
Maku *Iran*	59D1
Makumbi *Zaïre*	64C4
Makurazaki *Japan*	40C4
Makurdi *Nig*	63C4
Malabang *Phil*	45B4
Malabar Coast *India*	53A2
Malabo *Bioko*	55E7
Malaga *Colombia*	108C2
Málaga *Spain*	16B2
Malaimbandy *Madag*	67D3
Malaita, I *Solomon Is*	73F1
Malakal *Sudan*	65D2
Malakand *Pak*	50C2
Malang *Indon*	44C4
Malanje *Angola*	64B4
Malanville *Benin*	63C3
Mälaren, L *Sweden*	5H7
Malargüe *Arg*	110B3
Malaspina Gl *USA*	88F3
Malatya *Turk*	59G2
Malawi, Republic *Africa*	67C2
Malaybalay *Phil*	45C4
Malayer *Iran*	56A3
Malaysia, Federation *S E Asia*	36B3
Malazgirt *Turk*	59D2
Malbork *Pol*	24B2
Malchin *E Germ*	22C2
Malden *USA*	94C2
Maldives *Is Indian O*	49B5
Maldives Ridge *Indian O*	70B4
Maldonado *Urug*	105F2
Male *Italy*	13D1
Malegaon *India*	51C4
Malé Karpaty, Upland *Czech*	25B3
Malema *Mozam*	67C2
Malestan *Afghan*	50B2
Maleuz *USSR*	27J3
Malheur L *USA*	96C2
Mali, Republic *Africa*	63B3
Malinau *Indon*	44D1
Malindi *Kenya*	65E3
Malin Head, Pt *Irish Rep*	6B2
Malkala Range, Mts *India*	52A2
Malkapur *India*	51D4
Malkara *Turk*	21C2
Malko Turnovo *Bulg*	20C2
Mallaig *Scot*	10B3
Mallawi *Egypt*	61C2

Málles Venosta *Italy*	13D1
Mallorca, I *Spain*	17C2
Mallow *Irish Rep*	11B2
Malm *Nor*	4G6
Malmberget *Sweden*	4J5
Malmédy *W Germ*	12D1
Malmesbury *Eng*	9C4
Malmesbury *S Africa*	66A4
Malmö *Sweden*	5G7
Malmyzh *USSR*	27G2
Malolos *Phil*	45B3
Maloma *USA*	91D2
Maloti Mts *Lesotho*	67G1
Måløy *Nor*	4F6
Malpelo, I *Colombia*	104A2
Malpura *India*	51D3
Malta, Montana *USA*	84C2
Malta, Chan *Malta/Italy*	19B3
Malta, I *Medit S*	19B3
Maltahöhe *Namibia*	66A3
Malton *Eng*	8D2
Malung *Sweden*	5G6
Malvan *India*	53A1
Malvern *USA*	95B3
Malwa Plat *India*	51D4
Mama *USSR*	29D2
Mamadysh *USSR*	27H2
Mambasa *Zaïre*	65C2
Mamfé *Cam*	64A2
Mamou *Guinea*	63A3
Mampikony *Madag*	67D2
Mampong *Ghana*	64B4
Mamshit, Hist Site *Israel*	60B3
Mamuno *Botswana*	66B2
Man *Ivory Coast*	63B4
Mana *Hawaiian Is*	97C4
Manabo *Madag*	67D3
Manacapuru *Brazil*	109E4
Manacor *Spain*	17C2
Manado *Indon*	37D3
Managua *Nic*	101D3
Manakara *Madag*	67D3
Manambaru *Madag*	67D2
Mananjary *Madag*	67D3
Manapouri *NZ*	77A3
Manapouri, L *NZ*	77A3
Manas *Bhutan*	52C1
Manas *China*	48C1
Manas Hu, L *China*	31K5
Manaslu, Mt *Nepal*	52A1
Manasquan *USA*	92B2
Manaus *Brazil*	109F4
Manavgat *Turk*	58B2
Manbij *Syria*	59C2
Man, Calf of, I *Eng*	7C3
Mancheral *India*	53B1
Manchester, Connecticut *USA*	92D2
Manchester *Eng*	8C3
Manchester, New Hampshire *USA*	86C2
Manchester, Pennsylvania *USA*	91C2
Manchuria, Hist Region *China*	35E2
Manda *Tanz*	67C2
Mandaguari *Brazil*	111A2
Mandal *Nor*	5F7
Mandalay *Burma*	42B1
Mandalgovi *Mongolia*	34C2
Mandal Ovoo *Mongolia*	38A1
Mandalselva *India*	90A2
Mandera *Eth*	65E2
Mandeville *Jamaica*	102B3
Mandidzudzure *Zim*	66C2
Mandimba *Mozam*	65D5
Mandla *India*	52A2
Mandritsara *Madag*	67D2
Mandsaur *India*	51D4
Manduria *Italy*	19C2
Mandvi *India*	51B4
Mandya *India*	53B2
Manevichi *USSR*	24D2
Manfield *Eng*	8D3
Manfredonia *Italy*	19C2
Manga, Desert Region *Niger*	64B1
Mangakino *NZ*	78C1
Mangalia *Rom*	20C2
Mangalme *Chad*	64B1
Mangalore *India*	53A2
Manggar *Indon*	44B3
Manghnia *China*	34B3
Mangoche *Malawi*	65D5
Mangole, I *Indon*	37D4
Mangral *India*	51B4
Mangui *China*	29E2
Manhattan *USA*	84D3
Manhuacu *Brazil*	107C6
Manica *Mozam*	67C2
Manicouagan Res *Can*	83D4
Manifah *S Arabia*	57A4
Manila *Phil*	45B3
Manila *Aust*	75D2
Maninian *Ivory Coast*	63B3
Manipur, State *India*	52C2
Manisa *Turk*	58A2
Man, Isle of *Irish Sea*	7C3
Manistee *USA*	90A2
Manistique *USA*	90A1
Manitoba, Province *Can*	81H4
Manitoba, L *Can*	81J4
Manito L *Can*	89F2
Manitou Is *USA*	90A1
Manitoulin, I *Can*	83B5
Manitowoc *USA*	90A2
Maniwaki *Can*	91C1
Manizales *Colombia*	108B2
Manja *Madag*	67D3
Manjimup *Aust*	76A4
Mankato *USA*	86A2
Mankono *Ivory Coast*	63B4
Manley Hot Springs *USA*	88D2
Manly *NZ*	76B1
Manmad *India*	51C4
Manna *Indon*	44A3
Mannahill *Aust*	74A2
Mannar *Sri Lanka*	53B3
Mannar, G of *India*	53B3
Mannargudi *India*	53B2
Mannheim *W Germ*	23B3
Manning *Can*	89D1
Manning *USA*	93B1
Mannum *Aust*	74A2
Mano *Sierra Leone*	63A4
Manokwari *Indon*	37E4
Manono *Zaïre*	64C3
Manoron *Burma*	42B3
Manp'o *N Korea*	40B2
Mansa *India*	50D3
Mansa *Zambia*	66B2
Mansel I *Can*	82B3
Mansfield, Arkansas *USA*	95B2
Mansfield *Aust*	74C3
Mansfield, Louisiana *USA*	95B3
Mansfield, Massachusetts *USA*	92D1
Mansfield, Ohio *USA*	92D1
Mansfield, Pennsylvania *USA*	91C2
Mansyu Deep *Pacific O*	37E2
Manta *Ecuador*	108A4
Mantalingajan, Mt *Phil*	45A4
Manteca *USA*	92B2
Mantes *France*	14C2
Mantova *Italy*	18B1
Mantta *Fin*	4J6
Manturovo *USSR*	27F2
Manuel Ribas *Brazil*	111A2
Manukan *Phil*	45B4
Manukau *NZ*	76B1
Manus, I *Pacific O*	37F4
Manzanares *Spain*	16B2
Manzanillo *Cuba*	101E2
Manzanillo *Mexico*	100B3
Manzhouli *USSR*	29D3
Manzil *Jordan*	60C3
Manzini *Swaziland*	67C3
Mao *Chad*	64B1
Maomao Shan, Mt *China*	68A1
Maoming *China*	39C5
Mapai *Mozam*	67C3
Mapia, Is *Pacific O*	37E3
Maple Creek *Can*	81H5
Maputo *Mozam*	67H1
Maqu *China*	31A2
Maquela do Zombo *Angola*	64B3
Maquinchao *Arg*	105C4
Marabá *Brazil*	107B3
Maracaibo *Ven*	108C1
Maracay *Ven*	108C1
Maradah *Libya*	61A2
Maradi *Niger*	63C3
Maragheh *Iran*	56A2
Maralal *Kenya*	65D2
Maramasike, I *Solomon Is*	73F1
Maramba *Zambia*	66B2
Marand *Iran*	56A2
Maranhão, State *Brazil*	107B2
Marañón, R *Peru*	108B4
Marathon *Can*	83B5
Marathon, Florida *USA*	83B5
Maratua, I *Indon*	44D2
Maravato *Mexico*	99A2
Marawi *Phil*	45B4
Marayes *Arg*	110B2
Marbella *Spain*	16B2
Marble Bar *Aust*	72A3
Marblehall *S Africa*	66B3

Matane *Can*	83D5
Matanó *Spain*	17C1
Matanzas *Cuba*	101D2
Matara *Sri Lanka*	53C3
Mataram *Indon*	72A1
Matarani *Peru*	106B2
Mataura *NZ*	77A3
Matehuala *Mexico*	100B2
Matera *Italy*	19C2
Mátészalka *Hung*	25F3
Mathura *India*	51D3
Mati *Phil*	45C4
Matisiri, I *Indon*	44D3
Matlock *Eng*	7D3
Mato Grosso *Brazil*	109F6
Mato Grosso, State *Brazil*	109F6
Mato Grosso do Sul, State *Brazil*	106E2
Matola *Mozam*	67H1
Matrah *Oman*	57C5
Matrûh *Egypt*	58A3
Matsue *Japan*	40C3
Matsumae *Japan*	40E2
Matsumoto *Japan*	40D3
Matsusaka *Japan*	40D4
Matsuyama *Japan*	40C4
Mattawa *Can*	91C1
Matterhorn, Mt *Switz/Italy*	18A1
Matthew Town *Bahamas*	102C2
Mattituck *USA*	92C2
Mattoon *USA*	94C2
Matun *Afghan*	50B2
Maturín *Ven*	109E2
Mau *India*	52A1
Maúa *Mozam*	67C2
Maubeuge *France*	15C1
Maude *Aust*	74B2
Maud Seamount *Atlantic O*	69J8
Maui, I, *Hawaiian Is*	97C4
Maumee *USA*	90B2
Maun *Botswana*	66B3
Mauna Kea, Mt *Hawaiian Is*	97C4
Mauna Loa, Mt *Hawaiian Is*	97C4
Maunoir, L *Can*	4F3
Maunoir, L *Can*	46F3
Mauritania, Republic *Africa*	14C2
Mavinga *Angola*	66B2
Mawlaik *Burma*	43D3
Mawson *Base Ant*	112C10
Maya, I *Indon*	44B3
Mayadin *Syria*	59D2
Mayaguana, I *Bahamas*	87C4
Mayagüez *Puerto Rico*	103D3
Mayahi *Niger*	63C3
Mayama *Congo*	64B3
Mayamey *Iran*	56C2
Maybole *Scot*	8B2
Maydena *Aust*	75C4
Mayen *W Germ*	12D1
Mayenne *France*	14B2
Mayerthorpe *Can*	89D2
Mayfield *USA*	94C2
Maykop *USSR*	27E5
Maymaneh *Afghan*	31H6
Maymyo *Burma*	42B1
Mayo *Can*	80E3
Mayo, County *Irish Rep*	11B2
Mayo *USA*	92A3
Mayo, Mts of *Irish Rep*	11B1
Mayon, Mt *Phil*	45B3
Mayor, Mt *Spain*	15B1
Mayor Buratovich *Arg*	110C3
Mayor I *NZ*	76C1
Mayor P Lagerenza *Par*	106D2
Mayotte, I *Indian O*	67D2
Mayrhofen *Austria*	13D1
Mays Landing *USA*	92B3
Maysville *USA*	91B3
Mayumba *Gabon*	64B3
Mazabuka *Zambia*	66B2
Mazaffarnagar *India*	50D3
Mazar *China*	50B3
Mazar *Jordan*	60B3
Mazara del Vallo *Italy*	19B3
Mazar-i-Sharif *Afghan*	50B1
Mazatlán *Mexico*	100B2
Mazra *Jordan*	60B3
Mbabane *Swaziland*	67E2
Mbaïki *CAR*	64B2
Mbala *Zambia*	65D3
Mbale *Uganda*	65D3
Mbalmayo *Cam*	64B2
Mbamba Bay *Tanz*	67C2
Mbandaka *Zaïre*	64B2
Mbanza Congo *Angola*	64B3
Mbanza-Ngungu *Zaire*	64B3
Mbarara *Uganda*	65D3
Mbenza *Congo*	64B3
Mbeya *Tanz*	65D3
Mbinda *Congo*	64B3
Mbout *Maur*	63A3
Mbuji-Mayi *Zaïre*	64C3
Mbulu *Tanz*	65D3
Mcherrah, Region *Alg*	62B2
Mchinji *Malawi*	67C2
Mdrak *Viet*	42D3
Mead, L *USA*	85B3
Meadow Lake *Can*	81H4
Meadville *USA*	90B2
Mealy Mts *Can*	83E4
Meandarra *Aust*	75C1
Meander River *Can*	81G4
Meath, County *Irish Rep*	11B3
Meaux *France*	15C2
Mechanicville *USA*	92C1
Mechelen *Belg*	22A2
Mecheria *Alg*	62B1
Meconta *Mozam*	67C2
Mecubúri *Mozam*	67C2
Mecufi *Mozam*	67D2
Mecula *Mozam*	67C2
Medan *Indon*	36A3
Médanos *Arg*	110C3
Médanos *Arg*	110C2
Medecine Hat *Can*	89B2
Medellin *Colombia*	108B2
Medenine *Tunisia*	62D1
Medford *USA*	84A2
Medgidia *Rom*	21C2
Media Agua *Arg*	110C2
Medias *Rom*	20B1
Medical Lake *USA*	96C1
Medicine Hat *Can*	81G5
Medina *Brazil*	111C1
Medina *S Arabia*	58B3
Medinaceli *Spain*	16B1
Medina del Campo *Spain*	16B1
Medina de Río Seco *Spain*	16A1
Medinipur *India*	52B2
Mediterranean S *Europe*	54E4
Medley *Can*	89C2
Mednogorsk *USSR*	27J3
Médoc *France*	14B2
Médog *China*	52D1
Medouneu *Gabon*	64B2
Medvezh'yegorsk *USSR*	30E3
Meekatharra *Aust*	72A3
Meerut *India*	50D3
Mega *Eth*	65D2
Megalópolis *Greece*	21B3
Mégara *Greece*	21B3
Meghalaya, State *India*	52C1
Megido, Hist Site *Israel*	60B2
Mehrīz *Iran*	56B3
Meiganga *Cam*	64B2
Meiktila *Burma*	42B1
Meiringen *Switz*	13C1
Meishan *China*	39A4
Meissen *E Germ*	23C2
Mei Xian *China*	39D5
Meizhou *China*	39D5
Mejillones *Chile*	106B3
Mekambo *Gabon*	64B2
Meknès *Mor*	62B1
Mekong, R *Camb*	42D3
Melaka *Malay*	43C5
Melanesia, Region *Pacific O*	70F4
Melbourne *Aust*	73D4
Melbourne *USA*	87B4
Melchor Muzquiz *Mexico*	100B2
Melfi *Chad*	64B1
Melfort *Can*	81H4
Melilla *N W Africa*	62B1
Melimoyu, Mt *Chile*	105B4
Melincué *Arg*	110A2
Melipilla *Chile*	110A2
Melitopol' *USSR*	26E4
Melksham *Eng*	7C4
Mellmoth *S Africa*	67H1
Melo *Arg*	110C2
Melo *Urug*	105F2
Melones Res *USA*	98B2
Mels *Switz*	13C1
Melton Mowbray *Eng*	9D3
Melun *France*	15C2
Melville *Can*	81H4
Melville Hills, Mts *Can*	80F3
Melville I *Aust*	72C2
Melville I *Can*	80G2
Melville, L *Can*	83E4
Melvin, L *Irish Rep*	11B1
Memba *Mozam*	67D2
Memberg *E Germ*	23C3
Memmingen *W Germ*	23C3
Mempawan *Indon*	44B2
Memphis, Tennessee *USA*	87B3
Mena *USA*	95B3
Ménaka *Mali*	63C3
Menasha *USA*	90A2

Mehde France	15C3
Mendebo, Mts Eth	65D2
Mendip Hills, Upland Eng	9C4
Mendocino Seascarp Pacific O	71J2
Mendota, California USA	98B2
Mendoza Arg	105C2
Mendoza, State Arg	105C3
Menemen Turk	21C3
Menen Belg	12B1
Mengcheng China	38D3
Menggala Indon	44B3
Menghai China	42B1
Mengla China	39A5
Menglian China	42B1
Mengzi China	39A5
Menindee Aust	73D4
Menindee L Aust	74A3
Meningie Aust	74A3
Menominee USA	90A1
Menomonee Falls USA	90A2
Menongue Angola	66A2
Menorca, I Spain	17C1
Mentasta Mts USA	88F2
Mentawai Indon	42B1
Mentok Indon	44B3
Mentor USA	90B2
Ménu France	12B2
Menyuan China	38A2
Menzelinsk USSR	22B2
Meppen W Germ	18B2
Merah Indon	44D2
Merano Italy	18B1
Merauke Indon	37F4
Merced USA	84A3
Mercedario, Mt Chile	105B2
Mercedes Arg	105C2
Mercedes, Buenos Aires Arg	105E2
Mercedes, Corrientes Arg	106E4
Mercedes Urug	105E2
Mercury Is NZ	76C1
Mereghi Somalia	65E2
Mergui Burma	42B3
Mergui Arch Burma	42B3
Mérida Mexico	101D2
Mérida Spain	16A2
Mérida Ven	109C2
Meridian USA	87B3
Merimbula Aust	75C3
Meringur Aust	74B2
Merowe Sudan	61C3
Merredin Aust	72A4
Merrick, Mt Scot	8B2
Merrillville USA	90A2
Merritt Can	89C2
Merritt Island USA	93B2
Merriwa Aust	75D2
Mersa Fatma Eth	65E1
Mers el Kebir Alg	17B2
Merseyside, Metropolitan County Eng	8C3
Mersin Turk	58B2
Mersing Malay	55C5
Merta India	51C3
Merthyr Tydfil Wales	9C4
Mertola Port	16A2
Meru, Mt Tanz	65D3
Merzifon Turk	26E5
Merzig W Germ	12D2
Mesa USA	85B3
Meschede W Germ	12E1
Mescit Dag, Mt Turk	59D1
Meshik USA	88C3
Meshra Er Req Sudan	65C2
Mesocco Switz	13C1
Mesolóngion Greece	21B3
Mesquite, Texas USA	95A3
Messina Italy	19C3
Messina S Africa	66B3
Messini Greece	21B3
Messiniakós Kólpos, G Greece	21B3
Mestre Italy	18B1
Metairie USA	95B4
Metaline Falls USA	96C1
Metán Arg	106D4
Metangula Mozam	67C2
Metaponto Italy	19C2
Methil USA	10C3
Methuen USA	92D1
Methven NZ	76C2
Metlakatla USA	88H3
Metropolis USA	94C2
Mettur India	53B2
Metz France	15D2
Meulaboh Indon	36A3
Meulan France	12A2
Meuse, Department France	12C2
Meuse, R France	15D2
Mexia USA	95A3
Mexicali Mexico	100A1
Mexico, Federal Republic Central America	100B2
México Mexico	100C3
México, State Mexico	99A2
Mexico USA	94B2
Mezada, Hist Site Israel	60D3
Mezcala Mexico	99B2
Mezen' USSR	20F3
Mezhdusharskiy, I USSR	30G3
Mhow India	51D4
Miahuatlán Mexico	99B2
Miajadas Spain	16A2
Miami, Florida USA	87B4
Miami, Oklahoma USA	94B2
Miami Beach USA	87B4
Miandowab Iran	56A2
Miandrivazo Madag	67D2
Mianeh Iran	56A2
Mianwali Pak	56C2
Mianyang China	39A3
Mianyang China	39C3
Mianzhu China	39A3
Miaodao Qundao, Arch China	38E2
Miao Ling, Upland China	39B4
Miass USSR	27K3
Michalovce Czech	25C3
Miches Dom Rep	103D3
Michigan, State USA	86B2
Michigan, L USA	86B2
Michigan City USA	86B2
Michipicoten I Can	83B5
Michoacan, State Mexico	99A2
Michurnsk USSR	31F4
Michurin Bulg	20C2
Michurinsk USSR	27F3
Micronesia, Region Pacific O	70F3
Midai, I Indon	44B2
Mid Atlantic Ridge Atlantic O	68F4
Middelburg Neth	12B1
Middle Alkali L USA	96B2
Middleboro USA	92D2
Middleburg, Cape Province S Africa	66B4
Middleburg, Pennsylvania USA	92A2
Middleburg, Transvaal S Africa	67G1
Middleburgh USA	92B1
Middlebury USA	91D2
Middlesbrough USA	87B3
Middlesbrough Eng	8D2
Middletown, Connecticut USA	92C2
Middletown, Delaware USA	92B3
Middletown, New York USA	91D2
Middletown, Ohio USA	90B3
Middletown, Pennsylvania USA	92A2
Midelt Mor	62B1
Mid Glamorgan, County Wales	9C4
Mid Indian Basin Indian O	70B4
Mid Indian Ridge Indian O	70B4
Midland Can	83C5
Midland, Michigan USA	90B2
Midland, Texas USA	86C3
Midongy Atsimo Madag	67D3
Mid Pacific Mts Pacific O	71G2
Midvale USA	96C2
Midway Is Pacific O	71H2
Midwest City USA	94A3
Midžor, Mt Yugos	20B2
Mielec Pol	25B2
Miercures-Ciuc Rom	20C1
Mieres Spain	16A1
Mifflintown USA	92A2
Mihara Japan	42A2
Mihara-yama, Mt Japan	41A2
Mijun Shuiku, Res China	38D1
Mikhaylovka USSR	31F4
Mikhaylovgrad Bulg	20B2
Mikhaylovsk USSR	27F3
Mikhaylovskiy USSR	31J4
Mikkeli Fin	4K6
Mikonos, I Greece	21C3
Mikulov Czech	25B3
Mikumi Tanz	65?
Mikuni-sammyaku, Mts Japan	40D3
Mikura-jima, I Japan	41B2
Milagro Ecuador	108B4
Milana Alg	17C2
Milano Italy	18B1
Milas Turk	58A1
Mildura Aust	73D4
Mile China	39A5
Mileh Tharthar, L Iraq	59D3

Miles *Aust*	73E3	Minqin *China*	38A2
Miles City *USA*	84C2	Min Shan, Upland *China*	38A3
Milford, Connecticut *USA*	92C2	Minsk *USSR*	26C3
Milford, Delaware *USA*	91C3	Minsk Mazowiecki *Pol*	48E2
Milford, Massachusetts *USA*		Minto *USA*	88E2
Milford, Nebraska *USA*	94A1	Minto, L *Can*	83C4
Milford, Pennsylvania *USA*	92B2	Min Xian *China*	38A3
Milford Haven *Wales*	9B4	Miquelon *Can*	83E5
Milford L *USA*	94A2	Miraj *India*	53A1
Milk River *Can* R	9E2	Miramar *Arg*	105E3
Millau *France*	15C3	Miram Shah *Pak*	50B2
Millbrook *USA*	92C2	Miranda de Ebro *Spain*	16B1
Milledgeville *USA*	93B1	Mirandola *Italy*	13D2
Miller, Mt *USA*	88F2	Mir Bachcheh Kut *Afghan*	50B2
Millerovo *USSR*	27F4	Miri *Malay*	44D1
Millersburg *USA*	92A2	Mirnoye *USSR*	29A1
Millers Creek *Aust*	74A1	Mirnyy, Base *Ant*	112C9
Millers Falls *USA*	92C1	Mirnyy *USSR*	29D1
Millerton *USA*	92C2	Mirpur *Pak*	50C2
Millerton L *USA*	98C2	Mirpur Khas *Pak*	51B3
Millicent *Aust*	74B3	Mirtoan S *Greece*	21B3
Millimerran *Aust*	75D1	Miryang *S Korea*	40B3
Mill Valley *USA*	98A2	Mirzapur *India*	52A1
Millville *USA*	91D3	Misantla *Mexico*	50C1
Milne Land, I *Greenland*	82H2	Misgar *Pak*	50C1
Mililolii *Hawaiian Is*	97C4	Mishawaka *USA*	90A2
Milos, I *Greece*	21B3	Misheguk Mt *USA*	88B1
Milparinka *Aust*	73D3	Mi-shima, I *Japan*	41A2
Milroy *USA*	92A2	Misima, I *Solomon Is*	73E2
Milton *NZ*	77A3	Misiones, State *Arg*	106F4
Milton, Pennsylvania *USA*	92A2	Miskolc *Hung*	25C3
Milwaukee *USA*	86B2	Mismiyah *Syria*	60C2
Mina' al Ahmadi *Kuwait*	57C4	Misool, I *Indon*	37E4
Minab *Iran*	57C4	Misratah *Libya*	61A1
Minas *Indon*	40C4	Mission City *Can*	91C2
Minas *Indon*	44A2	Mississippi, State *USA*	87A3
Minas *Urug*	105E2	Mississippi, R *USA*	87A3
Minas Gerais, State *Brazil*	107B5	Mississippi Delta *USA*	95C3
Minas Novas *Brazil*	111C1	Missoula *USA*	84B2
Minatitlan *Mexico*	101C3	Missour *Mor*	62A1
Minbu *Burma*	42A1	Missouri, State *USA*	87A3
Minbu *Burma*	42A1	Missouri, R *USA*	86A2
Mincha *USA*	110A2	Mistassini, L *Can*	86C1
Minchumina, L *USA*	88D2	Misti, Mt *Peru*	106B2
Mindanao, I *Phil*	45B4	Mitchell *Aust*	75C3
Minden *W Germ*	95B3	Mitchell *USA*	84D2
Minden, Louisiana *USA*	22B2	Mitchell, Mt *USA*	87B3
Mindona L *Aust*	74B3	Mitchelstown *Irish Rep*	11B2
Mindoro, I *Phil*	45B3	Mithankot *Pak*	50C3
Minehead *Eng*	9C4	Mitilini *Greece*	21C3
Mineiros *Brazil*	106F2	Mitla *Mexico*	99B2
Mineola *USA*	95A3	Mito *Japan*	40D3
Mineral de Monte *Mexico*	99B1	Mitú *Colombia*	108C3
Minersville *USA*	92A2	Mitumba, Mts *Zaire*	65C3
Mingary *Aust*	74B2	Mitwaba *Zaire*	64C3
Minhe *China*	38A2	Mitzic *Gabon*	64B2
Minicoy, I *India*	53A3	Miyake, I *Japan*	35F3
Minkler *USA*	98C2	Miyake-jima, I *Japan*	41B2
Minlaton *Aust*	74A2	Miyako, I *Japan*	35E4
Minle *China*	38A2	Miyakonojo *Japan*	40C4
Minna *Nig*	63C4	Miyazaki *Japan*	40C4
Minneapolis *USA*	86A2	Miyazu *Japan*	41B1
Minnedosa *Can*	21A	Miyoshi *Japan*	40C4
Minnesota, State *USA*	86A2		
Minot *USA*	84C2		

Miyun *China*	38D1
Mizan Teferi *Eth*	65D2
Mizdah *Libya*	61A1
Mizil *Rom*	20C1
Mizo Hills *India*	52C2
Mizoram, Union Territory *India*	52C2
Mizpe Ramon *Israel*	60B3
Mizuho, Base *Ant*	112B1
Mizusawa *Japan*	40D3
Mjolby *Sweden*	5H7
Mkushi *Zambia*	66B2
Mkuzi *S Africa*	67H1
Mladá Boleslav *Czech*	23C2
Mlawa *Pol*	48E2
Mljet, I *Yugos*	18C2
Mmabatho *S Africa*	66B3
Mnadi *India*	50D2
Moab, Region *Jordan*	60B3
Moab *USA*	85C3
Moanda *Congo*	64B3
Moanda *Gabon*	64B3
Moba *Zaire*	65C3
Mobara *Japan*	41C1
Mobaye *CAR*	64C2
Mobayi *Zaire*	64C2
Moberly *USA*	86A3
Mobile *USA*	87B3
Mobridge *USA*	84C2
Mocambique *Mozam*	67D2
Moc Chau *Viet*	42C1
Mochudi *Botswana*	66B3
Mocimboa da Praia *Mozam*	67D2
Mocoa *Colombia*	108B3
Mococa *Brazil*	111B2
Mocuba *Mozam*	67C2
Modane *France*	13B2
Modena *Italy*	18B2
Modesto *USA*	84A3
Modesto Res *USA*	98B2
Modica *Italy*	19B3
Mödling *Austria*	25B3
Moe *Aust*	73D4
Moffat *Scot*	8D4
Moga *India*	50D2
Mogi das Cruzes *Brazil*	111B2
Mogilev *USSR*	26C3
Mogilev Podolskiy *USSR*	26C4
Mogi-Mirim *Brazil*	111B2
Mogincual *Mozam*	67D2
Mogliano *Italy*	13E2
Mogna *Arg*	110B2
Mogocha *USSR*	34D1
Mogochin *USSR*	31K4
Moguer *Spain*	16A2
Mohanganj *Bang*	52C2
Mohoro *Tanz*	65D3
Mointy *USSR*	31J5
Moi i Rana *Nor*	4C2
Moissac *France*	14C3
Mojave *USA*	97B2
Mojave Desert *USA*	85B3
Mojokerto *Indon*	44C4
Mokama *India*	52B1
Mokelumne Aqueduct *USA*	98B1
Mokelumne Hill *USA*	98B1
Mokhotlong *Lesotho*	67G1

Moknine *Tunisia*	62D1
Mokokchung *India*	52C1
Mokolo *Cam*	64B1
Mokp'o *S Korea*	48B4
Molango *Mexico*	99B1
Moláoi *Greece*	21B3
Moldavskaya SSR, Republic *USSR*	26C4
Molde *Nor*	4F6
Moldoveanu, Mt *Rom*	20B1
Molepolole *Botswana*	66B3
Molfetta *Italy*	19C2
Molina *Chile*	110A3
Mollendo *Peru*	106B2
Molodechno *USSR*	26C4
Molodezhnaya, Base *Ant*	112C1
Molokai, I *Hawaiian Is*	97C4
Molong *Aust*	75C2
Moloundou *Cam*	64B2
Molson L *Can*	84D1
Molucca, S *Indon*	37D4
Moluccas, Is *Indon*	37D4
Moma *Mozam*	67C2
Mombaca *Brazil*	107C3
Mombasa *Kenya*	65D3
Mompono *Zaïre*	64C2
Mon, I *Den*	22C2
Monach, Is *Scot*	5A3
Monaco, Principality *Europe*	15D3
Monadhliath, Mts *Scot*	10B3
Monaghan, County *Irish Rep*	11C1
Monaghan *Irish Rep*	11C1
Mona Pass *Caribbean*	103D3
Monarch Mt *Can*	89B2
Monashee Mts *Can*	81G4
Monastereven *Irish Rep*	7B3
Moncalieri *Italy*	13B2
Monção *Brazil*	107B2
Monchegorsk *USSR*	4L5
Mönchen-gladbach *W Germ*	22B2
Monclova *Mexico*	100B2
Moncton *Can*	83D5
Moncton *Mexico*	85C4
Mondovi *Italy*	18A2
Moneague *Jamaica*	103H1
Monessen *USA*	90C2
Monett *USA*	91D3
Monfalcone *Italy*	18B1
Monforte de Lemos *Spain*	16A1
Monga *Zaïre*	64C2
Mongalla *Sudan*	65D2
Mong Cai *Viet*	42D1
Mongo *Chad*	64B3
Mongolia, Republic *Asia*	34B2
Mongu *Zambia*	66B2
Mönhhaan *Mongolia*	29D3
Monitor Range, Mts *USA*	97B2
Monkoto *Zaïre*	64C3
Monmouth *Eng*	9C4
Monmouth *USA*	94B1
Monmouth, Mt *Can*	89C2
Mono L *USA*	97B2
Monopoli *Italy*	19C2
Monreal del Campo *Spain*	17B1
Monroe, Louisiana *USA*	95B3
Monroe, Michigan *USA*	90B2

Monroe, Washington *USA*	96B1
Monroe City *USA*	94B2
Monrovia *Lib*	63A4
Mons *Belg*	96B3
Monselice *Italy*	13D2
Monson *USA*	92C1
Mönsterås *Sweden*	24B1
Montagne d'Ambre, Mt *Madag*	67D2
Montagnes des Ouled Nail, Mts *Alg*	62C1
Montague I *USA*	88E3
Montaigu *France*	14B2
Montalto, Mt *Italy*	19C3
Montana, State *USA*	84B2
Montañas de León, Mts *Spain*	16A1
Montargis *France*	15C2
Montauban *France*	14C3
Montauk *USA*	91D2
Montauk Pt *USA*	91D2
Montbéliard *France*	15D2
Mont Blanc, Mt *France/Italy*	18A1
Montceau les Mines *France*	14C2
Montceny, Mt *Spain*	17C1
Mont Cinto, Mt *Corse*	15D3
Montcornet *France*	12C2
Mont-de-Marsin *France*	14B3
Montdidier *France*	14C2
Monteagudo *Bol*	106D2
Monte Alegre *Brazil*	109G4
Monte Amiata, Mt *Italy*	18B2
Monte Baldo, Mt *Italy*	13D2
Montebello *Can*	91C1
Monte Bello Is *Aust*	72A3
Montebelluna *Italy*	13D2
Monte Carlo *France*	15D3
Monte Carmelo *Brazil*	111B1
Monte Caseros *Arg*	110D2
Monte Cimone, Mt *Italy*	18B2
Mont Cinto, Mt *Corse*	18B2
Monte Corno *Arg*	110B2
Monte Corno, Mt *Italy*	18B2
Montecristi *Dom Rep*	103C3
Montecristo, I *Italy*	18B2
Monte Escobedo *Mexico*	99A1
Monte Gargano, Mt *Italy*	19C2
Montego Bay *Jamaica*	102B3
Monte Grappa, Mt *Italy*	13D2
Monte Lesima, Mt *Italy*	13C2
Montélimar *France*	15C3
Monte Miletto, Mt *Italy*	19B2
Montemo-o-Novo *Port*	16A2
Montemorelos *Mexico*	100C2
Montená *Colombia*	102B5
Montenegro, Region *Yugos*	20A2
Monte Pascoal, Mt *Brazil*	111D1
Monte Patria *Chile*	110A2
Monte Pollino, Mt *Italy*	19C3
Montepuez *Mozam*	67C2
Monterey, California *USA*	84A3
Monterey, Virginia *USA*	91C3
Montería *Colombia*	106B2
Montero *Bol*	106D2
Monte Rosa, Mt *Italy/Switz*	13B2

Monterrey *Mexico*	100B2
Montes Claros *Brazil*	107C5
Montes de Toledo, Mts *Spain*	16B2
Montevideo *Urug*	105E2
Monte Viso, Mt *Italy*	18A2
Mont Gimie, Mt *St Lucia*	103P2
Montgomery, Alabama *USA*	87B3
Mont Gréboun *Niger*	62C2
Montherme *France*	12C2
Monthey *Switz*	13B1
Monticello, Arkansas *USA*	95B3
Monticello, New York *USA*	92B2
Monticello, Utah *USA*	85B3
Monti del Gennargentu, Mts *Sardegna*	19A2
Monti Lessini, Mts *Italy*	13D2
Monti Nebrodi, Mts *Italy*	19B3
Mont-Laurier *Can*	83C5
Montluçon *France*	14C2
Montmagny *France*	14C2
Montmédy *France*	12C2
Mont Mézenc, Mt *France*	15C2
Montmirail *France*	12B2
Montoro *Spain*	16B2
Mont Pelat, Mt *France*	15D3
Montpelier, Ohio *USA*	90B2
Montpelier, Vermont *USA*	86C2
Montpellier *France*	15C3
Montréal *Can*	83C5
Montreuil *France*	14C1
Montreux *Switz*	18A1
Mont Risoux, Mt *France*	13B1
Montrose, Colorado *USA*	84C3
Montrose *Scot*	6C2
Mont-St-Michel *France*	14B2
Monts des Ksour, Mts *Alg*	62B1
Monts des Ouled Nail, Mts *Alg*	17C3
Monts du Hodna, Mts *Alg*	17C2
Montserrat, I *Caribbean*	103E3
Monument Mt *USA*	88B1
Monveda *Zaïre*	64C2
Monywa *Burma*	42B1
Monza *Italy*	18A1
Monze *Zambia*	66B2
Mool River S *Africa*	67G1
Moomba *Aust*	74B1
Moonbi Range, Mts *Aust*	75D2
Moonda L *Aust*	74B1
Moonie *Aust*	75D1
Moonie R *Aust*	74A2
Moonta *Aust*	72A3
Moore, L *Aust*	72A3
Moorfoot Hills *Scot*	8C2
Moorhead *USA*	84D2
Moorpark *USA*	98C3
Moose Jaw *Can*	81H4
Moosomin *Can*	81H4
Moosonee *Can*	83B4
Moosup *USA*	92D2
Mopeia *Mozam*	67C3
Mopti *Mali*	63B3
Moquegua *Peru*	106B2
Mora *Sweden*	10B6
Morada *Brazil*	107D3

Moradabad *India* 50D3
Morada Nova de Minas, L *Brazil* 111B1
Morafenobe *Madag* 67D2
Moramanga *Madag* 67D2
Morant Bay *Jamaica* 103J2
Morant Pt *Jamaica* 103J2
Moratuwa *Sri Lanka* 53B3
Moraveh Tappeh *Iran* 56C2
Moray Firth, Estuary *Scot* 6C2
Morbegno *Italy* 13C1
Morden *Can* 51C4
Mor Dag, Mt *Turk* 59D2
Morden *Can* 81J5
Mordovskaya ASSR, Republic *USSR* 27F3
Morecambe *Eng* 6C2
Moree *Aust* 73D3
Morehead *USA* 90B3
Morel *Switz* 13C1
Morelia *Mexico* 100B3
Morena *India* 51D3
Moresby I *Can* 81E4
Moreton I *Aust* 75D1
Moreuil *France* 12B2
Morez *France* 13B1
Morgan City *USA* 95B4
Morgan Hill *USA* 98B2
Morgantown *USA* 90C3
Morgenzon *S Africa* 91E3
Morges *Switz* 13B1
Morhange *France* 12D2
Mori *Japan* 40E2
Moriatio *Tobago* 103K1
Morice L *Can* 89B2
Morinville *Can* 89E2
Morioka *Japan* 40E4
Morisset *Aust* 75D2
Morlaix *France* 14B2
Morne Diablotin, Mt *Dominica* 103Q2
Morningtion, I *Aust* 72C2
Moro *Pak* 51B3
Morocco, Kingdom *Africa* 62E1
Moro G *Phil* 45B4
Morogoro *Tanz* 65D3
Moroleon *Mexico* 99A1
Morombe *Madag* 67D3
Morón *Cuba* 102B2
Morondava *Madag* 67D3
Moron de la Frontera *Spain* 15A2
Moroni *Comoros* 67D2
Moroni, I *Indon* 37D3
Moroto *Uganda* 65D2
Morozovsk *USSR* 27F4
Morpeth *Eng* 8D2
Morrilton *USA* 95B2
Morrinhos *Brazil* 111B1
Morrinsville *NZ* 76C1
Morristown, New Jersey *USA* 92B2
Morristown, New York *USA* 91C2
Morrisville, Pennsylvania *USA* 92C2
Morro Bay *USA* 97A2
Morro de Papanoa *Mexico* 99A2

Morro de Petatlán *Mexico* 99A2
Morrumbala *Mozam* 67C2
Morrumbene *Mozam* 67C3
Morshansk *USSR* 27F3
Mortara *Italy* 13C2
Morteros *Arg* 110C2
Mortlake *Aust* 74B3
Moruga *Trinidad* 103L1
Moruya *Aust* 75D3
Morven *Aust* 75C1
Morwell *Aust* 75C3
Moscos Is *Burma* 42B3
Moscow, Idaho *USA* 96C1
Moselle, Department *France* 12D2
Moses Lake *USA* 96C1
Mosgiel *NZ* 77B3
Moshi *Tanz* 65D3
Mosjøen *Nor* 4G5
Moskal'vo *USSR* 29G2
Moskva *USSR* 30E4
Moss *Nor* 5G7
Mossaka *Congo* 64B3
Mossel Bay *S Africa* 66B4
Mossendjo *Congo* 64B3
Mossgiel *Aust* 74B2
Mossoró *Brazil* 107D3
Most *Czech* 23C2
Mostaganem *Alg* 62C1
Mostar *Yugos* 20A2
Mosty *USSR* 24C2
Mosul *Iraq* 59D2
Motala *Sweden* 5H7
Motherwell *Scot* 8C2
Motihari *India* 52A1
Motilla del Palancar *Spain* 17B2
Motril *Spain* 16B2
Motueka *NZ* 77B2
Moudon *Switz* 13B1
Mouila *Gabon* 64B3
Moulamein *Aust* 74B2
Mould Bay *Can* 80J2
Moulins *France* 15C2
Moulmein *Burma* 42B2
Moultrie *USA* 93B1
Moultrie, L *USA* 93C1
Mound City, Illinois *USA* 94C2
Mound City, Missouri *USA* 94A1
Moundou *Chad* 64B3
Moundsville *USA* 90C3
Mountain Grove *USA* 94B3
Mountain Home, Arkansas *USA* 94B2
Mountain View *USA* 98A2
Mountain Village *USA* 88B2
Mount Airy, Maryland *USA* 92A3
Mount Carmel *USA* 92A2
Mount Dutton *Aust* 74A1
Mount Eba *Aust* 74A2
Mount Gambier *Aust* 74B3
Mount Holly *USA* 92B3
Mount Holly Springs *USA* 92A2
Mount Hope *Aust* 72C3
Mount Isa *Aust* 72C3
Mount Lofty Range, Mts *Aust* 74A2

Mount McKinley Nat Pk *USA* 88D2
Mount Magnet *Aust* 72A3
Mount Manara *Aust* 74B2
Mount Morgan *Aust* 73E3
Mount Pleasant, Texas *USA* 95B3
Mount Rainier Nat Pk *USA* 96B1
Mount Shasta *USA* 96B2
Mount Vernon, Illinois *USA* 87B3
Mount Vernon, Kentucky *USA* 95A3
Mount Vernon, Washington *USA* 96B1
Mourne Mts *N Ire* 9C2
Moussoro *Chad* 64B1
Mouth of the Indus *Pak* 51B4
Mouths of the Ganga *India/Bang* 52B2
Mouths of the Mekong *Viet* 43D4
Mouths of the Niger *Nigeria* 64C3
Moutier *Switz* 13B1
Moûtiers *France* 13B2
Mouydir, Mts *Alg* 62C2
Mouyondzi *Congo* 64B3
Moville *France* 12C2
Moyahua *Mexico* 99A1
Moyale *Kenya* 65D2
Moyamba *Sierra Leone* 63A4
Moyen Atlas, Mts *Mor* 62B1
Moyeni *Lesotho* 66B4
Moyo *Uganda* 65D2
Moyobamba *Peru* 108B5
Moyu *China* 50D1
Mozambique, Republic *Africa* 67C3
Mozambique Chan *Mozam/Madag* 67C3
Mozhga *USSR* 27H2
Mozyr *USSR* 26C3
Mpanda *Tanz* 65D3
Mpika *Zambia* 67C2
Mporokoso *Zambia* 65D3
Mposhi *Zambia* 66B2
Mpulungu *Zambia* 65D3
Mpwapwa *Tanz* 65D3
Mtsensk *USSR* 26E3
Mtubatuba *S Africa* 67H1
Mtwara *Tanz* 65E3
Muang Chainat *Thai* 42C2
Muang Chiang Rai *Thai* 42C2
Muang Kalasin *Thai* 42C2
Muang Khon Kaen *Thai* 42C2
Muang Lampang *Thai* 42B2
Muang Lamphun *Thai* 42B2
Muang Loei *Thai* 42C2
Muang Lom Sak *Thai* 42C2
Muang Nakhon Phanom *Thai* 42C2
Muang Nakhon Sawan *Thai* 42B2
Muang Nan *Thai* 42C2
Muang Phayao *Thai* 42C2
Muang Phetchabun *Thai* 42C2
Muang Phichit *Thai* 42C2
Muang Phitsanulok *Thai* 42C2
Muang Phrae *Thai* 42C2
Muang Roi Et *Thai* 42C2
Muang Sakon Nakhon *Thai* 42C2

Muang Samut Prakan *Thai*	42C3	Munger *India*	52B1	Muskoka, L *Can*	91C2
Muang Uthai Thani *Thai*	42C2	Mungindi *Aust*	75C1	Musmar *Sudan*	61C3
Muang Yasothon *Thai*	42C2	Munising *USA*	90A1	Musoma *Tanz*	65D3
Muar *Malay*	43C5	Munster, Region *Irish Rep*	11B2	Mussende *Angola*	66A2
Muara *Brunei*	44C2	Münster *Switz*	13C1	Mussidan *France*	14C2
Muara *Indon*	36B4	Münster *W Germ*	22B2	Mustafa-Kemalpasa *Turk*	21C2
Muaralakitan *Indon*	44A3	Muntii Apuseni, Mts *Rom*	20B1	Mustang *Nepal*	52A1
Muaratebo *Indon*	44A3	Muntii Calimanilor, Mts		Muswellbrook *Aust*	75D2
Muaratewah *Indon*	44C3	*Rom*	20B1	Mut *Egypt*	61B2
Muarenim *Indon*	44A3	Muntii Carpatii Meridionali,		Mutarara *Mozam*	67C2
Muaungmaya *Burma*	42A2	Mts *Rom*	20B1	Mutare *Zim*	67C2
Mubende *Uganda*	65D2	Muntii Rodnei, Mts *Rom*	20B1	Mutoko *Zim*	67C2
Muchinga, Mts *Zambia*	66C2	Muntii Zarandului, Mts *Rom*	20B1	Mutsamudu *Comoros*	67D2
Muck, I *Scot*	10A3	Munzur Silsilesi, Mts *Turk*	59C2	Mutshatsha *Zaïre*	66B2
Muckadilla *Aust*	75C1	Muomio *Fin*	30D3	Mutsu *Japan*	40E2
Mucuri *Brazil*	111D1	Muong Khoua *Laos*	42C1	Mutton, I *Irish Rep*	11B2
Mucusso *Angola*	66B2	Muong Man *Viet*	42D3	Mu Us Shamo Desert, *China*	38B2
Mudanjiang *China*	35E2	Muong Nong *Laos*	42D2	Muxima *Angola*	64B3
Mudgee *Aust*	75C2	Muong Ou Neua *Laos*	42C1	Muya *USSR*	29D2
Mudon *Burma*	42B2	Muong Sai *Laos*	42C1	Muyezerskiy *USSR*	4L6
Muéda *Mozam*	67C2	Muong Sen *Viet*	42C2	Muyinga *Burundi*	65D3
Mueo *Nouvelle Calédonie*	73F3	Muong Sing *Laos*	42C1	Muyumba *Zaïre*	64C3
Mufulira *Zambia*	66B2	Muong Son *Laos*	42C1	Muyun Kum, Desert *USSR*	48A1
Mufu Shan, Hills *China*	39C4	Muonio *Fin*	4J5	Muzaffarabad *Pak*	50C2
Mugadzhary, Mts *USSR*	27J4	Muqdisho *Somalia*	65E2	Muzaffargarh *Pak*	50C2
Mughayra *S Arabia*	59C4	Murakami *Japan*	40D3	Muzaffarpur *India*	52B1
Mugla *Turk*	58A2	Murallón, Mt *Chile/Arg*	109B5	Muzhi *USSR*	30H5
Mugodzhary, Mts *USSR*	31G5	Murashi *USSR*	27G2	Muztag, Mt *China*	48C2
Muguaping *China*	39A3	Muravera *Sardegna*	19A3	Muztagata, Mt *China*	48B2
Muhaywir *Iraq*	59D3	Murayama *Japan*	41C1	Mvuma *Zim*	66C2
Mühldorf *W Germ*	23C3	Murcheh Khvort *Iran*	56B3	Mwanza *Tanz*	65D3
Mühlhausen *E Germ*	22C2	Murchison *NZ*	77B2	Mwanza *Zaïre*	64C3
Muhos *Fin*	4K6	Murcia, Region *Spain*	17B2	Mweka *Zaïre*	64C3
Muine Bheag *Irish Rep*	11C2	Murcia *Spain*	17B2	Mwene Ditu *Zaïre*	64C3
Mujimbeji *Zambia*	66B2	Murgha Kibzai *Pak*	50B2	Mwenezi *Zim*	66C3
Mukacchevo *USSR*	25C3	Murgon *Aust*	75D1	Mwenga *Zaïre*	65C3
Mukah *Malay*	44C2	Muri *India*	52B2	Mweru, L *Zambia*	65C3
Muko-jima, I *Japan*	35G4	Muriaé *Brazil*	111C2	Mwinilunga *Zambia*	66B2
Muktinath *Nepal*	52A1	Muriege *Angola*	64C3	Myanaung *Burma*	49D4
Mukur *Afghan*	50B2	Murmansk *USSR*	30E3	Myanaung *Burma*	52D2
Mulberry *USA*	94B2	Murom *USSR*	27F2	Myingyan *Burma*	42B1
Mulchén *Chile*	110A3	Muroran *Japan*	40E2	Myingyao *Burma*	42B1
Mulgrave I *Aust*	37F5	Muros *Spain*	16A1	Myinmoletkat, Mt *Burma*	42B3
Mulhacén, Mt *Spain*	16B2	Muroto *Japan*	40C4	Myitkyina *Burma*	48D3
Mülheim *W Germ*	12D1	Murphy, Idaho *USA*	96C2	Myitta *Burma*	42B3
Mulhouse *France*	15D2	Murphys *USA*	98B1	Mymensingh *Bang*	52D2
Muli *China*	39A4	Murray, Kentucky *USA*	94C2	Myojin, I *Japan*	35F3
Mull, I *Scot*	10B3	Murray, R *Aust*	74B2	Myrdal *Nor*	5F6
Mullaitivu *Sri Lanka*	53D3	Murray Bridge *Aust*	74A3	Myrdalsjökur, Mts *Iceland*	4B2
Mullaley *Aust*	75C2	Murray, L *PNG*	37F4	Myrtle Beach *USA*	93C1
Mullewa *Aust*	72A3	Murray, L *USA*	93B1	Myrtle Creek *USA*	96B2
Mullingar *Irish Rep*	11C2	Murray Seacarp *Pacific O*	71J2	Mysen *Nor*	5G7
Mull of Kintyre, Pt *Scot*	8B2	Murrumburrah *Aust*	75C2	Mysiloborz *Pol*	22C2
Mullumbimby *Aust*	75D1	Murrumidi *Aust*	75D2	Myslenice *Pol*	25B3
Mulobezi *Zambia*	66B2	Murten *Switz*	13B1	Mysore *India*	53B2
Multan *Pak*	50C2	Murtoa *Aust*	74B3	Mystic *USA*	92D2
Mumbwa *Zambia*	66B2	Murupara *NZ*	76C1	Mys Tyub-Karagan, Pt	
Mumra *USSR*	27G4	Murwara *India*	52A2	*USSR*	27H5
Muna, I *Indon*	35F7	Murwillimbah *Aust*	75D1	Myrtle Point *USA*	96B2
München *W Germ*	23C3	Mus *Turk*	59D2	Mzimba *Malawi*	67C2
Muncie *USA*	90A2	Musala, Mt *Bulg*	20B2	Mzuzú *Malawi*	67C2
Muncy *USA*	91C2	Musan *N Korea*	40B2		
Münden *W Germ*	22B2	Muscat, Region *Oman*	57C5		
Mundubbera *Aust*	75D1	Musgrave Range, Mts *Aust*	72C3	**N**	
Mungallala *Aust*	75C1	Mushie *Zaïre*	64B3		
Mungbere *Zaïre*	65C2	Muskegon *USA*	90A2	Naalehu *Hawaiian Is*	97C4
Mungeli *India*	52A2	Muskogee *USA*	94A2	Naantali *Fin*	5J6
				Naas *Irish Rep*	11C2

Nabari Japan 41B2
Nabeul Tunisia 62D1
Nablus Israel 60B2
Nacala Mozam 67D2
Naches USA 96B1
Nachingwea Tanz 67C2
Nacogdoches USA 95B3
Nacondam, I Indian O 42A3
Nacozari Mexico 100B1
Nadiad India 51C4
Nador Mor 16B2
Nadushan Iran 56B3
Nadvornaya USSR 25C3
Naestved Den 22C1
Nafoora Libya 61B2
Nagahama Japan 41A2
Naga Hills Burma 48D3
Nagai Japan 41B1
Nagaland, State India 52C1
Nagano Japan 40D3
Nagaoka Japan 40D3
Nagappattinam India 53B2
Nagar Parbat Pak 51C4
Nagasaki Japan 40B4
Nagashima Japan 41B2
Nagato Japan 41A2
Nagaur India 51C3
Nagercoil India 53B3
Nagha Kalat Pak 51B3
Nagina India 50D3
Nagoya Japan 40D3
Nagpur India 51D4
Nagqu China 48D2
Nagykanizsa Hung 25B3
Nagykörös Hung 25B3
Naha Japan 35E4
Nahaimo Can 84A2
Nahan India 50D2
Nahanni Butte Can 80F3
Nahariya Israel 60B2
Nahavand Iran 56A3
Nahpu China 38D2
Naimen Qi China 38E1
Nain Can 83D4
Na'in Iran 56B3
Naini Tai India 50D3
Nairn Scot 10C3
Nairobi Kenya 65D3
Najafabad Iran 56B3
Najin N Korea 40C2
Nakama Japan 41A2
Nakaminato Japan 40E3
Nakamura Japan 41A2
Nakano Japan 41B1
Nakano-shima, I Japan 41A1
Nakatsu Japan 40C4
Nakatsu-gawa Japan 41B1
Nakfa Eth 61C3
Nakhichevan USSR 56E2
Nakhl Egypt 58B4
Nakhodka USSR 40C2
Nakhon Pathom Thai 42C3
Nakhon Ratchasima Thai 42C3
Nakhon Si Thammarat Thai 43C4
Nakina Can 83B4
Nakina, Ontario Can 83B4
Naknek USA 88C3

Naknek L USA 88C3
Nakrek USA 80C4
Nakskov Den 5G8
Nakuru Kenya 65D3
Nakusp Can 89D2
Nal'chik USSR 27F5
Nalgonda India 53B1
Nallamala Range, Mts India 53B1
Nalut Libya 61A1
Namaacha Mozam 67H1
Namak, L Iran 31G6
Namakzar-e Shadad, Salt Flat Iran 56C3
Namangan USSR 31J5
Namapa Mozam 67C2
Namaqualand, Region S Africa 66A4
Nambour Aust 75D1
Nambucca Heads Aust 75D2
Nam Can Viet 43D4
Namcha Barwa, Mt China 48D3
Nam Co, L China 48D2
Nam Dinh Viet 42D1
Nametil Mozam 67C2
Namhae-do, I S Korea 40G6
Namib Desert Namibia 66A2
Namibe Angola 66A2
Namibia, Dependency Africa 66A3
Namlea Indon 37D4
Nampa Can 89D1
Nampa USA 96C2
Nampala Mali 63B3
Nam Phong Thai 42C3
Namp'o N Korea 40B3
Nampula Mozam 67C2
Namson Nor 4G6
Namton Burma 42B1
Namtu Burma 52D2
Namu Can 12C1
Namuno Mozam 67C2
Namur Belg 12C1
Namutoni Namibia 66A2
Namwon S Korea 40B3
Nanaimo Can 89C3
Nanam N Korea 40B2
Nanango Aust 75D1
Nanatsu-jima, I Japan 41B1
Nanbu China 39A4
Nanchang China 39D4
Nanchong China 39B3
Nancy France 15D2
Nanded India 53B1
Nandewar Range, Mts Aust 75D2
Nandurbar India 51C4
Nandyal India 53B1
Nanga Eboko Cam 66A3
Nangapinoh Indon 44C3
Nangatayap Indon 44C3
Nangnim Sanmaek, Mts N Korea 40B2
Nang Xian China 52C1
Nangzhou China 33F3
Nangunguri India 53B2
Nanjing China 38D3

Nankoku Japan 41A2
Nan Ling, Region China 39C4
Nanning China 39B5
Nanortalik Greenland 82F3
Nanpara India 52A1
Nanping China 39D4
Nansio Tanz 65D3
Nantes France 14B2
Nanton Can 89C2
Nantong China 38E3
Nantucket, I USA 86C2
Nanuque Brazil 111C1
Nanyang China 38C3
Nanyang Hu, L China 38D2
Nanyuki Kenya 65D2
Naoetsu Japan 40D3
Naokot Pak 51B4
Napa USA 98A1
Napaiskak USA 88B2
Napanee Can 91C2
Napas USSR 31K4
Napassoq Greenland 82E3
Nape Laos 42D2
Napier NZ 76C1
Naples, Florida USA 91B4
Naples, Texas USA 95B3
Napo China 39B5
Napoli Italy 16C2
Naqadeh Iran 56A2
Naqb Ishtar Jordan 58C4
Nara Japan 41B2
Nara Mali 63B3
Naracoorte Aust 73D4
Naranjos Mexico 99B1
Narasaraopet India 53C1
Narathiwat Thai 43C4
Narayanganj Bang 52C2
Narayenpet India 53B1
Narbonne France 15C3
Narendranagar India 50D2
Narita Japan 41C1
Narnaul India 50D2
Naro Fominsk USSR 26E2
Narok Kenya 65D3
Narowal Pak 50C2
Narrabri Aust 73D4
Narran, L Aust 75C2
Narrandera Aust 75C3
Narrogin Aust 72A4
Narromine Aust 75C2
Narsimhapur India 51D4
Narsipatnam India 53C1
Narssalik Greenland 82F3
Narssaq Greenland 82F3
Narssarssuaq Greenland 82F3
Narugo Japan 41C1
Naruto Japan 41A2
Narva USSR 26C2
Narvik Nor 4H5
Narvik Nor 50D3
Narwana India 50D3
Nar'yan Mar USSR 30G3
Narylico Aust 74B1
Naryn USSR 31J5
Nasarawa Nig 63C4
Nasca Ridge Pacific O 69D5
Nashua USA 92D5
Nashville, Arkansas USA 95B3

Nashville, Tennessee *USA*	87B3	
Nasice *Yugos*	20A1	
Nasik *India*	51D4	
Nasir *Sudan*	65D2	
Nassau *Bahamas*	102B1	
Nassau *USA*	92C1	
Nasser, L *Egypt*	61C2	
Nässjö *Sweden*	5G7	
Nastapoka Is *Can*	83C4	
Nata *Botswana*	66B3	
Natal *Brazil*	107D3	
Natal *Indon*	36A3	
Natal, Province *S Africa*	67H1	
Natanz *Iran*	56B3	
Natashquan *Can*	83D4	
Natchez *USA*	95B3	
Natchitoches *USA*	95B3	
Nathalia *Aust*	74C3	
Nathorsts Land, Region *Greenland*	82H2	
National City *USA*	97B3	
Natori *Japan*	41C1	
Natoval'a *USSR*	24D2	
Natron, L *Tanz*	65D3	
Nauders *Austria*	13D1	
Nauen *E Germ*	22C2	
Naugatuck *USA*	92C2	
Naumburg *E Germ*	23C2	
Naur *Jordan*	60B3	
Nauru, I *Pacific O*	71G4	
Naushki *USSR*	29C2	
Nautla *Mexico*	99B1	
Navajo Res *USA*	85C3	
Navalmoral de la Mata *Spain*	16A2	
Navarino, I *Chile*	105C7	
Navarra, Province *Spain*	17B1	
Navasota *USA*	110D3	
Navasota *USA*	95A3	
Navidad *Chile*	110A2	
Navlakhi *India*	51C4	
Navlya *USSR*	26D3	
Navojoa *Mexico*	100B2	
Návpaktos *Greece*	21B3	
Návplion *Greece*	21B3	
Navsari *India*	51C4	
Nawá *Syria*	60C2	
Nawada *India*	52B1	
Nawah *Afghan*	50B2	
Nawrabshah *Pak*	51B3	
Naxi *China*	39B4	
Náxos, I *Greece*	21C3	
Nayar *Mexico*	99A1	
Nay Band *Iran*	56C3	
Nay Band *Iran*	57B4	
Nayoro *Japan*	40E2	
Nazareth *Israel*	60B2	
Nazay *France*	14B2	
Nazca *Peru*	108C6	
Nazilli *Turk*	58A2	
Nazimovo *USSR*	29B2	
Nazwa *Oman*	57C5	
Nazyvayevsk *USSR*	31J4	
Ndalatando *Angola*	64B3	
Ndélé *CAR*	64C2	
Ndendé *Gabon*	64B3	
N'Djamena *Chad*	64B1	
Ndjolé *Gabon*	64B3	
Ndola *Zambia*	66B2	
Neabul *Aust*	75C1	
Neápolis *Greece*	21B3	
Neath *Wales*	9C4	
Nebit Dag *USSR*	31G6	
Nebraska, State *USA*	84C2	
Nebraska City *USA*	94A1	
Necochea *Arg*	110D3	
Nédong *China*	52C1	
Needles *USA*	85B3	
Neenah *USA*	90A2	
Neepawa *Can*	81J4	
Neerpelt *Belg*	12C1	
Neftelensk *USSR*	29C2	
Negele *Eth*	65D2	
Negev, Desert *Israel*	60B3	
Negolu, Mt *Rom*	26B4	
Negombo *Sri Lanka*	53B3	
Negritos *Peru*	106B4	
Negros, I *Phil*	45B4	
Negru Voda *Rom*	20C2	
Nehbandan *Iran*	56D3	
Neijiang *China*	39B4	
Nei Monggol, Autononous Region *China*	38B1	
Neiva *Colombia*	108B3	
Nejo *Eth*	65D2	
Nelidovo *USSR*	26D2	
Nellore *India*	53B2	
Nel'ma *USSR*	35F2	
Nelson *Can*	89B3	
Nelson *NZ*	77B2	
Nelson, R *Can*	83A4	
Nelson I *USA*	88B2	
Néma *Maur*	63B3	
Nemagt Uul, Mt *Mongolia*	38A2	
Nemira, Mt *Rom*	20C1	
Nemuro *Japan*	40F2	
Nenagh *Irish Rep*	7B3	
Nenana *USA*	88E2	
Nenjiang *China*	35E2	
Neodesha *USA*	94A2	
Neosho *USA*	94B2	
Nepa *USSR*	29C2	
Nepal, Kingdom *Asia*	48C3	
Nepalganj *Nepal*	52A1	
Nephin, Mt *Irish Rep*	7B3	
Nequén, State *Arg*	110A3	
Nerchinsk *USSR*	34D1	
Nero Deep *Pacific O*	37F2	
Neskaupstaethur *Iceland*	4C1	
Nesle *France*	12B2	
Nesleyville *Can*	83E5	
Netanya *Israel*	60B2	
Netcong *USA*	92B2	
Netherlands, Kingdom *Europe*	22B2	
Netherlands Antilles, Is *Caribbean*	79M7	
Netrakona *Bang*	52C2	
Nettilling L *Can*	82C3	
Neubrandenburg *E Germ*	22C2	
Neuchâtel *Switz*	13B1	
Neufchâteau *Belg*	13C2	
Neuchâtel *France*	14C2	
Neufchâtel-en-Bray *France*	12A2	
Neumünster *W Germ*	22B2	
Neunkirchen *Austria*	18C1	
Neunkirchen *W Germ*	12D2	
Neuquén *Arg*	110B3	
Neuquén, State *Arg*	105B4	
Neuruppin *E Germ*	22C2	
Neuss *W Germ*	12D1	
Neustadt *W Germ*	12E2	
Neustadt *W Germ*	12E2	
Neustrelitz *E Germ*	22C2	
Neuwied *W Germ*	12D1	
Nevada, State *USA*	84B3	
Nevada *USA*	94B2	
Nevada de Chillán, Mts *Chile*	110A3	
Nevada de Colima *Mexico*	99A2	
Nevada de Toluca, Mt *Mexico*	99B2	
Nevatim *Israel*	60B3	
Nevel *USSR*	26C2	
Nevers *France*	15C2	
Nevertire *Aust*	75C2	
Nevis, I *Caribbean*	103E3	
Nevsehir *Turk*	58B2	
Nev'yansk *USSR*	27K2	
Newala *Tanz*	67C2	
New Albany, Indiana *USA*	91B3	
New Albany, Mississippi *USA*	95C3	
New Amsterdam *Guyana*	109F2	
New Angledool *Aust*	75C1	
Newark, Delaware *USA*	91C3	
Newark, New Jersey *USA*	92B2	
Newark, Ohio *USA*	90B2	
Newark-upon-Trent *Eng*	9D3	
New Bedford *USA*	91D2	
New Bella Bella *Can*	89B2	
Newberg *USA*	96B1	
New Bern *USA*	87C3	
Newberry *USA*	93B1	
New Bight *Bahamas*	102B2	
New Boston *USA*	90B3	
New Braunfels *USA*	85D4	
New Britain *USA*	92C2	
New Brunswick *USA*	92B2	
New Brunswick, Province *Can*	83D5	
New Burgh *USA*	92B2	
Newburgh *Eng*	9D4	
Newbury *Eng*	9D4	
Newburyport *USA*	92C1	
New Canaan *USA*	92C2	
Newcastle *Aust*	75D2	
New Castle, Indiana *USA*	90A3	
Newcastle *N Ire*	8B2	
New Castle, Pennsylvania *USA*	90B2	
Newcastle *S Africa*	67G1	
Newcastle, Wyoming *USA*	84C2	
Newcastle upon Tyne *Eng*	8D2	
Newcastle Waters *Aust*	72C2	
Newcastle West *Irish Rep*	11B2	
New Delhi *India*	50D3	
New England Range, Mts *Aust*	75D2	
New Forest, The *Eng*	9D4	
Newfoundland, Province *Can*	83D4	

Newfoundland, I Can	83E5
Newfoundland Basin Atlantic O	68F2
New Franklin USA	94B2
New Galloway Scot	8B2
New Georgia, I Solomon Is	73E1
New Glasgow Can	83D5
New Guinea SE Asia	37F4
New Hampshire, State USA	88D3
Newhall USA	98C3
New Hanover S Africa	67H1
Newhaven Eng	9E4
New Haven USA	91D2
New Hazelton Can	89B1
New Iberia USA	95B3
New Jersey, State USA	86C2
New Liskeard Can	83C5
New London USA	92C2
Newman USA	72A3
Newman USA	98B2
Newmarket Eng	9E3
Newmarket Irish Rep	11B2
New Market USA	91C3
New Mexico, State USA	85C3
New Milford, Connecticut USA	92C2
Newnan USA	93B1
New Norfolk Aust	75C4
New Orleans USA	87A3
New Paltz USA	92B2
New Philadelphia USA	90B2
Newport Eng	9D4
Newport, Arkansas USA	94B2
Newport, Kentucky USA	90B3
Newport, Oregon USA	96B2
Newport, Pennsylvania USA	92A2
Newport, Rhode Island USA	91D2
Newport, Vermont USA	91D2
Newport Wales	9C4
Newport, Washington USA	96C1
Newport Beach USA	98D4
Newport News USA	87D3
New Providence, I Caribbean	102B1
Newquay Eng	9B4
New Quebec Crater Can	82C3
New Ross Irish Rep	11C2
Newry N Ire	11C1
New Smyrna Beach USA	93B2
New South Wales, State Aust	73D4
Newton Stuyahok USA	88C3
Newton, Kansas USA	94A2
Newton, Massachusetts USA	92D1
Newton, Mississippi USA	95C3
Newton, New York USA	92B2
Newton Abbot Eng	9C4
Newton Stewart Scot	8B2
Newton Stewart N Ire	11C1
Newtown Wales	9C3
Newtownards N Ire	8B2
Newville USA	92A2
New Westminster Can	81F5
New York, State USA	86C2
New York USA	86C2
New Zealand, Dominion SW Pacific O	76
New Zealand Plat Pacific O	71G6
Neya USSR	27F2
Neyriz Iran	58F3
Neyshabur Iran	56C2
Nezeto Angola	64B3
Nezhin USSR	26D3
Ngabé Congo	64B3
Ngami, L Botswana	66B3
Ngauruhoe, Mt NZ	76C1
Ngo Congo	64B3
Ngoc Linh, Mt Viet	44D2
Ngoring Hu, L China	34B3
Ngorongoro Crater Tanz	65D3
Nguigmi Niger	64A2
Ngulu, I Pacific O	37E3
Nguru Nig	63D3
Nha Trang Viet	44D3
Nhill Aust	74B3
Nhlangano Swaziland	67J2
Nhommarath Laos	42D2
Nhulunbuy Aust	72C1
Niafounké Mali	63B3
Niagara USA	90A1
Niagara Falls Can	91C2
Niagara Falls USA	91C2
Niah Malay	56B3
Niakaramandougou Ivory Coast	63B4
Niamey Niger	63C3
Niangara Zaire	65C2
Nia Nia Zaire	64C2
Nias, I Indon	36A3
Nicastro Italy	21B2
Nice France	15D3
Nicholl's Town Bahamas	102B1
Nicobar Is Indian O	49D5
Nicosia Cyprus	58B2
Nidzica Pol	24D2
Niederbronn France	12D2
Niedersachsen, State W Germ	24B2
Niemba Zaire	65C3
Nienburg W Germ	24B2
Nieset, Mt Lib	63B4
Nieuw Amsterdam Surinam	109F2
Nieuw Nickerie Surinam	109F2
Nieuwpoort Belg	12B1
Nigde Turk	58B2
Niger, Republic Africa	63C3
Niger, R Nig	63C3
Nigeria, Federal Republic Africa	63C4
Nigrita Greece	21B2
Nihommatsu Japan	41C1
Niigata Japan	40D4
Niihama Japan	40C4
Nii-jima, I Japan	41B2
Niimi Japan	41A2
Niitsu Japan	40D3
Nijil Jordan	58C3
Nijmegen Neth	22B2
Nikel' USSR	30E3
Nikki Benin	63C3
Nikko Japan	40D3
Nikolayev USSR	26D4
Nikolayevsk USSR	27G4
Nikolayevsk-na-Amure USSR	29G2
Nikol'sk, RSFSR USSR	27G2
Nikopol USSR	26D4
Niksar Turk	58C1
Nikshahr Iran	57D4
Niksic Yugos	20A2
Nila, I Indon	37D4
Nile R N E Africa	46B3
Niles USA	90A2
Nilgiri Hills India	53B2
Nimach India	51C4
Nimbe Cam	64A2
Nîmes France	15C3
Nimmitabel Aust	75C3
Nimule Sudan	65D2
Nine Degree Chan Indian O	49B5
Ninety Mile Beach Aust	75C4
Ninetyeast Ridge Indian O	70C4
Ninety Mile Beach Aust	75C3
Ningde China	39D4
Ningdu China	39D4
Ningjing Shan, Mts China	34B3
Ningming China	42D1
Ningnan China	39A4
Ningxia, Province China	38B2
Ningxia China	38B2
Ning Xian China	38B2
Ninh Binh Vietnam	39B5
Ninigo Is PNG	73D1
Ninilchik USA	88D2
Nioki Zaire	64B3
Nioro du Sahel Mali	63B3
Niort France	14B2
Nipawin Can	81H4
Nipigon Can	83B5
Nipigon, L Can	83B5
Nipissing, L Can	90B1
Nirmal India	53B1
Nirmali India	53C2
Nis Yugos	21E2
Nisab S Yemen	47C4
Nishino-shima, I Japan	35F4
Nishino-shima, I Japan	41A1
Nishiwaki Japan	41A2
Nitchequon Can	83C4
Niterói Brazil	107C6
Nitra Czech	25B3
Nitro USA	90B3
Niut, Mt Malay	44C2
Nivelles Belg	12C1
Nivernais, Region France	15C2
Nizamabad India	53B1
Nizana, Hist Site Israel	60B3
Nizhniye Sergi USSR	27J2
Nizhniy Lomov USSR	27H4
Nizhniy Tagil USSR	31G4
Nizip Turk	59C2
Nizmennost USSR	26D4
Njombe Tanz	65D3
Nkambé Cam	64B2
Nkhata Bay Malawi	67C2
Nkongsamba Cam	64B2
N'Konni Niger	63C3

Noakhali *Bang*	52C2	North Battleford *Can*	89F2	Notikeulin *Can*	81G4
Noatak *USA*	88B1	North Bay *Can*	83C5	Noto *USA*	19C3
Nobeoka *Japan*	40C4	North Bend *USA*	96B2	Notodden *Nor*	5F7
Nochistlán *Mexico*	99A1	North Berwick *Scot*	10C3	Nottingham, County *Eng*	9D3
Nochistlán *Mexico*	99A1	North Carolina, State *USA*	87B3	Nottingham *Eng*	9D3
Nocona *USA*	95A3	North Cascade Nat Pk *USA*	96B1	Nottingham, I *Can*	82C3
Nogales, Sonora *Mexico*	100A1	North Chan *Can*	90B1	Nottingham Island *Can*	82C3
Nogales *USA*	85B3	North Chan *Ire/Scot*	8B2	Nouadhibou *Maur*	62A2
Nogales, Veracruz *Mexico*	99B2	North Dakota, State *USA*	84C2	Nouakchott *Maur*	63A3
Nogata *Japan*	41A2	North East *USA*	90C2	Nouméa *Nouvelle Calédonie*	73F3
Noginsk *USSR*	26E2	North East Atlantic Basin		Nouma *Burkina*	63B3
Nogoyá *Arg*	110D2	*Atlantic O*	68H2	Nouveau Comptoir *Can*	83C4
Nohar *India*	50C3	Northern Ireland *UK*	6B3	Nouvelle Anvers *Zaïre*	64B2
Nola *CAR*	64B2	Northern Range, Mts		Nouvelle Calédonie, I *S W*	
Nomans Land, I *USA*	92D2	*Trinidad*	103L1	*Pacific O*	73F3
Nome *USA*	88A2	Northern Territory *Aust*	72C2	Nova Caipemba *Angola*	64B3
Nomeny *France*	12D2	Northfield, Massachusetts		Nova Chaves *Angola*	66B2
Nomgon *Mongolia*	38B1	*USA*	92C1	Nova Esparança *Brazil*	111A2
Nonachol I, *Can*	81H3	North I *NZ*	76B1	Nova Friburgo *Brazil*	111C2
Nong Khai *Thai*	42C2	North Korea, Republic		Nova Gaia *Angola*	66A2
Nongoma *S Africa*	67H1	*S E Asia*	40B3	Nova Granada *Brazil*	111B2
Noorvik *USA*	88B1	North Little Rock *USA*	95B3	Nova Horizonte *Brazil*	111B2
Noqui *Angola*	64B3	North Magnetic Pole *Can*	1B4	Nova Lima *Brazil*	111C2
Noranda *Can*	83C5	North Miami *USA*	93B2	Nova Londrina *Brazil*	111A2
Nord, Department *France*	12B1	North Miami Beach *USA*	93B2	Nova Mambone *Mozam*	67C3
Nordaustlandet, I *Barents S*	32D1	North Platte *USA*	84C2	Novara *Italy*	13C2
Nordegg *Can*	89D2	North Pt *Barbados*	103R3	Nova Scotia, Province *Can*	83D5
Nordfjord, Inlet *Nor*	4F6	North Pt *USA*	90B1	Novato *USA*	98A1
Nordfriesiche, Is *W Germ*	5F8	North Rona, I *Scot*	6B2	Nova Venécia *Brazil*	111C1
Nordhausen *E Germ*	22C2	North Ronaldsay, I *Scot*	10C2	Nova Kakhovka *USSR*	26D4
Nordrhein Westfalen, State		North Sea *N W Europe*	6D2	Novaya Zemlya, I *Barents S*	30G2
W Germ	22B2	North Slope, Region *USA*	80D3	Novaya Russas *Brazil*	107C2
Nordre Greenland	82E3	North Stradbroke, I *Aust*	75D1	Nové Zámky *Czech*	20A1
Nord Strongfjället, Mt *Sweden*	4H5	North Truchas Peak, Mt *USA*	85C3	Novgorod *USSR*	26D2
Nordvik *USSR*	1B9	North Uist, I *Scot*	10A3	Novi *USA*	13C2
Norfolk, County *Eng*	9E3	Northumberland, County		Novi Ligure *Italy*	13C2
Norfolk, Nebraska *USA*	84D2	*Eng*	8C2	Novi Pazar *Bulg*	20C2
Norfolk, Virginia *USA*	87C3	Northumberland Is *Aust*	73E3	Novi Pazar *Yugos*	20B2
Norfolk I *Aust*	73F3	North Vancouver *Can*	96B1	Novi Sad *Yugos*	20A1
Norfolk L *USA*	87D1	North Walsham *Eng*	9E3	Novoalekseyevka *USSR*	27J3
Norfolk Ridge *Pacific O*	71G5	Northway *USA*	88F2	Novoanninskiy *USSR*	27F3
Noril'sk *USSR*	1C0	North West Frontier,		Novocherkassk *USSR*	27F4
Normal *USA*	94C1	Province *Pak*	50C2	Novograd Volynskiy *USSR*	26C3
Norman *USA*	95A2	North West River *Can*	83D4	Novogrudok *USSR*	24D2
Normandie, Region *France*	14B2	North West Territories *Can*	80F3	Novo Hamburgo *Brazil*	106F4
Normanton *Aust*	73D2	North York Moors Nat		Novokazalinsk *USSR*	31H5
Norman Wells *Can*	88F1	*Pk*	8D2	Novokuznetsk *USSR*	31K4
Norne *USA*	80B3	Norwalk, Connecticut *USA*	92C2	Novolazarevskaya, Base	
Norristown *USA*	91C2	Norwalk, Ohio *USA*	90B2	*Ant*	112B2
Norrköping *Sweden*	5H7	Norway, Kingdom *Europe*	5F6	Novo Mesto *Yugos*	18C1
Norrsundet *Sweden*	5H6	Norway House *Can*	81J4	Novomoskovsk *USSR*	26E2
Norrtälje *Sweden*	5H7	Norwegian Basin		Novorossiysk *USSR*	26E5
Norseman *Aust*	72B4	*Norwegian S*	68H1	Novosibirsk *USSR*	31K4
Norsk *USSR*	29F2	Norwegian S *N W Europe*	30A3	Novosibirskye Ostrova, I	
North, S N W Europe	68J2	Norwich *Eng*	9E3	*USSR*	1B8
Northallerton *Eng*	8D2	Norwich, Connecticut *USA*	92C2	Novotroitsk *USSR*	27J3
Northam *Aust*	72A4	Norwood, Massachusetts		Novo Uzensk *USSR*	27G3
North American Basin		*USA*	92D1	Novovolynsk *USSR*	25C2
Atlantic O	68E3	Norwood, Ohio *USA*	90B3	Novo Vyatsk *USSR*	27G2
Northampton *Aust*	72A3	Noshiro *Japan*	40D2	Novozybkov *USSR*	26D4
Northampton, County *Eng*	9D3	Noss, I *Scot*	10D1	Novyy Port *USSR*	30J3
Northampton *Eng*	9D3	Nostrabad *Iran*	57D4	Novyy Dwór Mazowiecki *Pol*	24C2
Northampton *USA*	91D2	Nosy Barren, I *Madag*	67D2	Novyy Port *USSR*	30J3
North Augusta *USA*	93B1	Nosy Bé, I *Madag*	67D2	Novyy Uzem *USSR*	27H5
North Aulatsivik, I *Can*	82D4	Nosy Boraha, I *Madag*	67E2	Nowa Sól *Pol*	18C2
		Nosy Varika *Madag*	67D3	Nowata *USA*	94A2

Nowgong *India*	52C1
Nowra *Aust*	75D2
Now Shahr *Iran*	56B2
Nowshera *Pak*	50C2
Nowy Sacz *Pol*	25C3
Noyes I *USA*	88H3
Noyon *France*	12B2
Nsawam *Ghana*	63B4
Nuba, Mts *Sudan*	65D1
Nubian Desert *Sudan*	47B3
Nueltin L *Can*	81J3
Nueva Gerona *Cuba*	102A2
Nueva Imperial *Chile*	110A3
Nueva Laredo *Mexico*	85C4
Nueva Palmira *Urug*	110D2
Nueva Rosita *Mexico*	100B2
Nuevitas *Cuba*	102B2
Nuevo Casas Grandes *Mexico*	100B1
Nuevo Laredo *Mexico*	100C2
Nugal, Region *Somalia*	65E3
Nógàtsàq *Greenland*	82E2
Nûgùssaq, I *Greenland*	82E2
Nukey Bluff, Mt *Aust*	74A2
Nukhayb *Iraq*	107C3
Nukus *USSR*	31G5
Nulato *USA*	88C2
Nullarbor Plain *Aust*	72B4
Numan *Nig*	63D4
Numata *Japan*	41B1
Numazu *Japan*	40D3
Numfoor, I *Indon*	37E4
Numurkah *Aust*	74C3
Nunapitchuk *USA*	88B2
Nunkun, Mt *India*	50D2
Nuoro *Sardegna*	19A2
Nurabad *Iran*	57B3
Nuriootpa *Aust*	74A2
Nuristan, Upland *Afghan*	50C1
Nurlat *USSR*	27H3
Nurmes *Fin*	4K6
Nürnberg *W Germ*	23C3
Nurri, Mt *Aust*	74C2
Nusaybin *Turk*	59D2
Nushki *Pak*	50B3
Nutak *Can*	83D4
Nutzotin Mts *USA*	88F2
Nuwakot *Nepal*	52A1
Nuwara-Eliya *Sri Lanka*	52C3
Nuyukjuak *Can*	82C3
Nyack *USA*	92C2
Nyahururu *Kenya*	65D2
Nyah West *Aust*	74B3
Nyala *Sudan*	50C3
Nyaingentanglha Shan, Mts *China*	34B3
Nyakabindi *Tanz*	65D3
Nyala *Sudan*	64C1
Nyalam *China*	52B1
Nyamlell *Sudan*	64C1
Nyanda *Zim*	66C3
Nyandoma *USSR*	30F3
Nyasa L *Malawi/Mozam*	67C2
Nyaunglebin *Burma*	42B2
Nyazepetrovsk *USSR*	27J2
Nyborg *Den*	5G7
Nybro *Sweden*	5H7
Nyda *USSR*	30J3
Nyeboes Land, Region *Can*	82D1
Nyeri *Kenya*	65D3
Nyimba *Zambia*	67C2
Nyingchi *China*	48D3
Nyiregyhaza *Hung*	25C3
Nyiru, Mt *Kenya*	65D2
Nykarleby *Fin*	4J6
Nykobing *Den*	5F7
Nykobing *Den*	5G8
Nyköping *Sweden*	5H7
Nylstroom *S Africa*	66B3
Nymagee *Aust*	75C2
Nynäshamn *Sweden*	5H7
Nyngan *Aust*	75C2
Nyon *Switz*	13B1
Nyons *France*	15D3
Nysa *Pol*	25B2
Nyssa *USA*	96C2
Nyurba *USSR*	29D1
Nzega *Tanz*	65D3
Nzérékore *Guinea*	63B4

O

Oaggsimiut *Greenland*	82F3
Oahe Res *USA*	84C2
Oahu, I *Hawaiian Is*	97C4
Oakbank *Aust*	74B2
Oakdale *USA*	98B2
Oakey *Aust*	75D1
Oakland, California *USA*	98B2
Oakland, Oregon *USA*	96B2
Oakland City *USA*	90A3
Oak Lawn *USA*	90A2
Oakley, California *USA*	99B3
Oakridge *USA*	96B2
Oakville *Can*	90C2
Oamaru *NZ*	77B3
Oates Land, Region *Ant*	112B7
Oatlands *Aust*	75C4
Ob', R *USSR*	31J3
Obama *Japan*	41B1
Oban *Scot*	10B3
Oban *NZ*	77A3
Obanazawa *Japan*	41C1
Oberammergau *W Germ*	13D1
Oberhausen *W Germ*	12D1
Oberstdorf *W Germ*	13D1
Obi, I *Indon*	37D4
Obidos *Brazil*	109F4
Obihiro *Japan*	44E2
Obo *CAR*	64C2
Obock *Djibouti*	65E1
Oborniki *Pol*	24B2
Oboyan *USSR*	29D2
O'Brien *USA*	96B2
Obshchiy Syrt, Mts *USSR*	27H3
Obuasi *Ghana*	63B4
Ocala *USA*	91C3
Ocana *Colombia*	108C2
Ocaño *Spain*	16B2
Ocean City, Maryland *USA*	95C3
Ocean City, New Jersey *USA*	92B3
Ocean Falls *Can*	81F4
Oceanside *USA*	98D4
Ocean Springs *USA*	95C3
Ocher *USSR*	27H2
Ochil Hills *Scot*	10C3
Ocho Rios *Jamaica*	103H1
Ocilla *USA*	90A2
Ocotlán, Jalisco *Mexico*	99A1
Ocotlán, Oaxaca *Mexico*	99B2
Oda *Ghana*	63B4
Oda *Japan*	41A1
Ódáðahraun, Region *Iceland*	4B2
Odate *Japan*	40E2
Odawara *Japan*	40D3
Odda *Nor*	5F6
Odemira *Port*	16A2
Odemiş *Turk*	21C3
Odendaalsrus *S Africa*	67G1
Odense *Den*	5G7
Oder, R *Pol/E Germ*	22C2
Odessa, Texas *USA*	85C3
Odessa *USSR*	26D4
Odessa, Washington *USA*	96C1
Odienné *Ivory Coast*	63B4
Oeiras *Brazil*	107C3
Offaly, County *Irish Rep*	10B3
Offenbach *W Germ*	15D2
Offenburg *W Germ*	15D2
Oga *Japan*	40D3
Ogaden, Region *Eth*	65E2
Ogaki *Japan*	40C4
Ogallala *USA*	84C2
Ogasawara Gunto, Is *Japan*	35C4
Ogbomosho *Nig*	63C4
Ogden, Utah *USA*	84B2
Ogdensburg *USA*	91C2
Ogilvie *Can*	88G1
Ogilvie Mts *Can*	80E3
Oglethorpe, Mt *USA*	93B1
Ogoja *Nig*	63C4
Ogre *USSR*	24C1
Ogulin *Yugos*	18C1
Ohai *NZ*	77A3
Ohakune *NZ*	77A2
Ohanet *Alg*	62C2
Ohau, L *NZ*	77A2
Ohio, State *USA*	86B2
Ohopoho *Namibia*	66A2
Ohrid *Yugos*	21B2
Ohridsko Jezero, L *Yugos/Alb*	21B2
Ohura *NZ*	76B1
Oiapoque *French Guiana*	109G3
Oijiaojing *China*	34B2
Oil City *USA*	92A2
Oildale *USA*	98B2
Oise, Department *France*	12B2
Oita *Japan*	40C4
Ojai *USA*	98C3
Ojinaga *Mexico*	100B2
Ojitlán *Mexico*	99B2
Ojiya *Japan*	41B1
Ojos del Salado, Mt *Arg*	106C4
Ojuelos *Mexico*	99B1
Okahandja *Namibia*	66A3
Okanagan Falls *Can*	96C1

Oron *Israel*	60B3	Ota *Japan*	41B1
Oroquieta *Phil*	45B4	Otaki *NZ*	76C2
Orosháza *Hung*	25C3	Otaru *Japan*	40E2
Oroville, California *USA*	97A2	Otavalo *Ecuador*	108B1
Oroville, Washington *USA*	96C1	Otavi *Namibia*	66A2
Orsières *Switz*	13B1	Otawara *Japan*	41C1
Orsk *USSR*	31G4	Othello *USA*	96C1
Ørsta *Nor*	4F6	Otira *NZ*	21B3
Orthez *France*	14B3	Otis, Massachusetts *USA*	92C1
Ortigueira *Spain*	16A1	Otish Mts *Can*	89D3
Orties, Mts *Italy*	13D1	Otisville *USA*	92B2
Oruro *Bol*	106C2	Otjiwarongo *Namibia*	66A3
Osa *USSR*	27J2	Otog Qi *China*	38B2
Osaka *Japan*	41B1	Otorohanga *NZ*	76C1
Osceola, Arkansas *USA*	94C2	Otranto *Italy*	21A2
Osceola, Iowa *USA*	9481	Otsego *USA*	90A2
Osgood Mts *USA*	96C2	Otsu *Japan*	41B1
Oshawa *Can*	91C2	Otta *Nor*	5F6
O-shima, I *Japan*	41B2	Ottawa *Can*	91C1
Oshkosh *USA*	86B2	Ottawa, Kansas *USA*	94A2
Oshogbo *Nig*	63C4	Ottawa Is *Can*	83B4
Oshosh *USA*	83B5	Otter Rapids *Can*	83B4
Oshwe *Zaïre*	64B3	Otto Fjord *Can*	82B1
Osijek *Yugos*	20A1	Ottosdal *S Africa*	67G1
Osinniki *USSR*	31K5	Ottumwa *USA*	94B1
Osipovichi *USSR*	24D2	Ottweiler *W Germ*	13D2
Oskaloosa *USA*	9481	Oturkpo *Nig*	63C4
Oskarshamn *Sweden*	26A2	Otusco *Peru*	108B5
Oslo *Nor*	5G7	Otwock *Pol*	24C2
Osmaniye *Turk*	58C2	Otztal *Austria*	13D1
Osnabrück *W Germ*	22B2	Otzal, Mts *Austria*	13D1
Osório *Brazil*	106F4	Ouachita, L *USA*	95B3
Osorno *Chile*	105B4	Ouachita Mts *USA*	95B3
Osorno *Spain*	16B1	Ouadane *Maur*	62A2
Osoyoos *Can*	96C1	Ouadda *CAR*	64B2
Ossa, Mt *Aust*	73D5	Ouaddaï, Desert Region	
Ossining *USA*	92C2	*Chad*	64C1
Ostashkov *USSR*	26D2	Ouagadougou *Burkina*	63B3
Östersund *Sweden*	4G6	Ouahigouya *Burkina*	63B3
Ostfriesische Inseln, Is		Ouaka *CAR*	64B3
W Germ	22B2	Oualam *Niger*	63C3
Östhammär *Sweden*	7H6	Ouallen *Alg*	62C2
Ostia *Italy*	19B2	Ouanda Djallé *CAR*	64C2
Ostiglia *Italy*	13D2	Ouarane, Region *Maur*	62A2
Ostrava *Czech*	25B3	Ouargla *Alg*	62C1
Ostróda *Pol*	24B2	Ouarzazate *Mor*	62B1
Ostroleka *Pol*	24B2	Oudenaarde *Belg*	12B1
Ostrov *USSR*	26C2	Oudtshoorn *S Africa*	66B4
Ostrov Belyy, I *USSR*	30H1	Oued Tlelat *Alg*	17B2
Ostrov Green Bell, I *Barents*		Oued Zem *Mor*	62B1
S	30H1	Ouesso *Congo*	64B2
Ostrov Kolguyev, I *USSR*	30F3	Ouezzane *Mor*	62B1
Ostrov Kunashir, I *USSR*	40F2	Ouidah *Benin*	63C4
Ostrov Mechdusharskiy, I		Oujda *Mor*	62B1
Barents S	30F2	Oulainen *Fin*	4J6
Ostrov Ogurchinskiy, I *USSR*	56B2	Oulu *Fin*	4K5
Ostrov Rudol'fa, I *Barents S*	30G1	Oulujärvi, L *Fin*	4K6
Ostrov Vaygach, I *USSR*	30G2	Oum Chalouba *Chad*	61B3
Ostrov Vrangelya, I *USSR*	1B7	Oum Hadjer *Chad*	64B3
Ostrów *Pol*	24B2	Ouninanga Kébir *Chad*	61B3
Ostrowiec *Pol*	25C2	Ouricuri *Brazil*	107C3
Ostrów Mazowiecka *Pol*	24C2	Ourinhos *Brazil*	111B2
Osuna *Spain*	16A2	Ouro Prêto *Brazil*	111C2
Oswego *USA*	91C2	Outer Hebrides, Is *Scot*	44A3
Oswego *USA*	91C2	Outer Santa Barbara, Chan	
Oswestry *Eng*	9C3	*USA*	98C4
Oświęcim *Pol*	25B2	Outjo *Namibia*	66A3

Outokumpu *Fin*	4K6
Ouyen *Aust*	74B3
Ovada *Italy*	13C2
Ovalle *Chile*	110A2
Ovamboland, Region	
Namibia	66A2
Ova Tyuleni, Is *USSR*	27H5
Övertorneå *Sweden*	4J5
Oviedo *Spain*	16A1
Ovruch *USSR*	26C3
Ovsyanka *USSR*	29E2
Owaka *NZ*	77A3
Owase *Japan*	41B2
Owensboro *USA*	87B3
Owen Falls *Uganda*	99D2
Owen, Mt *NZ*	21B2
Owen Sound *Can*	90B2
Owen Stanley Range, Mts	
PNG	73D1
Owerri *Nig*	63C4
Owo *Nig*	63C4
Owosso *USA*	90B2
Owyhee Mts *USA*	96C2
Oxapampa *Peru*	108B6
Oxelösund *Sweden*	5H7
Oxford, County *Eng*	9D4
Oxford *Eng*	9D4
Oxford, Massachusetts *USA*	92D1
Oxford, Mississippi *USA*	95C3
Ox Mts *Irish Rep*	11B1
Oxnard *USA*	98C3
Oyama *Japan*	40D3
Oyem *Gabon*	89E2
Oyen *Can*	6...
Oyonax *Gabon*	64B2
Øyre *Nor*	5F6
Ozamiz *Phil*	45B4
Ozark *USA*	93A1
Ozark Plat *USA*	14B3
Ozarks, L of the *USA*	14B3
:zd *Hung*	25C3
Ozero Alakol, L *USSR*	31K5
Ozero Balkhash, L *USSR*	31J5
Ozero Baykal, L *USSR*	29C2
Ozero Chany, L *USSR*	31J4
Ozero Chudskoye, L *USSR*	26C2
Ozero Il'men, L *USSR*	26D2
Ozero Imandra, L *USSR*	4L5
Ozero Issyk Kul', L *USSR*	39D4
Ozero Khanka, L *USSR/China*	35F2
Ozero Kovdozero, L *USSR*	4L5
Ozero Kuyto, L *USSR*	4L5
Ozero Pyazozero, L *USSR*	4L5
Ozero Tengiz, L *USSR*	31H4
Ozero Topozero, L *USSR*	4L5
Ozero Zaysan *USSR*	31K5
Ozuluama *Mexico*	99B1

P

Paarl *S Africa*	66A4
Pabbay, I *Scot*	10A3
Pabianice *Pol*	24B2
Pabna *Bang*	52B2
Pabrade *USSR*	24D2
Pacasmayo *Peru*	108B5
Pachuca *Mexico*	99B1
Pacific-Antarctic Ridge	
Pacific O	71K6

Pacific Grove USA	98B2		Palma Mozam	67D2		Panna India	52A2
Pacitan Indon	44C4		Palma de Mallorca Spain	17C2		Panorama Brazil	111A2
Padang Indon	36B4		Palmares Brazil	107D3		Pantelleria, I Medit S	19B3
Paderborn W Germ	22B2		Palmar Sur Costa Rica	102A5		Pantepec Mexico	99B1
Padilla Bol	108C1		Palma Soriano Cuba	102B2		Panuco Mexico	99B1
Padova Italy	13D2		Palm Bay USA	93B2		Pan Xian China	39A4
Padre I USA	85D4		Palm Beach USA	93B2		Paola Italy	19C3
Padstow Eng	9B4		Palmdale USA	98C3		Paola USA	94B2
Padthaway Aust	74B3		Palmeira dos Indos Brazil	107D3		Papa Hung	20B3
Paducah, Kentucky USA	90A3		Palmer USA	88E2		Papakura NZ	76B1
Paducah US	87B3		Palmer, Base Ant	112C3		Papantla Mexico	99B1
Padunskoye More, L USSR	4L5		Palmer Arch Ant	112C3		Papa Stour, I Scot	10D1
Paengnyong-do, I S Korea	40A3		Palmer Land, Region Ant	112B3		Papatoetoe NZ	76B1
Paeroa NZ	76C1		Palmerston NZ	77B3		Papa Westray, I Scot	10C2
Pafuri Mozam	66C3		Palmerston North NZ	76C2		Papua, G of PNG	73D1
Pag, I Yugos	18B2		Palmerton USA	93B2		Papua New Guinea, Republic S E Asia	73D1
Pagadian Phil	45B4		Palmetto USA	93B2		Papudo Chile	110A2
Pagai Selatan, I Indon	36B4		Palmi Italy	19C3		Para, State Brazil	109G4
Pagai Utara, I Indon	36B4		Palmira Colombia	108B3		Para, R Brazil	107B2
Pagan, I Pacific O	37F2		Palm Is Aust	73D2		Paraburdoo Aust	72A3
Pagatan Indon	44D3		Palm Springs USA	97B3		Paracatu Brazil	111B1
Pagondhas Greece	21C3		Palmyra, Missouri USA	94B2		Parachinar Pak	50C2
Pahiatua NZ	76C2		Palmyra, Pennsylvania USA	92A2		Paracin Yugos	20B2
Pahoa Hawaiian Is	97C4		Palmyras Pt India	52B2		Pará de Minas Brazil	111C1
Pahokee USA	93B2		Palo Alto USA	98A2		Paradise, California USA	97A2
Päijänna, L Fin	5K6		Paloich Sudan	44B2		Paragould USA	94B2
Pailola Chan Hawaiian Is	97C4		Palomar Mt USA	97B3		Paraguari Par	106E4
Painesville USA	90B2		Palopo Indon	36D4		Paraguay, Republic S America	106E3
Painted Desert USA	85B3		Palu Indon	36C4		Paraguay, R Par	106E3
Paisley Scot	8C4		Palu Turk	59C2		Paraiba, State Brazil	107D3
Paita Peru	108A5		Palwal India	50D3		Parakou Benin	63C4
Pajala Sweden	4J5		Pama Burkina	50D3		Parakylia Aust	74A2
Pakistan, Republic Asia	4J5		Pamekasan Indon	44C4		Paramakkudi India	53B3
Pak Lay Laos	42C2		Pameungpeuk Indon	44B4		Paramaribo Surinam	109F2
Pakokku Burma	52D2		Pamiers France	14C3		Paramushir, I USSR	35H1
Pakowki L Can	89E2		Pamir, Mts China	48B2		Paraná, State Brazil	106F3
Pakrac Yugos	20A1		Pampa USA	85C3		Paraná Urug	110C2
Paks Hung	42C2		Pampa de la Salinas, Salt Pan Arg	110B2		Paraná, R Arg	105E2
Pak Sane Laos	42C2		Pampa de la Varita Plain, Arg	110B3		Paraná, R Brazil	110B2
Pakse Laos	42D2		Pamplona Colombia	108C2		Paraná, R Arg	111A2
Pakwach Uganda	65D2		Pamplona Spain	16B1		Paranaguá Brazil	106G4
Pala Chad	64B2		Pana USA	94C2		Paranaiba Brazil	111A1
Palagruza, I Yugos	18C2		Panagyurishte Bulg	20B2		Paranavai Brazil	111A2
Palaiseau France	14B3		Panaji India	53A1		Parang Phil	45B4
Palangkaraya Indon	44C3		Panamá Panama	108B2		Paraparaumu NZ	76B2
Palani India	53B2		Panama Canal Panama	102J5		Parbhani India	53B1
Palanpur India	51C4		Panama City USA	93A1		Pardes Hanna Israel	60B2
Palapye Botswana	66B3		Panamint Range, Mts USA	97B2		Pardo Arg	110D3
Palatka USA	93B2		Panay, I Phil	45B3		Pardubice Czech	26B2
Palau Is Pacific O	43B3		Pancevo Yugos	20B2		Parece Vela, Reef Pacific O	35F4
Palawan, I Phil	45A4		Pandan Phil	45B3		Parent Can	86C2
Palawan Pass Phil	45A4		Pandie Pandie Aust	74A1		Parepare Indon	45A4
Palayankottai India	53B3		Panevezys USSR	24C1		Parera Arg	110C3
Paldiski USSR	5J7		Panfilov USSR	31K5		Pariaman Indon	36B4
Palembang Indon	44A3		Pangani Tanz	65D3		Paris France	14B3
Palencia Spain	16B1		Pangi Zaire	64C3		Paris, Kentucky USA	90B3
Paleokhorio Cyprus	60A1		Pangkalpinang Indon	44B3		Paris, Texas USA	95A3
Palermo Italy	19B3		Pangnirtung Can	82D3		Parkersburg USA	90B3
Palestine, Region Israel	56C3		Pangtara Burma	42B1		Parkes Aust	75C2
Palestine USA	95A3		Pangutaran Group, Is Phil	45B4		Parkesburg USA	89B3
Paletwa Burma	52C2		Panipat India	50D3		Park Forest USA	90A2
Palghat India	53B2		Panjao Afghan	50B2		Parksville Can	96B1
Pali India	51C3		P'anmunjom N Korea	40B3			
Palitana India	51C4						
Pallasovka USSR	27G3						
Pallastunturi, Mt Fin	4J5						

Penny Highlands, Mts Can	82D3
Penola Aust	74B3
Penong Aust	72C4
Penrith Eng	8C2
Pensacola USA	87B3
Pensacola Mts Ant	46E
Pensiangan Malay	44D1
Penticton Can	89D3
Pentland Firth, Chan Scot	10C2
Pentland Hills Scot	8C2
Penza USSR	27G3
Penzance Eng	9B4
Peoria USA	84B2
Perabumulih Indon	44A3
Perawang Indon	44A2
Pereira Colombia	108B3
Pereira Barreto Brazil	111A2
Perelazovskiy USSR	27F4
Pergamino Arg	110C2
Périgueux France	14C2
Perlas Arch de, Is Panama	101E4
Perm' USSR	27J2
Pernambuco, State Brazil	107D3
Pernik Bulg	20B2
Péronne France	12B2
Perote Mexico	23B2
Perpignan France	15C3
Perris USA	98D4
Perry, Florida USA	93B1
Perry, Georgia USA	93B1
Perry, Oklahoma USA	94A2
Perry River Can	80H3
Perrysburg USA	90B2
Perryville, Alaska USA	88C3
Perryville, Missouri USA	94C2
Perth Aust	72A4
Perth Can	10C3
Perth Scot	10C3
Perth Amboy USA	92B2
Peru, Republic S America	108C6
Peru USA	94C1
Peru-Chile Trench Pacific O	69E5
Perugia Italy	18B2
Perusic Yugos	18C2
Pervari Turk	59D2
Pervomaysk, RSFSR USSR	27F3
Pervomaysk, Ukraine SSR USSR	26D4
Pervoural'sk USSR	27J2
Pesaro Italy	18B2
Pescadero USA	98A2
Pescara Italy	18B2
Peschiera Italy	18B2
Peshawar Pak	50C2
Peshkopi Alb	20B2
Peshtigo USA	90A1
Pestovo USSR	26E2
Petah Tiqwa Israel	60B2
Petaluma USA	97A2
Pétange Lux	12C2
Petatlán Mexico	99A2
Petauke Zambia	67C2
Peterborough Aust	74A2
Peterborough Can	91C2
Peterborough Eng	9D3
Peterhead Scot	10D3
Petermann Gletscher, Gl Greenland	82D1
Petermann Range, Mts Aust	72B3
Peteroa, Mt Chile/Arg	109B3
Peter Pond L Can	89F1
Petersburg, Alaska USA	88H3
Petlad India	51C4
Petlalcingo Mexico	99B2
Peto Mexico	101D2
Petomskoye Nagor'ye, Upland USSR	25O3
Petorca Chile	110A2
Petoskey USA	90B1
Petra, Base Ant	112C2
Petrolina Brazil	107C3
Petropavlovsk USSR	31H4
Petrópolis Brazil	111C2
Petrovsk USSR	30E3
Petrovsk USSR	27G3
Petrovsk Zabaykal'skiy USSR	34C1
Petrozavodsk USSR	30E3
Petrus S Africa	67G1
Petrusburg S Africa	67G1
Pevek USSR	1B7
Pfälzer Wald, Region W Germ	12D2
Pforzheim W Germ	23B3
Phagwara India	50D2
Phalodi India	51C3
Phalsbourg France	13D3
Phaltan India	53A1
Phangnga Thai	43B4
Phan Rang Viet	42D3
Phan Thiet Viet	42D3
Phnom Dang, Mts Camb	42C3
Phet Buri Thai	42B3
Phiafay Laos	43D2
Philadelphia, Mississippi USA	13E1
Philadelphia, Pennsylvania USA	95C3
Philippeville Belg	12C1
Philippine S Pacific O	37D2
Philippines, Republic S E Asia	37D2
Philippine Trench Pacific O	70E3
Philipsburg, Pennsylvania USA	91C2
Philip Smith Mts USA	12C2
Philippine S Phil	45B2
Phillipsburg, New Jersey USA	92B2
Phitsanulok Thai	21B3
Phnom Penh Camb	42C3
Phoenix, Arizona USA	85B3
Phoenixville USA	92B2
Phong Saly Laos	42C1
Phu Bia, Mt Laos	42C2
Phu Cuong Viet	42D3
Phuket Thai	43B4
Phulbani India	52A2
Phu Miang, Mt Thai	42C2
Phu Set, Mt Laos	42D2
Phu Tho Viet	42D1
Phu Vinh Viet	43D4
Piacenza Italy	13C2
Pianosa, I Italy	18B2
Pianosa, I Italy	18C2
Piassezno Pol	24C2
Piatra-Neamt Rom	20C1
Piauí, State Brazil	107C3
Pibor Post Sudan	65D2
Picardie, Region France	12B1
Picayune USA	95C3
Pic de Rochebrune, Mt France	13B2
Pichilemu Chile	110A2
Pichi Mahuida Arg	110C3
Pickering Eng	8D2
Pickle Lake Can	83A4
Pico, I Açores	62A1
Pico Bernina, Mt Switz	13C1
Pico de Anito, Mt Spain	17C1
Pico del Infernillo, Mt Mexico	100B3
Pico Duarte, Mt Dom Rep	103C3
Picos Brazil	107C3
Picos de Europa, Mt Spain	16B1
Picton Aust	75D2
Picton NZ	77B2
Pic Toussidé, Mt Chad	61A2
Piedade Brazil	111B2
Piedra USA	98C2
Piedras Negras Mexico	100B3
Piešt'any Czech	25B3
Pietermaritzburg S Africa	67H1
Pietersburg S Africa	66B3
Piet Retief S Africa	67H1
Pietrosu, Mt Rom	26B4
Pietrosul, Mt Rom	20C1
Pieve di Cadore Italy	13E1
Pigeon L Can	89E2
Piggott USA	94B2
Pihani India	50D3
Pikangikum L Can	83A4
Pikes Peak USA	84C3
Piketberg S Africa	66A4
Pikintaleq Greenland	82F3
Pierre USA	84C2
Pik Kommunizma, Mt USSR	48B2
Pikounda Congo	64B2
Pik Pobedy, Mt China/USSR	48C1
Pila Arg	110D3
Piła Pol	24B2
Pilar Par	106E4
Pilibhit India	50D3
Pilos Greece	21B3
Pilot Point USA	88C3
Pilot Station USA	88B2
Pilottown USA	95C3
Pimenta Brazil	109F4
Pinang, I Malay	43C4
Pinar del Rio Cuba	102A2
Pinas Arg	110B2
Pinche Belg	12C1
Pincher Creek Can	89E2
Pindhos, Mts Greece	21B3
Pine Bluff USA	95B3
Pine Creek Aust	72C2
Pinecrest USA	98C1

Pond, Inlet *Can*	82C2
Ponferrade *Spain*	16A1
Ponnani *India*	53B2
Ponnyadoung Range, Mts *Burma*	52C2
Ponoka *Can*	89E2
Ponoy *USSR*	30F3
Pons *France*	14B2
Ponta da Baleia, Pt *Brazil*	111D1
Ponta Delgada *Acores*	62A1
Ponta do Padrao, Pt *Angola*	64B3
Ponta dos Búzios, Pt *Brazil*	111C2
Ponta Grossa *Brazil*	106F4
Pontal *Brazil*	111B2
Pontà-à-Mousson *France*	13D3
Ponta Pora *Brazil*	106E3
Pontarlier *France*	15D2
Pontchartrain, L *USA*	95B3
Pontedera *Italy*	18B2
Ponte Lecca *Corse*	18A2
Pontevedra *Spain*	16A1
Pontiac, Illinois *USA*	94C1
Pontiac, Michigan *USA*	90B2
Pontianak *Indon*	44B3
Pontivy *France*	14B2
Pontoise *France*	12B2
Pontotoc *USA*	95C3
Pontypool *Wales*	9C4
Pontypridd *Wales*	9C4
Poole *Eng*	9D4
Pooncarie *Aust*	74B2
Poopelloe, L, L *Aust*	74B2
Poorman *USA*	88C2
Popayán *Colombia*	108B3
Poperinge *Belg*	12B1
Popilta L *Aust*	74B2
Poplar Bluff *USA*	94B2
Poplarville *USA*	95C3
Popndetta *PNG*	73D1
Popocatepetl, Mt *Mexico*	99B2
Popokabaka *Zaïre*	64B3
Popondetta *PNG*	37F4
Popovo *Bulg*	20C2
Porbandar *India*	51B4
Porcher I *Can*	89A2
Porec *Yugos*	18B1
Porecatu *Brazil*	111A2
Pori *Fin*	5J6
Porirua *NZ*	75J
Porjus *Sweden*	4H5
Poronaysk *USSR*	35G2
Porrentruy *Switz*	13B1
Porsangen, Inlet *Nor*	4K4
Porsgrunn *Nor*	5F7
Portadown *N Ire*	11C1
Portage la Prairie *Can*	84D2
Port Alberni *Can*	89C3
Portalegre *Port*	16A2
Portales *USA*	85C3
Port Alfred *Can*	
Port Alfred *S Africa*	66B4
Port Alice *USA*	89B2
Port Allen *USA*	95B3
Port Angeles *USA*	96B1
Port Antonio *Jamaica*	102B3
Portarlington *Irish Rep*	11C2
Port Arthur *USA*	95B4
Port Augusta *Aust*	74A2
Port-au-Prince *Haiti*	102C3
Port Austin *USA*	90B2
Port Campbell *Aust*	75B3
Port Canning *India*	52B2
Port Cartier *Can*	83D5
Port Chalmers *NZ*	77B3
Port Charlotte *USA*	93B2
Port Chester *USA*	92C2
Port Colborne *Can*	91C2
Port Credit *Can*	91C2
Port Davey *Aust*	75C4
Port-de-Paix *Haiti*	102C3
Port Dickson *Malay*	43C5
Port Edward *S Africa*	66C4
Porteirinha *Brazil*	111C1
Port Elgin *Can*	90B2
Port Elizabeth *S Africa*	66B4
Porter Pt *St Vincent*	103N2
Porterville *USA*	97B2
Port Fairy *Aust*	75B3
Port Gentil *Gabon*	64A3
Port Gibson *USA*	95B3
Port Graham *USA*	88D3
Port Hammond *Can*	96B1
Port Harcourt *Nigeria*	55E7
Port Hardy *Can*	89B2
Port Hawkesbury *Can*	83D5
Port Hedland *Aust*	72A3
Porthmadog *Wales*	9B3
Port Hope Simpson *Can*	83E4
Port Hueneme *USA*	98C3
Port Huron *USA*	90B2
Portimao *Port*	16A2
Port Jefferson *USA*	92C2
Port Jervis *USA*	92B2
Port Kembla *Aust*	75D2
Portland, Indiana *USA*	90B2
Portland, Maine *USA*	86C2
Portland, New South Wales *USA*	75C2
Portland, Oregon *USA*	96B1
Portland, Victoria *Aust*	74B3
Portland Bill, Pt *Eng*	9C4
Portland Canal *USA/Can*	89A1
Portland I *NZ*	76C1
Portland Pt *Jamaica*	103H2
Port Laoise *Irish Rep*	11C2
Port Lincoln *Aust*	74A2
Port Loko *Sierra Leone*	63A4
Port Louis *Mauritius*	67E3
Port MacDonnell *Aust*	74B3
Port McNeill *Can*	89B2
Port Macquarie *Aust*	75D2
Port Moller *USA*	88B3
Port Moresby *PNG*	73D1
Port Nolloth *S Africa*	66A3
Port Norris *USA*	92B3
Port Novo *Benin*	55E7
Pôrto Alegre *Brazil*	106F5
Porto Artur *Brazil*	109F6
Pôrto 15 de Novembro *Brazil*	111A2
Pôrto E Cunha *Brazil*	106F3
Portoferraio *Italy*	18B2
Port of Spain *Trinidad*	103E4
Portomaggiore *Italy*	13D2
Porto Novo *Benin*	63C4
Port Orchard *USA*	96B1
Port Orford *USA*	96B2
Port Saint S, *Medeira*	62A1
Porto Seguro *Brazil*	107D6
Porto Torres *Sardegna*	19A2
Porto Vecchio *Corse*	19A3
Pôrto Velho *Brazil*	109E5
Port Phillip B *Aust*	75B3
Port Pirie *Aust*	74A2
Portree *Scot*	10A3
Port Renfrew *Can*	96B1
Port Royal *Jamaica*	103J2
Portrush *N Ire*	11C1
Port Said *Egypt*	58B3
Port St Joe *USA*	93A2
Port St Johns *S Africa*	66B4
Port Saunders *Can*	83E4
Port Shepstone *S Africa*	66C4
Port Simpson *Can*	89A2
Portsmouth *Dominica*	103E3
Portsmouth *Eng*	9D4
Portsmouth, Ohio *USA*	90B3
Portsmouth, Virginia *USA*	87C3
Port Sudan *Sudan*	61C3
Port Sulphur *USA*	95C3
Porttipahan Tekojärvi, Res *Fin*	4K5
Portugal, Republic *Europe*	16A2
Port Washington *USA*	90A2
Port Weld *Malay*	43C5
Porvenir *Bol*	108D6
Posadas *Arg*	106E4
Posadas *Spain*	16A2
Poschiavo *Switz*	13D1
Posht-e Badam *Iran*	56C3
Poso *Indon*	37D4
Postavy *USSR*	24D1
Post Clinton *USA*	90B2
Poste-de-la-Baleine *Can*	83C4
Postmasburg *S Africa*	66B3
Postojna *Yugos*	18B1
Pos'yet *USSR*	40C2
Potchefstroom *S Africa*	67G1
Poteau *USA*	95B2
Potenza *Italy*	19C2
Potgietersrus *S Africa*	66B3
Potiskum *Nig*	63D3
Potosi *USA*	96C1
Potosi *Bol*	106C6
Potrerillos *Chile*	106C4
Potsdam *E Germ*	22C2
Pottstown *USA*	92B2
Pottsville *USA*	92A2
Poughkeepsie *USA*	92C2
Pouso Alegre *Brazil*	111B2
Povorino *USSR*	27F3
Poyungnituk *Can*	83C4
Powell Creek *Aust*	72C2
Powell, L *USA*	85B3
Powell River *Can*	89C2
Powys, County *Wales*	9C3
Poyang Hu, L *China*	39D4
Poza Rica *Mexico*	9D4

Quesnel Can	89C2	Radauti Rom	25D3	Ramsar Iran	56B2
Quetta Pak	50B2	Radhanpur India	51C4	Ramsey Eng	8B2
Quezaltenango Guatemala	101C3	Radix, Pt Trinidad	103L1	Ramsey USA	92B2
Queziot Israel	60B3	Radom Pol	24C2	Ramsey I Wales	9B4
Quezon City Phil	45B3	Radomsko Pol	25B2	Ramsgate Eng	9E4
Quibala Angola	66A2	Radviliskis USSR	24C1	Ramtha Jordan	60C2
Quibdó Colombia	108B2	Rae Can	80G3	Rancagua Chile	110A2
Quiberon France	14B2	Rae Bareli India	52A1	Ranchi India	52B2
Quicama Nat Pk Angola	64B3	Rae Isthmus Can	82B3	Ranchi Plat India	52A2
Quijing China	39A4	Rae L Can	80G3	Randers Den	5G7
Quilino Arg	110A2	Raetihi NZ	76C1	Randfontein S Africa	67G1
Quilimane Peru	108C6	Rafaela Arg	110C2	Randolph, Vermont USA	91D2
Quillacollo Bol	106C2	Rafah Egypt	60B3	Ranfurly NZ	77B3
Quillan France	14C3	Rafai CAR	64C2	Rangamati Bang	52C2
Quill L Can	81H4	Rafha Al Jumaymah S Arabia	59D3	Rangiora NZ	77B2
Quill Lakes Can	81H4	Rafsanjan Iran	57C3	Rangoon Burma	42B2
Quillota Chile	110A2	Raga Sudan	64C3	Rangpur India	52B1
Quilon India	53B3	Ragged Pt Barbados	103R3	Ranibennur India	53B2
Quilpie Aust	74B1	Raguba Libya	61A2	Ranier, Mt, USA	44A2
Quilpué Chile	110A2	Ragusa Italy	19B3	Raniganj India	52B2
Quimbele Angola	64B3	Rahimyar Khan Pak	50C3	Rankins Springs Aust	75C2
Quimper France	14B2	Rahjerd Iran	56B3	Ranklin Inlet Can	82A3
Quimperlé France	14B2	Raichur India	51B4	Rann of Kachchh, Flood Area India	51B4
Quincy, California USA	97A2	Raigarh India	53B1	Ranong Thai	43B4
Quincy, Illinois USA	86A3	Rainbow Aust	74B3	Rantauprapat Indon	36A3
Quincy, Massachusetts USA	92D1	Rainbow City USA	93A1	Rantoul USA	94C1
Quines Arg	110B2	Rainier USA	96B1	Rapallo Italy	15D3
Quinhagak USA	88B3	Rainier, Mt USA	96B1	Rapid City USA	84C2
Qui Nhon Viet	42D3	Rainy L Can	86A2	Rapid River USA	90B2
Quintanar de la Orden Spain	16B2	Rainy P USA	88D2	Rapti R India	52A1
Quintero Chile	110A2	Rainy River Can	86A2	Rapla USSR	13C1
Quirihue Chile	110A3	Raipur India	52A2	Ra's al 'Ayn Syria	59D2
Quirima Angola	66A2	Rajahmundry India	53C1	Ras al Kaimah UAE	57C4
Quirindi Aust	75D2	Rajapur Pak	50D3	Ras Dashan, Mt Eth	65D1
Quissanga Mozam	67D2	Rajapalaiyam India	53B3	Ra's-e-Barkan, Pt Iran	56A3
Quissico Mozam	67C3	Rajasthan, State India	50D3	Râs el Kenâyis, Pt Egypt	60B1
Quito Ecuador	108B4	Rajgarh India	50D3	Ras Ghârib Egypt	61C2
Quixadá Brazil	107D2	Rajgarh, State India	51D4	Rashad Sudan	65D1
Quorn Aust	74A2	Rajkot India	51C4	Rashadiya Jordan	60B3
Quseir Egypt	61C2	Rajmahal Hills India	52B2	Rashid Egypt	58B3
Qutdligssat Greenland	82E3	Raj Nandgaon India	53B1	Rasht Iran	56A2
Qu Xian, Sichuan China	39B3	Rajpipla India	51C4	Ras Koh, Mt Pak	50B3
Qu Xian, Zhejiang China	39D4	Rajshahi Bang	52B2	Rasshua, I USSR	35H2
Quynh Luu Viet	42D2	Rajur India	51B4	Rasskazovo USSR	27F3
Quzhou China	38C2	Raka,I Indon	44B4	Ra's Tannurah S Arabia	57B4
Qüzü China	52C1	Rakhov USSR	25C3	Rastatt W Germ	23B3
		Rakops Botswana	66B3	Ratangarh India	50C3
		Rakov USSR	24D2	Rat Buri Thai	42B3
R		Raleigh USA	87C3	Rath India	51D3
		Ralny L Can	83A5	Ratherow E Germ	22C2
Raahe Fin	4J6	Rama Israel	60B2	Rathkeale Irish Rep	11B2
Raasay, I Scot	10A3	Ramallah Israel	60B3	Rathlin, I N Ire	11C1
Raasay, Sound of, Chan Scot	10A3	Ramanathapuram India	53B3	Ráth Luirc Irish Rep	11B2
Rab, I Yugos	18B2	Ramapo Deep Pacific Oc	35G3	Ratlam India	51D4
Raba Indon	44D4	Ramat Gan Israel	60B2	Ratnagiri India	53A1
Raba't Mor	62B1	Ramgarh, Bihar India	52B2	Ratnapura Sri Lanka	53C3
Rabba Jordan	60B3	Ramgarh, Rajasthan India	51C3	Ratno USSR	24C2
Rabigh S Arabia	46B3	Ramhormoz Iran	56A3	Rattenberg Austria	23B3
Racconigi Italy	18B2	Ramla Israel	60B3	Rättvik Sweden	5H6
Rachaya Leb	60B2	Ramlat Al Wahibah, Region Oman	57C5	Ratz, Mt Can	88H3
Rachel, Mt W Germ	23C3	Ramona USA	97B3	Rauch Arg	110D3
Rach Gia Viet	42D3	Rampur India	50D3	Raukumara Range, Mts NZ	76C1
Racine USA	90A2	Rampura India	51D4	Raul Soares Brazil	111C2
				Rauma Fin	5J6
				Raurkela India	52A2
				Ravansar Iran	56A3
				Ravar Iran	56C3

Ringkobing *Den*	5F7
Rio Benito *Eq Guinea*	64A2
Rio Branco *Brazil*	108D5
Riochacha *Colombia*	108C1
Rio Claro *Brazil*	111B2
Rio Claro *Trinidad*	103L1
Rio Cuarto *Arg*	110C2
Rio de Janeiro *Brazil*	107D4
Rio de Janeiro *Brazil*	111C2
Rio de Janeiro, State *Brazil*	111C2
Rio de la Plata, Est *Arg/Uru*	105E3
Rio Gallegos *Arg*	105C6
Rio Grande *Arg*	105C6
Rio Grande *Brazil*	106F5
Rio Grande *Nic*	102A4
Rio Grande, R *USA/Mexico*	100B2
Rio Grande de Santiago *Mexico*	99A1
Rio Grande do Norte, State *Brazil*	107D3
Rio Grande do Sul, State *Brazil*	106F4
Riohacha *Colombia*	102C4
Riom *France*	15C2
Riombamba *Ecuador*	108B4
Rio Mulatos *Bol*	105C3
Rio Negro, State *Arg*	105C2
Rio Tercero *Arg*	110C2
Rio Turbio *Arg*	105B6
Rio Verde *Brazil*	111A1
Rio Verde *Mexico*	99A1
Ripley, Ohio *USA*	90B3
Ripley, West Virginia *USA*	90B3
Ripon *Eng*	8D2
Ripon *USA*	90B3
Rishon le Zion *Israel*	69B3
Rising Sun *USA*	92A3
Risor *Nor*	7C7
Ritenbek *Greenland*	82E2
Ritter, Mt *USA*	98C2
Ritzville *USA*	96C1
Rivadavia *Arg*	110A3
Rivadavia *Chile*	110A1
Rivadavia Gonzalez Moreno *Arg*	110C3
Riva de Garda *Italy*	13D2
Rivera *Arg*	110C3
Rivera *Urug*	105E2
Riverbank *USA*	98B3
River Cess *Lib*	63B4
Riverhead *USA*	92C2
Riverina *Aust*	74B3
Riversdale *NZ*	77A3
Riverside *USA*	98D4
Rivers Inlet *Can*	89B2
Riverton *Aust*	77A3
Riverton *USA*	84C2
Riviera Beach *USA*	93B2
Rivigny-sur-Ornain *France*	12C2
Riyadh *S Arabia*	57A5
Rize *Turk*	59D1
Rizhao *China*	38D2
Rjukan *Nor*	5F7
Roanne *France*	15C2

Roanoke, Alabama *USA*	93A1
Roanoke, Virginia *USA*	87C3
Robertsfors *Sweden*	4J6
Robert S Kerr Res *USA*	95B2
Robertsport *Lib*	63A4
Roberval *Can*	83C5
Robinvale *Aust*	74B2
Robson, Mt *Can*	89D2
Roca Partida, I *Mexico*	100A3
Rocas, I *Atlantic O*	69G5
Rocas, I *Atlantic O*	107E2
Rocha *Urug*	105F2
Rochechouart *France*	8C3
Rochefort *France*	14B2
Rocher River *Can*	89H3
Rochester *Aust*	74B3
Rochester *Can*	83C5
Rochester *Eng*	9E4
Rochester, Minnesota *USA*	91D2
Rochester, New Hampshire *USA*	91D2
Rochester, New York *USA*	86C2
Rockford *USA*	86B2
Rock Hill *USA*	87B3
Rock Island *USA*	86A2
Rocklands Res *Aust*	74B3
Rockledge *USA*	93B2
Rock Rapids *USA*	91B2
Rock Springs, Wyoming *USA*	84C2
Rocks Pt *NZ*	76B2
Rock, The *Aust*	75C3
Rockville, Connecticut *USA*	94B2
Rockville, Indiana *USA*	90A3
Rockville, Maryland *USA*	94B3
Rocky Island L *Can*	90B1
Rocky Mountain House *Can*	89E2
Rocky Mts *Can/USA*	84B1
Rocky Pt *NZ*	88B2
Rodbyhavn *Den*	22C2
Rodeo *Arg*	110C2
Rode *France*	15C3
Ródhos *Greece*	21C3
Ródhos, I *Greece*	21C3
Rodi Garganico *Italy*	16B2
Rodopi Planina, Mts *Bulg*	20B2
Roebourne *Aust*	72A3
Roebuck B *Aust*	72B2
Roermond *Neth*	12C1
Roeselare *Belg*	12B1
Rogers *USA*	94B2
Rogers City *USA*	90B1
Rohn Pak	51B3
Rohtak *India*	60D3
Roja *USA*	24C1
Rolândia *Brazil*	111A2
Rolla *USA*	94B2
Roma *Aust*	75C1
Roma *Italy*	18B2
Romagnano *Italy*	13C2
Roman *Rom*	20C1
Romanche Gap *Atlantic O*	69H5
Romang, I *Indon*	37D4
Romania, Republic *E Europe*	26B4
Romans sur Isère *France*	15D2
Romblon *Phil*	45B2
Rome, Georgia *USA*	93A1
Rome, New York *USA*	91C2

Romilly-sur-Seine *France*	15C2
Romney *USA*	91C3
Romny *USSR*	26D3
Romo, I *Den*	22B1
Romont *Switz*	13B1
Romoratin *France*	14C2
Ronda *Spain*	16A2
Rondônia *Brazil*	109B6
Rondônia, State *Brazil*	100F6
Rondonópolis *Brazil*	106F2
Rong'an *China*	39B4
Rongcheng *China*	39B4
Rongcheng *China*	39B4
Rongjiang *China*	39B4
Rongklang Range, Mts *Burma*	42A1
Ronne *Denmark*	5G7
Ronneby *Sweden*	5G7
Ronne Ice Shelf *Ant*	112B2
Ronse *Belg*	12B1
Ronthieu, Region *France*	12A1
Roof Butte, Mt *USA*	85C3
Roorkee *India*	12C1
Roosendaal *Neth*	12C1
Roosevelt I *Ant*	46E8
Roraima, State *Brazil*	109E3
Roraima, Mt *Ven*	109E2
Roros *Nor*	4G6
Rorschach *Switz*	13C1
Rorvik *Nor*	4G6
Rosalie *Dominica*	103Q2
Rosamond L *USA*	98C3
Rosario *Arg*	110C2
Rosario del Tala *Arg*	110C2
Roscoff *France*	14B2
Roscommon, County *Irish Rep*	11B2
Roscommon *Irish Rep*	7B3
Roscrea *Irish Rep*	11C2
Roseau *Dominica*	103E3
Rosebery *Aust*	75C5
Roseburg *USA*	96B2
Rosenberg *USA*	95A4
Rosenheim *W Germ*	23C3
Rosetown *Can*	89F2
Rosiorii de Verde *Rom*	20B2
Roskilde *Den*	5G7
Roslavl' *USSR*	26D3
Roslyatino *USSR*	27E2
Ross *NZ*	77B2
Rossan, Pt *Irish Rep*	6B3
Rossano *Italy*	19C3
Ross Barnet Res *USA*	95C3
Rosseau L, L *Can*	91C1
Rossel, I *Solomon Is*	73E2
Ross Ice Shelf *Ant*	46E
Rossiyskaya S.F.S.R., Republic *USSR*	26D2
Ross L *USA*	96B1
Rossland *Can*	89D3
Rosslare *Irish Rep*	11C2
Rosso *Maur*	63A3
Rosso *Maur*	63A3
Ross-on-Wye *Eng*	9C4
Rossosh *USSR*	26E4
Ross River *Can*	80E3

Ross S *Ant*	112B6	Rue *France*	12A1		
Rostaq *Iran*	57B4	Ruffec *France*	14C2		
Rostock *E Germ*	22E2	Rufino *Arg*	110C2	**S**	
Rostov *USSR*	28E2	Rufisque *Sen*	63A3	Sa'adatabad *Iran*	57B3
Rostov-na-Donu *USSR*	27E4	Rufunsa *Zambia*	66B2	Saanen *Switz*	13B1
Roswell, Georgia *USA*	93B1	Rugby *Eng*	9D3	Saarbrücken *W Germ*	12D2
Roswell, New Mexico *USA*	85C3	Rügen, I *E Germ*	5G8	Saarburg *W Germ*	12D2
Rota *Pacific O*	39D4	Ruijin *China*	39D4	Saaremaa, I *USSR*	5J7
Rotenburg, Niedersachsen		Rujen, Mt *Bulg/Yugos*	20B2	Saarland, State *W Germ*	12D2
W Germ	22B2	Rukwa, L *Tanz*	65D3	Saarlouis *W Germ*	12D2
Rothaar-Geb, Region		Rum, I *Scot*	10A3	Saavedra *Arg*	110C3
W Germ	12E1	Ruma *Yugos*	20A1	Sabac *Yugos*	20A2
Rothera, Base *Ant*	112C3	Rumah *S Arabia*	57A4	Sabadell *Spain*	17C1
Rotherham *Eng*	8B2	Rumbek *Sudan*	62D3	Sabae *Japan*	41B1
Rothesay *Scot*	8B2	Rum Cay, I *Caribbean*	102C2	Sabah, State *Malay*	44D1
Rotl, I *Indon*	37D5	Rumilly *France*	13A2	Sabanalarga *Colombia*	102C4
Roto *Aust*	74C2	Rum Jungle *Aust*	72C2	Sabang *Indon*	36A3
Rotoiti, L *NZ*	77B2	Rumphi *Malawi*	67C2	Sabastiya *Israel*	60B2
Rotorua *NZ*	77B2	Runanga *NZ*	77B2	Sabaya *Bol*	106C2
Rotorua *NZ*	76C1	Rundu *Namibia*	66A2	Sab'Bi'ar *Syria*	59C3
Rotorua, L *NZ*	76C1	Rungwa *Tanz*	65D3	Sabha *Jordan*	60C2
Rotterdam *Neth*	22A2	Rungwe, Mt *Tanz*	65D3	Sabha *Libya*	61A2
Roubaix *France*	12B1	Ruoqiang *China*	48C2	Sabinas *Mexico*	100B2
Rouen *France*	14C2	Rupea *Rom*	20C1	Sabinas Hidalgo *Mexico*	100B2
Round I *Mauritius*	67E3	Rurrenabaque *Bol*	100B5	Sabine L *USA*	95B4
Round Mt *Aust*	75D2	Rusape *Zim*	67C2	Sabkhat Matti, Salt Marsh	
Roundup *Aust*	84C2	Ruse *Bulg*	20C2	*UAE*	57B5
Rousay, I *Scot*	10C2	Rushville, Illinois *USA*	94B1	Sablayan *Phil*	45B3
Roussillon, Region *France*	14C3	Rushworth *Aust*	74B3	Sable I *Can*	83D5
Rouyn *Can*	86C2	Rusk *USA*	95A3	Sabzevar *Iran*	56C2
Rovaniemi *Fin*	4K5	Ruskin *USA*	93B2	Sacajawea Peak *USA*	96C1
Rovereto *Italy*	13D2	Russell *NZ*	76B1	Sachs Harbour *Can*	80F2
Rovigo *Italy*	13D2	Russellville, Arkansas		Säckingen *W Germ*	13B1
Rovinj *Yugos*	18B1	*USA*	94B2	Sacramento *USA*	98B1
Rovno *USSR*	25D2	Russellville, Kentucky		Sacramento Mts *USA*	85C3
Row'an *Iran*		*USA*	94C2	Sa'dah *Yemen*	47C4
Rowena *Aust*	75C1	Russian Socialist Federated		Sadanski *Bulg*	20B2
Rowley I *Can*	82C3	Soviet Rep *USSR*	26B3	Sadiya *India*	48D3
Rowley Shoals *Aust*	72A2	Rustavi *USSR*	59E1	Sado-shima, I *Japan*	40D3
Roxas, Palawan *Phil*	45A3	Rustenburg *S Africa*	67G1	Sadri *India*	51C3
Roxas, Panay *Phil*	45B3	Ruston *USA*	95B3	Safed Koh, Mts *Afghan*	50A2
Roxburgh *NZ*	78A3	Rutana *Burundi*	65C3	Saffle *Sweden*	5G7
Royal Canal *Irish Rep*	11C2	Rüthen *W Germ*	12E1	Safi *Mor*	58C3
Royal Leamington Spa *Eng*	9D3	Rutla *Mexico*	99B2	Safi *Jordan*	62B1
Royal Oak *USA*	90B2	Rutland *USA*	91D2	Safidabeh *Iran*	56D3
Royal Tunbridge Wells *Eng*	9E4	Rutog *China*	50D2	Safita *Syria*	60C1
Royan *France*	14B2	Ruwenzori Range, Mts		Safwan *Iraq*	59E3
Royat *France*	12B2	*Uganda/Zaire*	65D2	Saga *Japan*	41A2
Royston *Eng*	9D3	Ruzomberok *Czech*	25B3	Sagaing *Burma*	42B1
Roznava *Czech*	25C3	Rwanda, Republic *Africa*	65C3	Sag *India*	51D4
Rozoy *France*	12B2	Ryazan' *USSR*	26E3	Sagar *India*	50C2
Rtishchevo *USSR*	25F5	Ryazhsk *USSR*	27F3	Saginaw *USA*	90B2
Ruaha Nat Pk *Tanz*	65D3	Rybinsk *USSR*	26E2	Sag Harbor *USA*	91D2
Ruahine Range, Mts *NZ*	76C1	Rybinskoye		Sagleouc *Can*	82D3
Ruapehu, Mt *NZ*	76C1	Vodokhranilishche,		Sagua de Tanamo *Cuba*	102B2
Rub al Khali, Desert		Res *USSR*	26E2	Sagua la Grande *Cuba*	102B2
S Arabia	31D3	Rycroft *Can*	89D1	Sagunto *Spain*	17B2
Rubha Hunish *Scot*	10A3	Ryde *Eng*	9E4	Sahab *Jordan*	60C3
Rubinéia *Brazil*	111A2	Rye Patch Res *USA*	96C2	Sahagún *Spain*	16B1
Rubtsovsk *USSR*	31K4	Ryl'sk *USSR*	26D3	Sahara, Desert *N Africa*	62C2
Ruby *USA*	88C2	Ryn Peskt, Desert *USSR*	27G4	Saharanpur *India*	50D3
Rudan *Iran*	57C4	Ryotsu *Japan*	29D3	Sahiwal *Pak*	50C3
Rudbar *Iran*	57C4	Ryukyu Retto, Arch *Japan*	35E4	Sahra al Hijarah, Desert	
Rudnaya Pristan' *USSR*	35F2	Rzeszów *Pol*	25C2	Region *Iraq*	59D3
Rudoka Planina, Mt *Yugos*	20B2	Rzhev *USSR*	26D2	Sahuayo *Mexico*	99A1
Rudong *China*	38E3			Saibai I *Aust*	73D1
Rudyard *USA*	90B1			Saida *Alg*	62C1
				Saïda *Leb*	60B2

Sa'idabad *Iran*	57C4	
Saidia *Mor*	17B2	
Saidpur *India*	52B1	
Saidu Pak	50C2	
Saigo *Japan*	41A1	
Saigon *Viet*	42D3	
Saiha *India*	52C2	
Saihan Tal *China*	34D2	
Saijo *Japan*	41A1	
Saiki *Japan*	40C4	
St Abb's Head, Pt *Scot*	8C2	
St Albans *Eng*	9D4	
St Albans, Vermont *USA*	91D2	
St Albans, West Virginia *USA*	90B3	
St Albert *Can*	89E2	
St Amand-les-Eaux *France*	12B1	
St Amand-Mont Rond *France*		
St Andrews *Scot*	10C3	
St Ann's Bay *Jamaica*	103H1	
St Anthony *Can*	83E4	
St Arnaud *Aust*	74B3	
St Augustine *USA*	93B2	
St Austell *Eng*	9B4	
St-Avold *France*	12D2	
St Bees Head, Pt *Eng*	8C2	
St-Bonnet *France*	13B2	
St-Brieuc *France*	14B2	
St Catherines *Can*	91C2	
St Catherine, Mt *Grenada*	103M2	
St Catherines I *USA*	93B1	
St Catherines Pt *Eng*	9D4	
St Chamond *France*	15C2	
St Charles, Missouri *USA*	94B2	
St Clair *USA*	90B2	
St Clair, L *USA/Can*	90B2	
St Clair Shores *USA*	90B2	
St Claud *France*	15D2	
St Cloud *USA*	86A2	
Ste Croix *Switz*	13B1	
St Croix, I *Caribbean*	103E3	
St Davids Head, Pt *Wales*	9B4	
St Denis *France*	12B2	
St Denis *Réunion*	67E3	
St Dizier *France*	12C2	
St Elias, Mt *USA*	88F2	
St Elias Mts *Can*	88G2	
Saintes *France*	14B2	
St Étienne *France*	15C2	
St Gallen *Switz*	13C1	
St Gaudens *France*	14C3	
St George *Aust*	75C1	
St George, South Carolina *USA*	93B1	
St George, Utah *USA*	85B3	
St George I, Florida *USA*	93B2	
St George, Pt *USA*	96B2	
St-Georges *Can*	91D1	
St George's *Grenada*	103E4	
St Georges Chan *Irish Rep/ Wales*	11C3	
St Germain-en-Laye *France*	12A2	
St-Gervais *France*	13B2	
St Gotthard, P *Switz*	13C1	
St Govans Head, Pt *Wales*	9B4	
St Helena *USA*	98A1	
St Helena, I *Atlantic O*	69H5	
St Helens *Aust*	75C4	
St Helens *Eng*	8C3	
St Helens *USA*	96B1	
St Helens, Mt *USA*	96B1	
St Helier *Jersey*	14B2	
St Hippolyte *France*	13B1	
St Hyacinthe *Can*	12C1	
St-Hyacinthe *Can*	83C5	
St Ignace *USA*	90B1	
St Ives *Eng*	9B4	
St James, Missouri *USA*	94B2	
St Jean *Can*	91D1	
St-Jean d'Angely *France*	14B2	
St-Jean-de-Maurienne *France*	13B2	
St Jean, L *Can*	86C2	
St-Jérôme *Can*	91D1	
Saint John *Can*	83D5	
St John's *Can*	83E5	
St Johns, Michigan *USA*	90B2	
St Johnsbury *USA*	91D2	
St-Joseph *Can*	91D1	
St Joseph, Louisiana *USA*	95B3	
St Joseph, Michigan *USA*	90A2	
St Joseph, Missouri *USA*	94B2	
St Joseph *Trinidad*	103L1	
St Joseph I *Can*	90B1	
St Joseph, L *Can*	83A4	
St Julien *France*	13B1	
St-Junien *France*	14C2	
St-Just-en-Chaussée *France*	12B2	
St Kilda, I *Scot*	80B2	
St Kitts, I *Caribbean*	103E3	
St-Laurent *France*	13A1	
St Lawrence, R *Can*	83D5	
St Lawrence I *USA*	80A3	
St Lawrence Seaway *Can/USA*		
St Lo *France*	91C2	
St Louis *Sen*	63A3	
St Louis *USA*	87A3	
St Lucia, I *Caribbean*	103E4	
St Lucia, L *S Africa*	67H1	
St Malo *France*	14B2	
St Maries *USA*	96C1	
St Martin, I *Caribbean*	103E3	
St Mary Peak, Mt *Aust*	74A2	
St Marys *Aust*	75C4	
St Marys *USA*	91C2	
Ste-Menehould *France*	12C2	
St Michael *USA*	88B2	
St Michaels *USA*	92A3	
St-Michel *France*	13B2	
St-Mihiel *France*	12C2	
St Moritz *Switz*	13C1	
St-Nazaire *France*	14B2	
St-Niklaas *Belg*	12C1	
St-Omer *France*	12B1	
St-Pol-Sur-Ternoise *France*	12B1	
St Pölten *Austria*	25B3	
St Quentin *France*	12B2	
St Raphaël *France*	15D3	
St Simons I *USA*	93B1	
St Stephen *USA*	93B1	
St Thomas *Can*	90B2	
St-Tropez *France*	15D3	
St Truiden *Belg*	12C1	
St-Valéry-sur-Somme *France*	12A1	
St Vincent, I *Caribbean*	103E4	
St Vincent, G *Aust*	74A2	
St-Vith *W Germ*	12D1	
St Wendel *W Germ*	12D2	
Saipan, I *Pacific O*	37F2	
Saïydabad *Afghan*	50B2	
Sajama, Mt *Bol*	106C2	
Sakai *Japan*	40D4	
Sakaidi *Japan*	41A2	
Sakaiminato *Japan*	41A1	
Sakakah *S Arabia*	59D4	
Sakami *Can*	86C1	
Sakania *Zaïre*	66B2	
Sakaraha *Madag*	67D3	
Sakasleja *USSR*	24C1	
Sakata *Japan*	40D3	
Saketél *Benin*	63C4	
Sakhalin, I *USSR*	35G1	
Sakishima gunto, Is *Japan*	35E4	
Sal, I *Cape Verde*	63A4	
Sala *Sweden*	5H7	
Saladillo *Arg*	110D3	
Salaga *Ghana*	63B4	
Sala Hintoun *Camb*	42C3	
Salal *Chad*	64B1	
Salalah *Oman*	47D4	
Salamanca *Chile*	110A2	
Salamanca *Mexico*	99A1	
Salamanca *Spain*	16A1	
Salamanca *USA*	91C2	
Salamaua *PNG*	37F4	
Salamonie, R *USA*	91C2	
Salang *Indon*	44D1	
Salangen *Nor*	4H5	
Salar de Arizaro *Arg*	106C3	
Salar de Atacama, Salt Pan *Chile*		
Salar de Coipasa, Salt Pan *Bol*	106C2	
Salar de Uyuni, Salt Pan *Bol*	106C3	
Salasomaggiore *Italy*	13C2	
Salavat *USSR*	27J3	
Salayar *Indon*	38D4	
Sala y Gomez, I *Pacific O*	71L5	
Salazar *Arg*	110C3	
Salbris *France*	14C2	
Saldanha *S Africa*	66A4	
Saldhad *Syria*	60C2	
Saldungaray *Arg*	110C3	
Saldus *USSR*	24C1	
Sale *USA*	75C3	
Salem, Illinois *USA*	94C2	
Salem *India*	53B3	
Salem, Massachusetts *USA*	92D1	
Salem, New Jersey *USA*	92B3	
Salem, Oregon *USA*	96B2	
Salembu Besar, I *Indon*	44C4	

Salen *Sweden*	5G6
Salerno *Italy*	19B2
Salford *Eng*	8C3
Salgót *Hung*	20A1
Salgotarjan *Hung*	25B3
Salgueiro *Brazil*	107D3
Salihli *Turk*	21C3
Salima *Malawi*	67C2
Salimaa, L *Fin*	5K6
Salina, Kansas *USA*	9A2
Salina, I *Italy*	19B3
Salina Cruz *Mexico*	99B2
Salina de Arizato *Arg*	108C3
Salina Grande, Salt Pan *Arg*	110B3
Salina La Antigua, Salt Pan *Arg*	110B2
Salinas *Brazil*	107B2
Salinas *USA*	98B2
Salinas de Llancaneb, Salt Pan *Arg*	110B3
Salinas Grandes, Salt Pan *Arg*	110B2
Salines, Pt *Grenada*	103M2
Salinópolis *Brazil*	107B2
Salins *France*	13A1
Salisbury *Eng*	9D4
Salisbury, Maryland *USA*	91C3
Salisbury *I Can*	82C3
Salisbury Plain *Eng*	9D4
Salla *Fin*	4K5
Sallanches *France*	13B2
Sallisaw *USA*	9A82
Sallyana *Nepal*	52A1
Salmas *Iran*	59D2
Salmi *USSR*	4L6
Salmo *Can*	96C1
Salmon *USA*	8A82
Salmon Arm *Can*	89D2
Salmon River Mts *USA*	8A82
Salo *Fin*	5J6
Salò *Italy*	15D3
Salon-de-Provence *France*	15D3
Salonta *Rom*	20B1
Salpausselka, Region *Fin*	4K6
Salsacate *Arg*	110B2
Sal'sk *USSR*	27F4
Salt *Jordan*	60B2
Salta *Arg*	106C3
Salta, State *Arg*	106C3
Saltillo *Mexico*	100B2
Salt Lake City *USA*	8A82
Salto *Arg*	110C2
Salto *Urug*	110C2
Salto Angostura, Waterfall *Colombia*	108C3
Salto da Divisa *Brazil*	111D1
Salto del Angel, Waterfall *Ven*	109E2
Salto del Guaira, Waterfall *Brazil*	106E3
Salto Grande, Waterfall *Colombia*	108C4
Salt Range, Mts *Pak*	50C2
Salt River *Jamaica*	103H2
Saluda *USA*	93B1
Saluzzo *Italy*	13B2

Salvador *Brazil*	107D4
Salvador, L *USA*	95B4
Salvatierra *Mexico*	99A1
Salwah *Qatar*	57B5
Salween, R *Burma*	42B1
Sal'yany *USSR*	59E2
Salzburg *Austria*	23C3
Salzgitter *W Germ*	22C2
Salzwedel *E Germ*	22C2
Samagaltay *USSR*	34B1
Samales Group, Is *Phil*	45B4
Samaná *Dom Rep*	103D3
Samandagi *Turk*	58C2
Samangan *Afghan*	50B1
Samar, I *Phil*	45C3
Samarai *PNG*	73E2
Samarinda *Indon*	44D3
Samarkand *USSR*	46E2
Samarra' *Iraq*	59D3
Samar S *Phil*	45B3
Sambalpur *India*	52A2
Sambas *Indon*	44B2
Samba Madag	67E2
Sambhal *India*	50D3
Samboja *Indon*	44D3
Sambor *USSR*	43E3
Samch'ok S *Korea*	40B3
Same *Tanz*	65D3
Samedan *Switz*	13C1
Samer *France*	12A1
Samfya *Zambia*	66B2
Samka *Burma*	42B1
Sam Neua *Laos*	42C1
Sámos, I *Greece*	21C3
Samothráki, I *Greece*	21C2
Sampacho *Arg*	110C2
Sampaga *Indon*	44D3
Sampit *Indon*	44D3
Sam Rayburn Res *USA*	95B3
Samrong *Camb*	42C3
Samso, I *Den*	22C1
Samsun *Turk*	58C1
Sam *Mali*	63B3
San'a *Yemen*	47C4
San Agustín *Arg*	105C2
Sanandaj *Iran*	56A2
San Andreas *USA*	98B1
San Andrés Tuxtla *Mexico*	101C3
San Angelo *USA*	85C3
San Antioco *Sardegna*	19A3
San Antioco, I *Medit S*	19A3
San Antonio *Chile*	110A2
San Antonio *Phil*	45B2
San Antonio Abad *Spain*	17C2
San Antonio de los Banos *Cuba*	102A2
San Antonio, Mt *USA*	97C3
San Antonio Oeste *USA*	105C4
San Augustin *Arg*	110D3
San Agustín de Valle Féril *Arg*	110B2
Sanawad *India*	51D4
San Bartolo *Mexico*	99A1
San Benedicto, I *Mexico*	100A3
San Benito Mt *USA*	98B2

San Bernardino *USA*	98D3
San Bernardo *Chile*	110A2
San Carlos *Chile*	110A3
San Carlos *Nic*	108A1
San Carlos *Phil*	45B2
San Carlos de Bariloche *Arg*	105B4
San-chung *Taiwan*	35E4
Sanchursk *USSR*	27G2
San Clemente *Chile*	110A3
San Clemente *USA*	98D4
San Clemente I *USA*	97B3
San Cristóbal *Arg*	110C2
San Cristóbal *Mexico*	101C3
San Cristóbal *Ven*	108C2
San Cristóbal, I *Ecuador*	108J7
San Cristóbal, I *Solomon Is*	73F2
Sancti Spiritus *Cuba*	101E2
Sandai *Indon*	44C3
Sandakan *Malay*	36C3
Sanday, I *Scot*	10C2
Sanderson *USA*	85C3
Sandfly L *Can*	89F1
San Diego *USA*	97B3
Sandikli *Turk*	58B2
Sandila *India*	52A1
Sandnes *Nor*	5F7
Sandnessjoen *Nor*	4G5
Sando *Faroes*	4D3
Sandoa *Zaire*	64C3
Sandomierz *Pol*	25C2
Sandpoint *USA*	96C1
Sandrio *Italy*	15D2
Sand Springs *USA*	94A2
Sandstone *Aust*	72A3
Sandu *China*	39C4
Sandusky *USA*	90B2
Sandviken *Sweden*	5H6
Sandy L *Can*	83A4
San Elcano *Arg*	110C2
San Felipe, Baja Cal *Mexico*	85B3
San Felipe *Chile*	110A2
San Felipe, Guanajuato *Mexico*	99A1
San Felipe *Ven*	103D4
San Feliu de Guixols *Spain*	17C1
San Felix, I *Pacific O*	104A5
San Fernando *Chile*	110A2
San Fernando *Phil*	45B2
San Fernando *Phil*	45B2
San Fernando *Spain*	16A2
San Fernando *Trinidad*	103E4
San Fernando *USA*	98C3
San Fernando *Ven*	108D2
Sanford, Florida *USA*	93B2
Sanford, Mt *USA*	88F2
San Francisco *Arg*	110C2
San Francisco *Dom Rep*	103C3
San Francisco *USA*	98A2
San Francisco del Oro *Mexico*	100B2
San Francisco del Rincon *Mexico*	99A1
San Gabriel Mts *USA*	98D3
Sanganner *India*	51C5
Sangan, I *Pacific O*	37F2
Sangareddi *India*	53B1

Sangeang, I *Indon* 44D4
Sanger *USA* 98C2
Sangau *Indon* 44C2
Sanghar *Pak* 51B3
Sangkhla Buri *Thai* 42B3
Sangkulirang *Indon* 44D2
Sangli *India* 53A1
Sangmélima *Cam* 64B2
San Gorgonio Mt *USA* 85B3
San Gregorio, Mts *USA* 85C3
San Gregorio *USA* 110C2
San Gregorio *USA* 98A2
Sangrur *India* 50D2
San Ignacio *Arg* 106E4
San Isidro *Arg* 45B3
San Jacinto *Colombia* 108B2
San Jacinto Peak, Mt *USA* 9783
San Javier *Chile* 110A3
San Javier, Sante Fe *Arg* 110D2
Sanjo, I *Japan* 40D3
San Joao del Rei *Brazil* 107C6
San Joaquin Valley *USA* 98C2
San José *Costa Rica* 103A1
San José *Guatemala* 101C3
San Jose, I *Phil* 45B2
San Jose, Mindoro *Phil* 45B3
San José *USA* 98B2
San José, I *Mexico* 85B4
San José de Chiquitos *Bol* 106D2
San José de Feliciano *Arg* 110D2
San José de Jachal *Arg* 110B2
San José de la Dormida
  Arg 110C2
San José do Rio Prêto
  Brazil 107B6
San José del Cabo *Mexico* 100B2
San Juan *Arg* 110B2
San Juan *Puerto Rico* 103D3
San Juan, State *Arg* 110B2
San Juan *Trinidad* 103L1
San Juan *Ven* 108D2
San Juan, Mt *USA* 84C3
San Juan Bautista *Mexico* 99B2
San Juan Bautista *Par* 106E4
San Juan Bautista *USA* 98B2
San Juan del Norte *Nic* 101D3
San Juan de los Cayos *Ven* 103D4
San Juan de loz Lagoz
  Mexico 99A1
San Juan del Rio *Mexico* 99A1
San Juan del Sur
  Nicaragua 101D3
San Juan Is *USA* 96B1
San Juan Tepozcolula
  Mexico 99C2
San Julián *Arg* 105C5
San Justo *Arg* 110C2
San Leandro *USA* 98A2
San Lorenzo *Ecuador* 108B3
San Lorenzo *Arg* 110C2
San Lucas *USA* 98B2
San Luis *Arg* 110B2
San Luis, State *Arg* 110B2
San Luis de la Paz *Mexico* 99A1
San Luis Obispo *USA* 97A2
San Luis Potosi *Mexico* 99A1

San Luis Res *USA* 98B2
Sanluri *Sardegna* 19A3
San Maigualida, Mts *Ven* 108D2
San Manuel *Arg* 110D3
San Marcos *Chile* 110B2
San Marcos *Mexico* 99B2
San Marino, Republic
  Europe 18B2
San Martin, Mendoza *Arg* 110B2
San Martin, Base *Ant* 112C3
San Martino di Castroza
  Italy 13D1
San Martin Tuxmelucan
  Mexico 99B2
San Mateo *USA* 98A2
San Matias *Bol* 106E2
Sanmenxia *China* 38C3
San Miguel *El Salvador* 101C3
San Miguel, I *USA* 98B3
San Miguel del Allende
  Mexico 99A1
San Miguel del Monte *Arg* 110D3
San Miguel de Tucumán
  Arg 106C4
Sanming *China* 39D4
San Nicolas, I *USA* 85B3
San Nicolás de los Arroyos
  Arg 110D2
Sannicshof *S Africa* 67G1
Sanniquellie *Lib* 63B4
Sanok *Pol* 25C3
San Onofre *Colombia* 102B5
San Onofre *USA* 98D4
San Pablo *Phil* 45B3
San Pedro, Buenos Aires *Arg* 110D2
San Pédro *Ivory Coast* 63B4
San Pedro, Jujuy *Arg* 106D3
San Pedro *Par* 106E3
San Pedro Chan *USA* 98C4
San Pedro de las Colonias
  Mexico 85C4
San Pedro Sula *Honduras* 101D3
San Pietro, I *Medit S* 19A3
San Quintin *Mexico* 100A1
San Rafael *Arg* 110B2
San Rafael *USA* 98A2
San Rafael Mts *USA* 98C3
San Remo *Italy* 15D3
San Salvador *Arg* 110D2
San Salvador, I *Caribbean* 102C2
San Salvador, I *Ecuador* 108J7
San Salvador de Jujuy *Arg* 106C3
San Sebastian *Spain* 17B1
San Severo *Italy* 19C2
Santa Ana *Bol* 106C2
Santa Ana *Guatemala* 101C3
Santa Ana *USA* 98D4
Santa Ana Mts *USA* 98D4
Santa Bárbara *Chile* 110A3
Santa Barbara *Mexico* 100B2
Santa Barbara *USA* 98C3
Santa Barbara, I *USA* 98C4
Santa Barbara Chan *USA* 98B3
Santa Barbara Res *USA* 98C4
Santa Catalina, I *USA* 98C4
Santa Catalina, G of *USA* 98C4

Santa Catarina, State *Brazil* 106F4
Santa Clara *Cuba* 102B2
Santa Clara *USA* 98B2
Santa Cruz *Arg* 105C6
Santa Cruz *Bol* 106D2
Santa Cruz *Chile* 110A2
Santa Cruz *Phil* 45B3
Santa Cruz, State *Arg* 105B5
Santa Cruz, I *USA* 98C4
Santa Cruz Cabrália *Brazil* 111D1
Santa Cruz Chan *USA* 98C3
Santa Cruz de la Palma
  Canary Is 62A2
Santa Cruz del Sur *Cuba* 102B2
Santa Cruz de Tenerife
  Canary Is 62A2
Santa Cruz do Cuando
  Angola 66B2
Santa Cruz do Rio Pardo
  Brazil 111B2
Santa Cruz Mts *USA* 98A2
Santa Elena *Arg* 110D2
Santa Elena *Ven* 109E3
Santa Fe *Arg* 110C2
Santa Fe, State *Arg* 110C2
Santa Fe *USA* 85C3
Santa Helena de Goiás
  Brazil 111A1
Santai *China* 39B3
Santa Inés, I *Chile* 105B6
Santa Isabel, La Pampa *Arg* 110B3
Santa Isabel, Sante Fe *Arg* 110C2
Santa Isabel, I *Solomon Is* 73E1
Santa Lucia Ra, *USA* 97A2
Santa Lucia Range, Mts *USA* 97A2
Santa Luzia, I *Cape Verde* 63A4
Santa Margarita, I *Mexico* 85B4
Santa Maria *Brazil* 106F4
Santa Maria *Colombia* 102C4
Santa Maria *USA* 97A3
Santa Maria, I *Acores* 69A1
Santa Maria del Rio *Mexico* 99A1
Santa Marta *Colombia* 108C1
Santa Monica *USA* 98C3
Santana do Livramento
  Brazil 105E2
Santander *Colombia* 108B3
Santander *Spain* 17C2
Santañy *Spain* 17C2
Santa Paula *USA* 98C3
Santa Quitéria *Brazil* 107C2
Santarém *Brazil* 109G4
Santarém *Port* 17A2
Santa Rosa, California *USA* 98A2
Santa Rosa *Honduras* 101D3
Santa Rosa, La Pampa *Arg* 110B3
Santa Rosa, Mendoza *Arg* 110B2
Santa Rosa, San Luis *Arg* 110B2
Santa Rosa, I *USA* 98B3
Santa Rosalia *Mexico* 100A2
Santa Rosa Range, Mts
  USA 96C2
Santa Talhada *Brazil* 107D3
Santa Teresa *Brazil* 111C1
Santa Teresa di Gallura
  Sardegna 19A2

Santa Ynez Mts USA	98B3	Sao Vicente Brazil	111B2	Sasebo Japan	40B4
Santhia Italy	13C2	Sao Vincente, I Cape Verde	63A4	Saskatchewan, Province Can	81H4
Santiago Chile	110A2	Sápai Greece	21C2	Saskatchewan, R Can	81H4
Santiago Dom Rep	103C3	Sape Indon	44D4	Saskatoon Can	81H4
Santiago Panama	108A2	Sapele Nig	63C4	Sasolburg S Africa	67G1
Santiago Phil	45B2	Sapporo Japan	40E2	Sasovo USSR	27F3
Santiago de Compostela Spain	16A1	Sapri Italy	19C2	Sassandra Ivory Coast	63B4
Santiago de Cuba Cuba	102B2	Sapulpa USA	94A2	Sassari Sardegna	19A2
Santiago del Estero Arg	110B2	Saqqez Iran	56A2	Sassnitz E Germ	22C2
Santiago del Estero, State Arg	106D4	Sarab Iran	56A2	Sassuolo Italy	13D2
Santiago Peak, Mt USA	98D4	Sarafa USSR	20C1	Sastre Arg	110C2
Santo, State Brazil	107C5	Sarajevo Yugos	20A2	Satara India	53A1
Santo Anastatácio Brazil	111A2	Sarakhs Iran	56B3	Satengar, Is Indon	44D4
Santo Angelo Brazil	106F4	Saraktash USSR	27J3	Säter Sweden	5H6
San Antao, I Cape Verde	63A4	Sarala USSR	29A2	Satkhira Bang	27J2
Santo Antonio da Platina Brazil	111A2	Saranac L USA	91D2	Satna India	52A2
Santo Domingo Dom Rep	103D3	Saranac Lake USA	91D2	Satpura Range, Mts India	51C4
Santos Brazil	111C2	Sarandë Alb	21B3	Satu Mare Rom	20B1
Santos Dumont Brazil	111C2	Sarangani Is Phil	45C4	Sauce Arg	110D2
Santo Tomé Arg	106E4	Saransk USSR	27G3	Sauda Nor	5F7
San Valentin, Mt Chile	105B5	Sarapul USSR	27G3	Saudi Arabia, Kingdom Arabian Pen	46C3
San Vicente Chile	110A2	Sarasota USA	93B2	Sauerland, Region W Germ	12D1
Sanza Pomba Angola	64B3	Saratoga Springs USA	91D2	Sauethárkrókur Iceland	4B1
Sao Borja Brazil	106E4	Saratok Malay	44C2	Saugatuck USA	90A2
Sao Carlos Brazil	111B2	Saratov USSR	27G3	Saugerties USA	92C1
Sao Félix, Mato Grosso Brazil	109G5	Saratovskoye Vodokhranilishche, Res USSR	27G3	Saugstad, Mt Can	89B2
Sao Fidélis Brazil	111C2	Sarawak, State Malay	33F4	Sault Sainte Marie Can	83B5
Sao Francisco Brazil	111C1	Saraykoy Turk	58A2	Sault Ste Marie Can	90B1
Sao Francisco, R Brazil	107D3	Sarbisheh Iran	56C3	Sault Ste Marie USA	90B1
Sao Francisco do Sul Brazil	106G4	Sardalais Libya	61A2	Saumlaki Indon	37E4
Sao Gotardo Brazil	111B1	Sar Dasht Iran	56A2	Saumur France	14B2
Sao Hill Tanz	65D3	Sardegna, I Medit S	18A2	Saurimo Angola	64C3
Sao Joao da Barra Brazil	111C2	Sarektjåkkå, Mt Sweden	4H5	Sauteurs Grenada	103M2
Sao Joao de Boa Vista Brazil	111B2	Sargodha Pak	50C2	Savalou Benin	63C4
Sao Joao da Ponte Brazil	111C1	Sarh Chad	64B2	Savannah, Georgia USA	93B1
Sao Joao del Rei Brazil	111C2	Sari Iran	56B2	Savannakhet Laos	42C2
Sao Joaquim da Barra Brazil	111B2	Sarikamis Turk	59D1	Savanna la Mar Jamaica	102B3
Sao Jorge, I Acores	62A1	Sarina Aust	73D3	Savant Lake Can	83A4
Sao José do Rio Prêto Brazil	111B2	Sar-i-Pul Afghan	50B1	Savarane Laos	42D2
Sao José dos Campos Brazil	111B2	Sarir Libya	61B2	Savé Benin	63C4
Sao Luis Brazil	107C2	Sarir Tibesti, Desert Libya	61B2	Saveh Iran	56B3
Sao Maria do Suacui Brazil	111C1	Sariwon N Korea	40B3	Saverne France	12D2
Sao Mateus Brazil	111D1	Sark, I UK	14B2	Savigliano Italy	13B2
Sao Miguel, I Acores	62A1	Sarkisla Turk	58C2	Savoie, Region France	12B2
Sao Nicolau, I Cape Verde	63A4	Sarmi Indon	37E4	Savona Italy	15D3
Sao Paulo Brazil	111B2	Sarmiento Arg	105C5	Savonlinna Fin	4K6
Sao Paulo, State Brazil	111A2	Särna Sweden	5G6	Savoonga USA	80A3
Sao Raimundo Nonato Brazil	107C3	Sarnen Switz	13C1	Savukoski Fin	4K5
Sao Romao Brazil	111B1	Sarnia Can	90B2	Savu S Indon	37D4
Sao Sebastia do Paraiso Brazil	111B2	Sarny USSR	24D2	Saw Burma	43D3
Sao Simao, Goias Brazil	111A1	Saroaq Greenland	82E2	Sawai Madhopur India	51D3
Sao Simao, Sao Paulo Brazil	111B2	Sarobi Afghan	50B2	Sawang Indon	44A2
Sao Tiago, I Cape Verde	63A4	Sarolangun Indon	44A3	Sawankhalok Thai	42B2
Sao Tomé, I W Africa	63C4	Saronikós Kólpos, G Greece	21B3	Sawara Japan	41C1
Sao Tomé and Principe, Republic W Africa	63C4	Saronno Italy	13C2	Sawtooth Mt USA	88E1
		Sarpsborg Nor	5G7	Sawu, I Indon	72B2
		Sarralbe France	12D2	Say Niger	63C3
		Sarrebourg France	12D2	Sayghan Afghan	50B2
		Sarreguemines France	12D2	Sayhut S Yemen	47D4
		Sarre-Union France	12D2	Saykhin USSR	27G4
		Sarrion Spain	17B1	Saynshand Mongolia	39H2
		Sartanahp Pak	51B3	Say-Utes USSR	39G5
		Sartène Corse	19A2	Sayville USA	92C2
		Sarykamys USSR	27H4		
		Sasaram India	52A2		

Sayward Can	89B2	
Scafell Pike, Mt Eng	8C2	
Scalloway Scot	10D1	
Scarborough Can	91C2	
Scarborough Eng	8D2	
Scarborough Tobago	103E4	
Scarp, I Scot	10A2	
Scarriff Irish Rep	11B2	
Schaffhausen Switz	18A1	
Scharding Austria	23C3	
Scharteberg, Mt W Germ	12D1	
Schefferville Can	83D4	
Schenectady USA	86C2	
Schio Italy	13D2	
Schleiden W Germ	12D1	
Schleswig W Germ	22B2	
Schleswig Holstein, State W Germ	22B2	
Schoharie USA	92B1	
Schouten, Is PNG	37F4	
Schreiber Can	85B5	
Schurz USA	97B2	
Schuykill Haven USA	92A2	
Schwabische Alb, Upland W Germ	23B3	
Schwarzwald, Mts W Germ	15D2	
Schwäbisch Upland, W Germ	23B3	
Schwatka Mts USA	88C1	
Schwaz Austria	13D1	
Schweinfurt W Germ	23C2	
Schweizer Reneke S Africa	67G1	
Schwerin E Germ	22C2	
Schwyz Switz	13C1	
Sciacca Italy	19B3	
Scone Aust	75D2	
Scotia Ridge Atlantic O	69F7	
Scotia S Atlantic O	69F7	
Scotland, Country U K	10B3	
Scott, Base Ant	112B7	
Scott City USA	85C2	
Scott I Ant	112C6	
Scott, Mt USA	96B2	
Scott Reef Timor S	72B2	
Scottsbluff USA	84C2	
Scottsboro USA	93A1	
Scottsdale Aust	75C4	
Scranton USA	86C2	
Scuol Switz	13D1	
Sea Lake Aust	74B3	
Searcy USA	94B2	
Seaside, California USA	98B2	
Seaside, Oregon USA	98A1	
Seaside Park USA	92B3	
Seat USA	96B1	
Sebastopol USA	98A1	
Sebez USSR	24D1	
Sebring USA	93B2	
Secretary I NZ	77A3	
Sedalia USA	94B2	
Sedan France	12C2	
Seddonville NZ	77B2	
Sede Boqer Israel	60B3	
Sederot Israel	60B3	
Sédhiou Sen	60A3	
Sedom Israel	60B3	
Seeheim Namibia	66A3	
Sefton, Mt NZ	77B2	
Segamat Malay	43C5	
Segorbe Spain	17B2	
Ségou Mali	63B3	
Segovia Spain	63B3	
Séguéla Ivory Coast	63B4	
Seguntur Indon	44D2	
Sehwan Pak	51B3	
Seinäjoki Fin	4J6	
Seine, R France	14C2	
Seine-et-Marne, Department France	12B2	
Sekenke Tanz	65D3	
Selah USA	96B1	
Selaru, I Indon	37F4	
Selat Wetar, Chan Indon	37D4	
Selawik USA	88B1	
Selawik L USA	88B1	
Selby Eng	8D3	
Selcuk Turk	21C3	
Seldovia USA	88D3	
Selebi Pikwe Botswana	66B3	
Selfoss Iceland	4B2	
Selima Oasis Sudan	61B2	
Selkirk Can	81J4	
Selkirk Scot	8C2	
Selkirk USA	96B1	
Selma, California USA	98C2	
Selouane Mor	16B2	
Selous, Mt Can	88H2	
Selvas, Region Brazil	108C5	
Selwyn Aust	73D3	
Selwyn Mts Can	80E3	
Semarang Indon	44C4	
Semenov USSR	27E2	
Semidi Is USA	88C3	
Semiluki USSR	28F3	
Seminole, Oklahoma USA	95A2	
Seminole, L USA	93B1	
Semipalatinsk USSR	31K4	
Semirara Is Phil	45B3	
Semnan Iran	56B3	
Semitau Indon	44C2	
Semnan Iran	56B2	
Sempopala, Hist Site Mexico	99D2	
Sena Madureira Brazil	108D5	
Senanga Zambia	66B2	
Senatobia USA	95C3	
Sendai, Honshu Japan	40E3	
Sendai, Kyushu Japan	40C4	
Sendwha India	51D4	
Seneca Falls USA	92B1	
Senegal, Republic Africa	63A3	
Senekal S Africa	67G1	
Senhor do Bonfim Brazil	107D4	
Senigallia Italy	18B2	
Senj Yugos	18C2	
Senkaku Gunto, Is Japan	38C4	
Senlis France	12B2	
Sennar Sudan	65D1	
Senneterre Can	83C5	
Sennes France	15C2	
Senta Yugos	20A1	
Sentery Zaïre	64C3	
Sentinel Peak, Mt Can	89C2	
Seoni India	51D4	
Separation Pt NZ	76B2	
Sepone Laos	42D2	
Sept-Iles Can	83D4	
Séquédine Niger	61A2	
Sequoia, Nat Pk USA	97B2	
Seram, I Indon	37D4	
Serang Indon	44B4	
Serasan, I Indon	44B2	
Serbia, Region Yugos	20A2	
Serdobsk USSR	27F3	
Seremban Malay	43C5	
Serengeti Nat Pk Tanz	65D3	
Serenje Zambia	66C2	
Sergach USSR	27G2	
Sergino USSR	31H3	
Sergipe, State Brazil	107D4	
Seria Brunei	44C2	
Serian Malay	44C2	
Sérifos, I Greece	21B3	
Serir Calanscio, Desert Libya	61B2	
Sermaize-les-Bains France	12C2	
Sermata, I Indon	37D4	
Sernovodsk USSR	27H3	
Serov USSR	31H4	
Serowe Botswana	66B3	
Serpa Port	16B2	
Serpukhov USSR	26E3	
Serra da Canastra, Mts Brazil	111A4	
Serra da Mantiqueira, Mts Brazil	111B2	
Serra da Mombuca Brazil	111A1	
Serra do Cabral, Mt Brazil	111C1	
Serra do Cachimbo, Mts Brazil	109F5	
Serra do Caiapó, Mts Brazil	111A1	
Serra do Cantu, Mts Brazil	111A2	
Serra do Caparaó, Mts Brazil	111C2	
Serra do Chifre Brazil	107C5	
Serra do Espinhaço, Mts Brazil	111C1	
Serra do Mar, Mts Brazil	111B2	
Serra do Mirante, Mts Brazil	111A2	
Serra do Navio Brazil	109G3	
Serra do Paranapiacaba, Mts Brazil	111B2	
Serra dos Caiabis, Mts Brazil	109F6	
Serra dos Dourados, Mts Brazil	111A2	
Serra dos Parecis, Mts Brazil	109E6	
Serra dos Piloes, Mts Brazil	111B1	
Serra Dourada, Mts Brazil	111A1	
Serra Formosa, Mts Brazil	109F6	
Sérrai Greece	21B2	
Serrana Bank, Is Caribbean	101D3	
Serrana de Cuenca, Mts Spain	17B1	
Serranópolis Brazil	111A1	
Serra Pacaraima, Mts Brazil/Ven	109E3	
Serra Parima, Mts Brazil	109E3	
Serra Tumucumaque Brazil	109G3	

Serrezuela Arg	110B2	
Serrinha Brazil	107D4	
Serrmilik Greenland	82G3	
Serro Brazil	111C1	
Sertanópolis Brazil	111A2	
Sértar China	38C1	
Sesfontein Namibia	66A2	
Sesheke Zambia	66B2	
Sestriere Italy	13B2	
Setana Japan	41B1	
Sete France	15C3	
Sete Lagoas Brazil	111C1	
Sétif Alg	62C1	
Seto Japan	41B1	
Seto Naikai, S Japan	41A2	
Settat Mor		
Settle Eng	8C2	
Settler Can	81G4	
Setúbal Port	16A2	
Sevan, Oz, L USSR	59E1	
Sevastopol' USSR	26D5	
Severn, R Eng	9C3	
Severnaya Zemlya, I USSR	1B9	
Severo-Baykalskoye Nagorye, Mts USSR	29C2	
Severo Donets USSR	26E4	
Severodvinsk USSR	30E3	
Sevier L USA	84B3	
Sevilla Spain	16A2	
Sevlievo Bulg	20C2	
Seward, Alaska USA	88E2	
Seward, Nebraska USA	94A1	
Sexsmith Can	89D1	
Seychelles, Is Indian O	55K8	
Seyethisfjörethur Iceland	4C1	
Seyhan Turk	58C2	
Seymour Aust	74C3	
Seymour, Connecticut USA	92C2	
Seymour, Indiana USA	90A3	
Sézanne France	12B2	
Sfax Tunisia	62D1	
Sfinto Gheorghe Rom	20C1	
's-Gravenhage Neth	22A2	
Shaanxi, Province China	38B3	
Shabunda Zaire	64C3	
Shache China	48B2	
Shackleton Ice Shelf Ant	112C9	
Shadadkot Pak	51B3	
Shaftesbury Eng	9C4	
Shag Rocks, Is South Georgia	105G8	
Shahabad Iran	56A3	
Shahba Syria	60C2	
Shahdap Iran	57C3	
Shahdol India	50C4	
Shahin Dezh Iran	56A2	
Shah Kuh Iran	56C3	
Shahr-e Babak Iran	57C3	
Shahr Kord Iran	56B3	
Shajabad India	50D3	
Shajapur India	51D4	
Shakhty USSR	27F4	
Shakhun'ya USSR	27G2	
Shaki Nig	63C4	
Shaktoolik USA	88B2	
Shamary USSR	27J2	

Shambe Sudan	65D2	
Shamokin USA	92A2	
Shandaken USA	92B1	
Shandong, Province China	38D2	
Shangchuan Dao, I China	39C5	
Shangdu China	38C1	
Shanghai China	39E3	
Shangnan China	38C3	
Shangombo Zambia	66B2	
Shangra China	39D4	
Shangsi China	39B5	
Shang Xian China	38C3	
Shanqiu China	38D3	
Shansonggang China	40B2	
Shantarskiye Ostrova, I USSR	29F2	
Shantou China	39D5	
Shanxi, Province China	38C2	
Shan Xian China	38D3	
Shaoguan China	39C5	
Shaoxing China	39E4	
Shaoyang China	39C4	
Shapinsay, I Scot	10C2	
Shaqqa Syria	60C2	
Sharifabad Iran	56C2	
Sharjah UAE	57C4	
Sharlauk USSR	56B2	
Sharon, Plain of Israel	60B2	
Sharya USSR	27G2	
Shashamanna Eth	65D2	
Shashi China	39C3	
Shasta L USA	96B1	
Shasta, Mt USA	96B2	
Shaubak Jordan	60B3	
Shaunavon Can	89F3	
Shaver L USA	98C2	
Shawangunk Mt USA	92B2	
Shawinigan Can	91D1	
Shawnee, Oklahoma USA	95A2	
Sha Xian China	39D4	
Shay Gap Aust	72B3	
Shaykh Miskin Syria	60C2	
Shaykh 'Uthman S Yemen	55F8	
Shchigry USSR	26E3	
Shchors USSR	26D3	
Shchuchinsk USSR	31J4	
Sheboygan USA	90A2	
Shebshi, Mts Nig	64B2	
Sheep Haven, Estuary Irish Rep	11C1	
Sheerness Eng	9E4	
Shefar'am Israel	60B2	
Sheffield Eng	8D3	
Shekhupura Pak	50C2	
Shelagyote Peak, Mt Can	89B3	
Shelburne Falls USA	92C1	
Shelby, Michigan USA	90A2	
Shelby, Montana USA	84B2	
Shelbyville, Indiana USA	90A3	
Sheldon, Mt Can	75D2	
Shellharbour Aust	77A3	
Shelton USA	96B1	
Shemakha USSR	59E1	
Shenandoah USA	94A1	
Shenandoah Nat Pk USA	91C3	
Shendam Nig	63C4	

Shendi Sudan	61C2	
Shenmu China	38C2	
Shenyang China	38E1	
Shenzhen China	39C5	
Sheopur India	51D3	
Shepetovka USSR	25D2	
Shepparton Aust	74C3	
Sherborne Eng	9C4	
Sherbro I Sierra Leone	63A4	
Sherbrooke Can	91D1	
Shergarh India	51C3	
Sheridan, Arkansas USA	95B3	
Sheridan, Wyoming USA	84C2	
Sherman USA	95A3	
s-Hertogenbosh Neth	22B2	
Sheslay Can	88H3	
Shetland, Is Scot	6C1	
Shevchenko USSR	27H5	
Sheyk Sho'eyb, I Iran	57B4	
Shiashkotan, I USSR	35H2	
Shibarghan Afghan	50B1	
Shibetsu Japan	40D3	
Shibin el Kom Egypt	61C1	
Shijiazhuang China	38C2	
Shikarpur Pak	50B3	
Shikoku, I Japan	33G3	
Shikoku-sanchi, Mts Japan	41A2	
Shiliguri India	52B1	
Shilka USSR	34D1	
Shillington USA	92B2	
Shillong India	52C1	
Shilovo USSR	27F3	
Shimabara Japan	41A2	
Shimada Japan	41B2	
Shimanovsk USSR	35E1	
Shimizu Japan	40D3	
Shimoda Japan	41B2	
Shimoga India	53B2	
Shimonoseki Japan	40C4	
Shinas Oman	57C5	
Shingu Japan	40D4	
Shinjo Japan	41C1	
Shinminato Japan	40D3	
Shinshar Syria	60C1	
Shinyanga Tanz	65D3	
Shiogama Japan	40E3	
Shiping China	39A5	
Shippensburg USA	92A2	
Shiquan China	38B3	
Shirakawa Japan	41C1	
Shirane-san, Mt Japan	41B1	
Shirani-san, Mt Japan	41B1	
Shiraz Iran	57B4	
Shir Kuh Iran	56B3	
Shirotori Japan	41B1	
Shirvan Iran	56C2	
Shishmaref USA	88A1	
Shishmaref Inlet USA	88A1	
Shishmaret USA	80B3	
Shitanjing China	38B2	
Shively USA	90A3	
Shivpuri India	51D3	
Shivta, Hist Site Israel	60B3	
Shiwa Ngandu Zambia	67C2	
Shiyan China	38C3	
Shizuishan China	38B2	

Sinkat *Sudan*	61C3
Sinkiang, Autonomous Region	48C1
Sinnamary *French Guiana*	109G2
Sinop *Turk*	58C1
Sintana *Rom*	20B1
Sintang *Indon*	44C2
Sintra *Port*	16A2
Sinuiju *N Korea*	40A2
Siofok *Hung*	25B3
Sion *Switz*	13B1
Sioux City *USA*	84D2
Sioux Falls *USA*	84D2
Sioux Lookout *Can*	86A2
Sipalay *Phil*	45B4
Siparia *Trinidad*	103L1
Siping *China*	35E2
Siple Base, *Ant*	112B3
Siple I *Ant*	112B5
Sipocot *Phil*	45B3
Sipora *Indon*	36A4
Siquijor, I *Phil*	45B4
Sira *India*	53B2
Siracusa *Italy*	19C3
Sirajganj *Bangl*	52B2
Sir Alexander, Mt *Can*	89C2
Sir Bani Yas, I *UAE*	65C3
Sir Edward Pellew Group, Is *Aust*	72C2
Sir James McBrien, Mt *Can*	88J2
Sir Kalahasti *India*	53B2
Sir Laurier, Mt *Can*	89D2
Sirnak *Turk*	59D2
Sirohi *India*	51C4
Sironcha *India*	53B1
Sironj *India*	51D4
Siros, I *Greece*	21B3
Siri, I *Iran*	65C4
Sirsa *India*	50D3
Sir Sandford, Mt *Can*	89D2
Sirsi *India*	53A2
Sirt *Libya*	61A1
Sirte Desert *Libya*	61A1
Sirte, G of *Libya*	61A1
Sisak *Yugos*	18C1
Sisaket *Thai*	42C2
Sisophon *Camb*	42C2
Sissonne *France*	12B2
Sistan, Region *Iran/Afghan*	56D3
Sisteron *France*	14D3
Sistig Khem *USSR*	39B2
Sitapur *India*	52A1
Sitia *Greece*	21C3
Sitka *USA*	80E4
Sitkalidak I *USA*	88D3
Sitkinak, I *USA*	88D3
Sittard *Neth*	12C1
Sittwe *Burma*	52C2
Situbondo *Indon*	44C4
Sivas *Turk*	59C2
Siverek *Turk*	59C2
Sivrihisar *Turk*	59C1
Siwa *Egypt*	61B2
Siwalik Range, Mts *India*	52C1
Siwalik Range, Mts *Nepal*	52A1
Siyang *China*	38D3
Sjaelland, I *Den*	22C1
Skagen *Den*	5G7
Skagit Mt *Can*	96B1
Skagway *USA*	80E4
Skara *Sweden*	5G7
Skarzysko-Kamienna *Pol*	25C2
Skeena Mts *Can*	89B1
Skegness *Eng*	8E3
Skelleftea *Sweden*	4J6
Skiathos, I *Greece*	21B3
Skibbereen *Irish Rep*	11B3
Skidegate *Can*	81E4
Skiemiewice *Pol*	24C2
Skien *Nor*	5F7
Skikda *Alg*	62C1
Skikoku, I *Japan*	40C4
Skipton *Eng*	8D3
Skiros, I *Greece*	21B3
Skive *Den*	5F7
Skjern *Den*	22B1
Skjoldungen *Greenland*	82F3
Skokie *USA*	90A2
Skópelos, I *Greece*	21B3
Skopje *Yugos*	20B2
Skövde *Sweden*	5G7
Skovorodino *USSR*	29E2
Skwentna *USA*	88C3
Siwierzyna *Pol*	24B2
Skye, I *Scot*	6B2
Slagelse *Den*	5G7
Slatina *Rom*	20B2
Slaung *Indon*	44C4
Slav Brod *Yugos*	20A1
Slave Lake *Can*	89E1
Slavgorod, Rossiyskaya *USSR*	31J4
Slavuta *USSR*	25D2
Slavyansk *USSR*	26E4
Sleat, Sound of, Chan *Scot*	10B3
Sleetmute *USA*	88C2
Sleeve Bloom, Mts *Irish Rep*	11C2
Slidell *USA*	95C3
Slide Mt *USA*	92B2
Sligo, County *Irish Rep*	11B1
Sligo *Irish Rep*	7B3
Sliven *Bulg*	20C2
Slobozia *Rom*	20C2
Slocan *Can*	89D3
Slonim *USSR*	24D2
Slovensko, Region *Czech*	25B3
Slubice *Pol*	22C2
Sludyanka *USSR*	34C1
Slupsk *Pol*	24B2
Slutsk *USSR*	24D2
Slyne Head, Pt *Irish Rep*	7A3
Slyudyanka *USSR*	29C2
Smallwood Res *Can*	83D4
Smara *Mor*	62A2
Smederevo *USA*	20B2
Smederevska Palanka *Yugos*	20B2
Smela *USSR*	26D4
Smethport *USA*	91C2
Smith *Can*	89E1
Smithers *Can*	89B2
Smith I *Can*	83C3
Smiths Falls *Can*	91C2
Smithton *Aust*	75C4
Smoky Lake *Can*	89E2
Smola, I *Nor*	4F6
Smolensk *USSR*	26D3
Smolikas, Mt *Greece*	21B2
Smolyan *Bulg*	20B2
Smorgon' *USSR*	24D2
Smyrna, Delaware *USA*	92B3
Smyrna, Georgia *USA*	93B1
Snaefell, Mt *Eng*	8B2
Snaefel, Mt *Iceland*	4B2
Snake River Canyon *USA*	84B2
Sneek *Neth*	22B2
Sneem *Irish Rep*	11B3
Snelling *USA*	98B2
Snezka, Mt *Pol/Czech*	25C2
Snohetta, Mt *Nor*	4F6
Snohomish *USA*	96B1
Snoqualmie F *USA*	96B1
Snoul *Camb*	42D3
Snowdon, Mt *Wales*	9B3
Snowdonia Nat Pk *Wales*	9B3
Snowdrift *Can*	80G3
Snow Lake *Can*	81H4
Snowtown *Aust*	74A2
Snowy Mts *Aust*	75C3
Snyder *USA*	85C3
Soan, I *S Korea*	40B4
Sobral *Brazil*	107C2
Sochaczew *Pol*	24C2
Sochi *USSR*	27E5
Socorro *USA*	85C3
Socorro, I *Mexico*	100A3
Socos *Chile*	110A2
Socotra, I *S Yemen*	47D4
Sodankylä *Fin*	4K5
Soddo *Eth*	65D2
Söderhamn *Sweden*	5H6
Södertälje *Sweden*	5H7
Sodiri *Sudan*	65C1
Soest *W Germ*	12E1
Sofala *Mozam*	67C2
Sofiya *Bulg*	20B2
Sofu Gan, I *Japan*	35G4
Sogamoso *Colombia*	108C2
Sognefjorden, Inlet *Nor*	5F6
Sog Xian *China*	48D2
Sohâg *Egypt*	61C2
Sohipat *India*	50D3
Soignies *Belg*	13B2
Soissons *France*	12B2
Sojat *India*	51C3
Söke *Turk*	58A2
Sokodé *Togo*	63C4
Sokol *USSR*	27E2
Sokolka *Pol*	24C2
Sokolo *Mali*	63B3
Sokongens Oy, I *Greenland*	82H3
Sokota *Eth*	65D1
Sokoto *Nig*	63C3
Solander I *NZ*	77A3
Solano *Phil*	45B2
Solapur *India*	53B1
Solbad Hall *Austria*	102C1
Sölden *Austria*	18B1
Soldotna *USA*	88D2
Soledad *Colombia*	102D4
Solesmes *France*	12B1

Soligorsk USSR 24D2
Solikamsk USSR 27J2
Solimoes Peru 108C4
Solingen W Germ 12D1
Sol'Itsek USSR 31G4
Solleftea Sweden 16H6
Sol'Iletsk USSR 27H3
Solok Indon 36B4
Solomon, Is Pacific O 71G4
Solothurn Switz 13B1
Soltau W Germ 5F8
Solvang USA 98B3
Solway Firth, Estuary Scot/Eng 8C2
Solwezi Zambia 66D2
Soma Japan 41C1
Soma Turk 21C3
Somalia, Republic E Africa 47C5
Sombor Yugos 20A1
Somerset Aust 73D2
Somerset, County Eng 9C4
Somerset, Massachusetts USA 92D2
Somerset East S Africa 66B4
Somers I Can 82A2
Somers Point USA 92B3
Somerville USA 92B2
Somerville USA 95A3
Somme, Department France 12B2
Sommesous France 12C3
Somon'n N Korea 40A3
Sonch'on N Korea 40A3
Sonderborg Den 5F8
Sondre Stromfjord Greenland 82E3
Sondrio Italy 13C1
Song Cau Viet 42D3
Songea Tanz 67C2
Songjiang China 39E3
Songkhla Thai 43C4
Songnim N Korea 40B3
Songpan China 38A3
Sonid Youqi China 38A1
Son La Viet 42C1
Sonmiani Pak 51B3
Sonmiani Bay Pak 51B3
Sonoma USA 98A1
Sonora, California USA 99B3
Sonoran Desert USA 85B3
Sonora P USA 98C1
Sonsonate El Salvador 101D3
Sonsorol, I Pacific O 37E3
Soo Canals USA/Can 86B2
Sooke Can 89C3
Sopot Pol 24B2
Sopron Hung 25B3
Soquel USA 98B2
Sora Italy 19D2
Sorel Can 91D2
Sorell Aust 75C4
Sorgun Turk 58C2
Soria Spain 16B1
Sorkjosen Nor 4J5
Sorksop, I Barents S 30C2
Sor Mertvyy Kultuk, Plain USSR 27H4

Sorocaba Brazil 111B2
Sorochinsk USSR 27H3
Soroi, I Pacific O 37F3
Sorok USSR 26C4
Sorong Indon 37E4
Sorong, Province Indon 37E4
Soroti Uganda 65D2
Soroya, I Nor 4J4
Sorrento Italy 19B2
Sorsatunturi, Mt Fin 4K5
Sorsele Sweden 4H5
Sorsogon Phil 45B3
Sortavala USSR 4L6
Sosan S Korea 40B3
Sosnowiec Pol 25B2
Sos'va USSR 31H4
Soubré Ivory Coast 63B4
Souderton USA 92B2
Soufriere St Lucia 103P2
Souillac France 14C3
Souk Ahras Alg 62C1
Soul S Korea 40B3
Sources, Mt aux Lesotho 67G1
Sousa Brazil 107D3
Sousse Tunisia 62D1
South Africa, Republic Africa 66B4
South Amboy USA 92B2
Southampton Eng 9D4
Southampton USA 92C2
Southampton I Can 83D4
South Atlantic O 104F6
South Aulatsivik I Can 83D4
South Australia, State Aust 72C3
South Australian Basin Indian O 70E5
South Bay USA 95C3
South Baymouth Can 90B1
South Bend, Indiana USA 90A2
South Bend, Washington USA 96B1
Southbridge USA 92D1
South Carolina, State USA 87B3
South China S S E Asia 36C2
South Dakota, State USA 84C2
South Deerfield USA 92D1
South Downs Eng 9D4
Southern Alps, Mts NZ 77A2
Southend Can 81H4
Southend-on-Sea Eng 9E4
Southern Alps, Mts NZ 77A2
Southern Cross Aust 72A4
Southern Indian L Can 81J4
Southfield Jamaica 103H2
South Fiji Basin Pacific O 71G5
South Georgia, I S Atlantic O 104F8
South Glamorgan, County Wales 9C4
South Haven USA 90A2
South Henik L Can 81J3
South Honshu Ridge Pacific O 70F3
South I NZ 77A2

Southington USA 92C2
South Korea, Republic S E Asia 40B3
South Lake Tahoe USA 97A2
South Magnetic Pole Ant 112C8
South Miami USA 93B2
South Mt USA 92A3
South Negril Pt Jamaica 102G1
South Orkney, Is Atlantic O 69F8
South Pole Ant 46E
Southport Eng 8C3
South Pt Barbados 103R3
South River USA 92B2
South Ronaldsay, I Scot 10C2
South Sandwich Trench Atlantic O 69G7
South San Francisco USA 98A2
South Shields Eng 8D2
South Uist, I Scot 10A3
South West Pacific Basin Pacific O 71J5
South West Peru Ridge Pacific O 69D5
South Yemen, Republic Arabian Pen 47C4
South Yorkshire, County Eng 9D3
Sovetsk, RSFSR USSR 24C1
Sovetsk, RSFSR USSR 27G2
Soyo Congo Angola 64B3
Spa Belg 12C1
Spain, Kingdom 3
Spalding Eng 9D3
Spanish Town Jamaica 103H2
Sparks USA 97B2
Spartanburg USA 87B3
Sparti Greece 21B3
Spassk Dal'niy USSR 35F2
Speightstown Barbados 103R3
Spenard USA 88E2
Spencer, Indiana USA 90A3
Spencer, Iowa USA 84D2
Spencer Bay Can 82A3
Spencer G Aust 74A2
Spencer I Can 82C3
Spencer Mts NZ 77B2
Sperrin, Mts N Ire 11C1
Speyer W Germ 23B3
Speyside Tobago 103K1
Spiez Switz 18B1
Spike Mt USA 88F1
Spirit Lake USA 96C1
Spirit River Can 81G4
Spitsbergen, I Barents S 30C2
Spittal Austria 23C3
Spjelkavik Nor 4F6
Split Yugos 18C2
Splügen Switz 13C1
Spokane USA 96C1
Sporádhes, Is Greece 21B3
Spray USA 96C2
Springbok S Africa 66A3
Springdale USA 94B2
Springfield, Illinois USA 86B3
Springfield, Massachusetts USA 86C2
Springfield, Missouri USA 94B2
Springfield, Ohio USA 90B3

Springfield, Oregon USA	96B2
Springfield, Vermont USA	91D2
Springfontein S Africa	66B4
Springs S Africa	67G1
Spurn Head, Pt Eng	7D3
Squamish Can	89C3
Sredne-Russkaya Vozvyshennost, Upland USSR	26E3
Sredne Sibirskoye Ploskogorye Tableland USSR	29B1
Sredniy Ural, Mts USSR	27J2
Sretensk USSR	34D1
Sre Umbell Camb	42C3
Sri Lanka, Republic S Asia	49C5
Srinagar Pak	50C2
Srivardhan India	53A1
Sroda Pol	24B2
Sta Clara, I Chile	109E6
Sta Cruz, I Ecuador	108J7
Stade W Germ	22B2
Staffa, I Scot	10A3
Stafford, County Eng	9C3
Stafford Eng	9C3
Stafford Springs USA	92C2
Stalowa Wola Pol	25D2
Sta Maria, I Ecuador	108J7
Stamford, Connecticut USA	92C2
Stamford, New York USA	92B1
Stampriet Namibia	66A3
Standerton S Africa	67G1
Standish USA	92B2
Stanger S Africa	67H1
Stanke Dimitrov Bulg	20B2
Stanley Aust	75C4
Stanley Falkland Is	105E6
Stanley Res India	53B3
Stanovoy Khrebet, Mts USSR	29E2
Stans Switz	13C1
Stanthorpe Aust	75D1
Starachowice Pol	25C2
Stara Planiná, Mts Bulg	20B2
Staraya Russa USSR	26D2
Stara Zagora Bulg	20C2
Stargard Pol	24B2
Starkville USA	95C3
Starnberg W Germ	23C3
Starogard Gdanski Pol	24B2
Starokonstantinov USSR	25D3
Start Pt Eng	9C4
Staryy Oskol USSR	26E3
State College USA	91C2
Staten I USA	92B2
Statesboro USA	93B1
Staunton USA	91C3
Stavanger Nor	5F7
Stavelot Belg	12C1
Stavropol' USSR	27F4
Stawell Aust	74B3
Stawno Pol	24B2
Stayton USA	96B2
Stebbins USA	88B2
Steele, Mt Can	88F2
Steelton USA	92A2
Steens Mt USA	96C2
Steenstrups Gletscher, Gl Greenland	82E2
Stefansson I Can	80H2
Stegi Swaziland	67H1
Steinach Austria	13D1
Steinbach Can	84D2
Steinkier Nor	4G6
Stein Mt Can	89C2
Stemaco Mexico	99B2
Stenay France	13C3
Stendal E Germ	22C2
Stephens Creek Aust	74B2
Stephenson USA	90A1
Stephens Pass USA	88H3
Stephenville Can	86B4
Sterkstroom S Africa	66B4
Sterling, Colorado USA	84C2
Sterling Heights USA	90B2
Sterlitamak USSR	27J3
Stettler Can	89E2
Steubenville USA	90B2
Stevens Village USA	88D3
Stewart Can	89B1
Stewart Crossing Can	88G2
Stewart I NZ	77A3
Stewart Is Solomon Is	71F1
Stewart River Can	80E3
Stewartstown USA	92A3
Steyn S Africa	67G1
Steyr Austria	23C3
Stika USA	88G3
Stikine Ranges, Mts Can	88H3
Stillwater, Oklahoma USA	94A2
Stillwater Range, Mts USA	97B2
Stirling Aust	74A2
Stirling Scot	10C3
Stockbridge USA	92C1
Stockerau Austria	25B3
Stockport Eng	8C3
Stockton, California USA	98B2
Stockton Eng	8D2
Stockton I, USA	64B2
Stoke-on-Trent Eng	9C3
Stokkseyri Iceland	4A2
Stokmarknes Nor	4G5
Stolbtsy USSR	5K8
Stolin USSR	24D2
Stone Harbor USA	92B3
Stonehaven Scot	10C3
Stonewall USA	95A3
Storavan, L Sweden	4H5
Storen Nor	4G6
Stornoway Scot	10A2
Storozhinets USSR	25D3
Storrs USA	92C2
Storsjon, L Sweden	4G6
Storuman Sweden	4H5
Stoughton USA	92D1
Stowmarket Eng	9E3
Strabane N Ire	11C1
Strahan Aust	75C4
Stralsund E Germ	22C2
Stranda Nor	4F6
Strängnäs Sweden	5H7
Stranraer Scot	8B2
Strasbourg France	15D2
Strasburg USA	91C3
Stratford Can	90B2
Stratford, Connecticut USA	92C2
Stratford NZ	76B1
Stratford-on-Avon Eng	9D3
Strathalbyn Aust	74A3
Strathclyde, Region Scot	8B2
Strathmore Can	89E2
Streator USA	94C1
Stresa Italy	13C2
Stroboli, I Italy	19C3
Stromfjord Greenland	82E3
Stromness Scot	10C2
Stromo Faroes	4D3
Stromsburg USA	94A1
Stromsund Sweden	4H6
Stroms Vattudal, L Sweden	4G6
Stronsay, I Scot	10C2
Stroud Eng	9C3
Stroudsburg USA	92B2
Strumble Head, Pt Wales	9B3
Strumica Yugos	21B2
Stryy USSR	25C3
Stuart, Florida USA	93B2
Stuart I USA	88B2
Stuart L Can	89C2
Stubaier Alpen, Mts Austria	13D1
Stung Sen Camb	42D3
Stung Treng Camb	42D3
Sturgeon Bay USA	90A2
Sturgeon Bay USA	90C1
Sturgis, Kentucky USA	94C2
Sturgis, Michigan USA	90A2
Sturt Desert Aust	74B1
Stutterheim S Africa	66B4
Stuttgart USA	95B3
Stuttgart W Germ	23B3
Stykkishólmur Iceland	4A1
Suakin Sudan	47B4
Su-ao Taiwan	39E5
Suardi Arg	110C2
Subi I, Indon	44B2
Subotica Yugos	20A1
Suceava Rom	26C4
Sucre Bol	106C2
Sudan, Republic Africa	64C1
Sudbury Can	90B1
Sudbury Eng	9E3
Sudd, Swamp Sudan	64C2
Suddie Guyana	109F2
Suez Egypt	58B4
Suez Canal Egypt	58B3
Suez, G of Egypt	58B4
Suffern USA	92B2
Suffolk, County Eng	9E3
Sugarloaf Pt Aust	75D2
Suhar Oman	57C5
Sühbaatar Mongolia	34C1
Sui Pak	50B3
Suide China	38C2
Suihua China	35E2
Suining China	39B3
Suippes France	12C2
Sui Xian China	39C3

Suizhong China	38E1	Superior, Wisconsin USA	86A2	Swallow Reef, I S E Asia	36C3
Sujangarth India	51C3	Superior, L USA/Can	86B2	Swamihalli India	53B2
Sukabumi Indon	44B4	Suphan Buri Thai	42C3	Swan, I Honduras	101D3
Sukadana, Borneo Indon	44C3	Süphan Dag Turk	59D2	Swanage Eng	9D4
Sukadana, Sumatra Indon	44B4	Supiori, I Indon	37E4	Swan Hill Aust	75B3
Sukagawa Japan	40E3	Suq ash Suyukh Iraq	59E3	Swan Hills Can	89D2
Sukaraya Indon	44C3	Suqian China	38D3	Swan Hills, Mts Can	89D2
Sukhinichi Shchekino USSR	26E3	Sur Oman	57C5	Swan I Caribbean	102A3
Sukhumi USSR	27F5	Surabaya Indon	44C4	Swan River Can	81H4
Sukkertoppen Greenland	82E3	Surakarta Indon	44C4	Swansea Wales	9C4
Sukkertoppen, L Greenland	82E3	Surat Aust	75C1	Swartruggens S Africa	67G1
Sukkozero USSR	4L6	Surat India	51C4	Swaziland, Kingdom S Africa	67H1
Sukkur Pak	51B3	Suratgarh India	50C3	Sweden, Kingdom N Europe	5G7
Sukma India	53C1	Surendranagar India	51C4	Sweet Home USA	96B2
Sukses Namibia	66A3	Surf City USA	92B3	Sweetwater USA	96C3
Sukumo Japan	41A2	Surgut USSR	30J3	Swellendam S Africa	66B4
Sulaiman Range, Mts Pak	50B3	Suriapet India	53B1	Swidnica Pol	25B2
Sulawesi, I Indon	36C4	Surigao Phil	45C4	Swidwin Pol	24B2
Sulaymaniyah Iraq	59E3	Surin Thai	42C3	Swiebodzin Pol	24B2
Sulina Rom	20C1	Surinam, Republic	109F3	Swiecie Pol	24B2
Sulitjelma Nor	4H5	Surrey, County Eng	9D4	Swift Current Can	81H4
Sullana Peru	108A4	Sursee Switz	13C1	Swindon Eng	9D4
Sullivan USA	94B2	Surtsey, I Iceland	4A2	Swinford Irish Rep	11B2
Sullivan Bay Can	89B2	Surulangan Indon	44A3	Swinoujscie Pol	22C2
Sullivan L Can	89E2	Susa Italy	13B2	Switzerland, Federal Republic Europe	15D2
Sulmona Italy	18B2	Susah Libya	49D1	Swords Irish Rep	11C2
Sulphur, Louisiana USA	95B3	Susaki Japan	41A2	Sydero Faeroes	4D3
Sulphur, Oklahoma USA	95A3	Susanville USA	97A1	Sydney Aust	75D2
Sulphur Springs USA	95A3	Süsch Switz	13D1	Sydney Can	83D5
Sultanpur India	52A1	Sussex USA	92B2	Syktyvkar USSR	30G3
Sulu Arch Phil	45B4	Sussex West Eng	9D4	Sylacauga USA	93A1
Sulu S Philip	45B4	Susut Peak, Mt Can	89B1	Sylarna, Mt Sweden	4G6
Sumampa Arg	106D4	Sutherland S Africa	66B4	Sylhet Bang	52C2
Sumba, I Indon	36C4	Sutter Creek USA	97A2	Sylt, I W Germ	22B1
Sumba, I Indon	44D4	Sutton USA	90B3	Sylvania USA	90B2
Sumbawa Besar Indon	44D4	Sutwik I USA	88C3	Syowa, Base Ant	112C1
Sumbawanga Tanz	65D3	Suwa Japan	40D3	Syracuse, New York USA	86C3
Sumbe Angola	66A2	Suwalki Pol	24C2	Syracuse USA	91C2
Sumburgh Head, Pt Scot	10J2	Suweilih Jordan	60B2	Syrdal'ya, R USSR	31H5
Sumenep Indon	44C4	Suwon S Korea	40B3	Syria, Republic S W Asia	59C2
Sumisu, I Japan	35G3	Su Xian China	38D3	Sysert' USSR	27J2
Summerland Can	89D3	Suzaka Japan	41B1	Syzran' USSR	27G3
Summit Lake Can	81F4	Suzhou China	39E3	Szczecin Pol	22C2
Summit Mt USA	94B3	Suzu Japan	40D3	Szczecinek Pol	22C2
Sumner, L NZ	77B2	Suzuka Japan	41B2	Szczytno Pol	24B2
Sumoto Japan	41A2	Svalbard, Is Barents S	30C2	Szeged Hung	25C3
Sumter USA	93B1	Svalyava USSR	25C3	Székesfehérvar Hung	25B3
Sumy USSR	26D3	Svartisen, Mt Nor	4G5	Szekszard Hung	25B3
Sunbury USA	92A2	Svay Rieng Camb	42D3	Szolnok Hung	25B3
Sunchales Arg	110C2	Sveg Sweden	4G6	Szombathely Hung	25B3
Sunch'on N Korea	40B3	Svendborg Den	5G7	Szprotawa Pol	24B2
Sunch'on S Korea	40B4	Sverdlovsk USSR	31H4		
Sundargarh India	52A2	Sverdrup Chan Can	82A1	**T**	
Sunderbans, Swamp India	52B2	Svetlaya USSR	35F2		
Sunderland Eng	8E2	Svetlogorsk USSR	24C2	Tabas Iran	56C3
Sundre Can	89E2	Svetogorsk USSR	5K6	Tabasco Mexico	99A1
Sundridge Can	91C1	Svetozarevo Yugos	20B2	Tabatinga Brazil	108D4
Sundsvall Sweden	4H6	Svilengrad Bulg	20C2	Tabelbala Alg	62B2
Sungaianyar Indon	44D3	Svobodnyy USSR	35E1	Tabeng Camb	42C3
Sungaisalak Indon	44A3	Svolvaer Nor	4G5	Tabira, I Phil	89E2
Sunnyside USA	96C1	Swain Reefs Aust	73E3	Tablas, I Phil	89E2
Sunnyvale USA	97A2	Swainsboro USA	93B1	Table Mt S Africa	66A3
Suntar USSR	29D1	Swakopmund Namibia	66A3	Table Mt USA	88F1
Sunyani Ghana	63B4			Table Rock Res USA	94B2
Suonenjoki Fin	4K6			Taboali Indon	44B3
Supaul India	52B1				
Superior, Nebraska USA	94A1				

Tábor Czech	23C3		Takestan Iran	56A2		Tandaho Eth	65E1
Tabora Tanz	65D3		Taketa Japan	41A2		Tandil Arg	110D3
Tabou Ivory Coast	63B4		Takingeun Indon	43A2		Tandjong Datu, Pt Indon	44B2
Tabriz Iran	56A2		Takijvak L Can	89B1		Tando Adam Pak	51B3
Tabuk S Arabia	56A2		Takla Landing Can	89B1		Tando Muhammad Khan Pak	51B3
Tacámbaro Mexico	99A2		Taklesluk L USA	88B2		Tandou L Aust	74B2
Tacheng China	48C1		Tala Mexico	99A1		Tandur India	53B1
Tacloban Phil	45C2		Talabanya Hung	25B3		Taneatua NZ	76C1
Tacna Peru	106B2		Talagang Pak	60C2		Tanen Range, Mts Burma/Thai	42B2
Tacoma USA	84A2		Talagante Chile	110A2		Tanezrouft, Desert Region Alg	63C2
Tadjoura Djibouti	65E1		Talaimannar Sri Lanka	53B3		Tang Iran	57C4
Tadpatri India	53B2		Talak, Desert Region Niger	63C3		Tanga Tanz	65D3
Tadzhen USSR	31H6		Talangbetutu Indon	44A3		Tanganyika, L Tanz/Zaire	65C4
Tadzhikskaya SSR, Republic USSR	48A2		Talara Peru	106B4		Tanger Mor	62B1
Taebaek Sanmaek, Mts S Korea	40B3		Talavera de la Reina Spain	16B2		Tanggula Shan, Mts China	48C2
Taegu S Korea	40B3		Talca Chile	110A3		Tangjungpinang Indon	44A2
Taehuksan, I S Korea	40B4		Talcahuano Chile	110A3		Tangra Yumco, L China	48C2
Taejon S Korea	40B3		Talcher India	52B2		Tangshan China	38D2
Tafalla Spain	17B1		Taldy Kurgan USSR	48B1		Tangub Phil	45B4
Tafila Jordan	60B3		Talibabu Indon	37D4		Tanguy USSR	29C2
Tagant, Region Maur	63A3		Taligan Afghan	50B1		Tanjay Phil	45B4
Tagbilaran Phil	45B4		Tali Post Sudan	65D2		Tanjung Indon	44D3
Tagula, I Solomon Is	73E2		Taliwang Indon	44D4		Tanjungbalai Indon	36A3
Tagum Phil	45C4		Talkeetna USA	88B2		Tanjung Jabung, Pt Indon	44B3
Tahat, Mt Alg	62C2		Talkeetna Mts USA	88B3		Tanjungpandan Indon	44B3
Tahiti, I Pacific O	71J4		Talladega USA	93A1		Tanjung Priok Indon	44B4
Tahlequah USA	94A2		Tall 'Afar Iraq	59D2		Tanjungredeb Indon	44D2
Tahoe City USA	97A2		Tallahassee USA	93B1		Tanjungselor Indon	44D2
Tahoe, L USA	97A2		Tall Bisah Syria	60C1		Tank Pak	50C2
Tahoua Niger	63C3		Tallinn USSR	26B2		Tannu Ola, Mts USSR	34B1
Tahuna Indon	37D3		Tall Kalakh Syria	58C3		Tanout Niger	63C3
Tai'an China	38D2		Tallulah USA	95B3		Tanquian Mexico	99B1
Taibai Shan, Mt China	38B3		Tal'noye USSR	26D4		Tan-shui Taiwan	39E4
Taibus Qi China	38D1		Talpaki USSR	24C2		Tansing Nepal	52A1
T'ai-chung Taiwan	39E5		Taltal Chile	106B4		Tanta Egypt	61C1
Taihang Shan China	38C2		Talwood Aust	75C1		Tan-Tan Mor	62B1
Taihape NZ	78C1		Tamabo Range, Mts Malay	43E4		Tanunak USA	80B3
Tai Hu, L China	38E3		Tamale Ghana	63B4		Tanzania, Republic Africa	65B3
Tailem Bend Aust	74A3		Tamanrasset Alg	62C2		Taolanaro Madag	67D3
Tain Scot	10B3		Tamaqua USA	92B2		Taole China	38B2
T'ai-nan Taiwan	39E5		Tamazula, Jalisco Mexico	99A2		Taourirt Mor	62B1
Taiobeiras Brazil	111C2		Tamazulápan Mexico	99B1		Tapa USSR	26C2
T'ai pei Taiwan	39E5		Tamazunchale Mexico	99B1		Tapachula Mexico	101C3
Taiping Malay	43C5		Tambacounda Sen	63A3		Tapalquén Arg	110C3
Taira Japan	41C1		Tambov USSR	27F3		Tapan Indon	44B3
Tais Indon	44A3		Tambura Sudan	64C2		Tapanui NZ	77B2
Taisha Japan	41A1		Tamchaket Maur	63A3		Taplejung Nepal	52B1
Tai-tung Taiwan	39E5		Tamiahua Mexico	99B1		Tapuaenuku, Mt NZ	77B2
Taivelkoski Fin	4K5		Tamil Nadu, State India	53B2		Tapul Group, Is Phil	45B4
Taiwan, Republic China	35E4		Tam Ky Viet	42D2		Tapurucuara Brazil	109E4
Taiyuan China	38C2		Tampa USA	93B2		Tara Aust	75D1
Taizhou China	38D3		Tampere Fin	5J6		Tara, R USSR	31J4
Tak Thai	42B2		Tampico Mexico	99B1		Tarabuco Bol	106D2
Takada Japan	40D3		Tamsagbulag Mongolia	34D2		Tarancón Spain	16B1
Takahashi Japan	41A2		Tamuis Mexico	99B1		Tarakan Indon	44D2
Takaka NZ	76B2		Tamworth Aust	75D2		Taransay, I Scot	10A3
Takamatsu Japan	40C4		Tamworth Eng	9D3		Taranto Italy	19C2
Takaoka Japan	40D3		Tana Nor	4K4		Tarapoto Peru	108B5
Takapuna NZ	76B1		Tana, L Eth	65D1		Tarare France	16C2
Takasaki Japan	40D3		Tanabe Japan	41B2		Tararua Range, Mts NZ	76C2
Takayama Japan	41B1		Tanafjord, Inlet Nor	4K4		Tarat Alg	62C2
Takefu Japan	40D3		Tanahgrogot Indon	44D3			
Takeo Camb	42C3		Tanahmerah Indon	37E4			
Takeo Japan	41A2		Tanch'on N Korea	38B1			

Timimoun Alg 62C2
Timisoara Rom 20B1
Timmins Can 86B2
Timor, I Indon 72B1
Timor S Aust/Indon 72B2
Timote Arg 110C3
Tinaca Pt Phil 45C4
Tinaco Ven 103D5
Tindivanam India 53B2
Tindouf Alg 62B2
Tinfouchy Alg 62B2
Tin Fouye Alg 62C2
Tingmiarmiut Greenland 82F3
Tingo Maria Peru 108B5
Tingrela Ivory Coast 63B3
Tingri China 52B1
Tinian Pacific O 37F2
Tinogasta Arg 106C4
Tinos, I Greece 21C3
Tintagel Head, Pt Eng 9B4
Tintinara Aust 74B3
Tin Zaouaten Alg 62C2
Tioga P USA 98C2
Tioman, I Malay 43C5
Tione Italy 18B2
Tipperary, County Irish Rep 11C2
Tipperary Irish Rep 7B3
Tipton, Missouri USA 94B2
Tiptur India 53B2
Tiquicheo Mexico 99A2
Tirané Alb 21A2
Tirano Italy 13D1
Tiraspol USSR 26C4
Tirohchirappalli India 53B2
Tire Turk 21C3
Tirebolu Turk 59C1
Tiree, I Scot 10A3
Tirgoviste Rom 20B2
Tirgu Jiu Rom 20B1
Tirgu Mures Rom 20B1
Tirich Mir, Mt Pak 50C1
Tiris, Region Mor 62A2
Tirlyanskiy USSR 27J3
Tirnaveni Rom 20B1
Tirnavos Greece 21B3
Tirodi India 51D4
Tirol, Province Austria 13D1
Tiruchchendur India 53B3
Tirunelveli India 53B3
Tirupati India 53B3
Tiruppattur India 53B2
Tiruppur India 53B2
Tiruvannamalai India 53B2
Tishomingo USA 95A3
Tisiyah Syria 60C2
Titlagarh India 52A2
Titograd Yugos 20A2
Titov Uzice Yugos 20A2
Titov Veles Yugos 20A2
Titule Zaïre 64C2
Titusville USA 93B2
Tiverton Eng 9C4
Tivoli Italy 18B2
Tixtla Mexico 99B2
Tiyeglow Somalia 65E2
Tizayuca Mexico 99B2
Tizimin Mexico 101D2

Tizi Ouzou Alg 62C1
Tiznit Mor 62B2
Tizpan el Alto Mexico 99A1
Tlacolula Mexico 99B2
Tlacotalpan Mexico 99B2
Tlalchapa Mexico 99A2
Tlalnepantla Mexico 99B2
Tlalpan Mexico 99B2
Tlaltenango Mexico 99A1
Tlancualpican Mexico 99B2
Tlapa Mexico 99B2
Tlapacoyan Mexico 99B2
Tlaquepaque Mexico 99A1
Tlaxcala Mexico 99B2
Tlaxcala, State Mexico 99B2
Tlaxiaco Mexico 99B2
Tlemcen Alg 62B1
Toamasina Madag 67D2
Toay Arg 110C3
Toba Japan 41B2
Toba and Kakar Ranges, Pak 50B2
Tobago, I Caribbean 103E4
Tobelo Indon 37D3
Tobermory Can 90B1
Tobi, I Pacific O 37E3
Tobin, Mt USA 97B1
Toboli Indon 36D4
Tobol'sk USSR 31H4
Tocantins, R Brazil 107B2
Toccoa USA 93B1
Tocopilla Chile 106B3
Tocorpuri, Mt Chile 106C3
Toda India 51D3
Tödi, Mt Switz 13C1
Todong S Korea 41A1
Todos Santos Mexico 85B4
Tofield Can 89E2
Tofino Can 89B3
Togiak USA 88B3
Togo, Republic Africa 63C4
Togtoh China 38C1
Tok USA 88F2
Tokamachi Japan 41B1
Tokara Retto, Arch Japan 35E4
Tokat Turk 58C1
Tokchok-kundo, Arch S Korea 40B3
Tok-do, I S Korea 41A1
Tokmak USSR 48B1
Tokomaru Bay NZ 76C1
Tokung Indon 44C3
Tokuno, I Japan 35E4
Tokushima Japan 40C4
Tokuyama Japan 41A2
Tokyo Japan 40D3
Tolaga Bay NZ 76C1
Toledo Brazil 106F3
Toledo Spain 16B2
Toledo USA 90B2
Toledo Bend Res USA 95B3
Toliara Madag 67D3
Toliman Mexico 99B1
Tolina, Mt Colombia 108B3
Tolosa Spain 17B1

Toltén Chile 105B3
Toluca Mexico 99B2
Tol'yati USSR 27G3
Tomakomai Japan 40E2
Tomani Malay 44D1
Tomaszow Mazowiecka Pol 24C2
Tomboco Angola 64B3
Tombos Brazil 111C2
Tomboctou Mali 63B3
Tombua Angola 66A2
Tome Chile 110A3
Tomelloso Spain 16B2
Tomé, Port Arg 16A2
Tomkinson Range, Mts Aust 72B3
Tommot USSR 29E2
Tomorrit, Mt Alb 21B2
Toms River USA 16C2
Tonalá Mexico 101C3
Tonasket USA 96C1
Tonawanda USA 91C2
Tonga, Is Pacific O 71H4
Tongaat S Africa 67H1
Tongcheng China 39D3
Tongchuan China 38B2
Tongde China 38A2
Tongeren Belg 12C1
Tonggu Jiao, I China 42E2
Tonghai China 39A5
Tonghua China 40B3
Tongjoson-man N Korea 40B3
Tongkin, G of Viet/China 42D1
Tongling China 39D3
Tongo Aust 74B2
Tongren, Guizhou China 39B4
Tongren, Qinghai China 38A2
Tongsa Bhutan 52D1
Tongta Burma 42B1
Tongue Scot 10B2
Tong Xian China 38D2
Tongxin China 38B2
Tonhil Mongolia 29B5
Tonichi Mexico 85B3
Tonj Sudan 65C2
Tonk India 51D3
Tonkawa USA 94A2
Tonle Sap, L Camb 42C3
Tonopah USA 97B2
Tonsina USA 88E2
Tooele USA 84B2
Toogoolawah Aust 75D1
Toompine Aust 74B1
Toowoomba Aust 75D1
Topaz L USA 98C1
Topeka USA 94A2
Topolobampo Mexico 85C4
Toppenish USA 96B1
Tor India 51D3
Torbat-e-Heydariyah Iran 56C2
Torbat-e Jam Iran 56D2
Torbay Eng 9C4
Torbert, Mt USA 88D2
Tordesillas Spain 16A1
Torgau E Germ 22C2

Tsogt Ovoo Mongolia	38B1
Tsu Japan	41B2
Tsubata Japan	41B1
Tsuchira Japan	40E3
Tsumeb Namibia	66A2
Tsumis Namibia	66A3
Tsunugi Japan	41B1
Tsuruga Japan	40D3
Tsuruoka Japan	40D3
Tsushima Japan	41B1
Tsushima, I Japan	40B4
Tsuyama Japan	40C3
Tuam Irish Rep	11B2
Tuapse USSR	26E5
Tuatapere NZ	77A3
Tubarao Brazil	106G4
Tubas Israel	60B2
Tubbataha Reefs, Is Phil	45A4
Tübingen W Germ	23B3
Tubruq Libya	61B1
Tucacuare USA	92B3
Tucson USA	85B3
Tucumán, State Arg	106C4
Tucunuco Arg	110B2
Tucupita Ven	109E2
Tudela Spain	17B1
Tudmur Syria	59C3
Tuggerah, L Aust	75D2
Tugidak, I USA	88D3
Tuguegarao Phil	45B2
Tugur USSR	29F2
Tuktoyaktuk USA	80E3
Tukums USSR	24C1
Tukuyu Tanz	65D3
Tuxzar Afghan	50B1
Tula USSR	26E3
Tulancingo Mexico	99B1
Tulcán Colombia	108B3
Tulcea Rom	26C5
Tuli Zim	66B2
Tulkarm Israel	60B2
Tulle France	14C2
Tullos USA	95B3
Tullow Irish Rep	11C2
Tulsa USA	94A2
Tulul ash Shamiyah, Desert Region Syria/S Arabia	59C3
Tulun USSR	29C2
Tulungagung Indon	44C4
Tumaco Colombia	108B3
Tumbarumba Aust	75C3
Tumbes Ecuador	108A4
Tumby Bay Aust	74A2
Tumen China	40B2
Tumkur India	53B2
Tumpat Malay	43C4
Tumsar India	51D4
Tumu Ghana	63B3
Tumut Aust	75C3
Tunapuna Trinidad	103L1
Tunceli Turk	59C2
Tunduma Zambia	65D3
Tunduru Tanz	67C2
Tung-Chiang Taiwan	34D4
Tungnafellsjökull, Mts Iceland	4B2
Tungsten Can	88J2
Tuni India	53C1
Tunis Tunisia	62D1
Tunisia, Republic N Africa	54E4
Tunja Colombia	108C2
Tunttutilak USA	88C2
Tununak USA	88C2
Tunungayualok, I Can	110B2
Tunxi China	39D4
Tuolumne Meadows USA	98C2
Tupa Brazil	111A2
Tupaciguara Brazil	111B1
Tupelo USA	95C3
Tupiza Bol	106C3
Tupper Lake USA	91D2
Tupungato Arg	110B2
Tupungato, Mt Arg	105C2
Tura India	52C1
Tura USSR	56C2
Turan Iran	56C2
Turayf S Arabia	59C3
Turbat Pak	57B3
Turbo Colombia	108B2
Turda Rom	26B1
Turfan Depression China	29A3
Turgay USSR	31H4
Turgen Uul, Mt Mongolia	29B3
Turgutlu Turk	58C1
Turhal Turk	58C1
Türi USSR	5K7
Turinsk USSR	27K2
Turiy Rog USSR	35F2
Turkana, L Kenya/Eth	65D2
Turkestan USSR	48A1
Turkey, Republic W Asia	58B2
Turkmenskaya, SSR Republic USSR	46D1
Turks Is Caribbean	103C2
Turku Fin	5J6
Turlock USA	98B2
Turlock L USA	98B2
Turneffe I Belize	101D3
Turners Falls USA	91D2
Turnor L Can	89F1
Turnu Magurele Rom	54B2
Turnu-Severin Rom	20B2
Turpan China	29A3
Turquino, Mt Cuba	102B2
Turtkul' USSR	46E1
Turtle Creek Res USA	94A2
Turtle L Can	89F2
Turukhansk USSR	29A1
Turuntayevo USSR	34C1
Tuscaloosa USA	95C3
Tuscola USA	94C2
Tusharik Iran	58C1
Tuticorin India	53B3
Tutrakan Bulg	20C2
Tuttlingen W Germ	23B3
Tuvalu, Is Pacific O	71G4
Tuvinskaya, Republic USSR	29B2
Tuxpan, Jalisco Mexico	99A2
Tuxpan, Nayarit Mexico	100B2
Tuxpan, Veracruz Mexico	99C2
Tuxtepec Mexico	99C2
Tuxtla Gutiérrez Mexico	101C3
Túy Spain	16A1
Tuy Hoa Viet	42D3
Tuz Gölü, Salt Lake Turk	58B2
Tuz Khurmatu Iraq	59D3
Tuzla Yugos	20A2
Tweed Heads Aust	75D1
Tweedsmuir Hills Scot	8C2
Twillingate Can	83E5
Twin Falls USA	84B2
Twins, The, Mt NZ	77B2
Two Rivers USA	90A2
Tygda USSR	29E2
Tyler USA	95A3
Tymovskoye USSR	35G1
Tyne and Wear, Metropolitan County Eng	8D2
Tynemouth Eng	8D2
Tynset Nor	4G6
Tyonek USA	88D3
Tyr Leb	60B2
Tyrone, County N Ire	11C1
Tyrrell, L Aust	74B3
Tyrrhenian S Italy	19B2
Tyumen' USSR	31H4
Tywyn Wales	9B3
Tzoumérka, Mt Greece	21B3

U

Uarsciek Somalia	65E2
Uba Brazil	111C2
Ubai Brazil	111C1
Ube Japan	41A2
Ubeda Spain	16B2
Ubekendt Ejland, I Greenland	82E2
Uberaba Brazil	111B1
Uberlândia Brazil	111B1
Ubon Ratchathani Thai	42C2
Ubundi Zaire	64C3
Uch Pak	50C3
Udaipur India	51C4
Udaipur Garhi Nepal	52B1
Udaquoila Arg	110D3
Uddevalla Sweden	5G7
Uddjaur, L Sweden	4H5
Udgir India	53B1
Udhampur India	50D2
Udmurtskaya ASSR Republic USSR	27H2
Udon Thani USA	42C2
Udupi India	53A2
Ueda Japan	41B1
Uelzen W Germ	22C2
Ufa USSR	27J3
Uganda, Republic Africa	65D2
Ugashik L USA	88C3
Ugine France	13B2
Uglegorsk USSR	35G2
Uglich USSR	20A3
Ug Scot	10A3
Uige Angola	64B3
Uil USSR	27H4
Uinta Mts USA	84B2
Uitenhage S Africa	66B4
Ujfehértó Hung	25C3
Uji Japan	41B2

Ujiji *Tanz* **65C3**
Ujina *Chile* **106C3**
Ujjain *India* **51D4**
Ujung Pandang *Indon* **36C4**
Ukerewe, I *Tanz* **65C3**
Ukhrul *India* **52C1**
Ukiah, California *USA* **97A2**
Ukiah, Oregon *USA* **96C1**
Ukmerge *USSR* **24C1**
Ukrainskaya, Republic *USSR* **26C4**
Ulaanbaatar *Mongolia* **32B2**
Ulaangom *Mongolia* **34B2**
Ulaan Ul *Mongolia* **38C1**
Ulangar Hu, L *China* **48C1**
Ulan Ude *USSR* **34C1**
Ulan Ul Hu, L *China* **38C1**
Ulapes *Arg* **110B2**
Ulchin *S Korea* **40B3**
Ulcinj *Yugos* **20A2**
Uldz *Mongolia* **34D2**
Uliastay *Mongolia* **34B2**
Ulla *USSR* **24D1**
Ulladulla *Aust* **75D3**
Ullapool *Scot* **10B3**
Ullsfjorden, Inlet *Nor* **4H5**
Ullswater, L *Eng* **8C2**
Ullung-do, I *S Korea* **40C3**
Ulm *W Germ* **18C3**
Uloowaranie, L *Aust* **74A1**
Ulsan *S Korea* **40B3**
Ulster, Region *N Ire* **11C1**
Ulungur Hu, L *China* **31K5**
Ulva, I *Scot* **10A3**
Ulverston *Eng* **8C2**
Ulverstone *Aust* **75C4**
Ul'yanovsk *USSR* **27G3**
Uman *USSR* **26D4**
Umanak *Greenland* **52A2**
Umaria *India* **52A2**
Umarkot *Pak* **51B3**
Umaroona, L *Aust* **74A1**
Umatilla *USA* **96C1**
Umba *USSR* **4L5**
Umea *Sweden* **4J6**
Umiat *USA* **80C3**
Umm al Qaiwain *UAE* **57C4**
Umm as Samim, Salt Marsh *Oman* **57C5**
Umm Bell *Sudan* **65C1**
Umm Hagar *Eth* **66D3**
Umm Keddada *Sudan* **64C1**
Umm Ruwaba *Sudan* **65D1**
Umm Sa'id *Qatar* **57B5**
Umred *India* **51D4**
Umtata *S Africa* **66B4**
Umuarama *Brazil* **111A2**
Unai *Brazil* **111B1**
Unalakleet *USA* **88B2**
Unayzah *S Arabia* **46C3**
Uncasville *USA* **92C2**
Underberg *S Africa* **66B3**
Unecha *USSR* **26D3**
Uneisa *Jordan* **60B3**
Uniao de Vitória *Brazil* **106F4**
Unión *Arg* **110B3**
Union, Missouri *USA* **94B2**
Union, S Carolina *USA* **93B1**

Union City, Pennsylvania *USA* **90C2**
Union of Soviet Socialist Reps *Asia* **28C3**
Union Springs *USA* **93A1**
Uniontown *USA* **91C3**
United Arab Emirates *Arabian Pen* **57B5**
United Kingdom, Kingdom *W Europe* **2C3**
United States of America **78H4**
United States Range, Mts *Can* **82B1**
Unity *Can* **89F2**
Unity *USA* **96C2**
Unna *W Germ* **12D1**
Unnao *India* **52A1**
Unst, I *Scot* **10D1**
Unye *Turk* **58C1**
Upata *Ven* **109E2**
Upemba Nat Pk *Zaire* **64C3**
Upernavik *Greenland* **55N2**
Upington *S Africa* **98D3**
Upland *USA* **98C3**
Uplington *S Africa* **66B3**
Upper Arlington *USA* **90B2**
Upper Hutt *NZ* **77C2**
Upper Klamath L *USA* **96B2**
Upper L *USA* **96B2**
Upper Lough Erne, L *N Ire* **11C1**
Upper Manzanilla *Trinidad* **103L1**
Upper Seal, L *Can* **83C4**
Uppsala *Sweden* **5H7**
Upstart B *Aust* **75A3**
Urairah *S Arabia* **57A4**
Ural, R *USSR* **27H3**
Uralla *Aust* **75D2**
Ural'sk *USSR* **27H3**
Uralskiy Khrebet, Mts *USSR* **31G4**
Uranium City *Can* **81H4**
Urawa *Japan* **41B1**
Urbana, Illinois *USA* **94C1**
Urbana, Ohio *USA* **90B2**
Urbino *Italy* **16C2**
Uren' *USSR* **27G2**
Urfa *Turk* **59C2**
Urgench *USSR* **46E1**
Urgun *Afghan* **50B2**
Urla *Turk* **21C3**
Urosevac *Yugos* **20B2**
Uruaçu *Brazil* **107B4**
Uruapan *Mexico* **99A2**
Uruguaiana *Brazil* **106E4**
Uruguay, Republic *S America* **105E2**
Ürümqi *China* **48C1**
Urup, I *USSR* **35H2**
Uruzgan *Afghan* **50B2**
Uryupinsk *USSR* **27F3**
Urzhum *USSR* **27H2**
Urziceni *Rom* **21C3**
Usa *China* **48C1**
Usa *Japan* **41A2**
Uşak *Turk* **58A2**
Usakos *Namibia* **66A3**
Ushashi *Tanz* **65D3**
Ush Tobe *USSR* **31J5**

Ushuaia *Arg* **105C6**
Ushumun *USSR* **29E2**
Üsküdar *Turk* **58A1**
Usol'ye Sibirskoye *USSR* **29C2**
Uspallata *Arg* **110B2**
Ussuriysk *USSR* **35F3**
Uster *Switz* **13C1**
Ustica, I *Italy* **19B3**
Ústi nad Labem *Czech* **2xC2**
Ust'Ishim *USSR* **31J4**
Ustka *Pol* **18D2**
Ust'-Kamenogorsk *USSR* **31K5**
Ust Karabula *USSR* **29B2**
Ust'Katav *USSR* **27J2**
Ust'-Kut *USSR* **29C2**
Ust Labinsk *USSR* **29F2**
Ust'Maya *USSR* **29F1**
Ust'Nera *USSR* **1C8**
Ust'Nyukzha *USSR* **29E2**
Ust'Ordynskiy *USSR* **29C2**
Ust'Tsil'ma *USSR* **30G3**
Ust'Umal'ta *USSR* **29F2**
Usuki *Japan* **41A2**
Utah, State *USA* **84B3**
Utah L *USA* **84B3**
Utena *USSR* **24D1**
Utica *USA* **86C2**
Utiel *Spain* **15B2**
Utikuma L *Can* **89D1**
Utrecht *Neth* **22B2**
Utrecht *S Africa* **67H1**
Utrera *Spain* **15A2**
Utsjoki *Fin* **4K5**
Utsunomiya *Japan* **40D3**
Uttaradit *Thai* **42C2**
Uttar Pradesh, State *India* **52A1**
Uval *USSR* **31H4**
Uvéa, I *Nouvelle Calédonie* **73F3**
Uvinza *Tanz* **65D3**
Uvira *Zaire* **65C3**
Uvkusigssat *Greenland* **82E2**
Uusikaupunki *Fin* **5J6**
Uvs Nuur, L *China* **34B2**
Uwajima *Japan* **40C4**
Uxin Qi *China* **38B2**
Uyar *USSR* **29B2**
Uyuni *Bol* **106C3**
Uzbekskaya, S.S.R. Republic *USSR* **46E1**
Uzerche *France* **14C2**
Uzhgorod *USSR* **25C3**
Uzlovaya *USSR* **26E3**
Uzunköprü *Turk* **58A1**

V

Vaal Dam, Res *S Africa* **67G1**
Vaalwater *S Africa* **66B3**
Vaasa *Fin* **4J6**
Vác *Hung* **25B3**
Vacaria *Brazil* **106F4**
Vacaville *USA* **97A2**
Vadodara *India* **51C4**
Vadso *Nor* **4K4**
Vaduz *Leichtenstein* **13C1**
Va Gesell *Arg* **105E3**

Victoria *Hong Kong*	39C5	
Victoria *Malay*	44D1	
Victoria, State *Aust*	74B3	
Victoria *USA*	85D4	
Victoria, State *Aust*	73D4	
Victoria de las Tunas *Cuba*	100B2	
Victoria Falls *Zambia/Zim*	66B2	
Victoria I *Can*	74B2	
Victoria, L *Aust*	74B2	
Victoria Land, Region *Ant*	112B7	
Victoria, Mt *Burma*	52A1	
Victoria Range, Mts *NZ*	77B2	
Victoria River Downs *Aust*	70C2	
Victoriaville *Can*	91D1	
Victoria West *S Africa*	66B3	
Victorica *Arg*	110B3	
Victorville *USA*	97B3	
Vicuña *Chile*	110A2	
Vicuña Mackenna *Arg*	110C2	
Vidalia *USA*	93B1	
Videle *Rom*	20B2	
Vidin *Bulg*	20B2	
Vidisha *India*	51D4	
Vidzy *USSR*	24D1	
Viedma *Arg*	105D4	
Viejo *Costa Rica*	102A4	
Vielha *Spain*	17C1	
Vienna, Illinois *USA*	94C2	
Vienna, W Virginia *USA*	90B3	
Vienne *France*	15C2	
Vientiane *Laos*	42C2	
Vierwaldstätter See, L *Switz*	13D1	
Vierzon *France*	15C2	
Vieste *Italy*	19C2	
Vietnam, Republic *S E Asia*	42D1	
Vietri *Viet*	36B2	
Vieux Fort *St Lucia*	103P2	
Vigan *Phil*	36B2	
Vigevano *Italy*	13C2	
Vignemale, Mt *France*	14B3	
Vigo *Spain*	16A1	
Vijayawada *India*	53C1	
Vik *Iceland*	4B2	
Vikhren, Mt *Bulg*	20B2	
Viking *Can*	89E2	
Vikna, I *Nor*	4G6	
Vila da Maganja *Mozam*	67C2	
Vila Machado *Mozam*	67C2	
Vila Real *Port*		
Vilanculos *Mozam*	67C3	
Vila Vasco da Gama *Mozam*	67C2	
Vila Velha *Brazil*	111C2	
Vileyka *USSR*	24D2	
Vilhelmina *Sweden*	4H6	
Vilhena *Brazil*	109E6	
Viljandi *USSR*	26C2	
Viljoenskroon *S Africa*	67G1	
Vilkovo *USSR*	25D3	
Villa Ahumada *Mexico*	85C3	
Vila Atuel *Arg*	110B2	
Villaba *Spain*	16A1	
Villa Carranza *Mexico*	99A2	
Villach *Austria*	18B1	
Villa Colon *Arg*	110B2	
Villa Constitución *Arg*	110C2	
Villa de Maria *Arg*	110C1	
Villa de Reyes *Mexico*	99A1	
Villa Dolores *Arg*	110B2	
Villafranca di Verona *Italy*	13D2	
Villa General Mitre *Arg*	110C2	
Villa General Roca *Arg*	110B2	
Villaguay *Arg*	110D2	
Villahermosa *Mexico*	101C3	
Villa Hidalgo *Mexico*	99A1	
Villa Iris *Arg*	110C3	
Villa Maria *Arg*	110C2	
Villa Montes *Bol*	106D3	
Villanueva *Mexico*	99A1	
Villa Nova de Gaia *Port*	16A1	
Villanueva de la Serena *Spain*	16A2	
Villanueva-y-Geltrú *Spain*	17C1	
Villa Regina *Arg*	110B3	
Villarreal *Spain*	17B2	
Villarrica *Chile*	105B3	
Villarrica *Par*	106E4	
Villarrobledo *Spain*	16B2	
Villa San José *Arg*	110D2	
Villa Valeria *Arg*	110C2	
Villavicencio *Colombia*	108C3	
Villefranche *France*	15C2	
Ville-Marie *Can*	83C5	
Villena *Spain*	17B2	
Villeneuve-St-Georges *France*	12B2	
Villeneuve-sur-Lot *France*	14C3	
Ville Platte *USA*	95B3	
Villers-Cotterêts *France*	12B2	
Villeurbanne *France*	15C2	
Villiers *S Africa*	67G1	
Villupuram *India*	53B2	
Vilnius *USSR*	24D2	
Vilyuy *USSR*	29D1	
Vilyuysk *USSR*	28F1	
Viña del Mar *Chile*	110A2	
Vinaroz *Spain*	17C1	
Vincennes *USA*	90A3	
Vindhya Range, Mts *India*	51D4	
Vineland *USA*	92D2	
Vineyard Haven *USA*	92D2	
Vinh *Viet*	42D2	
Vinh Loi *Viet*	43D4	
Vinh Long *Viet*	43D3	
Vinita *USA*	94A2	
Vinkovci *Yugos*	20D1	
Vinnitsa *USSR*	26C4	
Vinson Massif Upland, *Ant*	112B3	
Vioolsdrift *S Africa*	66A3	
Vipiteno *Italy*	13D1	
Virac *Phil*	45B3	
Virddhachalam *India*	53B2	
Virei *Angola*	66A2	
Virgem da Lapa *Brazil*	111C1	
Virginia *S Africa*	67G1	
Virginia, State *USA*	86C3	
Virginia *USA*	86A2	
Virginia City *USA*	97B2	
Virgin Is *Caribbean*	103E3	
Virovitica *Yugos*	18C1	
Virton *Belg*	12C2	
Virudunagar *India*	53B3	
Vis, I *Yugos*	18C2	
Visalia *USA*	97B2	
Visayan S *Phil*	45B3	
Visby *Sweden*	5H7	
Visegrad *Yugos*	20A2	
Viseu *Port*	16A1	
Vishakhapatnam *India*	46C4	
Visp *Switz*	13B1	
Vissingen *Neth*	15C1	
Vista *USA*	97B3	
Vitebsk *USSR*	26D2	
Viterbo *Italy*	18B2	
Vitigudino *Spain*	16A1	
Vitora *Spain*	16B1	
Vitoria *Brazil*	107C6	
Vitoria da Conquista *Brazil*	107C4	
Vitré *France*	14B2	
Vitry-le-Francois *France*	12C2	
Vittangi *Sweden*	4J5	
Vittoria *Italy*	19B3	
Vittorio Veneto *Italy*	13E2	
Vityaz Depth *Pacific O*	39B7	
Vivero *Spain*	16A1	
Vivorata *Arg*	110D3	
Vizhne-Angarsk *USSR*	29C2	
Vizianagaram *India*	49C4	
Vladeasa, Mt *Rom*	20B1	
Vladimir *USSR*	31F4	
Vladimir Volynskiy *USSR*	25C2	
Vladivostok *USSR*	40C2	
Vlieland, I *Neth*	22A2	
Vlissingen *Neth*	12B1	
Vlorë *Alb*	21A2	
Vöcklabruck *Austria*	23C3	
Voeune Sai *Camb*	42D3	
Voghera *Italy*	13C2	
Vohibinany *Madag*	67D2	
Vohimarina *Madag*	67E2	
Voi *Kenya*	65D3	
Voinjama *Lib*	63B4	
Voiron *France*	15D2	
Volcán Baru, Mt *Panama*	102A5	
Volcán Citlaltepetl, Mt *Mexico*	99B2	
Volcano Lullaillaco, Mt *Chile*	106C3	
Volcano Copahue, Mt *Chile*	110A3	
Volcano Domuyo, Mt *Arg*	110A3	
Volcano Lanin, Mt *Arg*	105B3	
Volcano Ollagüe, Mt *Chile*	106C2	
Volcano Llaima, Mt *Chile*	110A3	
Volcano Maipo, Mt *Chile*	110B2	
Volcano Peteroa, Mt *Chile*	110A3	
Volcán Parícutin, Mt *Mexico*	99A2	
Volcán Purace, Mt *Colombia*	108B3	
Volcán Tinguiririca, Mt *Chile/Arg*	110A2	
Volchansk *USSR*	27J2	
Volga, R *USSR*	27G4	
Volgodonsk *USSR*	27F4	
Volgograd *USSR*	27F4	
Volgogradskoye Vodokhranilishche, Res *USSR*	27G3	
Volkhov *USSR*	26D2	
Volkovysk *USSR*	24C2	
Volksrust *S Africa*	67G1	

Vologda *USSR* 27F2
Volognes *France* 14B2
Vólos *Greece* 21B3
Vol'sk *USSR* 27G3
Volta *USSR* 98B2
Volta, L *Ghana* 63B4
Volta Redonda *Brazil* 111C2
Volynskiy *USSR* 26C3
Volzhskiy *USSR* 27F4
Von Frank Mt *USA* 88D2
Vopnafjördur *Iceland* 82J3
Voralberg, Province *Austria* 13C1
Vordingborg *Den* 22C1
Vorkuta *USSR* 30H3
Voronezh *USSR* 26E3
Voroshilovgrad *USSR* 26E4
Voru *USSR* 5K7
Vosges, Mt *France* 15D2
Voshnyy Saytocan, Mts *USSR* 34B1
Voss *Nor* 5F6
Vostochnyy Sayan, Mts *USSR* 29B2
Vostok, Base *Ant* 112B9
Votkinsk *USSR* 27H2
Vouziers *France* 12C2
Voznesensk *USSR* 26D4
Vranje *Yugos* 20B2
Vratsa *Bulg* 20B2
Vrbas *Yugos* 20A1
Vrbovsko *Yugos* 18B1
Vrede *S Africa* 67G1
Vreed en Hoop *Guyana* 109F2
Vrsac *Yugos* 20B1
Vrtoce *Yugos* 18C2
Vryburg *S Africa* 66B3
Vryheid *S Africa* 67H1
Vukovar *Yugos* 20A1
Vulcan *Can* 89E2
Vulcano, I *Italy* 19B3
Vung Tau *Viet* 43D3
Vuollerim *Sweden* 4J5
Vyartsilya *USSR* 4L5
Vyartsilya *USSR* 18B1
Vyazemskiy *USSR* 35F2
Vyaz'ma *USSR* 26D2
Vyazniki *USSR* 27F2
Vyborg *USSR* 26C1
Vyshiy Volochek *USSR* 25B3
Vyskov *Czech* 26E1
Vytegra *USSR* 26E1

W

Wa *Ghana* 63B3
Wabasca *Can* 89E1
Wabasca L *Can* 89E1
Wabash *USA* 90A2
Wabowden *Can* 81J4
Wabush *Can* 83D4
Wachusett Res *USA* 92D1
Waco *USA* 95A3
Wad *Pak* 51B3
Waddan *Libya* 61A2
Waddington, Mt *Can* 81F4
Wadi es Sir *Jordan* 60B3
Wad Medani *Sudan* 65D1
Wafra *Kuwait* 59E4

Wager Bay *Can* 82A3
Wagga Wagga *Aust* 75C3
Wagin *Aust* 72A4
Waha *Libya* 61A2
Wahaiwa *Hawaiian Is* 97C4
Wahoo *USA* 94A2
Wahpeton *USA* 84D2
Wai *India* 53A1
Waiau *NZ* 77B2
Waigeo, I *Indon* 37E3
Waihi *NZ* 76C1
Waikaremoana, L *NZ* 76C1
Waikerie *Aust* 74A2
Waikouaiti *NZ* 77B3
Wailuku *Hawaiian Is* 97C4
Waimate *NZ* 77B2
Waimea *Hawaiian Is* 97C4
Waingapu *Indon* 36D1
Wainwright *Can* 89E2
Wainwright *USA* 80B2
Waipara *NZ* 77B2
Waipukurau *NZ* 76C2
Wairarapa, L *NZ* 77C2
Wairoa *NZ* 76C1
Waitara *NZ* 76C1
Waitomo *NZ* 76C1
Waiuku *NZ* 76B1
Wajima *Japan* 41B1
Wajir *Kenya* 65E2
Wakatipu, L *NZ* 77A3
Wakayama *Japan* 40D4
Wakde, Country *U K* 9C3
Wakefield *Eng* 8D3
Wakefield *Jamaica* 103H1
Wakefield, Rhode Island *USA* 92D2
Wakema *Burma* 43B2
Wakkanai *Japan* 35G2
Wabrzych *Pol* 25B2
Walcha *Aust* 75D2
Walcz *Pol* 25B2
Waldbröl *W Germ* 12D1
Walden *USA* 92B2
Waldia *Eth* 65D1
Wales, Country *U K* 9C3
Wales *USA* 88A1
Wales I *Can* 82B3
Walgett *Aust* 75C2
Walgreen Coast, Region *Ant* 112B4
Walikale *Zaïre* 65C3
Walker, L *USA* 97B2
Walkerton *Can* 90B2
Wallace *USA* 84B2
Wallaroo *Aust* 74A2
Walla Walla *Aust* 75C3
Walla Walla *USA* 96C1
Wallingford *USA* 92C2
Wallis and Futuna, Is *Pacific O* 71H4
Wallowa *USA* 96C1
Wallowa Mts, Mts *USA* 96C1
Wallumbilla *Aust* 75C1
Walnut Ridge *USA* 94B2
Walouru *NZ* 76C1
Walsall *Eng* 9D3
Walsenburg *USA* 85C3
Walsenburgh *USA* 85C3

Walterboro *USA* 93B1
Walter F George Res *USA* 93A1
Waltham *USA* 92D1
Walvis Bay *S Africa* 66A3
Walvis Ridge *Atlantic O* 69J6
Wamba *Nig* 63C4
Wamego *USA* 94A2
Wana *Pak* 50B2
Wanaaring *Aust* 74B1
Wanaka *NZ* 77A2
Wanaka, L *NZ* 77A2
Wanapitei L *Can* 90B1
Wandoan *Aust* 75C1
Wanganella *Aust* 74B3
Wanganui *NZ* 76B1
Wanganui *NZ* 76C1
Wangaratta *Aust* 75C3
Wanle Weyne *Somalia* 65E2
Wanning *China* 42E2
Wanparti *India* 53B1
Wanxian *China* 39B3
Wanyuan *China* 39B3
Wappapello, L *USA* 94B2
Wappingers Falls *USA* 92C2
Warangal *India* 53B1
Waratah *Aust* 75C4
Warburton *Aust* 74C3
Warder *S Africa* 67G1
Warder *Eth* 65E2
Wardha *India* 51D4
Ward, Mt *NZ* 77A3
Ware *Can* 81F4
Ware *USA* 92C1
Wareham *USA* 92D2
Warialda *Aust* 75D1
Warin Chamrap *Thai* 42C2
Warmbad *S Africa* 66B3
Warminster *USA* 92B2
Warm Springs *USA* 97B2
Warnemünde *E Germ* 22C2
Warner Mts *USA* 96B2
Warner Robins *USA* 93B1
Warracknabeal *Aust* 74B3
Warrandirinna, L *Aust* 74A1
Warren, Arkansas *USA* 95B3
Warren *Aust* 75C2
Warren, Massachusetts *USA* 92D2
Warren, Ohio *USA* 90B2
Warren, Pennsylvania *USA* 91C2
Warrenpoint *N Ire* 11C1
Warrensburg *USA* 94B2
Warrenton *S Africa* 67F1
Warrenton *USA* 91C3
Warri *Nig* 63C4
Warrina *Aust* 74A1
Warrington *Eng* 8C3
Warrnambool *Aust* 74B3
Warszawa *Pol* 24C2
Warwick *Aust* 75D1
Warwick, County *Eng* 9D3
Warwick *Eng* 9D3
Warwick, New York *USA* 92B2
Warwick, Rhode Island *USA* 92D2
Wasatch Range, Mts *USA* 84B3
Wasbank *S Africa* 67H1
Wasco *USA* 97B2
Washburn L, *Can* 80H2